ALEXANDRIA GOES TO WAR

ALEXANDRIA GOES TO WAR

*** *Beyond Robert E. Lee* ***

GEORGE G. KUNDAHL

THE UNIVERSITY OF TENNESSEE PRESS / KNOXVILLE

Library of Congress Cataloging-in-Publication Data

Kundahl, George G., 1940–
Alexandria goes to war : beyond Robert E. Lee / George G. Kundahl.—1st ed.
    p. cm.
Includes bibliographical references and index.
ISBN 1-57233-320-0 (alk. paper)
1. Alexandria (Va.)—Biography. 2. Alexandria (Va.)—History—
19TH century. 3. Alexandria (Va.)—History, Military—19TH century.
4. Virginia—History—Civil War, 1861–1865. 5. Secession—Virginia.
6. Virginia—Politics and government—1775–1865. I. Title.
F234.A3K86 2004
975.5'29603—DC22

2004001951

With love for Joy, my personal Clio,
who, given a choice,
would have been born an Alexandrian

Contents

Figures

Maps

Acknowledgments

IT IS SAID SO FREQUENTLY THAT THIS PERSON OR THAT was indispensable to the successful completion of a project, program, or proposition that it is tempting to discount such compliments. The kudos are absolutely true in the composition of this book, however, as it would not have been possible without the wholehearted support of T. Michael Miller, research historian for the city of Alexandria, Virginia. Michael has been studying life on both sides of the Potomac River since childhood, including momentous events, the lineages of families, origins of buildings, and roadways and waterways. This unique knowledge of his hometown and his extraordinary memory enabled him to identify obscure articles in newspapers and periodicals containing information lost to most contemporaries, and priceless primary sources on the community and its past. Repeatedly, he was called upon to find or verify a particular fact, and never once did he hesitate or admit defeat. Michael is determined that the rich heritage of Alexandria shall not wither for lack of attention, and I am but one of countless beneficiaries of his kindness and generosity.

The staff of the Alexandria Library's Special Collections has been exceptional as well. Librarians Joyce McMullin and George Combs, in particular, have proven to be a credit to their profession—resourceful, deeply knowledgeable, and ever helpful. They repeatedly surfaced collections, volumes, and data I would not have had the wit to seek. At times, they thoughtfully applied their editing skills to particularly vexing segments of the manuscript. In so doing, their assistance far exceeded what is expected from custodians of a community's literature and lore. Their assistants—Heather Muller, Rita Holtz, Kathy Chappell, Leslie Morales, and Barbara Winters—all provided help and displayed composure far beyond the call of duty.

Craig Kellermann spent countless hours reading, reflecting upon, and commenting on the manuscript. As he has done with earlier projects, Craig served not only as a sounding board and informal editor but also as an alter ego to the author. His contributions are invisible to the reader but were invaluable to the writer.

I must also acknowledge aid from a variety of other individuals who went beyond the normal bounds of their jobs or our friendship to assist me. In alphabetical order, this list includes, but by no means ends, with Susan Abbott, Carter Batcheller, Edwin Bearss, John and Ruth Coski, Tom Craig, Cooper Dawson, John De Pue, Mary Beth Horton, Suzanne Warfield Johnson, Wendy Kail, John Komoroske, Becky Kusserow, Horace Mewborn, Mike Musick, and Marion Dawson Phillips. I am truly indebted to each of these benevolent souls for their expertise, helpfulness, and patience.

Finally, my thanks to Jennifer Siler and her staff at the University of Tennessee Press, most competent, always cooperative.

Key Events in the
Formative Years of Alexandria

1749	Founding of settlement on Potomac River near Hunting Creek
1779	Incorporation of the town of Alexandria by the general assembly
1799	Death of George Washington; memorial service in Alexandria
1801	Alexandria County created and annexed into District of Columbia
1814	English naval squadron threatens Alexandria and receives a ransom
1824–25	Visit by the Marquis de Lafayette
1846	Alexandria County retroceded to Virginia Local militia march off to Mexican War
NOVEMBER 6, 1860	Alexandrians vote for Bell; Lincoln elected president
FEBRUARY 4, 1861	Alexandria sends a unionist to Virginia secession convention
APRIL 17, 1861	Richmond convention votes to withdraw from Union
MAY 23, 1861	Alexandrians join other Virginia voters in confirming secession
MAY 24, 1861	Federal troops occupy Alexandria; city militia leaves town
APRIL 9, 1865	Gen. R. E. Lee surrenders Army of Northern Virginia
1870	City of Alexandria legally separated from Alexandria County
1889	Dedication of Confederate memorial, "Appomattox"
1920	Alexandria County renamed "Arlington County"
1934	Alexandria's last Civil War veteran dies

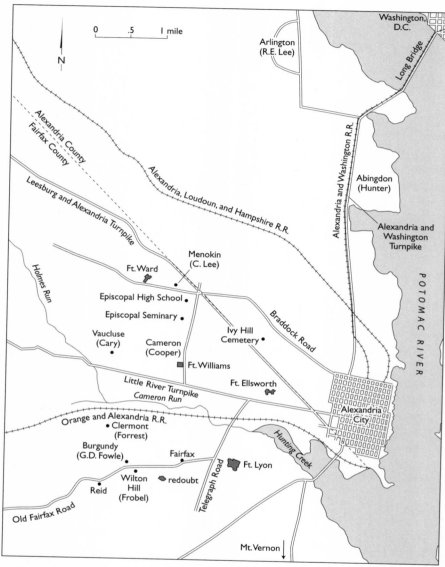

Alexandria County and environs, c. 1860–65.

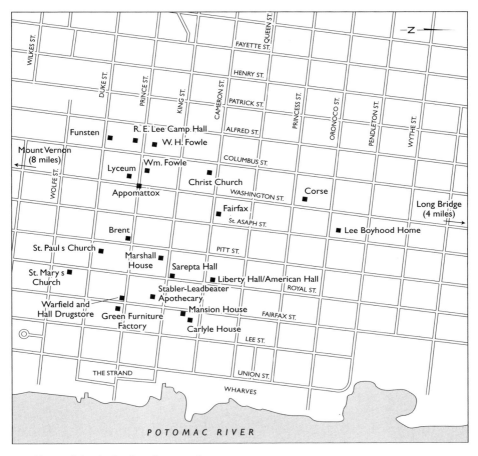

Alexandria city in the nineteenth century.

INTRODUCTION

THE WITHDRAWAL OF COTTON STATES IN LATE 1860 AND early 1861 left eight remaining slave states in the Union with popular majorities opposed to secession. The history of Alexandria before Virginia's departure is generally representative of border communities in the Upper South that hesitated to abandon the Union. The day after voting to confirm the state convention's decision to secede, however, Alexandria was invaded by soldiers in blue and started down a path divergent from other towns within the borders of the Confederacy.

The city quickly lost its placid colonial character and became an active Federal supply depot, convalescent center, and campground. A labyrinth of wharves, quartermaster storehouses, commissaries, marshaling yards, and railroad shops blanketed the area. Churches, public buildings, and abandoned mansions were converted into hospitals, prisons, and headquarters. Units assembled on the hillsides surrounding Alexandria prior to deployment and recovered there after military engagements. Sprawling clusters of contrabands added to the congestion.

Overwhelmed by the presence of the Federal army, Alexandria residents could generally offer little more to the cause they had voted to support beyond the five hundred or so of their husbands, sons, and brothers serving in the Southern army and navy. Most had become members of a local regiment like so many others organized in towns throughout the North and South. What made Alexandria exceptional was the quality and variety of the talent it provided to Confederate nationalism.

A look at the city and county on the eve of war and a study of the lives of sixteen citizens during the conflict yields an appreciation of the unique contributions Alexandrians made to the rebel effort. In many cases, these stories reflect sacrifices made throughout the South for a cause that would prove to be hopeless. Taken as a whole, the profiles might be viewed as a microcosm of the region's desperate gamble to secede from the Union and form its own nation.

The popular misconception of "the solid South" was as inaccurate in 1860 as it is today. Striking contrasts existed between plantation and town, farming and manufacturing, Whig and Democrat, black and white. These differences distinguished the Deep South from the border states, even separating people living in built-up surroundings from those in rural areas within the same county. Alexandria, Virginia, represented one strain of Dixie, in many respects typical of the Upper South at the outset of the Civil War, but with some notable anomalies.

Viewed through a nineteenth-century kaleidoscope, Alexandria conjured up varying images, depending on how the bits of glass were arrayed. The most recognizable picture was the city as hometown of George Washington, whose estate, Mount Vernon, overlooked the Potomac River just a few miles to the south. The colonial community of stately Federal and Georgian residences, large shade trees, and ivy-covered walls was a familiar sight to many spectators. Through the eyes of a mercantilist, Alexandria represented a thriving seaport accessible to multiple modes of transportation, close to agricultural production, with a large natural harbor well up the Potomac near its fall line. At mid-century, the perception of Alexandria acquired a new face for its strategic location across the river from the capital of the United States.

The community was by no means old by European standards. Alexandria only dated back to 1749, when a settlement by that name was established near the Hunting Creek warehouse on the south shore of the Potomac. The village was originally governed as a part of Fairfax County, which, by direction of the governor's council, moved its court to Alexandria in 1752. A town was incorporated by the general assembly in 1779.

An 1801 act of Congress created Alexandria County out of the Virginia portion of that ten-mile square designated as the nation's capital city and fixed its seat at the town of Alexandria. The entire entity was annexed into the new District of Columbia. For a variety of reasons, Alexandrians were unhappy in the Federal enclave and repeatedly sought to return to Virginia. This was finally accomplished after Congress voted in 1846 to retrocede Alexandria County. Then its residents approved the proposition in a referendum, and, finally, in 1847, the state agreed to extend its jurisdiction over the area once again.[1]

The commitment of Alexandrians to the nation was generally unquestioned.[2] Their forefathers fought with George Washington to secure the independence of Virginia and the other colonies. After the Revolution, Alexandrians were Federalists, almost to a man, and proponents of a strong central government, especially respecting regulation of trade and commerce. Yet, as the nineteenth century progressed, national cohesion

The city of Alexandria, 1863.

wore thin. The veil that obscured sharp divisions between North and South on the issue of slavery was torn aside irreparably in October 1859, when John Brown and his band of abolitionists occupied the arsenal at Harpers Ferry. In contrast to their neighbors in nearby jurisdictions such as Loudoun and Prince William Counties, however, the citizens of Alexandria remained calm and continued to support their national leaders.

A visitor in July 1860 observed, "We do not believe that there is any place in the whole bounds of the Union where the people enjoy more of the real comforts of life than in Alexandria."[3] The joy of living in Alexandria was enhanced by the grand buildings spotted around the city center. Federal architecture was sprinkled with Greek Revival and other classical designs. A stunning example was the Lyceum with its Doric portico supported by fluted columns. This elegant edifice served as a lecture hall, as well as home for the Alexandria Library Society, which boasted 5,100 volumes on its shelves. The single building that contained the post office, court, and custom house at Prince and South St. Asaph Streets was another rectangular structure with aesthetic lines, Doric pilasters, and an entablature. Built in 1851–52 as a bank, the Athenaeum replicated a Greek temple. The Italianate style was most evident in the city's largest and most prestigious hotel, James Green's Mansion House at North Fairfax and Cameron Streets. An octagonal cupola topped the flat-roofed building with eighteen windows across its front.[4]

The splendor of the city's churches was a further reminder of a rich cultural heritage. The most renowned house of worship was Christ Church, the brick colonial edifice with "pepper pot" steeple and George Washington's pew identified by a brass plaque. Under the leadership of an energetic Episcopal rector, the parish at St. Paul's was a strong moral force in the community. The simple Presbyterian Meeting House had been the site of the first president's memorial service in 1799. The Catholic presence, centered at St. Mary's Church, was augmented by the large influx of Irish immigrants in the 1830s and 1840s. Baptists, Methodists, and Quakers were also well known as civic leaders. Separate Baptist and Methodist churches ministered to blacks.[5]

While not as cosmopolitan as the coastal cities of the Northeast or as industrial as Richmond and Norfolk, Alexandria nevertheless kept step with advances in municipal services in the mid-nineteenth century. A fire department was created to unite the independent companies that had raced through the streets since colonial times. Lighting fueled by the city's new gasworks illuminated the traditional lamp posts. City conduits carried pure water to residents from Cameron Run.

The community was renowned for its excellent private schools. The Alexandria Academy traced its origin to George Washington and his contemporaries. The Alexandria Boarding School enjoyed prominence under the tutelage of the Quaker Benjamin Hallowell, another leader in civic affairs. St. John's Academy was established and operated by Roman Catholic priests to educate children from all strata of society.

The most noted academic institution, however, was Episcopal High School. Located just outside the city line (now bounded by North Braddock Road and Quaker Lane), its classical curriculum was among the finest in the South, attracting students from across the region as well as in Alexandria. Among its alumni were three young men who would compile notable records in the war on the horizon: Randolph Fairfax, attending the university at Charlottesville when the claxon sounded; Frank Stringfellow, teaching in Mississippi those subjects he had learned at "Episcopal on the Hill"; and Orton Williams, an aide to the U.S. Army's general in chief, Bvt. Lt. Gen. Winfield Scott. Alexander Hunter, another Alexandrian still enrolled as a student, would compose endearing accounts of the conflict for future generations based on his service in uniform.

On the eve of war, Alexandria's economy was booming. The hometown newspaper characterized 1860 as "the most prosperous year we have had since retrocession."[6] The preceding two decades saw the completion of the Alexandria Canal and the Aqueduct Bridge, connecting it to the Chesapeake and Ohio Canal at Georgetown, construction of three principal rail links, expansion of scheduled boat service with other ports, and the appearance of factories and foundries throughout the city. Economic expectations for Alexandria seemed unlimited when the firestorm of secession and military occupation swept across the county, ravaging everything in its path.

Heightened prosperity had begun with improvements in transportation. Where goods are transferred from one means of transport to another, commerce tends to flourish, although Alexandria experienced a false start before realizing the rewards of transshipping. The city fathers invested heavily in the Alexandria Canal, only to find that the introduction of rail lines made this means of conveyance obsolete for carrying agricultural produce to market. The Baltimore and Ohio Railroad funneled wheat to Baltimore, Alexandria's rival port. Extension of the Chesapeake and Ohio Canal to Cumberland, Maryland, however, opened up coal fields across the Appalachians to shipment eastward. The canal's access to Northern Virginia subsequently piled anthracite high on the city wharves. The *Alexandria Gazette* enthusiastically called its port "the natural depot for the coal trade of the Chesapeake and Ohio Canal."[7]

Even more important to Alexandria as a transportation hub were the rail lines brought into the city during the 1850s. The Orange and Alexandria Railroad provided a link to the West through a switch at Lynchburg. For the wide-eyed visionary, the ultimate terminus was not the Mississippi River, but San Francisco, Mexico, or even Hong Kong.[8] The rails of the Orange and Alexandria connected with the Manassas Gap Railroad to provide access to the grain, livestock, and coal of the Shenandoah Valley. As a result, in 1859 the city recorded its best year ever in wheat trading, if far behind Richmond, the state's leader in exporting grain.[9] Virginia produced more than thirty-eight million bushels of corn in 1860, and much of that, too, passed through the Potomac port.[10] At the opening of the war, another primary rail link, the Alexandria, Loudoun, and Hampshire Railroad, had reached Leesburg to the northwest, thirty-seven miles in the direction of the coal fields of western Virginia.[11] Among the innovators who planned and laid iron tracks across Northern Virginia was Wilson Presstman, a railroad engineer soon to be transformed into a military engineer.

The presence of these commercial arteries encouraged an increase in river traffic. First, steamer service was opened between Alexandria and Baltimore in 1854. Then, a New York City ship company inaugurated a regular schedule of voyages. Travel southward was facilitated by daily departures for Aquia Creek, where connections could be made to Fredericksburg, Richmond, and other points. More frequent ferries plied back and forth across the Potomac to Washington and Georgetown.

What freight was being carried? Alexandria had lost much of the tobacco trade that introduced prosperity to the community in the eighteenth century. Now Alexandrians exported fertilizer, fish, and slaves. Railcars and canal boats returning to the West carried manufactured products and guano imported from South America by William Fowle and Company to enrich depleted soil.[12] Herring and shad from the Potomac became a staple of Alexandria's trade with cities in the Mid-Atlantic region. The shift in agricultural production in the Upper South from tobacco to grains reduced the requirement for field hands and therefore lessened dependence on slaves. Home to Franklin and Armfield, the nation's largest slave trading company earlier in the nineteenth century, by the war's outbreak Alexandria had surrendered to Richmond its preeminence as the state's primary transshipment point for human cargo. Yet Alexandria's slave pens on Duke Street were filled regularly with human beings for wholesale to Deep South marketers.[13]

As unity began to fray, Alexandria's economy was expanding from commerce into manufacturing. The introduction of railroads led to the establishment of a foundry to produce steam engines. The city's leading merchants joined together to form the Mount Vernon Cotton Manufacturing Company, which in 1860 employed 135 workers at a large factory on Washington Street, the city's major north-south axis. The Pioneer Flour Mill was the community's first venture into converting wheat that heretofore had been shipped elsewhere for milling. Other plants fermented malt, tanned leather, processed food, made shoes and clothing, and baked biscuits. One of Alexandria's several cabinet shops, James Green's furniture factory, produced sofas, chairs, and tables, among other items, with the help of young men like Patrick O'Gorman, an Irish immigrant soon faced with grave personal decisions attendant to civil strife. The 1860 census reported ninety-six manufacturing concerns operating in the city, many, like Green's, utilizing steam power.

Financial institutions prospered with the growth in commercial activity. Firms such as the Potomac Insurance and Fire Insurance Company located their headquarters in the city. The Exchange Bank, Farmers Bank, Potomac Bank, and Old Dominion Bank were all established there as well. In 1852, John W. Burke and Arthur Herbert founded a bank that is still prominent in the community. Acting as financiers for some of the state's railroad enterprises were the Corse brothers, one of whom, Montgomery, would lead Alexandrians into battle.

Merchants and businessmen dominated Alexandria's leadership. Historian David R. Goldfield considered the city fathers of Alexandria different from many urban moguls in their monopolistic control of civic activities and the importance of family ties to their success. The preponderance of these elites were Virginians, unusual so near the Northern states. Even more surprising, Goldfield found slaveholding less common within this oligarchy than in comparable maritime communities of the Upper South. In their prosperity, property holding, and social position, these former Whigs resembled secessionists. What distinguished the patricians from their planter counterparts elsewhere in Virginia and the Upper South was their reliance upon pursuits involving mercantilism rather than on wealth derived from slavery.[14]

The demographics of the black population of Alexandria, as reported in the 1860 census, reflected the city's location on the fringe of the Upper South. Free blacks and slaves each accounted for 11 percent of the city's 12,652 total inhabitants at a time when slaves alone constituted 31 percent of Virginia's overall population. Of the other eleven cities in the Confederate states with more than 10,000 inhabitants, a smaller proportion of slaves was found only in New Orleans.[15] Less than one-seventh of all Alexandria households contained slaves, three being the median number of human chattel held. Without a heavy industrial base as, for example, in Richmond, slavery in Alexandria was centered on females performing domestic tasks. The city's racial profile therefore resembled Georgetown and Annapolis, two other small maritime centers in the border area, rather than communities elsewhere in Virginia.[16]

Alexandria's manufacturing attracted more blacks and fewer immigrants than its Northern competitors. Free blacks were drawn to the Virginia seaport because of work opportunities there. On one end of the black social spectrum at the war's outset were forty-one property owners who earned their livelihood primarily as shopkeepers, blacksmiths, and skilled construction workers. At the other extreme were hundreds of men and women covered with scales and offal while cutting and cleaning fish on the docks at the foot of Oronoco and Princess Streets. This area consequently acquired the nickname of "Fishtown," as well as a savory reputation.

While black and white residents toiled, the chief opinion maker in this part of Virginia was the man who controlled the main means of communication, Edgar Snowden, editor and publisher of the *Alexandria Gazette*. Like most Alexandrians, Snowden had been an ardent Whig. In earlier years, Snowden waved his baton to conduct the city's electorate behind the Whig agenda of promoting economic growth through making internal improvements, building railroads and canals, enacting tariffs to protect industrial development, and chartering banks. His political positions consistently reflected the mercantilism that formed the backbone of the city's economy. He beat the drums for his party's candidates in the 1840s and, like many Whigs throughout the border states, transferred allegiance in 1860 to its successor party, the Constitutional Unionists.

With the campaign of 1860 came political discord, although the vibrancy of the multi-party system within Alexandria was characteristic of Upper South politics in the election of 1860.[17] The Breckinridge wing of the Democratic Party convened at Sarepta Hall on King Street in August. For most local residents, John C. Breckinridge's platform was considered too radical since it championed states' rights and favored aggressive expansion of slavery into the territories. The Stephen A. Douglas faction assembled in the same meeting room in September. This arm of the Democrats favored popular sovereignty in the new lands to the west and consequently received only tepid support.

Alexandria's Whigs endeavored to downplay the issue of slavery and shun the propaganda of Northern abolitionists and Southern radicals. On September 27, they organized a grand demonstration in support of national unity. The *Gazette* reported, "If there has ever been a doubt of the intense enthusiasm which the Union cause and its candidates have created in this good old town, that doubt must have been dissipated by the outpouring of popular sentiment witnessed upon our streets last night."[18]

Because of a firm belief in preservation of the Union, as well as their own financial self-interest, it came as no surprise that when Alexandrians went to the polls in November, they cast the majority of their votes (1,011) for the Constitutional Unionist candidate, John Bell of Tennessee, former speaker of the U.S. House of Representatives. Breckinridge and Douglas garnered the support of 565 and 140 electors, respectively. Republican Abraham Lincoln's name was entered on only sixteen ballots, fourteen of which were in the county, an indication of the differences in political sentiment between urban and rural Alexandrians. This dichotomy would continue to be evident.

Alexandria reported 58 percent of its ballots marked for the Constitutional Unionist. This result was not out of the ordinary for a city in the Upper South and border slave states. The counties containing Louisville, Kentucky, and Annapolis, Maryland, for example, hovered around 50 percent in favor of Bell. Urbanized counties in his home state supported Bell less evenly, reflecting their varying slave populations and consequent support for Breckinridge and Douglas: Knoxville, 72 percent; Nashville, 58 percent; and Memphis, 45 percent. Baltimore City registered 42 percent for Bell. Within the state of Virginia, Bell garnered 60 percent or more of the votes cast in 14 of the 147 counties, located mainly in the Tidewater and the mountains, plus the city of Norfolk. In Northern Virginia, only Loudoun County, with its large population of Germans and Quakers, mostly from Pennsylvania, topped Alexandria's support for Bell by posting 69 percent for that candidate.[19] Across the state, he registered 46 percent of the votes, enough to claim Virginia's 15 votes in the electoral college by a plurality.

Virginians west of the Blue Ridge Mountains and in the northern tier of counties, where slavery was far less common than in more agricultural areas, performed differently at the polls than their slaveholding counterparts. Upland inhabitants traded their former Whig sympathies for adherence to unionism; in contrast, the Democrat loyalties of plantation owners and other slaveholders in the eastern part of the state led them to favor withdrawing from the Union.

After the election, Snowden published a series of editorials from newspapers across the border states to reassure his readers that folks in St. Louis, Nashville, Louisville, and Centreville, Maryland, were united with Alexandrians in withstanding the temptation to join "this glorious confederacy."[20] As early as October, the respected Richmond *Daily Enquirer* had declared that the Southern states had every right to secede if Lincoln won the national election. At a time when other dailies around the state began bowing to extremism, Snowden held firm in supporting the Union. His determination and that of other leaders like him in areas without high concentrations of slaves encouraged former Whigs to vote pro-Union almost without exception.[21]

The next test of public sentiment came on February 4, 1861, when Virginians elected delegates to a convention called by the state legislature to meet in Richmond and determine the commonwealth's position on the incendiary issue of secession. Alexandria's performance mirrored the state as a whole, as voters in the seaport gave 72 percent of their votes to a union man, compared with 69 percent statewide. Both candidates were noted Democrats, the unionist George Brent who had campaigned for Douglas in November, and the secessionist David Funsten, a party official earlier pledged to Breckinridge. In other parts of the South, this contest tended to pit a Whig unionist against a Democrat in favor of withdrawing.[22] The competition between two Democrats in Alexandria violated the norm. Brent and Funsten would play different roles in the war but at last be supporting the same cause.

Of particular note was the scant 3 percent drop in participation from the prior November, as contrasted with an increase of more than 10 percent in absenteeism across the commonwealth.[23] There is no way of knowing if this difference was due to a greater proportion of Alexandrians than Virginians as a whole viewing secession as a life-or-death issue, whether the closeness of the community gave its voters a personal familiarity with candidates not common elsewhere, or if the issues were drawn more sharply in the city by the Potomac.

Regarding the companion question on the ballot, 86 percent of Alexandria voters favored submitting the convention's final determination to a referendum. The preference expressed by Alexandrians fit nicely with the western part of the state, which recorded 83 percent support for a referendum. Voters east of the Blue Ridge divided almost evenly on the issue.[24]

Unionists had been buoyed by Bell's win in Virginia, albeit by a slim plurality. The overwhelming selection of unionist delegates to the state convention further reassured conservatives.[25] Less than one-third of the specially elected representatives went to Richmond in favor of leaving the Union.[26] Secessionists across the state were thrown on the defensive. They would not regain momentum until the firing on Fort Sumter in April. During the interim, unionists in Alexandria offered the same arguments in support of their position as those expressed across the border states.

The point man, of course, was Alexandria's representative at the meeting to consider the issue of secession. In December, long before the formal call for a state convocation, Brent had gone on record as equating union with peace and disunion to war. Like most Virginia anti-secessionists, he reminded his fellow citizens of the leadership exercised by their forefathers at the constitutional convention of 1787, declaring that the union of states was by no means the exclusive property of Northerners. He also acknowledged the special predicament of the border states, caught between abolitionists in front and secessionists to the rear.[27]

When he delivered his definitive statement before the convention in March, Brent was quite direct in accusing the cotton states, and South Carolina in particular, of pursuing schemes of disunion to effect a policy of free trade. In his mind, it was fueled more by a desire to relieve the system of protective tariffs than concern for the institution of slavery that motivated the Deep South to leave the national government. Brent recognized that Northern states like Massachusetts were the rivals of England, the target market for Southern cotton, and would therefore work against the agricultural interests of the nascent nation. At the same time, Brent pointed out that fugitive slave problems were almost exclusively confined to the border areas, as the Deep South had two tiers of slaveholding states to insulate them from abolitionists. Secession would bring the doom of slavery in the Upper South, he argued, as the North would no longer feel any compunction to return runaway blacks. Nor was Brent convinced that goods manufactured in Virginia and the other border states would receive preferential treatment in the new confederacy, as that would undercut agreements encouraging France and England to enter into reciprocal commercial treaties with the independent cotton states. As so many others were doing, Brent called upon Virginia to act as a mediator in the crisis at hand and not be drawn onto the side of the disunionists.[28]

Brent's arguments reflected those published in his hometown newspaper and circulated throughout the South in tracts intended to keep the secessionists at bay. A popular pamphlet by a Marylander, John Pendleton Kennedy, developed the thesis that the border states had distinctive characteristics and their own welfare to protect. The mechanical arts and manufacturing capability of the Upper South bore no semblance to "one vast cotton field," as Kennedy characterized the Gulf States.[29]

Snowden published the sentiments of another thoughtful unionist in Alexandria, who predicted that the Deep South would expect high prices for cotton and cheap prices for Negroes, which was diametrically opposed to Virginia's interest as a consumer of the former and supplier of the latter. Nor would the Southern confederacy recognize fair market value for the staples, wheat, livestock, and tobacco offered by Virginia. The cotton states would, however, look to the Old Dominion to contribute freely of her sons and treasure in the war sure to come.[30]

A different writer to the *Alexandria Gazette* emphasized the importance of Virginia and the other border states in constituting a buffer between the two opposing sides.[31] Their retention in the Union would, in his mind, encourage the North to be more conciliatory toward the seceding states. A stated condition, however, was that the Federal government not attempt to coerce the secessionists, for in that case, Virginia would have no choice but to vote with her Southern sisters.[32] Even the most ardent unionist seemed to concede that the region's non-slaveholders would stand up and fight if they perceived their rights being violated or feared the South would be invaded.

The dream of avoiding bloodshed evaporated on April 12, 1861. First, Southern troops fired on Fort Sumter. Then, President Lincoln called for seventy-five thousand militia, including six thousand troops from Virginia. These developments persuaded the Richmond convention to vote in favor of secession.

The loyalties of a vast number of Alexandrians immediately shifted from nation to state. James W. Jackson, proprietor of the city's John Marshall House hotel, had permitted townsfolk to raise a huge Confederate flag on the pole atop its roof to the huzzahs of an enthusiastic crowd. Paid for through public subscription, the banner was an emblem of Southern patriotism and a defiant challenge to Lincoln's newly installed administration.

At Arlington House, Col. Robert E. Lee composed his letter of resignation from the U.S. Army and took the train to Richmond to accept command of the military and naval forces of Virginia. Other higher-ranking officers from Alexandria had already left the service of the United States. Samuel Cooper was in Montgomery, Alabama, advising Jefferson Davis and would soon be recognized as the senior officer in the Confederate States Army. Commodore French Forrest captured the Gosport Navy Yard in Norfolk and assumed command of the facility. His son, Douglas, was still in Alexandria, however, where he practiced law when not drilling with a newly activated militia outfit, the Old Dominion Rifles.

In February 1861 a battalion was created to combine the militia units being formed in Northern Virginia. It would later be designated the

Seventeenth Virginia Infantry.[33] Its nickname, the "Alexandria Regiment," was, however, patently inaccurate, as recalled later by one member.[34] The grouping encompassed as many companies from rural communities between the Potomac and Shenandoah Rivers as units within Alexandria city and county. A total of 938 men volunteered to join the regiment prior to the opening battle at Bull Run.[35] The portrait of Alexandrians coming to the colors is enriched by viewing their demographics in comparison with other volunteers.

Three of the Alexandria companies bore the earmarks of their urban environment. The city's financial and mercantile character was reflected in the Alexandria Riflemen (Company A), as 87 percent of its members can be classified as professional, white collar, or students in their civilian pursuits. Of the regiment's thirty-one students, a dozen were found in Company A, not surprising in light of the proximity of Episcopal High School. Interestingly, the Warren Rifles (Company B) from Front Royal had the other significant concentration of ten student-soldiers, undoubtedly due to the unit's organizer and commander, Robert H. Simpson, a graduate of the Virginia Military Institute who was the founder and headmaster of a nearby military academy. Alexandria's Mount Vernon Guards and Old Dominion Rifles (Companies E and H) consisted largely (71 percent) of the skilled labor necessary for Alexandria's growing manufacturing. Concentrations of carpenters, cabinetmakers, machinists, and shoemakers reflected trades utilized in the city's industry. In contrast, unskilled Irishmen populated the Emmett Guards and O'Connell Guards (Companies G and I), organized in the seaport early in 1861. These men were overwhelmingly (83 percent) unskilled, most of Company I consisting of railroad hands and day laborers.

The differences between these enlistees and those in the non-Alexandria outfits were striking. The rural companies contained 92 percent (144 men) of the regiment's farmers. Only 14 percent of the white-collar workers and 25 percent of the skilled laborers hailed from outside the seaport. All the non-Irish companies averaged just 9 percent common laborers. The demographic disparity was evident in one other measure as well. The average age of the city's three companies of educated and skilled soldiers was only twenty-four years; the mean for the out-of-towners was almost twenty-five years. The 121 Irishmen, however, were over thirty years old on average. Twenty-three of the enlistees in these companies had already celebrated their fortieth birthday.

The data for the Alexandria companies differ considerably from that seen across the South. The sample of more than nine thousand soldiers drawn by Bell Irvin Wiley from seven Southern states (including Virginia) is the best counterpoint. Only 7 percent of his men were classified as white collar, as compared to a substantial 31 percent of the three non-Irish companies of Alexandrians. Wiley identified only fifty-one lawyers in his universe, whereas the smaller Alexandria figures show fourteen attorneys in its ranks.[36] Wiley and James McPherson, in a far more limited survey of 390 men, each found almost 62 percent of the rebels engaged in agriculture, as contrasted with only 19 percent of the Seventeenth Virginia's volunteers. Wiley's data reflect 8.5 percent unskilled laborers, exactly half of the proportion making up the Northern Virginia regiment.[37] In terms of age, according to Wiley, four-fifths of the men who joined Confederate units in 1861–62 were in the eighteen to twenty-nine range. Before First Manassas, that proportion in the five Alexandria companies was a comparable three-fourths.[38]

The presence of other nationalities in the Alexandria units was not dissimilar to typical Southern outfits. Most foreigners who joined the military were infantrymen, like those in the Seventeenth Virginia.[39] The fifty-one enlistees born in Ireland were by far the regiment's largest contingent of immigrants. They were spread throughout the ranks of nine of its ten companies, although concentrated most heavily in two Alexandria units. Native-born Germans were a distant second in number (twelve).

What motivated Alexandrians to volunteer? In the absence of specific information, the overall findings of Wiley and McPherson may be consulted to speculate on reasons underlying enlistments in Alexandria. The motives in Northern Virginia were no doubt similar to those of other Southern men caught up in what McPherson calls the *rage militaire* or patriotic fervor sweeping the country in the wake of the firing on Fort Sumter.[40] Strong opinions on slavery or a desire for liberty from Northern domination were undoubtedly less important to Alexandria residents than to their counterparts in the Lower South. Conversely, protection of hearth and home or, after May 24, defense of the Old Dominion, must have seemed far more compelling. Some viewed the conflict as a religious crusade.[41] In a study of seven young Virginians, John G. Selby identified two themes in his subjects' experiences: responses to hardships were determined by character, not circumstances, and the protagonists were sustained by faith in the cause of Southern independence, reinforced by a belief in the righteousness of their undertaking.[42] McPherson found references to duty and honor most often in the letters of upper-class soldiers and officers. This same pull was noticed among naturalized Americans who wanted to stand up beside their new countrymen.[43] Wiley may have been closer to the mark, however, when citing simple human feelings like wanting to join chums and seeking adventure or escape from humdrum lives.[44]

The rebels posted pickets on the turnpike toward Washington.[45] Theologians at the Episcopal Seminary west of Alexandria solemnly packed their belongings and headed north and south, not to be reunited in their religious studies for five long years. A procession of troops and supplies steamed up the Potomac past Alexandria on its way to the Washington Navy Yard. Federal authorities sought to curtail communication among the insurgents by establishing a Potomac flotilla to restrict traffic between the Maryland and Virginia shores and by seizing the four steamboats ferrying between Alexandria and Aquia Creek.[46] Marines manning Fort Washington on the Maryland shore attempted to inspect all vessels on the river. Assigned to supervise improvements in the fort's defenses, an engineer officer from Alexandria, Lt. G. W. Custis Lee, completed the task before resigning his commission and offering his services to the army organizing in Richmond.

The referendum on May 23, 1861, was the final and most crucial of the state's prewar political contests. Voter participation plummeted in Alexandria. Many of the electors had already fled the city in anticipation of the conflagration to come. It is also possible that, after the seminal events of April, anti-secessionists had difficulty mustering the enthusiasm and courage to appear at the polls and cast an unpopular vote that could be interpreted as favoring Abe Lincoln. Only 1,089 ballots were recorded in Alexandria, well below the 1,500 or more in an ordinary election, 983, or 90 percent, confirming the convention's conclusion. Across the state, 75 percent of the electorate backed the action taken in Richmond.

In this plebiscite, the political dichotomy evident between the Upper and Lower South and between populous and less-concentrated slave counties in Virginia was exhibited in Alexandria itself. The advocates of change resided in the seaport, where Publisher Snowden had shifted his position to conform with the action taken by the Richmond convention. "The madmen at the Federal Capital," read the *Alexandria Gazette,* "have struck a fatal blow, at Peace and Union. . . . Virginia, now, in defence of her honor, and her rights [employing two buzz words common to secessionist tracts], whatever may have been the differences of opinion as to the expediency or propriety of separate state secession, will assume an impregnable position defying the power of all enemies."[47] At this crucial juncture, Snowden was a follower, not a molder of public opinion. The blind optimism expressed in his commentary was not shared by military leaders at the port. The commander of volunteers recognized the unpreparedness of his troops, observed the forces being marshaled across the Potomac, and, most terrifying to him, knew of a secret order stating the Federals' intention to occupy Alexandria.[48]

In a landslide, the city of Alexandria supported secession, 958–48. Voters elsewhere in Alexandria County, however, preferred to remain in the Union by a margin of better than two to one: 58 opposed to secession, 25 in favor.[49] Rural folk tended to be more cautious, and withdrawing from the national government of their fathers and grandfathers was certainly a radical move. Residents originally from up North undoubtedly shared this view. The 1860 census identifies the birthplaces of the heads of only 101 of the 209 county households outside the city. Of this number, 27 came from the northeastern states above the Mason-Dixon line, and the place of birth of another 19 was Washington, D.C., or Maryland, where sentiments could go either way. Another 31 were born in Europe. All of these men originating outside the Commonwealth might have had unionist leanings, and, considering the incomplete census data, their actual numbers could have been twice as large. Interestingly, only 24 heads of household are listed as being of Virginia origin.[50] Perhaps these country people realized better than city dwellers that armed confrontations would take place in the first instance on their own soil.

The night after the Virginia referendum, Federal troops streamed across the Long Bridge and Aqueduct Bridge and headed into Alexandria. The Eleventh New York Volunteers approached the city by boat and climbed onto the wharves at the foot of King and Cameron Streets. Accompanied by a detail of men, Col. Elmer Ellsworth proceeded directly to the Marshall House and hauled down the offensive national flag of the Confederacy. He was shot and killed by Jackson, the proprietor, who, in turn, was mortally wounded by a Zouave, providing both the North and South with their first martyrs.

Camped apart from the rest of its command at Peyton's Grove on upper King Street, the Old Dominion Rifles did not hear the alarm and were late in leaving their quarters. They became the battalion's final element as the militiamen scrambled down Duke Street and out of town to elude the invaders. Patriotic eighteen-year-old Edgar Warfield, a prime mover in activating the outfit, was thus one of the city's last infantrymen to leave, just as he would become one of the nation's last survivors of the Civil War.[51]

Days before the invasion by Federal troops, a Northern visitor had lamented, "A more people-forsaken and desolate city I have never seen than Alexandria. The houses are low, dirty, and closed; the streets are narrow, filthy, and rough, and the people in the sackcloth of sullen humiliation. . . . The withering blight of secession had stamped its seal upon all around."[52] Stores were boarded up, wharves deserted, and most of the better families gone to the homes of friends or relatives in safer parts of Virginia. Those left behind, like Anne Frobel at Wilton Hill just south of the city, suddenly felt deserted by their friends and all alone in a fight against overwhelming military, economic, and social forces.

Alexandria quickly underwent a metamorphosis from a ghost town into a major supply depot, military railroad hub, and convalescent center for Federal soldiers. The accessibility of Alexandria to Virginia's blacks also made it a destination for slaves fleeing servitude. The Union army utilized those contrabands as unskilled labor in operating its logistical base. Huge increases in freed people and the infusion of missionaries and teachers from the North led to the organization of public schools for blacks, whereas only private instruction had been provided on a limited basis before the conflict. Nineteen free educational programs were in operation at one time or another during the early 1860s, even though "keeping a school for Negroes" was in violation of Virginia law.[53]

Another consequence of the community's burgeoning black population was heightened interest in military service. Late in the war, when the Northern army expanded its enlistment base, a recruiting station was activated in Alexandria. A local judge subsequently boasted of raising a company of 150 soldiers from among the city's blacks.[54]

Every black did not identify with the Yankee intruders, and all white Alexandrians were not Southern sympathizers. "Reverend" William Mack Lee, for example, was a body servant who cooked for Robert E. Lee during his four years in the field.[55] Loyal white Alexandrians greeted the invading soldiers and assisted them in finding quarters and provisions. The Union Association soon began meeting weekly. Many of the anti-secessionists had migrated to Alexandria from the North. For example, James Close and H. S. Martin, both originally from New York, were selected by the unionists to represent them at the convention in Wheeling to form a new state in western Virginia.[56] The most visible pro-Federal, Lewis McKenzie, was a native Alexandrian, however, and an enterprising merchant, civic booster, innovator, and politician, in addition to being president of a bank and railroad. Elected unionist mayor in November 1861 after the incumbent was unseated by the bluecoats, McKenzie was ostracized by many townsfolk following the conflict for assisting the Yankees.[57]

Despite these examples of pro-unionism, the breadth and depth of the residents' loyalty were subject to question. An effort to form a home guard in December 1861 failed when only three men volunteered to join the outfit.[58] Alexandrians with little sympathy for their conquerors were apparently willing to do just enough to make the best of a very difficult situation. If anything, the Federal occupation solidified the sympathies of the local populace behind the rebel government struggling for survival to the south.

Alexandria was unique in the Civil War experience. Despite being in a state that joined the Confederacy, the city never spent an entire day under the Stars and Bars. Its streets were occupied by Federal troops from the beginning of the conflict until its conclusion in Virginia, forty-five days short of four years later.

How did Alexandria figure in the buildup to hostilities? Michael F. Holt, the foremost scholar of the Whig Party in America, hypothesizes that its demise contributed to the outbreak of hostilities. As long as Whigs were the principal opposition to Democrats, his argument goes, sectional divisions would never have reached the boiling point that led ultimately to civil war. When Republican extremism supplanted Whiggery as the alternative to the Democratic Party, armed conflict was not far in the future.[59]

Alexandria might be thought of as a Whig stronghold right up until April 1861. Civic enterprise, new technology, accumulating savings—practices that encouraged trade and commerce were supported by citizens whose livelihood depended directly or indirectly on mercantilism. As is often the case, religion was important for explaining and justifying the status quo. The community placed a premium on education, as reflected in the number and quality of its academies. These values were not necessarily those of cities across the South, but more common to the border areas of the Upper South and Lower North that drew from both the Cavalier and Puritan traditions.

Consequently, the men dispatched by Alexandria to support their state's decision to withdraw from the Union did so, not motivated by vengeance, but with a culture and reserve uncommon in the usual breeding grounds for Confederates. Like so many individual participants in the national bloodletting, Alexandrians going to war were simply fulfilling their duty, upholding personal honor, not caught up in the political argument over a state's right to secede or the moral question of owning slaves. Their community's electorate had rejected sectional extremism and radical notions of government by supporting the Constitutional Unionist party in November 1860 and the unionist candidate in February 1861. Like their neighbors in the other slaveholding states of the Upper South, they strove for reconciliation between the antagonists to their north and south. It was clear who would be caught in the middle of a shooting war.

Alexandrians were part of the majority of Virginians in favor of moderation until Lincoln's call for militia in response to Confederate batteries opening fire on Fort Sumter. The excitement generated throughout the nation led to the state's decision to secede. Even when faced with an overwhelming 88–55 vote in favor of secession at the convention in Richmond, the delegate from Alexandria continued to represent accurately the feelings of his fellow citizens, when not under stress, by voting to stay in the Union. Afterward, pushed to the limit, most Alexandrians chose state over nation. The citizens of Tennessee, North Carolina, and Arkansas joined those of Virginia in seceding. For various reasons, the other slaveholding border states—Missouri, Kentucky, Maryland, and Delaware—remained a part of the Union.

A noted scholar on the politics of the secession crisis identifies two primary reasons for differences in attitudes between the Upper and Lower South—slaveholding and previous patterns of party allegiance.[60]

To these, in the case of Alexandria, must be added a third factor, financial considerations. Alexandria's elite could envision their city's economy moving in the direction of the North, rather than that of the Deep South's agriculture society. Steamships and a canal tied the port to Northern markets. Civic leaders consequently counseled caution. Like other communities in the Upper South, Alexandria was therefore able to withstand the initial disunionist impetus while a Southern confederacy was being formed in Montgomery, because of the existence of a rival political element to the Democratic Party in power.

From the countless Alexandrians who took action, officially or informally, in support of one side or the other, the experiences of sixteen individuals are representative of contributions made by patriotic Southerners throughout the Confederate States.[61] These examples constitute a cross-section of white Alexandrians, coming from different social and economic strata, educational levels, and ethnic backgrounds. The sample includes the scion of a First Family of Virginia and a resident born in the North, professional military officers and an immigrant, and a banker and a store clerk from the working class. Their roles reflect the range of talents elicited by the consortium of states trying to emerge as a separate nation. At the same time, one might view their credentials and accomplishments as disproportionate for a mid-sized community like Alexandria on the perimeter of the Confederacy.

The convictions that underpinned their service are not known in every case, but they were not necessarily those of the ordinary private marching west out Duke Street to fight for Virginia. A contemporary newspaper observed that "the young, the ardent, the impulsive" tended to be lured by the "contagious madness" of secession excitement. Like any revolution, the conservative majority was cowed into "passive acquiescence."[62] Alexandrians were not immune to this fever. Alexander Hunter related that in the city, "Political questions of the hour seethed and bubbled in a very maelstrom of excitement."[63] David Funsten was obviously committed to the cause of secession. Robert E. Lee and George Brent, on the other hand, were deeply troubled by the idea of leaving the Union and foresaw to some extent what lay ahead. Virginia's decision to secede was certainly a hard blow for them. In their personal commitment to Southern independence, the remaining individuals in the profiles that follow fall somewhere along the spectrum defined by these pillars of certainty. Regardless of whether we now perceive their principles to have been right or wrong, it is important that succeeding generations of Americans not forget the willingness of these men and women to make extraordinary personal sacrifices for what they believed. Hopefully, this degree of patriotism will never again be required.

CHAPTER ONE

GENERAL IN CHIEF
✯✯✯ ROBERT E. LEE

"THERE IS NO COMMUNITY TO WHICH MY AFFECTIONS more strongly cling than that of Alexandria, composed of my earliest and oldest friends, my kind school-fellows, and faithful neighbors."[1] Robert E. Lee's sentiments, expressed in his last year, reflect a lifetime of associations with his hometown. His feelings were reciprocated by the local citizenry. Its residents and their leaders spoke out on Lee's behalf at critical junctures—when he sought admission to West Point, while facing a wrenching personal decision as the nation divided, and upon his passing. Lee's military career has been thoroughly chronicled. His ties with Alexandria, stretching almost from birth to death, are less well known. Indeed, a recent biography expressed regret that "almost nothing is known of Robert's boyhood."[2] Fortunately, that is a misconception.

Robert became an Alexandrian at the age of three, when his family moved to the port city from Stratford Hall, his birthplace in Westmoreland County, Virginia. He was born on January 19, 1807, to Anne Hill Carter Lee, daughter of one of the state's richest men, and Henry ("Light Horse Harry") Lee, George Washington's favorite cavalryman during the War of Independence. Several factors contributed to the relocation. Robert's father had just been released from debtors' prison, and his wife's trust fund was insufficient to support the family at the large manor house on the banks of the lower Potomac. Ann was pregnant with their sixth child and may have wished to settle closer to her kinfolk in Northern Virginia.[3] Late in life, the general explained that his parents wanted to provide a better education for their children than possible at a remote plantation.[4]

The carriage carrying the family, some books, Robert's cradle, and a few other possessions pulled up in front of a house at what is now

611 Cameron Street. The new quarters were soon cramped with the addition of baby Mildred and, in 1812, Mrs. Lee moved into a larger, two-story, brick townhouse on Oronoco Street (now 607). This would be the residence Robert would remember as his boyhood home.

Robert's father did not remain long in Alexandria. As America entered another war with England, Light Horse Harry was seriously injured by a mob in Baltimore during a dispute concerning freedom of the press and the new nation's involvement in the conflict. Scarred almost beyond recognition, the old cavalier sailed to the Caribbean to restore his broken health. His thoughts frequently turned to his distant family, however, as indicated by two reflections on his youngest son in letters sent home: "Robert was always good, and will be confirmed in his happy turn of mind by his ever-watchful and affectionate mother. Does he strengthen his native tendency?" And, "Robert is as good as ever I trust; it is his nature, he always seemed to me to be a copy of my brother Edmund."[5]

In his father's absence, Edmund Lee was one of several male role models for Robert. A prominent attorney, Uncle Edmund served as mayor of Alexandria from 1815 to 1818 and was best remembered for his unbending application of the city's ordinances. Edmund's son, Cassius, became one of Robert's favorite playmates. Another uncle, Charles Lee, attorney general in both the Washington and Adams administrations, lived nearby on North Washington Street. Robert's two older brothers, Charles Carter Lee and Sydney Smith Lee must have taken an active interest in the youngster's welfare as well, as the general expressed special affection for them later in life. In addition, there were the Fitzhugh cousins at Ravensworth, ten miles west of the city, and the branches of his mother's family, the Carters living in nearby Fairfax and Loudoun Counties.

Robert's personal hero, however, was not a mortal of human proportions but one whose greatness was visible in his mind's eye. Historians seem to agree that this figure was George Washington, who had also considered Alexandria his hometown.[6] Robert was surrounded by reminders of the commanding general of the Continental army. As Joseph L. Harsh observed, "It was impossible to walk the streets of Alexandria, Virginia, where Lee spent much of his youth, without encountering the ghost of Washington at every corner."[7] Christ Protestant Episcopal Church, where Robert worshipped, contained Washington's Bible and pew. The square, tavern, firehouse, and post office all had connections to the squire of Mount Vernon, eight miles down the Potomac. Townspeople were still alive who remembered the first president. While the boy would have recalled war stories related by his father, it is more likely that the youngster gained greater inspiration from a mother deserted by her husband and anxious to provide a stellar male role model for her son. Mrs. Lee reportedly enjoyed telling her children about Washington and, in particular, of her meeting with him.[8]

This fascination remained a critical element of Lee's personality. As recognized by Thomas L. Connelly, "Washington was the central hero of Lee's life. His practice of duty, tact, and self-discipline often seemed a conscious effort to emulate Washington."[9] Virginia Gov. Henry Wise once teased him, "General Lee, you certainly play Washington to perfection."[10] Nor was Wise alone among Southerners in making this linkage. Gary W. Gallagher marshals statements by soldiers, civilians, and even a novelist, John Esten Cooke, to illustrate the popular affection for Lee as a latter-day Washington.[11] Another historian, Richard B. McCaslin, adds:

> Lee lived within the shadow of Washington, who had been presented to him from birth as a role model. When Lee like Washington faced a call for revolution, he read the most recent work about Washington for answers. Called to lead, Lee like Washington made himself the principal military leader in an effort to found a new nation. Lee wore a colonel's uniform as Washington had done, rode a horse bearing the name of one of his idol's mounts, Traveller; and packed one of Washington's swords in his baggage. Crushed by defeat, Lee became president of Washington College and devoted the rest of his life to enhancing his idol's legacy.[12]

The lifelong connection with Washington had its roots embedded in Lee's Alexandria days.

In addition to infusing the lore of Washington, Ann Lee taught her son the catechism before he was able to read.[13] Basic sums and Christian morals were learned at her knee. There was a limit, however, to what his mother could teach Robert at home, so she soon sent him to her sister's plantation, Eastern View, outside the city, to be instructed by the Carter family's tutor. The lad seemed a bit headstrong at one point, although Aunt Elizabeth insisted she always found him to be "a most engaging child," not at all difficult to handle.[14] Robert next entered the Alexandria Academy on Wolfe Street, where he learned Greek and Latin, the classics, and mathematics, all the while exhibiting "gentlemanly deportment" under the inspired instruction of the Irishman, William B. Leary.[15] Years later, Robert wrote to his childhood mentor, "I beg to express the gratitude I have felt all my life for the affectionate fidelity which characterised your teaching and conduct toward me."[16]

Growing up in Alexandria offered a great deal to a boy. The youth swam, skated, and fished on the Potomac and hunted ducks, geese, quail, and rabbits outside town. In August 1814, an English squadron appeared at the undefended port and demanded a ransom, which it received before sailing off down the waterway. This experience, combined with the burning of Washington City just up the river, surely left a lasting impression on Robert of the terrible cost of war.

The country's economic downturn in 1816–17 reduced the income derived from Mrs. Lee's trust, forcing her to move into the late Charles Lee's house at what is now 407 North Washington Street. Tradition holds that while playing in the yard in 1818, the eleven-year-old boy learned of his father's death on Cumberland Island, Georgia, during the journey to rejoin the family. The Lees returned to Oronoco Street in 1820.

This relocation coincided with increased responsibilities. Carter was practicing law in New York City; Smith obtained a midshipman's commission and went to sea. The health of his older sister, Ann, was poor, and so Robert was relied upon to tend the household and care for his mother, who was gradually becoming bedridden with tuberculosis.[17] Robert's time was divided among serving as nurse, overseeing his younger sister, doing the daily marketing, securing the pantry, and tending to the horses. He also accompanied his mother on daily drives in the carriage.

When considering his mother's tenuous financial situation, the young man's prospects for educational advancement did not appear promising. Robert therefore looked to the military, the arena in which both his father and his boyhood hero had distinguished themselves. Letters in support of his application to attend the U.S. Military Academy were sent by an impressive list of notables. The Virginia congressional delegation signed a joint letter to the secretary of war who recommended candidates to the president. The young Alexandrian met with Secretary John C. Calhoun in February 1824 to promote his own case. Individual members of Congress added their own personal endorsements. These declarations, plus those of Robert's brother, Carter, and half brother, William H. Fitzhugh, made reference to the candidate's amiable disposition and to the patriotic sacrifices of his father. It is even said that Lee garnered the support of Andrew Jackson.[18] William Leary wrote as well, testifying to the applicant's extraordinary conduct and academic accomplishment. Consequently, in March, Robert was offered an appointment to West Point for the class reporting in June of the following year. With his mother's blessing, he accepted.[19]

While waiting to enroll, Robert witnessed a high point in the young nation's history. During his triumphal tour of the United States in 1824–25, the Marquis de Lafayette stopped in Alexandria and visited with Mrs. Lee, the widow of his old comrade in arms. Surely, the nobleman's dialogue with the matriarch afforded Robert added insight into General Washington, his relationship with Light Horse Harry, and the

Marquis de Lafayette
in later life, as he
would have looked
when visiting Alexan-
dria in 1824–25.

importance of duty and honor. The youngster served as a marshal when
the French idol rode in a carriage through the city streets during a
parade in his honor the following Saturday.[20]

With the advent of a new year, Robert acknowledged the need to
strengthen his proficiency in mathematics in preparation for the academic examination administered to incoming plebes and West Point's
demanding engineering curriculum. He chose to study with Benjamin
Hallowell, a Quaker educator who had recently opened a school in the
residence adjoining the Lees' home on Oronoco Street. The enrollment
of Cousin Cassius no doubt added to the course's appeal. The tutorial
continued for only four months. Years after his pupil had achieved lasting fame, Hallowell wrote:

> Robert E. Lee entered my school in Alexandria, Va., in the winter of
> 1824–25, to study mathematics preparatory to his going to West Point.
> He was a most examplary student in every respect. He was never behind

time at his studies; never failed in a single recitation; was perfectly obser-
vant of the rules and regulations of the institution; was gentlemanly, unob-
trusive, and respectful in all his deportment to teachers and his fellow
students. His specialty was finishing up. He imparted a finish and a neatness, as he proceeded, to everything he undertook ... He drew the dia-
grams on a slate; and although he well knew that the one he was drawing
would have to be removed to make room for another, he drew each one
with as much accuracy and finish, lettering and all, as if it were to be
engraved and printed.[21]

The fifteen formative years of Robert's residence in Alexandria came
to a close in June 1825. By this time he was considered a handsome lad,
five foot ten inches in height, with brown eyes and wavy black hair. He
avoided smoking and intoxicating beverages, except for an occasional
glass of wine, and had no use for profane or immoral language. His character, values, self-discipline, and rigid economy in financial affairs had
been formed through his mother's strong influence, formal instruction,
and the family responsibilities thrust onto his shoulders at an early age.
As he departed, his mother was said to exclaim, "How can I live without
Robert? He is both son and daughter to me."[22]

Cadet Lee graduated second in the West Point class of 1829 and, consequently, received a commission as second lieutenant in the Corps of
Engineers. Two years later, he was in Alexandria once again, this time on
an important mission of a personal nature. His mother's cousin, Anne,
resided with her husband and daughter at Arlington House in Alexandria County on the Potomac River four and a half miles above the port.
George Washington Parke Custis relished the distinction of being the
patriot's adopted son and filled his home with former possessions and
mementos of the father of his country. During countless visits as a youth,
Robert had listened to stories of George Washington from the lord of the
manor while, at the same time, developing a deep affection for young
Mary Custis. On June 30, 1831, with his brother Smith as best man,
Robert married Mary at Arlington under the arches in the parlor. Coin-
cidentally, in 1804 Mary's mother and father had wed in the house on
Oronoco Street where Lee grew to manhood.

Over the next three decades, Lee went off to a series of postings across
the expanding country but returned periodically to Arlington. On one
such visit in 1853, occasioned by the death of his mother-in-law, Lee was
confirmed as an Episcopalian in a ceremony at Christ Church. He was
concluding two years of extended leave at the estate in October 1859
when he learned some sobering news. While conducting business at
Leadbeater's apothecary shop on South Fairfax Street in Alexandria,
Lee received a dispatch from the War Department ordering him to take
charge of military operations at Harpers Ferry, where an anti-slavery

Robert E. Lee in the dress uniform of a lieutenant of engineers, U.S. Army.
Portrait by William Edward West, 1838. Washington-Custis-Lee Collection,
Washington and Lee University.

extremist, John Brown, had seized the U.S. armory. Lee hurried away to
confront this threat to national unity.

In the spring of 1861, as the Virginia convention debated secession,
Lee, in residence again at Arlington, faced one of the most important
decisions of his life. Francis Preston Blair, President Lincoln's intermediary, had spoken with the colonel about taking field command of
the seventy-five thousand troops being raised to confront the growing

challenge to the Union. With loyalties divided between nation and state, Lee confided his inner conflict to Bvt. Lt. Gen. Winfield Scott, the army's general in chief and his mentor since the Mexican War. It was still possible that Virginia would not secede and that Lee would be spared from taking up arms against the Commonwealth, but he could still be ordered to lead Federal forces against other Southerners. Tormented about what to do, Lee sought the advice of friends whose counsel he valued.

On his way out of Washington on April 18, he stopped to confer with his brother Smith, now on duty at the capital. They could come to no resolution and decided to meet again. Lee also consulted with his childhood chum Cassius Lee, a strong advocate of remaining in the Union. After several hours, they, too, could not agree on a course of action. The cousins reportedly parted with the understanding that Lee would resign from the army but remain neutral in any conflict to come.[23]

Like the majority of Alexandrians, Lee hoped that delegates to the Richmond convention would resist the temptation to secede. His fears were realized on the morning of April 19, when he learned that the convention had voted two days earlier to withdraw from the Union and scheduled a referendum in late May to put the decision before the state's electorate. Tending to business in Alexandria, Lee stopped to settle an account with his friend, John Leadbeater. Opposite the record of payment in the apothecary ledger is the annotation that Lee remarked dejectedly, "I must say that I am one of those dull creatures that cannot see the good of secession."[24] The tormented colonel wrestled with the predicament late into the night in his room at Arlington and by morning had signed a letter surrendering his commission.[25]

Lee's dilemma was hardly a secret to Alexandrians. Edgar Snowden, publisher of the *Alexandria Gazette,* addressed the matter in an editorial. He assured readers that whatever the outcome, considering the man making the decision, it "will be conscientious and honorable." The commentary went on to declare that, should Lee resign his commission, the state of Virginia would be wise to turn to him for military leadership, as he would command the people's respect.[26]

The most authoritative statement of what happened next is that of Harriotte Lee, the twenty-one-year-old daughter of Cassius Lee, who arrived at her parents' home on North Washington Street on Saturday, April 20. Her father was nonresponsive when asked about Cousin Robert. The next morning, Robert was seated as usual in his pew at Christ Church. After the service, Harriotte stopped at the nearby home of a relative, where she found one of Robert's daughters (presumably Mary, the eldest) and engaged her in a long talk. The cousin revealed that her father had submitted his resignation, to which Harriotte expressed great delight. "It is no gratification to us, it is like a death in the house," the young woman retorted. "Since my father went to West Point, the army had been his home and his life, he expected to live and die belonging to it, and only his sense of duty made him leave it."[27]

Continuing up Washington Street to her own house, Harriotte found her father absent. He returned after a walk along the canal with Robert, who was concerned about being offered command of Virginia's forces. Cassius advised him to await the outcome of the referendum on the ordinance of secession, but they both knew that a difficult decision loomed ahead. Gov. John Letcher had serially dispatched David Funsten and Judge John Robertson to invite Lee to Richmond, where he would be offered leadership of the state's military at the convention still in session.[28] When he departed by train for the Virginia capital on April 22, Lee did not realize that it would be eight years before he once again passed over the cobblestones of his hometown.

Contact with friends behind Federal lines was almost impossible for the Lees during the four long years that followed. As the country settled into war, in June 1862 the Alexandrian was appointed to command what became the Army of Northern Virginia. In January 1865, by act of the Confederate Congress, he was designated general in chief of all its armies. Once the conflict was over, their hometown was never far from the Lees' thoughts. Mary Custis Lee was pleased to renew correspondence with her cousin, Louisa Snowden, wife of the newspaper publisher. Robert wrote to James Green, owner of the city's largest furniture company, about obtaining furnishings for the president's house at Washington College, where he now resided. In correspondence to another Alexandrian, Lee took the opportunity to laud the Episcopal Theological Seminary just outside town, praising its purpose and professors.[29]

When traveling from his postwar home in Lexington, Virginia, to Washington, D.C., Lee transferred from the Orange and Alexandria Railroad to a Potomac steamer in Alexandria but did not take time to stop and see his friends there until May 1869.[30] On that occasion, he had gone to Baltimore with backers of a proposed railroad in the Shenandoah Valley and then paid a call on President U. S. Grant at the White House. The return to Lexington included a visit to Alexandria. Arriving at the wharf on a boat from the capital, the old rebel chieftain walked up King Street and turned right on Washington Street to the residence of Mrs. Anna Maria Fitzhugh on the southeast corner of Queen Street, where he was to stay. Astonished passers-by uncovered their heads in respect, and word spread quickly that the revered son of Alexandria had come home.

So many residents flocked to his aunt's door to see the celebrity that a reception was scheduled the following evening in the parlor of Mr. Green's Mansion House hotel. For three hours, boyhood chums, friends and admirers, former soldiers, and the curious streamed by to shake Lee's hand. Montgomery Corse, the Alexandrian who commanded a brigade in Pickett's division, introduced those well-wishers who had never met the honoree.[31] Among those delighted to see the former Confederate general in chief, it was reported, was one of his former slaves. "It was more like a family meeting than anything else—for we here regard Gen. Lee as one of our Alexandria boys," opined the local newspaper. "We have never seen a more lovely exhibition of the grateful and unbought homage of the heart to worth and high character than was exhibited last evening. It was a scene long to be remembered."[32]

The following day, the elderly general met with John Janney, the unionist who had presided over the 1861 state convention that voted for secession and confirmed Lee's selection as commander of Virginia's military and naval forces. According to local lore, the pilgrim returned to his childhood home on Oronoco Street and peered over the garden wall to see if the viburnum, or snowball bushes, were in bloom. Lee also drove out to see Samuel Cooper and spend the night with Cousin Cassius at Menokin, his country estate on Seminary Hill. On Ascension Sunday (May 6), Lee worshiped at Christ Church with Smith, who had ridden in from his farm to be with Robert. It was the last time the brothers would be together. General Lee's hectic three days in Alexandria closed with another social, this time at the home of John B. Daingerfield, a prosperous merchant.

Although relatively brief, the visit was an opportunity to enjoy one last period of fellowship with those who had meant so much and, in turn, to receive their adulation. Lee expressed his gratitude in a letter to his son Rooney: "I had, upon the whole, a pleasant visit, and was particularly glad to see again our old friends and neighbours in Alexandria and vicinity; though should have preferred to enjoy their company in a more quiet way."[33]

Seven weeks later, Smith Lee died suddenly at his home in Stafford County. The body was brought to the city by steamboat on July 23, accompanied by his niece, Robert's daughter Mary, among others. Included as pallbearers were two former leaders of the old Seventeenth Virginia—Montgomery Corse and Arthur Herbert. General Lee took the train from Staunton but was terribly disappointed not to arrive until the evening of July 24, too late to attend the burial service earlier that day at Christ Church. The two brothers had been very close, sharing, in Mary's words, "a nobility of character and goodness of heart" acquired from their mother at a simpler time in Alexandria's life.[34]

Lee made one last trip to the seaport, arriving by train on July 1, 1870. He continued on to Baltimore for a medical examination and then visited relatives in Maryland before finally recrossing the Potomac for the last time on July 14. Back in his hometown, Lee's first order of business was consulting with his attorney, Francis Lee Smith, about the prospects of recovering Arlington from the U.S. government. Lee's complaints about the "piping hot" Mansion House elicited an invitation to move into the lawyer's majestic three-story residence on Wolfe Street, where friends once again stopped by to pay respects to the aging warrior. Among the admirers was the former partisan leader John S. Mosby, who recalled that Lee's adieu was, "Colonel, I hope we shall have no more wars."[35]

It is said that Lee made a final stop at his childhood home on Oronoco Street, where the present occupant kept Mrs. Lee's bedroom just as she had left it. The devoted son paused there for prayer.[36]

The general then rode out to Seminary Hill to visit Cassius Lee, his trusted confidant of long standing. According to Cazenove, his host's young son, the retiring warrior uncharacteristically revealed personal feelings about the war and its commanders. He spoke of "Stonewall" Jackson's failing at Mechanicsville and the inestimable absence of his leadership at Gettysburg. This was the conversation during which Lee was alleged to have identified George B. McClellan as the ablest of Federal generals. The childhood chums also spent a few moments fondly remembering Mr. Leary, their old teacher at the Alexandria Academy.[37]

The rigors of campaigning had taken its toll on the sexagenarian, and he did not have long to live. The general had complained to Corse, Francis Lee Smith, and other Alexandrians about increasing feebleness over the past winter.[38] Robert Edward Lee joined his illustrious ancestors on the morning of October 12, 1870. By late afternoon, word of his death reached Alexandria. Press accounts stated that the city was traumatized, people talking of nothing else, joined in grief irrespective of politics, united in sorrow for a loss that seemed personal to each individual.[39] The city council met and asked businesses to close on October 15, the date set for services in Lexington. Offices and private residences were draped in mourning, ships in port displayed flags at half mast, church and fire bells tolled intermittently, and portraits of the Confederate icon hung with crape throughout the city.

On the day of the funeral, a public meeting convened outside the Methodist Church on South Washington Street. On a platform erected for the remembrance, Mayor Hugh Latham was joined by the city's old guard—publisher Edgar Snowden, former general Corse, and Confederate colonels Herbert and Morton Marye, among others. The gathering heard the report of a citizens committee appointed the previous day at Liberty Hall. Its members included such civic leaders as George Brent, another war veteran. Resolutions expressing the community's sorrow were prefaced by a statement explaining Lee's special relationship with the people of Alexandria: "It was here that he received a portion of his early education, it was here that his tenderest associations were created and maintained, it is here that cherished friendships were formed which lasted through life, and towards this place and its people, he always showed deep attachment."[40] In the days following Lee's interment in Lexington, Alexandrians continued to speculate about whether his mortal remains would be returned to their city to be enshrined among those of his relatives and friends.[41]

Under Snowden's direction, the local newspaper printed a series of accounts and editorials from Lexington, Richmond, and cities in the North concerning Lee's lifetime of accomplishments, his final hours, reactions to his passing, and commemorative ceremonies in his honor. The paper praised Lee's "unselfish course, his modest and retiring deportment, his devotion to duty and to principle." As the accolades mounted, the first signs appeared of the Alexandrian's transformation from Southern idol to a hero of national proportions. The *New York Herald* recognized traits transcending sectionalism:

> Here in the North . . . we have long since ceased to look upon him as the Confederate leader, but have claimed him as one of ourselves; have cherished and felt proud of his military genius as belong to us; have recounted and recorded his triumphs as our own; have extolled his virtues as reflecting honor upon us—for Robert Edmund [*sic*] Lee was an American, and the great nation which gave him birth would be to day unworthy of such a son if she regarded him lightly. . . . In his death our country has lost a son in whom she might well be proud.[42]

Of all the tributes, however, it is likely that the Confederacy's general in chief would have derived the greatest pride from references to his childhood hero. "Never, since General Washington died, has any death produced, in this city, such manifestations of universal regret as that of General Robert Edward Lee," the *Alexandria Gazette* reported. Rising to the occasion, the newspaper concluded an editorial tribute: "The people of Virginia are in mourning for the illustrious dead—the man for whom they have felt an affectionate reverence similar to that which their fathers felt for George Washington."[43]

As the most renowned Alexandrian to serve the South, General Lee was well known to his fellow citizens, who closely followed his accomplishments during the war and visited with him whenever the opportunity arose. But Lee was by no means the only prominent Alexandria resident to devote his energies to the Lost Cause. Others of high and low station volunteered for duty, performed honorably, and interacted with one another throughout the long ordeal and afterward. The story of the roles played by Alexandrians in the conflict transcends Lee's service and encompasses a variety of men and women, some still known and others no longer familiar.

CHAPTER TWO

SENIOR GENERAL
✷✷✷ SAMUEL COOPER

WHO WAS SAMUEL COOPER, THE SENIOR-RANKING GENERAL in the Confederate army?[1] "A man as pure in heart as he was sound in judgment," as described by his patron, Jefferson Davis, or "that slow coach," as characterized by one Richmonder.[2] Why did this veteran of forty-six years in the U.S. Army resign his commission and risk considerable personal wealth as the first senior officer to join the rebels forming the Confederate States of America? What role did Cooper play in the Southern war effort?

The answers to these questions have their roots in Hackensack, New York, on the banks of the Hudson, where Samuel Cooper was born on June 12, 1798, to a veteran of the same name who had served in George Washington's Continental army. Young Sam entered West Point in 1813 and, two years later, graduated thirty-sixth in a class of forty cadets. He was commissioned an artillery officer, like his father, and served with batteries in Boston, the Washington, D.C., area, and Old Point Comfort, Virginia, at the mouth of Chesapeake Bay. Cooper's experiences during his first thirty-three years in uniform (1818–51) were recounted in an autobiography that he began after the Civil War but never completed.[3]

During a tour in the nation's capital as a first lieutenant in the Office of the Adjutant and Inspector General, 1818–25, Cooper made the acquaintance of Sarah Maria Mason, granddaughter of the patriot George Mason. On April 4, 1827, they were married at her family's estate on Analostan (now Teddy Roosevelt) Island in the Potomac River opposite Georgetown. The festivities resumed the following afternoon, when the bride's eldest brother, John, wed the daughter of Brig. Gen. Alexander Macomb. The "frolicking" continued for two more days.[4]

At this point, fact gives way to gossip. Washington society was small and inbred in the early days of the republic. Maria's mother allegedly missed her newly married daughter when she moved to the Norfolk area, where her husband was stationed. Mrs. Mason reportedly suggested to Macomb that she would use her influence to have him appointed the army's general in chief if he would select her son-in-law as his aide, thereby returning Maria and her husband to the capital. A sister of Mrs. Mason was married to Richard Rush, secretary of the treasury under President John Quincy Adams. Adeptly using that connection, the socialite mother reportedly ensured that Macomb was the selection in 1828 over the ambitious brevet Maj. Gen. Winfield Scott.[5] Years later, Cooper emphatically denied this explanation of his appointment.[6] Nonetheless, the careers of the veteran of the War of 1812 and the socially connected young officer would repeatedly converge in the small army of the antebellum years.

In 1835, Cooper received acclaim for authoring the *Concise System of Instructions and Regulations for the Militia and Volunteers of the United States* (popularly known as "Cooper's Infantry Tactics"), which adapted the French model to the American army. The manual was subsequently used by American troops in Mexico. Scott had earlier translated the French version into English and resented its distillation by a novice who had never appeared on a battlefield. Shortly thereafter, in 1836–37, Cooper served as the judge advocate who presented the case before a court of inquiry against Scott's conduct in the Seminole and Creek campaigns. Scott was found innocent of serious wrongdoing. Cooper subsequently recalled a confrontation with the accused over what documents should be appended to the report of the proceedings.[7] Two years later, Cooper was brevetted a major and made assistant adjutant general, serving as military aide to the secretary of war and functioning as acting secretary in his absence.[8]

Macomb died in 1841 and was immediately succeeded by Scott as the army's commanding general—perhaps not coincidentally, about the same time Cooper left Washington for his only tour of duty with a field command engaged in combat. He was assigned to the headquarters of Col. William J. Worth, a longtime friend of Scott who commanded forces in Florida charged with rounding up the Seminole Indians. Worth had a reputation for being vain, self-centered, rash, and impetuous.[9]

Worth's force numbered about five thousand men, almost half on sick call during July 1841. The new commander divided his companies into detachments of twenty or so to be used as partisans to ferret out Indians resisting resettlement to the west. Given Cooper's background, it is not surprising that he was assigned as acting adjutant general and functioned as chief of staff.[10] The following February, he was dispatched to the War

Department carrying a letter from Worth recommending that military operations be terminated. Cooper added his own notes to Scott, pointing out that the number of warriors still in opposition did not exceed 120 and supporting his commander's conclusions. A council of officers, chaired by the secretary, decided against Worth's proposal, however.[11]

Cooper returned to duty in Florida for the conflict's last major battle, which, considering the numbers involved, was hardly an epic struggle. On April 19, 1842, Worth directed a force of four hundred soldiers, blacks, and friendly Indians against a band of forty Seminoles dug in on a dense hummock near the army's Camp Palaklakaha. The defenders were soon routed. Cooper reported one man killed, plus a sergeant and three privates wounded.[12] Ten days later, the native chieftain came into the soldiers' camp with his wives and children and organized resistance ceased. It was not long thereafter that Washington decided to declare victory and remove U.S. troops from the area.[13]

Cooper was then assigned by Scott to the military headquarters at St. Louis. A letter to his wife at this time reiterates the friction he felt with Scott: "The Governor (Moultrie) [Alexandre Mouton of Louisiana] . . . was pleased to compliment me in respect to my book on Tactics, telling me that he was indebted to the work for the little knowledge he had acquired in the military. You must not tell this to a certain General S in Washington lest I might make him feel a little more hostile towards me than is already the case."[14] After serving in various staff positions in the West for four years, Cooper was reassigned back to the War Department to serve as assistant to the secretary and was brevetted lieutenant colonel in 1847.

Returning from Mexico the following year, Scott was displeased to find that Cooper had stayed home but was nevertheless promoted to colonel for his role in prosecuting the war from Washington. The general in chief ordered Cooper into the field on inspection duties. A yearlong odyssey ensued, taking Cooper to Louisiana, Florida, Texas, Arkansas, Kansas, and, finally, the Wyoming Territory. He inspected posts along the Rio Grande, met gold miners returning from California, and helped organize an Indian powwow at Fort Laramie.[15]

In 1852 Cooper returned to Washington to be appointed adjutant general of the army with the rank of colonel. The following year, President Franklin Pierce selected Jefferson Davis as secretary of war. Cooper and Davis molded a close working relationship that the Mississippian warmly recalled years later:

> My personal acquaintance with General Cooper began at the time when he was associated with Mr. [Joel] Poinsett in the War Office, where his professional knowledge was made available to the Secretary, in those army

details of which a civilian was necessarily but little informed. His sterling character and uniform courtesy soon attracted the attention and caused him to be frequently resorted to by members of Congress having business with the War Office. Ex-President Pierce, who was then a Senator, spoke in after years of the favorable impression which General Cooper had made upon him, and said his habit had been when he "wanted information to go to Cooper instead of to the Secretary;" but while he thus brought to the service of the Secretary his professional knowledge, the latter eminently great in other departments of learning, no doubt did much to imbue General Cooper's mind with those political ideas which subsequently marked him as more profoundly informed upon the character of our Government than most others of his profession. . . .

I never, in four years of constant consultation, saw Cooper manifest prejudice, or knew him to seek favors for a friend, or to withhold what was just from one to whom he bore reverse relations. This rare virtue— this supremacy of judgment over feeling—impressed as being so exceptional . . . that it deserves to be known by all men.[16]

During these prewar years, Cooper's assistants included Joseph Hooker, Irvin McDowell, Don Carlos Buell, Fitz John Porter, and Lorenzo Thomas, all of whom would soon achieve varying measures of fame while fighting for the Union.

Cooper maintained quarters in Washington City and, in July 1839, purchased property across the river outside Alexandria County. The estate known as "Cameron" was situated on a ridge overlooking Cameron Valley not far from the Episcopal Seminary. The holding consisted of twenty-one acres with a mansion, various outbuildings, and a number of slaves.[17] At Cameron resided Cooper's wife, two daughters, Jennie and Marie, and son, Samuel, along with a pair of matronly Mason sisters. Not surprisingly, the Coopers were socially active, entertaining notables like their neighbor at Arlington House, Lt. Col. Robert E. Lee, when he returned to Northern Virginia on a visit in 1854 while serving as superintendent of the U.S. Military Academy.[18]

As a new nation began forming to the south, Cooper must have been torn as to what to do. Jennie had married a lieutenant from Rhode Island, Frank Wheaton, and she sided with her husband, who would quickly rise to general officer rank. Yet Cooper's home outside Alexandria and his wife's family, with whom he was very close, pulled him in another direction. One of Cooper's last acts as adjutant general was to sign an order dismissing brevet Maj. Gen. David E. Twiggs from the U.S. Army, whereupon he received an equivalent permanent rank in the Provisional Army of the Confederate States, becoming the oldest officer of the old army to take up arms for the South. Another historic act was to communicate the secretary of war's instructions to Maj. Robert Anderson at Fort Sumter, S.C.[19] On March 7, 1861, six weeks before Lee left the army and more than two months in advance of Virginia's formal secession, Cooper resigned his commission.[20]

Without his lost personal papers to consult, Cooper's motives for defecting from the Union must be based purely on speculation. Several reasons have been advanced. The first is the influence of his two brothers-in-law, U.S. Sen. James Murray Mason and Comdr. Sydney Smith Lee. The former was Cooper's wife's brother. He sat for a while in the Confederate Congress before being sent to Paris as diplomatic representative of the government in Richmond.[21] The naval officer was Robert E. Lee's brother, who was married to Mrs. Cooper's sister. He resigned from the U.S. Navy after forty-four years to join the Virginia navy. These prominent American leaders were committing themselves and their fortunes to the new Southern nation. A second attraction for Cooper must have been the election in February 1861 of Jefferson Davis as provisional president of the infant government. Cooper had formed a close personal bond with Davis at the War Department in Washington. Conversely, Cooper was never comfortable working with Scott, who remained general in chief of the Union army at the war's outset.[22]

Not to be discounted is another reason that modern-day students of the war may undervalue. Cooper believed in states' rights. Many Southerners without chattel shared this now-unfashionable view of the federal system. Cooper reportedly objected to what he considered a misuse of national power. Davis recalled that his old friend and aide "foresaw the storm, which was soon to burst upon the seceding states— . . . the power to use the military arm of the General Government to coerce a State, was to be employed without doubt, and conscientiously believing that would be violative of the fundamental principles of the compact of Union, he resigned his commission, which was his whole wealth."[23] The issues that caused states to secede were clearly of utmost importance to the old soldier residing in what would become the city of Alexandria.

Arriving in Montgomery, Alabama, where a government was being organized, Cooper offered his services to the new nation on March 14. Davis immediately appointed him to the position of adjutant and inspector general of the Confederate army. In August, the president placed his name at the top of a list of five officers recommended for the rank of full general—Cooper, Albert Sydney Johnston, Lee, Joseph E. Johnston, and P. G. T. Beauregard. Davis reasoned that Cooper was senior as a colonel to Sydney Johnston and Lee in the old army, despite Johnston's brevet rank as brigadier general under special circumstances. Davis considered the designation of Joseph E. Johnston, the army's quartermaster general, as brigadier general to be a "protective rank," as he was prohibited

Samuel Cooper in a Confederate general's uniform. Virginia Historical Society.

from exercising command. Furthermore, Davis noted that Lee and J. E. Johnston had transferred into the Confederate army from the Virginia army, where Lee had been accorded senior status.[24]

The Confederate Congress confirmed the nominations on August 31. Scant notice was given the rankings in the Southern press. For once, even the Richmond diarist, Mary Chesnut, was silent. Joseph E. Johnston strongly objected, however, in a letter to Davis that the secretary of the navy, Stephen Mallory, characterized as "intemperate." He termed the president's reply "very sharp."[25] Thus began the animosity between the two Southern leaders that lasted throughout the war and well afterward.[26]

Cooper's most important role was that of confidant to the Confederate president. The two men were seen conferring over breakfast and dinner in Montgomery.[27] They attended church together. When the capital relocated to Richmond, the two colleagues departed in the same coach from the West Point depot outside Montgomery. The pairing was significant, as members of the cabinet did not leave until some time thereafter.[28] Once in Virginia, Cooper's office shared occupancy with the War Department in a brick building formerly used by the Mechanics Institute. Davis and Cooper reportedly met regularly at eleven each morning.[29]

Cooper's greatest contribution to the Southern war effort may well have been his leadership in organizing and deploying an army in 1861 and 1862. As a senior staff officer experienced at the pinnacle of power, Cooper was an invaluable resource to a nascent nation needing defense against its parent government to the north. Within days of his appointment, Cooper communicated with Col. William J. Hardee and Brig. Gen. Braxton Bragg, commanding Forts Morgan and Pensacola, respectively, concerning defenses along the Gulf of Mexico. Cooper transmitted the intention of the secretary of war to send Bragg five thousand infantrymen from Georgia and the nearby Gulf States.[30] Carrying out the cabinet's decision to acquire arms and supplies in Europe, Cooper and the chief of ordnance, Col. Josiah Gorgas, met with Caleb Huse to provide instructions and money to execute this mission. Cooper also conferred with the secretary of war regarding the number and disposition of regiments in the field.[31]

After the government relocated to Richmond, Cooper continued to work to build force structure. Cooper sent Tennessee Gov. Isham Harris and Maj. Gen. Leonidas Polk directions on receipt of the provisional army of Tennessee into Confederate States service.[32] Even in the first year of conflict, the South needed the service of every possible soldier. In November, Cooper responded to a Polk inquiry regarding exchange of prisoners from the battle of Belmont with the guidance, "Make full exchange if possible; if not exchange on equal terms."[33]

In February 1862, Cooper wrote to Gen. Joseph E. Johnston and the other commanding generals asking for the names and units of soldiers needed to satisfy the requirement identified by the chief of ordnance for two hundred additional gunsmiths and machinists to keep the Richmond armory working around the clock.[34] Early in the mobilization, Cooper established a bureau for volunteers and conscription, and its agents fanned out across the South in search of recruits. By 1864, problems with conscripts and deserters were being reported to Cooper.

In March, then–Lieutenant General Polk complained about the ineffi-
ciency of the Conscript Bureau and asked that, as department commander, he be given oversight of their activities in his area. Cooper
referred the matter to Secretary of War James A. Seddon with the observation, "To comply with the suggestions in this letter would but add to the
military responsibilities of General Polk, and would not lessen the evil
complained of, inasmuch as it would require the same amount of force to
enforce conscription and apprehend deserters, to which the general
here objects."[35] The secretary of war responded directly to Polk, putting
his proposal to rest. Later in the war, in the South's desperation to fill its
depleted ranks, Cooper sought to enlarge the population of potential
recruits by writing to units in the field encouraging them to welcome with
open arms Northerners crossing the lines out of sympathy for the Southern cause.[36] This initiative proved equally ineffective.

Not every commander was pleased with the help coming from headquarters. The exemplary reputation enjoyed by W. H. C. Whiting at the
war's outset, plus their personal friendship, emboldened the brigadier
general to complain to Cooper in November 1861: "What are they sending me unarmed and new regiments for? Don't want them. They will only
be in my way. Can't feed them nor use them. I want re-enforcements, not
recruits. Please to put those new regiments somewhere else. They can do
no good here, and will only seriously embarrass all operations."[37]

A well-documented episode illustrated Cooper's marginal involvement
in strategic planning early in the conflict. Brig. Gen. P. G. T. Beauregard
sent Col. James Chesnut to Richmond to present a grandiose "plan of
operations" to join his forces with those of Joseph E. Johnston in a series
of offensive forays intended to capture Washington and end the conflict.
On July 14, 1861, in the parlor of Richmond's Spotswood Hotel, Chesnut
met to discuss the concept with Davis, Cooper, and Brig. Gen. Robert E.
Lee, then serving as military adviser to the president. Beauregard was subsequently informed that the triumvirate considered the proposal "brilliant and comprehensive" but impractical.[38]

Once fighting erupted outside Washington, Davis telegraphed Cooper
from Manassas Junction at midnight after the battle to inform him of the
Southern victory. Mrs. Chesnut recorded how she learned the outcome
of the confrontation. "At the foot of [the stairs] stood General Cooper,
radiant, one finger nervously arranging his shirt collar, or adjusting his
neck to it, after his fashion. He called out: 'Your South Carolina man bon-
homme [Beauregard] has done a capital thing at Bulls Run—driven back
the enemy if not defeated him, killed, and prisoners—&c&c&c.'"[39]

As the conflict intensified and field commanders gained more experience and, in some cases, greater confidence and credibility, Cooper's limited input to strategy appeared to wane. The decline in his influence may

have begun with Lee's assignment in June 1862 to head the Southern army on the Peninsula. In an attempt to deny intelligence to Northern agents, the new commander clamped down on dissemination of information concerning his regiments and their whereabouts. Consequently, even the adjutant general's office was in the dark as to where to direct officers and men returning from leave.[40] A consummate military politician, Lee kept the president fully informed. As Lee's star ascended, gratuitous commentary diminished from the general staff in Richmond.

There were, of course, occasional opportunities late in the war for the adjutant general to become involved in military policy. One instance occurred in the spring of 1864, when Brig. Gen. William N. Pendleton returned from Dalton, Georgia, to report on the status of artillery in the Army of Tennessee. After conferring with Davis, Cooper, General Bragg, and the secretary of war, Pendleton was sent to the front to consult with Lee.[41] On another occasion late that year, Davis, Lee, Seddon, and Cooper each agreed upon a plan of mutual support between Bragg and Hardee, by that time commanding at Wilmington and Charleston, respectively, should either come under attack.[42] After the conflict, an anonymous government observer best summarized Cooper's limited role: "Though often consulted as to the policy of a campaign, or as to the disposition to be made of any officer for whom, or against whom, the people and press clamored, his advice was not invariably asked on things outside of his direct line; when asked it was seldom acted on."[43]

Even if they did not solicit his advice, commanders could satisfy their requirement to keep headquarters informed by filing reports, however brief, with the nonconfrontational adjutant general. Beauregard initially dismissed Cooper's inquiry about his withdrawal from Corinth in late May 1862 by replying that he was too busy to write.[44] Bragg used the same approach the following year, sending a series of brief communiqués to Cooper to report the retreat of his army from Tullahoma to Chattanooga, thereby understating the strategic significance of the withdrawal of Confederate forces from the breadbasket of Tennessee.[45] A third example took place in the Department of Western Virginia, when Maj. Gen. John C. Breckinridge took command there in early 1864. After initially trying to provide for his men and horses, consistent with the food and forage policies of the commissary general, but receiving no outside aid in return, Breckinridge determined to ignore his past instructions from Richmond. He informed Cooper that unless directed otherwise by the War Department, supplies obtained within his area of responsibility would be used to provision his own command.[46]

It was clear that the president was the supreme authority, but, despite a voracious appetite for military matters, the other demands on his time prevented Davis from becoming personally involved in every issue presented to the War Department. In theory, lines of authority were clearly drawn, from the president through the secretary of war and adjutant general to commanders in the field. In reality, responsibility was initially blurred, as illustrated by the frustration encountered by an emissary from Northern Virginia in mid-June 1861. With Beauregard's endorsement at Manassas, Capt. J. Morris Wampler of the Virginia militia was sent to Richmond by the regimental commander in Leesburg to warn of the Federal threat to occupy Loudoun County, thereby isolating Harpers Ferry and its armory from the South. The messenger carried a request that more troops be assigned to this sector. He was shuffled from the secretary of war to the president's office and then to the adjutant general, who referred him to the commander of Virginia state forces. Cooper proved no more helpful than the others, and the supplicant returned home empty-handed.[47]

Establishing an officer corps was the first order of business. In May 1861, the Southern congress provided for dramatic expansion in its miniscule regular army by creating the Provisional Army of the Confederate States. The president reserved the authority to appoint generals, leaving the secretary of war to commission other officers, with certain exceptions. Beauregard ran afoul of this system when he began making appointments to his army in Northern Virginia in the fall of 1861. Informed of his transgression, the Creole assured Cooper that it was not his intention to usurp the president's authority. It was less intimidating to complain to the adjutant general than to confront the president or secretary of war. At the war's outset, when a Texan believed he had been unjustly denied a captaincy in the regular army that had been promised, he did not hesitate to charge into Cooper's office, express his outrage, and tear up the unsatisfactory commission.[48] A clear case of overreaching occurred later, in June 1863, when Secretary of War James Seddon instructed the adjutant general to reassign Maj. Gen. D. H. Hill. The old general returned the communiqué without action, advising Seddon to consult with Davis, as Cooper believed the president held other views.[49]

To most officers in the field lacking personal acquaintance with President Davis, Adjutant General Cooper was the obvious addressee for correspondence regarding their careers. Clearly, his office was responsible for personnel placements and promotions. Consequently, after Brig. Gen. Richard Garnett clashed with Maj. Gen. Thomas J. "Stonewall" Jackson during the early spring of 1862, he asked Cooper for a court-martial and, if that was impractical, orders anywhere else.[50] When Lt. Gen. Edmund Kirby Smith could stand working for Bragg no longer, he pleaded for any other assignment.[51] Maj. Gen. B. Franklin Cheatham felt the same way at one point, but given a choice of retaining his rank or being reassigned to a position of lesser importance, he chose to remain with Bragg.[52] Disgusted with the same martinet, Lt. Gen. James Longstreet also asked Cooper to be transferred to some other command.[53]

Feelings about promotions could be equally emotional, which would have created awkward situations for an adjutant general less experienced than Cooper. On occasion, his office would request that commanders submit nominations to fill senior vacancies. Politicking would take place initially in the field, but it would not take long for Cooper to be placed in the middle between commanding generals and, occasionally, members of the Confederate Congress. At other times, ambitious officers would confront Cooper on their own initiative. In December 1862, Brig. Gen. Isaac Trimble bluntly wrote to the adjutant general, whom he knew very well, "If I am to have promotion I want it *at once* and I particularly request, that my date may be from 26th August [1862], the date of the capture of [Second] Manassas."[54] Trimble's subsequent promotion provided an effective date of rank of January 17, 1863. Perhaps not surprisingly, disappointed officers sometimes suspected the adjutant general's office of favoritism. One such claimant wrote, "I am still a Maj whilst almost every acquaintance in Lees Army has since that time been promoted from one to three grades."[55]

The adjutant general served as a buffer for the president and secretary of war. Good news came from the politicians; an unpleasant message would often be dispatched over the signature of Samuel Cooper. A prime example occurred with the change of leadership in the Confederate army defending Atlanta in July 1864. The adjutant general signed the message to Gen. Joseph E. Johnston, relieving him of command of the Army of Tennessee. Secretary Seddon sent greetings to Gen. John B. Hood on his new assignment as commanding general.[56]

Throughout the war, Cooper was constantly involved in deliberations evaluating and assigning senior officers. Cooper knew many of these individuals from his long service in the headquarters of the old army, and consequently his opinions carried weight with Davis. For example, in 1862 General Johnston took advantage of his prewar friendship with Cooper to try to resolve Jackson's discontent by ceding his own responsibility for the Valley District to "Stonewall."[57] Johnston asked Cooper to present the matter to the president, obviously hoping that he would use his personal influence in the process. If Davis ever lost respect for the old general's views, it is doubtful that Cooper would have remained a member of the president's inner circle for the entire war.

Despite Davis's praise for his impartiality, outside observers occasionally speculated that Cooper held some officers in less esteem than others. One such subordinate was Brig. Gen. Gideon Pillow, a friend of President James K. Polk and fellow member of the bar in Maury County, Tennessee, and unsuccessful aspirant for the vice presidency in 1852 and 1856. War clerk J. B. Jones detected that Pillow was unpopular in the adjutant general's office, whether because of his political connections or for his abysmal military record at Belmont, Missouri, and Fort Donelson, Tennessee, is unclear. Almost a century later, biographer Douglas Southall Freeman noted Cooper's coolness toward another Confederate chieftain, James Longstreet.[58]

Two incidents in early 1864 illustrate Cooper's involvement in the never-ending stream of personnel matters that, through default, reverted to the adjutant general, as questions pertaining to the very survival of the Confederacy occupied more and more of the president's time. An application of a captain to become a lieutenant colonel was recommended by Col. John Smith Preston, the assistant adjutant general at the time, and favorably endorsed by the secretary of war. Cooper objected on the grounds that his subordinate should not be directly involved, and the president consequently took no action.[59] Soon thereafter, Davis was gratuitously presented with a potential disciplinary action involving Maj. Gen. Nathan Bedford Forrest by the confrontational Braxton Bragg. Davis demurred, referring the matter to the adjutant general for his attention.[60]

Before Breckinridge was appointed secretary of war, Cooper was involved in several personnel decisions regarding the former vice president of the United States. In October 1861 Cooper received a letter from Brig. Gen. Simon Bolivar Buckner, informing the headquarters that Breckinridge was at Bowling Green, Kentucky, asking to be enrolled in the Confederate ranks as an enlisted soldier. Buckner recommended a commission as brigadier general.[61] Breckinridge appeared in Richmond and received such an appointment from Davis on November 2. Fourteen months later, as a major general, Breckinridge led a division into the battle at Stones River and soon found himself assigned the blame by Bragg for the unsatisfactory performance of Southern forces. Breckinridge wrote to Cooper, refuting Bragg's assertions and requesting that the adjutant general convene a court of inquiry to investigate the charges. The disharmony between Bragg and his subordinate commanders continued throughout the spring and summer and into autumn, despite the Army of Tennessee achieving its one solid victory of the war at Chickamauga. Not long thereafter, on November 30, 1863, Cooper was tasked to inform Bragg that the president had decided to relieve him of command.[62] The following winter, Breckinridge left the army in the West and reported to Richmond, where he conferred with Davis and Seddon about his next assignment. On February 25, 1864, Cooper published the order assigning the Kentuckian to command the Western Department of Virginia. A year later, he would become Cooper's superior in the War Department.

If there were one area in which Cooper did not suffer much outside interference, it was interpreting and implementing the minutia of army regulations. He must, after all, have been the acknowledged master of rules and discipline, based upon his extensive administrative experience in the old army. Cooper had no hesitancy in explaining to both Buckner and Longstreet the limits of their authority, for example, when they successively served as commander of the Department of East Tennessee. Cooper's experience did not deter him from soliciting advice from his superiors on matters that might acquire political overtones, however. Longstreet's relief of Maj. Gen. Lafayette McLaws, accompanied by a request for his own reassignment, was sensitive enough for the adjutant general to pass the communiqué up the chain of command through the secretary of war to the president. Before granting his request for a different posting, Davis was perceptive in asking who would succeed the popular lieutenant general, and deferred a decision on the McLaws matter. Seddon and Cooper were then left to debate where a court-martial would best be convened and who should sit on it.[63]

As war weariness wore down Richmonders, criticism of appointments began to be heard. The adjutant general must have been more than a figurehead in making these selections, for he, as well as the president, became the subject of this carping. The selection of Maj. Gen. Martin L. Smith as acting chief of the engineer bureau during the temporary absence of Maj. Gen. Jeremy Gilmer was interpreted by Robert G. H. Kean, chief of the bureau of war, as the work of Cooper and Davis, unbeknownst to Secretary of War Seddon.[64]

If this observation had been made by war clerk J. B. Jones, he no doubt would have related it to Smith's birth and upbringing in New York State. Early in the conflict, Jones had noted speculation that publication of the Southern order of battle in the *New York Herald* was due to the perfidy of the Yankee serving as adjutant general. Jones evidently did not give credence to Cooper's Southern leanings based upon his home in Alexandria and his wife's lineage to the revered Virginian George Mason. Rather, Jones thought he discerned a pattern of Northerners being assigned to key positions near the rebel capital, which he viewed as the influence of someone he considered an outsider, Samuel Cooper. The clerk criticized the elevation of Maj. Gen. Arnold Elzey, a Marylander, to command the Department of Richmond in December 1862, quite possibly because he soon organized a local defense brigade of government clerks. Jones was similarly suspicious of the placement of Maj. Gen. Samuel Gibbs French, born in New Jersey, in command at Petersburg the following month. In October 1864, Jones questioned Cooper's suggestion to the president that Maj. Gen. Mansfield Lovell, a native of Washington, D.C., be put in charge of all Southern prisons containing Federal captives.[65] Had Kean commented upon these appointments in his diary, he no doubt would have viewed them through the lens of what he considered the president's "irrepressible West Pointism," as all three officers, as well as Cooper, were graduates of Davis's alma mater.[66]

During the course of the conflict, Cooper served under five secretaries of war. He generally enjoyed good working relations with the politicians who held this office, but they must have been less than enamored of a subordinate who enjoyed an independent personal relationship with the president. While by no means unique to the Confederate bureaucracy, these kinds of arrangements rarely produce objective, straightforward policy making, and in worst cases create morale problems among other senior officials trying unsuccessfully for access to the decision maker.

The initial designee as secretary of war, Leroy Pope Walker, was considered a lightweight. One observer offered a popular explanation for his appointment: "Why was he selected for the post? Out of Alabama he was not known. . . . They who were posted surmised that he was appointed, primarily, because Mr. Davis only required a pliant agent in that office. He was, himself, very proud of a United States apprenticeship to its duties; therefore he sought for his Cabinet just such a representative of these duties as might be counted a dummy when not the Chief's echo. None appeared fitter for his purpose than the timid being chosen."[67]

Cooper was thought to regard Walker as inefficient. When the Alabamian left Richmond for an indefinite period in August 1861, the adjutant general drafted an order temporarily making A. T. Bledsoe acting secretary. Cooper reportedly was no more enamored with Walker's successor as head of the War Department, Judah Benjamin, the former attorney general, but, presumably, for other reasons.[68] Even though he freely acknowledged his unfamiliarity with things military, Benjamin's stature nonetheless remained intact in Davis's eyes, thereby quite possibly devaluing Cooper's counsel to the president. Benjamin did not remain in the position for long, however, being followed by George Wythe Randolph.

Although scarcely known in Confederate society, Randolph's credentials as grandson of Thomas Jefferson, prominent lawyer and engineer, pro-secession member of the state convention, organizer of the Richmond Howitzers, and brigadier general gave him the confidence to lock horns with Davis. Randolph's tenure was, consequently, of short duration, although during that period he did accomplish a reorganization of the war office.[69] By mid-November 1862, Davis wrote Randolph that his communications with general officers should be routed through Cooper's office. The confrontation may have been induced by Cooper or precipitated by a president dissatisfied with his own appointee.[70] In any event, Randolph resigned and Maj. Gen. Gustavus W. Smith was inserted as secretary of war ad interim. Cooper could relate well to his former comrade in the old army, but his high opinion did not suffice to keep Smith in office for more than three days before James A. Seddon was appointed secretary.

The selection of Seddon returned unchallenged supremacy in military matters to the president. The aloof aristocrat was no better than his predecessors in taking charge of the War Department. Two years later, as the military situation deteriorated to crisis proportions, Davis sought a lightning rod to attract some of the criticism directed at him. In mid-August 1864, Kean confided to his diary that Cooper had employed a subordinate to circulate a rumor "from the best authority" that the president desired for Seddon to resign.[71] The origin of the suggestion became confused, and nothing came of the matter until the following January, when Breckinridge replaced the irrelevant Seddon. The new incumbent brought to the duties of secretary a sterling résumé that showed service on Capitol Hill as, first, congressman and senator and, then, as vice president under James Buchanan, and, most recently, as one of the South's outstanding major generals in the volunteers.

Cooper's views of his final, most-qualified, political overseer are unknown. An outside observer, however, succinctly characterized the earlier appointees: "The secretaries were, of course, useful to arrange matters formally in their respective branches, but they had scarcely higher duties left them than those of their clerks."[72]

Before Smith's brief tenure, Cooper had attempted to reorganize the War Department and adjutant general's office, which, in the opinion of one key subordinate, "led to great confusion. The reformers neither understood themselves nor each other as the records of the Department from the 20th to the 30th [of October 1862] abundantly show."[73] Perhaps Cooper was directed by the president to rein in a department whose secretary might otherwise become too independent.

By early 1864 Cooper recognized a need to delineate the duties and responsibilities of the various offices under his direction. Consequently, on February 26 he published special orders providing an overview of his staff operation during the war.[74]

- The immediate office of the adjutant and inspector general safeguarded confidential records. It handled those extraordinary matters that could not be effectively addressed by the specified subject-matter office.
- The adjutant general's office provided staff support specially directed to the adjutant and inspector general, to include issuing general orders.

- The office of inspection was responsible for "enforcing obedience to the Laws, orders, regulations and usages of the Service," both in the field armies and staff departments.
- The office of organization handled matters relating to the raising, muster, consolidation, recruiting, and disbanding of units. It was also concerned with the succession of officers by election or promotion and questions of rank among officers of the line.
- The appointment office acted upon applications for commissions by issuing letters of appointment and posting the register of officers.
- The office of orders was charged with keeping the record of published orders. It issued special orders in response to requests for leaves of absence, furloughs, transfers, details, returns of soldiers, assignment of officers, and resignations.
- The judge advocate's office dealt with courts-martial and courts of inquiry, retaining files of related documents.
- The reception office had duties beyond handling visitors. It was tasked with opening, recording, and distributing incoming mail and maintaining the files and general records.

In the absence of a personal journal or memoirs by Cooper covering the war period, any insight into his outlook and the manner in which he performed his duties must come from observations by contemporaries in Richmond. The head of the bureau of war, Robert G. H. Kean, found his superior to be "uniformly courteous and uniformly non-committal," never deciding any matter without first consulting with a superior. Kean criticized Cooper for having no idea of the size of the Confederate armies, because he did not insist upon the submission of complete returns. Cooper was also said by Kean to be frequently out of the office.[75] There are accounts of Cooper inspecting the defenses at Charleston in the spring of 1862 and riding out to the Peninsula during the Yankee threat to Richmond in June of that year.[76] The full extent of his travels is unclear, but it is evident that, despite his designation as the army's inspector general, Cooper was not included among the emissaries dispatched by Davis to address important problems arising in the field, such as the festering discontent among western generals with Braxton Bragg in late 1862 and 1863.

Nevertheless, Cooper's tenure was secure. When Bragg was relieved as commanding general of the Army of Tennessee, gossip in Richmond speculated that he would be appointed to replace the aging adjutant general. Such a move must have made eminently good sense to Maj. Samuel W. Melton, Cooper's assistant adjutant general, who suggested the idea to the secretary of war.[77] Melton observed the incumbent regularly and yearned for a stronger figure as adjutant general, even someone as inept at interpersonal relations as the failed commander from the army in the West. Alas, it was not to be. The president retained his trusted ally of over a decade, and Bragg was added as a supernumerary to the senior command structure with the title of military adviser to the chief executive.

Cooper's performance as adjutant general may have best been summarized by an anonymous official in the Confederate government:

> General Samuel Cooper, of New York, the senior General, and the Adjutant and Inspector General of Dixie's armies, was really the great functionary of the War Office. A fine old soldier is he—a prepossessing type of military manhood, in the "sear and yellow" of its being. Of good stature, stately bearing, slim mould, Roman features, nervous in his motions, quick and often querulous in his words, he is much more accessible than many of his subordinates, and a more agreeable official with whom to have any business dealings. To his tact and knowledge and experience, nearly all the duty of organizing the different armies was confided. And in this duty he acquitted himself admirably. . . .
>
> He was left severely at his own specialty, and gradually came to act only as he was regarded—an excellent Adjutant, who had not a word to say beyond the routine of his office.[78]

After being introduced to Samuel Cooper as the senior ranking general in the South, the second distinction most likely to be cited is his farsightedness in preserving for posterity the war records of the fallen government. A careful reading of primary accounts of the final chapter in the life of the Confederacy casts Cooper's role in a somewhat different light. The old general was in his sixty-seventh year when the curtain lowered and was, by his own omission, in a physically reduced state of health. While involved as an agent of the failed regime, Cooper cannot rightfully be described as architect of the plan to protect documents of historical value.

The president and his cabinet fled Richmond as it was being occupied by troops under command of Lt. Gen. U. S. Grant. Moving through southern Virginia to Danville, the fugitives turned southward toward Greensboro, North Carolina. The president's secretary, Burton Harrison, secured an ambulance drawn by an old, broken-down team to transport members of the party unable to mount a horse. Among the passengers in the conveyance was the elderly adjutant general. Harrison recalled him "grumbling about the impudence of a subordinate officer ('only a brigadier-general, sir')" who had the audacity to take the place intended for Cooper in another wagon drawn by good horses.[79]

Harrison's most-amusing account involving Cooper concerned an overnight stop at a house without adequate accommodations for so large a group of guests:

A big negro man, with a candle in hand, then came into the room where we were gathered about a huge fire. Looking us over, he solemnly selected General Cooper, and, with much deference, escorted him into the "guest-chamber" through a door opening from the room we occupied. We could see the great soft bed and snowy white linen the old gentleman was to enjoy, and all rejoiced in the comfort they promised to aged bones, that for a week had been racked in the cars. The negro gravely shut the door upon his guest, and, walking through our company, disappeared. He came back after awhile with wood for our fire; and one of us asked him, "Aren't you going to give the President a room?" "Yes, sir, I done put him in thar," pointing to the "guest chamber," where General Cooper was luxuriating in delights procured for him by the mistaken notion of the darky that he was Mr. Davis! The President and one or two others were presently provided for elsewhere, and the rest of us bestowed ourselves to slumber on the floor, before the roaring fire.[80]

When the caravan reached Charlotte, Davis, Cooper, and others attended church, where they first learned of Lincoln's assassination. Kean recorded that as the retreat was about to resume, Breckinridge instructed him to "store the [War Department's] records there and surrender them to the U.S. officer who occupied Charlotte, if they found them, preserving them from being destroyed if I could."[81] Cooper was given similar responsibility, as he related to Gen. Joseph E. Johnston: "It was found impracticable to transfer the records of the War Department further than this place, and they remain here under my charge. The President and Secretary of War impressed me with the necessity of their preservation in our own hands, if possible; if not, then by the enemy, as essential to the history of the struggle. On account of your superior knowledge of the condition of affairs, I desire to have your advice as to the disposition that shall be made of them."[82]

The books and records of the War Department were left in a warehouse in Charlotte until found by occupying Federal troops and removed to Washington, D.C., where they constitute the bulk of the "Rebel Archives" used ever since by Civil War historians.[83] In a separate dispatch with the same date, April 27, 1865, Cooper asked Johnston to be included, along with his staff officer, in the surrender agreement just concluded with Maj. Gen. William T. Sherman.

On May 3, 1865, Cooper signed an oath not to take up arms against the United States and was paroled at Charlotte.[84] Cooper subsequently swore allegiance to the United States and then asked Secretary of State William H. Seward for the benefits of amnesty, namely, to recover ownership of Cameron.[85] The aged general resided in Mecklenburg County, Virginia, for nearly a year before returning to his property on the outskirts of Alexandria. He found his house had been torn down and replaced with a stronghold in the ring of defenses surrounding Washington, initially called "Fort Traitor" in his honor. In 1863 his son-in-law, by this time Brigadier General Wheaton, convinced Federal authorities to provide a proper name for the fortification, "Fort Williams," in remembrance of Brig. Gen. Thomas Williams, who had perished the year before commanding the Union defense at Baton Rouge. The Coopers first resided on the Episcopal Seminary grounds before eventually occupying the former manager's quarters on Cameron.

Cooper set about writing his memoirs but, unfortunately, never memorialized his experiences and observations at the heart of the Confederate military establishment. In 1869 Lee came to Alexandria and stopped at Cameron to visit with his elderly friend. They sat together on a bench under an old locust tree from ten in the morning until four in the afternoon, interrupted only by lunch prepared by Mrs. Cooper.[86] The reversal in Cooper's fortunes left him nearly destitute. Knowing of his financial distress, at a reunion of old Confederate officers in Savannah in 1870, Lee asked for contributions to help the past adjutant general. They collected three hundred dollars from former Brig. Gen. Alexander R. Lawton and others. Lee added one hundred dollars and sent the sum to Cooper "for the relief of any pressing necessity."[87]

Cooper remained at Cameron until his death there on December 3, 1876. He was laid to rest in the cemetery of Alexandria's Christ Church, the Episcopal sanctuary where Lee and Washington worshiped. Cooper's migration from Hackensack, New York, to Alexandria, Virginia, was complete.

CHAPTER THREE

FIELD COMMANDER

★★★ MONTGOMERY CORSE

MONTGOMERY CORSE WAS AN ALEXANDRIAN FROM BEGIN-
ning to end. He was born in the city, and he died there. In between, he
led a life of adventure in the major American epics of his day. Corse
marched his fellow Alexandrians out of town to participate in a war
against Mexico, panned gold in California during the famous rush for
wealth, and later led another exodus when the city was invaded by Northern troops. During the decades that followed the Civil War, no resident
was more popular than the old general who walked the streets each day,
greeting friends, acquaintances, and former comrades in arms. Corse's
life appealed to the imagination of generations of Alexandria men and
women, even if his efforts and the causes he served fell short of success.

Corse never wrote an account of his exploits, but he did the next best
thing. He shared the stories of his life with his eldest son, Montgomery
Beverley Corse, who recorded them in narrative form for their family.
Fortunately, this secondhand autobiography was subsequently shared
with the city's library, where the narrative allows others to appreciate
Corse for his extraordinary dedication and commitment.

The Corses of Alexandria descended from William Corse, who moved
from the Eastern Shore of Maryland to Kent County, Delaware, before
the American Revolution. He subsequently helped raise that colony's
first company of volunteers, thereby meriting dismissal from the pacifist
Quaker church. William's son, John, settled in Alexandria in time to
serve as a lieutenant of artillery in the War of 1812. One of his earliest
ventures there was publishing the *Alexandria Herald*. John's eldest son,
Montgomery Dent Corse, was born on March 14, 1816, in the family
home on the southwest corner of Pitt and Prince Streets.[1]

As a child, Montgomery was fascinated with everything martial. A band or drum and bugle corps never failed to thrill him. On the day of one military parade, fearing that the youngster would be lost or injured in the commotion, his mother, the former Julia Dent, took away his clothes and tied the youngster to a bedpost. The music of the procession inspired the unhappy youth to redouble his efforts to escape his bonds. Doing so, he donned a gingham apron and followed after the band. He was later found, wandering through the streets, his strange apparel and bare behind amusing onlookers.

Montgomery attended a military school operated by Maj. Bradley Lowe in the 1100 block of Oronoco Street and later studied with Benjamin Hallowell. The child was fascinated by the triumphal arch erected over Washington Street, near the corner of King Street, in recognition of the Marquis de Lafayette's visit to the city in 1824. As a member of the boys battery that participated in the inauguration of Andrew Jackson in 1829, Montgomery touched off a gun in the salute fired in honor of the new president. Years afterward, General Corse told his son that it was the proudest moment of his life. By the age of sixteen, the young centurion was commanding a company of boys armed with wooden guns and tin bayonets who marched through town on George Washington's birthday and Independence Day.[2]

Corse's fascination with military pomp continued into adult life. His stature was not imposing, as he was short and rather stout.[3] Yet throughout his life, Corse projected the image of a leader, repeatedly stepping forward as a citizen-soldier to meet military challenges when required. He was working with his father in the banking business when the Texas troubles erupted in 1846. Corse raised a company of volunteers and led his officers into Washington to offer their services in the oncoming war with Mexico. The contingent was received in the East Room of the White House by President James K. Polk, who commended them for their patriotism. The quota from the District of Columbia had already been satisfied, however, so Corse's unit was disbanded.[4]

Later that year, Congress retroceded Alexandria to Virginia. In November, the secretary of war levied one regiment from the state, and Gov. William Smith accepted the services of the "Alexandria Volunteers."[5] Organizational meetings took place at the old courtroom in the Market House, with Corse presiding. It was not surprising, therefore, that Corse was elected commander. On December 12, the unit marched to the city's wharf through crowds of cheering citizens, along with the Mount Vernon Guards, a cavalry escort, and two bands. Boarding the *Oceola,* soldiers shouted good-byes to family and friends as the vessel headed down the Potomac on its way to Richmond. The outfit was mustered into service as Company B of the First Virginia Volunteers. Before departing the state capital, Captain Corse was presented a sword by a delegation from Alexandria. The regiment embarked for Mexico from Fort Monroe on January 27, 1847.[6]

Corse's son recalled that his father always made light of his service in the Mexican War, despite exhibiting exceptional patriotism by volunteering twice to fight.[7] Corse's modesty was undoubtedly due to the fact that he saw no action under fire. Company B remained part of Maj. Gen. Zachary Taylor's reserve. For a while, the unit was under direct supervision of Taylor's second in command, Brig. Gen. John Wool, whom Corse described as "the most perfect martinet in the Army . . . he is determined to make us soldiers."[8] In addition to learning the school of the soldier, Corse demonstrated characteristics that would distinguish him in the bloodier conflict to come. Confronted by a march that promised to be grueling under the Mexican sun, he philosophized, "I never think I cannot stand anything that any other man can, and laugh at my sufferings after they are over."[9] The death and destruction attendant to a battlefield did not blind him to the beauty of the surrounding landscape, and in radiant terms he described the terrain at Buena Vista in a letter to his family. Corse also registered empathy for the common soldier, as his son later recorded:

> The most thrilling incident I ever heard him relate of the Mexican war was an account of a military execution. The victim was a soldier of excellent qualities, who for once had lost complete control of himself, and struck an officer. He was lead [*sic*] forth for execution and made to take his seat on his coffin which was sitting in front of the open grave. The officer in command of the execution went forward to blindfold him but was waved back, "I am not afraid to die," exclaimed the soldier, now sitting on his own coffin with the gaping grave just behind him. The command fire was given and the victim fell forward on the ground, but not dead, only wounded. Most of the firing squad out of a mistaken sense of kindness had fired wide. He slowly raised himself on his elbow, and exclaimed "Why are you butchering me in this way? Why don't you finish it?" The firing squad was then moved closer, the muskets reloaded, and another volley fired into the poor fellow lying on the ground.[10]

This was far from the last occasion on which Corse's heartstrings would be tugged by a military execution.

At the war's conclusion, Corse's company returned to Fort Monroe and, on August 1, 1848, mustered out of service.[11] The volunteers were greeted in Alexandria by flags flying, salutes firing, and an escort of citizens frolicking through the streets to a ceremony in the public square.[12] The celebration marked a beginning, not an end, for Corse's adventures were just getting underway.

Corse's time in Mexico piqued his wanderlust, and within six months he was sailing for California, drawn by fabulous stories of gold available for the taking. On the trip southward, forty men died of cholera. Crossing the Isthmus of Panama, Corse boarded another steamer and arrived in San Francisco on April 1, 1849. He would devote seven years to the gold rush.

The search for riches began modestly, bringing only $6.40 the first week. By the time he had accumulated $500.00, Corse was ready for a change. "No one has an idea of the labor of getting gold out of the earth until he tries it," he wrote home. "I have handled boulders enough since I have been here to pave King Street [in Alexandria] from one end to the other. . . . It is the hardest work in the world—Yet, I never enjoed [sic] better health then since engaged in it."[13]

Corse opened a store on the north fork of the Sacramento River, acted as a steamboat agent, customs officer, and deputy marshal, and even ran a hotel, sitting at the head of the dinner table to carve meat for the guests. A commitment by Corse to enforcing the law and preserving lives evolved during this period. Corse was asked three times to perform as the second in a duel, a practice he despised, and each time he talked the adversaries out of carrying through with their intentions. In 1852 the Alexandrian was elected captain of the Sutter Rifles, a company organized to assist in the maintenance of law and order as a counterweight to vigilantes who jeopardized the dispensation of justice.[14]

By 1856 Corse had lost his fascination with gold mining, and in December he was once again home in Alexandria. He immediately joined into a banking partnership with his brother and Edward Snowden, whose son would be a future military cohort. The firm helped finance some of the leading railroad enterprises then in progress in Virginia.[15] The city had not forgotten its military adventurer, nor had Corse lost his fascination for the profession of arms. In 1857 he was elected lieutenant colonel of the regional militia outfit, the 175th Virginia Regiment.[16] When the Prince of Wales toured the United States, Corse was designated to accompany him to Mount Vernon, where the royal visitor planted a tree.[17] Rank was apparently not all-important to the Alexandrian, for during the scare that attended John Brown's raid on Harpers Ferry, Corse was elected first lieutenant in the Home Guard organized to protect Alexandria in the absence of its militia, which had been dispatched to western Virginia.[18]

As tensions mounted in the wake of the 1860 presidential election, Corse was once again inspired to take a leadership role in his community's military preparations. Two enthusiastic youths, Edgar Warfield and Frank Wise, issued a call for volunteers to join a new company being formed in the city. Six days later, Corse presided over a meeting of sixty-eight young men at American Hall on Cameron Street to organize a unit they named the "Old Dominion Rifles." He was unanimously elected its captain, with Arthur Herbert, Delaware Kemper, and William H. Fowle Jr. selected for the three lieutenant positions.[19] As commander, Corse corresponded with the superintendent of the Virginia Military Institute concerning acquisition of arms for its cadet corps.[20]

By mid-February, the city's five militia companies were combined into a battalion with Corse as its major. In this capacity, he also served as assistant adjutant general to the succession of officers who functioned as military commanders in Alexandria—Brig. Gen. Philip St. George Cocke, Lt. Col. Sidney Taylor (nephew of Zachary Taylor), and Lt. Col. George Terrett.[21] On April 27, Corse's battalion was designated the Sixth Battalion of Virginia Volunteers and placed under Taylor's supervision.

Years later, in explaining his father's motivation for taking up arms against the Union, Montgomery B. Corse pointed out that allegiance to one's state was paramount for many Virginians. "He was not fighting for the maintenance of slavery but to repel the invasion of an Alien from his own sacred soil. He had never owned but one slave and him he had freed long before the war. He believed in the right of secession. His State had seceded. Hence, the war for him could have but one aspect."[22]

All did not go smoothly as Alexandrians learned the business of war. In late April a clerk misread an urgent message from the commander at Culpeper Court House to send the Alexandria Battery. Instead, the entire battalion hurried to the depot and entrained in a driving rainstorm, only to find out the mistake the next day and return sheepishly to the city.[23] In early May, when the battalion abruptly left a second time in response to false rumors that Federal troops were about to invade Northern Virginia, Taylor lost his command to Terrett. Corse was making himself known to the new military command structure forming in Richmond by, among other things, offering to serve as intermediary for messages sent to George H. Steuart, who was trying to arouse pro-Southern sentiment behind Federal lines in Maryland.[24] Finally, on May 24, Corse accompanied Alexandria's soldiers out of town for the last time. They boarded flatcars for Manassas Junction as blue-clad troops occupied the city.

Corse quickly found that no logistical arrangements had been made for his troops. The first night, the men slept in boxcars without supper or blankets. Many lacked arms or cooking utensils. The Alexandrians eventually settled into camp, and Corse requisitioned a wagon and horses to transport wood, water, and provisions.[25]

On June 10, the Sixth Battalion reorganized into the Seventeenth Virginia Regiment, consisting of ten companies, half hailing from Alexandria, the remainder from nearby counties. Corse was designated commander at the rank of colonel, with an effective date of May 17. In early July, the Seventeenth was assigned to Brig. Gen. James Longstreet's

Fourth Brigade, and the transformation of civilians into soldiers accelerated with regular brigade-level drills. The preparation paid off when the
Alexandrians were ordered to Bull Run on July 17 to confront a Federal
advance on Manassas Junction.

Corse's regiment was deployed above Blackburn's Ford to the left of
the First Virginia Volunteers. He reported that two detached companies
were positioned at the right of the First Regiment, with two more at
the crossing. At 1:00 P.M. the following day, the enemy appeared on
the opposite bank and opened fire. Corse pushed his remaining troops
forward to strengthen the line, and the Virginians answered the incoming barrage. Seizing the advantage, Corse dispatched three companies
across the stream and succeeded in driving back the enemy. His regiment killed fifteen Yankees, captured seven prisoners, and wounded
many more before being relieved by the Seventh Louisiana Volunteers.
The Alexandrians' only involvement in the more substantial action on
July 21 was to parry with enemy skirmishers in a diversion to the principal battle on Matthews, Buck, and Henry Hills behind them, known as
First Manassas.[26]

Blackburn's Ford constituted the Alexandrians' first and last engagement of 1861, despite subsequent alarms about Federal advances that
never occurred. Corse's men soon confronted the realities of war in the
wretchedness and discomfort they observed in hospitals full of sick and
wounded compatriots.[27] The regiment performed outpost duty around
Falls Church during the late summer and early fall before returning to
Centreville for the winter encampment. On October 28, Gov. John
Letcher presented a Virginia flag to the outfit. "Take it, and when you go
into Alexandria, drive out the invaders of our soil," he challenged. Corse
replied, "Governor, I accept this flag from our beloved old Mother, and
tender the thanks of the Regiment I have the honor to command; with
confidence I place it in their hands and promise you that it shall be
planted on the high places around Alexandria, or the blood of the Seventeenth shall flow freely in the attempt."[28] And flow freely it did.

First, the men of Corse's regiment had to endure a long winter away
from home in cantonment. On November 28, Gen. P. G. T. Beauregard
uncovered the new battle flag he had designed, which today is often mistaken for the Confederate national emblem. Two days later, these colors
were proudly carried in a review of now–Major General Longstreet's division. There followed four bitterly cold months and a wet spring, producing nearly impassable roads, over which Corse led his men to the Peninsula when the Federals deployed to southeast Virginia.

The march ended at Yorktown, where the Alexandrians suffered in
the trenches during more days of relentless rain. In this wet, foreboding
setting, the men of the Seventeenth Virginia elected officers in accor-

dance with legislation recently enacted by the Confederate Congress. Corse was retained as regimental commander, an outcome that was not a mere formality but the soldiers' confirmation that their leadership over the past ten months had succeeded in molding an effective military organization, while at the same time being mindful of troop welfare.

As May opened, Gen. Joseph E. Johnston began pulling his men back toward Richmond in the face of a superior Federal force. On the rainy morning of May 5, Johnston reversed direction, sending Brig. Gen. A. P. Hill's brigade, which included the Seventeenth Virginia, through Williamsburg to confront the enemy just outside town. Corse was deployed to the far left of the line of battle, opposite a regiment of U.S. regulars. The Confederates opened a steady fire before beginning to advance, the Seventeenth led by its commander. When the enemy retreated into a field of felled timber, it regrouped and made a stand. The Alexandrians stopped at a distance of thirty yards and exchanged fire with the Yankees for two hours. Corse narrowly escaped death when a twenty-one-year-old member of his outfit stepped on a log directly in front of him and was killed by a bullet in the chest.[29] The arrival of another brigade on its flank enabled the Seventeenth Virginia to move forward onto the ground defended by the enemy. Corse was directed to refill his men's cartridge boxes from those of the bluecoats lying about them. In seven hours of combat, many soldiers fired more than sixty rounds; 30 percent of Corse's outfit were killed or wounded. Hill characterized Corse's demeanor during the fighting as "calm and equable as a May morn, bore himself like a true soldier throughout."[30]

After the battle, Johnston's army continued its march back toward Richmond and established camp east of the capital. Pvt. Edgar Warfield remembered that many of the men entered the city using passes written by a comrade who forged Corse's signature so well that the commander himself could not tell the difference.[31]

On the last day of May, Southern forces once again closed with the invaders. Anticipating another fight, Corse reassured his men by repeating, "Keep cool, keep close, aim low."[32] It was late afternoon when the Alexandrians entered the fray on the left flank. They easily moved ahead through the enemy's campsite when another Virginia regiment opened a devastating crossfire into their adversaries. The tide soon turned, however, as the Federals rallied and drove back the attackers, almost overwhelming them before another Confederate flanking movement brought the action to a close. The Seventeenth Virginia suffered seventy-four casualties, the wounded including Maj. Arthur Herbert and three company commanders.[33] The losses at Seven Pines had a somber impact on the survivors from Alexandria, who later remembered with emotion Colonel Corse reading the burial service that followed.[34]

The men returned to camp near Richmond and resumed their daily regimen. Corse's anger soon exploded. Pvt. James Thomas Petty noted that the colonel broke his sword at drill one afternoon, presumably over inattention by his officers.[35] It was not long before the army defending Richmond was in combat once again, this time under a new commanding general, Robert E. Lee. The only contest in the Seven Days battles in which the Alexandrians were engaged was at Frayser's Farm on June 30.

After being held in reserve at Mechanicsville and Gaines Mill, Corse's Virginians were itching to become involved in what seemed to be a series of successful encounters driving the Federals away from Richmond. The Seventeenth was arrayed on the far right of the line of battle. Nervous about the enemy's whereabouts, Brig. Gen. James Kemper, the brigade commander, directed Corse to angle his regiment to the right and deploy two companies forward as skirmishers. About 5:00 P.M., Kemper ordered his entire brigade forward. What happened next is subject to interpretation. Kemper's report states that the troops misidentified enemy pickets as the Yankees' main line, and when they were driven in, the Confederates surged forward at double-quick time, cheering loudly and essentially acting out of control. After crossing a swamp, the alignment was completely lost in a thicket. Suddenly the attackers came under a withering fire from almost every direction.[36] The ragged elements of Kemper's brigade struggled back to safety, but at great loss. Corse's regiment suffered seventeen killed and another twenty-three wounded, with almost twice that total missing in action.[37] Among the captured were Lt. Col. Morton Marye, a company commander, and five other officers. Nor could Corse have been sanguine about the loss of the regimental flag. The broken brigade was not utilized at Malvern Hill the following day.

The failure at Frayser's Farm did not seem to hinder advancement of the officers involved. In August, Kemper was elevated to acting commander of Pickett's division while he recovered from a wound suffered at Gaines Mill. Corse was designated to lead Kemper's brigade, consisting of five regiments, to include his former command. Marye had been exchanged and returned to succeed Corse at the Seventeenth Virginia. Corse and his men now followed Longstreet on the way to join Maj. Gen. Thomas "Stonewall" Jackson in confronting Maj. Gen. John Pope and a portion of the Federal army operating in Virginia. Corse's elevation seemed to put him in a good mood, and on the march he teased men who broke ranks to gather fruit, shouting, "Come back here, you miserable stragglers." When the new brigade commander and his staff were seen chatting by the roadside with some ladies, "Come back from there, you miserable straggler," was the rejoinder from the troops tramping by.[38] Corse was lucky that he was not assigned to the no-nonsense Jackson or the movement would not have been so lackadaisical.

Corse's command passed through Thoroughfare Gap on the morning of August 29 and halted at Groveton, as a battle was under way nearby between Jackson and Pope. Ordered to move to the right of Longstreet's line, the brigade was subjected to heavy shelling from a battery 1,200 yards away. This was Corse's first test under fire as a brigade commander, and to maximize his chances of success, he turned to known and trusted subordinates. He dispatched Major Herbert to ascertain whether he had support on his right and deployed as skirmishers Company B, Seventeenth Virginia, commanded by Capt. R. H. Simpson, who had performed credibly in this role in the past. Receiving their assurances of no imminent threats, Corse crossed to the east of the Manassas Gap Railroad, joined the line of battle, and retired for the night.

It was late on the following afternoon that Longstreet advanced against Pope's left flank. Corse was assigned to support two brigades occupying woods near the Chinn house. Suddenly, orders arrived to move forward with haste. Corse pushed his men and came under heavy fire from infantry and artillery near the abandoned residence. Spotting an enemy battery to the left and rear, he ordered a charge along the whole line. The brigade surged forward, driving the artillerists from their guns. Herbert reported that the national colors were stripped from its Yankee color-bearer and given to Colonel Corse, who waved them in front his troops, giving "added life and renewed energy to our men." In the melee, Marye fell with a severe leg wound, requiring amputation. Corse was also hit, receiving an injury to the thigh, and his horse, "Bayonet," was shot and killed. Nevertheless, the day was a success, both for the Alexandrian and for the Army of Northern Virginia.[39]

With defeat had come promotion; with victory came demotion. As Lee's army continued northward, Kemper was returned to his old brigade, and Corse settled back as regimental commander, the pawns in a reorganization and consolidation under Maj. Gen. David R. Jones. Corse led the Seventeenth Virginia toward Leesburg and then across the Potomac River at White's Ford on September 6. The advance resumed four days later, taking the Seventeenth Virginia through Frederick, Middletown, Boonsborough, and Hagerstown, Maryland, before setting up camp. Unnecessary movements were prompted by false reports that the Yankees were attempting a flank maneuver.[40] On September 14, Kemper's brigade reversed direction, passing by Boonsborough again and ascending South Mountain to block Turner's Gap while Jackson invested Harpers Ferry.

About 4:00 P.M., Corse's regiment was placed on the right of the road leading to the summit and came under heavy enfilade shelling from a battery six hundred to eight hundred yards to its right. The Seventeenth was soon joined by the Fifty-sixth Virginia Infantry, commanded by

Col. William D. Stuart. Corse deployed the new command to a cornfield on the right, and it immediately absorbed the brunt of a flank attack that continued until after dark. Assessing his position to be untenable, as he could no longer see the enemy, Stuart proposed to Corse that they withdraw to a fence line twenty yards to the rear. From this position, both regiments engaged in a brisk firefight until exhausting their ammunition, at which point they began emptying the cartridge boxes of the dead and wounded. Stuart called for reinforcements. His messenger learned that Kemper's brigade had been ordered off the field. Stuart informed Corse, and the two regiments trudged away, leaving injured soldiers behind.[41] The Seventeenth Virginia had suffered thirteen casualties, including a slight wound to the mouth of its commander. His mustache covered the scar. It had not been an auspicious performance by the colonel from Alexandria.[42]

Kemper's troops moved back to join that portion of Lee's army near Sharpsburg. By the following evening, Corse's men had taken a position southeast of town, just to the north of the road to Harpers Ferry. Kemper moved his units behind a fence below the crest of a hill, beyond which was a stone bridge over Antietam Creek. At mid-afternoon, Maj. Gen. Ambrose Burnside launched an attack on the Georgians defending this crossing. A cacophony of artillery and firearms exploded, producing a cloud of smoke that enveloped the combatants.

During a brief lull in the fighting, Pvt. Alexander Hunter was sent back to Sharpsburg to fill canteens with water. He climbed into a church steeple for a quick look at the battlefield. Hurrying back to his regiment, he blurted out to Corse:

> "We are lost, Colonel; we haven't a single reserve."
> "Is it possible?" he said.
> I told him it was a fact; there was not a solitary Confederate soldier in sight. He clenched his teeth like a bulldog, and as the news ran along the line each man knew we had to stay there and, if needs be, die there.[43]

Over sixteen months of campaigning, Corse's regiment had dwindled to nine officers and forty-six enlisted men. These stalwarts now heard the sounds of enemy troops mounting the top of the hill. "Never did I feel, not even at Gettysburg, so much solicitude for the safety of our army," recalled a Confederate survivor of the encounter that followed.[44] Corse calmed his charges, "Steady, my men! Seventeenth, don't fire until they get above the hill." First flag staffs came into view, then the tops of caps appeared. Stationed on the extreme right of the line, Corse's formation was overlapped by the Yankee force approaching it. The bluecoats surged toward the defenders. "Keep cool, men, don't fire yet!" came the admonition. Not until the enemy was barely fifty yards away did Corse give the command. What seemed like a single volley erupted. Before the

Southerners could reload a third time, they received a barrage that settled the matter. Somehow, in the melee that ensued, the colors of the 103d New York Volunteers were captured by the Alexandrians. Seven officers and twenty-four men were killed or wounded, however, along with ten soldiers taken prisoner.[45]

Corse received a wound in the foot which prevented him from escaping. To avoid being identified as a senior leader, he turned down his collar, concealing the three stars designating him as a colonel. As the enemy gathered around, a soldier prepared to shoot him. At the last minute, a bluecoat intervened, driving off the brigand and promising Corse he would be properly treated as a prisoner of war. Shortly afterward, the Georgians, assisted by Kemper's brigade, launched a counterattack, driving back the Yankees. With bullets passing overhead, Corse raised himself onto one elbow and signaled to his comrades to come and rescue him.[46]

The Confederates avoided a complete rout at Antietam by the miraculous arrival of Maj. Gen. A. P. Hill's troops from Harpers Ferry. Lee's Maryland campaign ended the following evening when the Confederates began to withdraw back into Virginia. Better times lay ahead for Corse and his combat veterans. Corse achieved recognition when Secretary of War George W. Randolph received the two stands of colors captured by the Seventeenth Virginia from U.S. units at Second Manassas and Sharpsburg.[47] Longstreet referred to the Alexandrian as "one of the most gallant and worthy officers in this army. He and his regiment have been distinguished in at least ten of the severest battles of the war."[48] With the return of convalescents and stragglers, by the end of October the strength of the Seventeenth Virginia had grown to 198 officers and enlisted men.[49] Most important, General Lee submitted Corse's name to the War Department for advancement to the rank of brigadier general. On November 6, the promotion was announced, and Corse was assigned command of Maj. Gen. George E. Pickett's former brigade.[50]

Corse did not remain long in this billet, however, as a momentous event of another kind was about to occur in his life. He went to General Lee and asked for a furlough to get married. His superior tried to dissuade him, arguing that this was a bad time to make such a commitment, for months could pass before Corse saw his bride again. When asked how much longer the war would last, Lee was said to have replied, "About seven years," which caused an apoplectic Corse to renew his plea. The senior commander was amused and reluctantly granted permission. The groom proceeded at once to Charlottesville, where, on November 22, he married Elizabeth Beverley (known as "Lizzie"), whom he had first met in 1855 on a visit to Alexandria from California. Any honeymoon was short-lived, for by November 28 Corse had been called back to the army at Fredericksburg.[51]

Montgomery Corse
in a Confederate
general's uniform.
Special Collections,
Alexandria Library.

Corse returned to a different command than he left. A new brigade had been organized for him in Pickett's division, consisting of the Seventeenth plus regiments from Richmond, Fredericksburg, Tidewater, and Southwest Virginia. These troops were posted near the center of Lee's defensive line overlooking the Rappahannock River. When the Federals attacked on December 13, combat raged to their left and right. Corse's men enjoyed "a splendid view of the fight," in the words of one onlooker, but were never engaged. During much of the day, Corse stood talking with another of Pickett's subordinates, Brig. Gen. Lewis Armistead, each expecting orders any minute and both disappointed.[52]

The Virginians camped at nearby Guinea Station until mid-February, when the brigade began a series of relocations southward, first to Richmond, then to Petersburg, finally reaching the Suffolk area on March 25, 1863. The mission of Lieutenant General Longstreet's corps was to block access to Richmond to the concentration of Northern troops there, while at the same time gathering provisions from the rich Tidewater for the Army of Northern Virginia. To help keep the Federals bottled up in Suffolk, Corse's command was tasked with securing bridges over the Blackwater River. The brigade therefore dubbed itself "The Army of the Blackwater." Corse acknowledged that the duty would not be "arduous."[53]

In early April, Longstreet laid siege to Suffolk. This provoked several armed clashes over the next month before the Confederates declared the venture a success, in light of the meat and grain gathered, and withdrew. As they tramped back to rejoin the main body of the Army of Northern Virginia, Corse rode along the line, telling the news of Lee's stunning victory at Chancellorsville. With that triumph, of course, came the loss of Stonewall Jackson. Corse marched in the funeral procession accompanying Jackson's casket, along with other general officers and another Alexandrian, Capt. French Forrest of the Confederate navy.[54]

Corse had been left out of Lee's most celebrated battle, and now he would be denied participation in the invasion of Pennsylvania. Instead, Corse was ordered to remain behind at Hanover Junction to protect the railroad bridges over the North and South Anna Rivers from Yankee incursion. He bristled at the notion of missing what surely would be the greatest conquest of the confident Southern army. Lee and Pickett clearly wanted the Alexandrians with them, but the War Department was determined to retain protection for the Confederate capital and its transportation link to the north.[55] Corse's men therefore spent the next several weeks shuttling back and forth along the rail line connecting Richmond and Gordonsville, responding to reports of Federal raiders.[56]

Marriage had brought changes in the demeanor of the forty-six-year-old general.[57] Corse and his bride of six months were now carrying on regular correspondence. His seniority seemed to make stationery no problem at a time when most soldiers were resorting to cross-writing on small scraps of precious paper. When Lizzie experimented in this fashion, her husband quickly asked her to stop, as it "bothers me so to make them out."[58] To historians and other onlookers, the disappointing feature of Corse's letters was their focus on his affections as a new husband, to the exclusion of commentary on military matters transpiring around him. Was it just murmurs of romance or a genuine change in priorities that led Corse to write from Taylorsville on June 18 that he was about to "make arrangements to have you with me, my love," and "am now quite consoled at the idea of being left behind in anticipation of being with you."[59]

When he received orders to rejoin Lee on July 8, Corse drove his men for six days of hard marching to close at Winchester. It was there he learned what happened at Gettysburg. Afterward, according to Edgar Warfield, one of the Alexandrians in the ranks, Pickett wrote to LaSalle Corbell, the lady friend who would become his wife, that "if my other two brigades, [Albert G.] Jenkins' and Corse's, had been with me, we would now, I believe, have been in Washington and the war practically over."[60] Corse's son stated that his father knew better, realizing that his presence would have only added another decimated brigade and a dead brigadier. The heir also noted that the disappointed general said "he never felt that he belonged to Pickett's division after Gettysburg."[61]

For a few days, Corse's men remained in Winchester, "waiting for shoes & orders," as he put it.[62] Then, they were off to secure the Manassas and Chester Gaps for the defeated army to use as it dragged southward and to prevent the aggressors from descending upon the Confederate capital.[63] Corse's brigade succeeded in dislodging the skeletal Federal force attempting to hold both passages and then moved into central Virginia, occupying a series of bivouac sites throughout the month of August.

It was during the subsequent march to Culpeper Court House that the commissary clerk in Corse's brigade encountered the challenge of dealing with the sometimes noncommunicative commander: "Went to see the General (C.) about the advisability of bringing our live stock across tonight. After waiting 5 or 10 minutes received only a deep-toned *grunt* for answer; and went to sleep under an ambulance in a vain effort to penetrate the occult meaning of the characteristic grunt aforesaid."[64]

In early September, Corse's command was detached from duty with the Army of Northern Virginia and sent to Petersburg. The brigade was soon ordered to support Maj. Gen. Samuel Jones in defending against the threat posed by Burnside's forces in northeastern Tennessee to the mines at Saltville, as well as the rest of southwestern Virginia. By a circuitous route, Corse and his men traveled to Zollicoffer, Tennessee, arriving on September 17. In an area little touched by war, food was plentiful and soldier life enjoyable. The enemy probed the Confederate position over the next several days and, finding it strong, moved off in a different direction.[65]

Under mounting pressure to return Corse's troops to Lee as soon as possible, Jones released them by month's end, and they journeyed by rail back to Petersburg.[66] The brigade was divided, and the Seventeenth Virginia dispatched once again to the Suffolk area. But in southwest Virginia, Jones became nervous about the Yankee force assembling nearby and called for help once more. Pickett was directed to return Corse and the three regiments remaining with him, numbering twelve hundred men. On October 15, the infantrymen departed for Dublin, Virginia, where they met Brig. Gen. Gabriel C. Wharton's brigade. Both commands were poorly clad and badly shod, yet they marched southerly as best they could. Crossing into Tennessee, they were assigned to a division commanded by Maj. Gen. Robert Ransom and joined Longstreet's campaign to take Knoxville.

Corse declared himself "disgruntled" with the remote, mountainous terrain but deployed his men effectively against the elusive Yankees. At one point, his brigade was hurried back into Virginia to help Jones defend the rail bridge over the New River from a Federal raid that threatened the nearby saltworks. On Christmas Eve, Corse directed both brigades in a sharp skirmish at Dandridge, Tennessee, just east of Knoxville.[67] He proudly wrote to his wife, "I had the honor of commanding a Corps [Longstreet's] for a few days, & the left of Genl. L's line. It did not puff me up at all, on the contrary, only increased my solicitude."[68] Corse was temporarily commanding Ransom's division when orders arrived to move the infantry and artillery to Morristown and prepare to engage the enemy.[69] He established a temporary headquarters at Bull's Gap in the Bays Mountains, a ridge in the Appalachians northeast of Knoxville, but was prevented from foraging in the rich locale by the proximity of a considerable Federal force. In the new year, Longstreet's campaign was abandoned. On January 20, 1864, Corse received orders to return to Petersburg, as his brigade was required for an "emergency."[70] He marched his ragged command ninety miles through the snow to Bristol, where troops boarded the cars for southern Virginia.

Lee had approved a plan to capture the garrison at Newbern, North Carolina. It required the use of much of Ransom's division, in addition to the brigade of Brig. Gen. Robert Hoke, a North Carolinian familiar with the area. Specifying that the attack take place during the period January 25–30, Lee selected Maj. Gen. George Pickett to lead the expedition. The commander of the Army of Northern Virginia then telegraphed his son, Col. G. W. Custis Lee, aide to President Jefferson Davis, to ensure that Corse's brigade would be recalled from Tennessee to join the task force.[71]

It was January 30 before Corse's three regiments arrived at Petersburg and began the trip by rail into North Carolina. Pickett launched his attack the following day in a complex series of maneuvers that seemed destined to misfire. Two elements achieved success, however. As part of the demonstration in front of Newbern, Corse drove back an enemy maneuver to turn Pickett's right flank, and Comdr. John Taylor Wood's commandos captured the Federal steamer, *Underwriter*. Other components of the Confederate offensive did not accomplish their objectives, however. The result was a failure to take the river town at the cost of the element of surprise in any future attempts.[72]

Corse's troops went into camp at Goldsboro, the crossing point for two eastern Carolina rail lines. His brigade had grown to almost sixteen hundred effectives with the return of the Seventeenth Virginia.[73] On February 15, its members reenlisted for the duration of the war. To encourage them to do so, Corse addressed his old regiment, imploring them to rally around the Southern Cross. As he was leaving the field, his horse reared and fell backward, bruising its rider but avoiding serious injury.[74] The following week, the Seventeenth was dispatched by rail to

Lexington, North Carolina, to quell a disturbance that was over by the time the Virginians arrived. Instead of soldiering, therefore, they enjoyed some local hospitality.[75]

By early March, Corse was established as commander of the military district at Kinston, where the rail line crossed the Neuse River. He had been buoyed by Lizzie joining him in Goldsboro but was now frustrated at not finding lodging for her at his new posting. There was plenty to keep him busy. Recurring reports told of Federal reinforcements being sent into Newbern. At one point, Corse sent Pickett a message that Burnside was on his way with fourteen regiments of infantry. Estimates of the number of Yankees being deployed to North Carolina ran as high as twenty thousand troops. Enemy attacks on Confederate pickets were common, but the Southerners also went on the offensive. Corse congratulated a North Carolina unit for capturing a flatcar from the enemy, demonstrating the vulnerability of the Yankees' rail stock and thereby magnifying their task of physical security. Rebel raiders made their way to the Atlantic, where they destroyed one of the lighthouses at Cape Lookout and badly damaged the other, thereby removing important aids to northern navigation along that treacherous coastline. A more vexing concern for Corse, however, was the theft and destruction of private property by his soldiers. He issued stern orders restricting egress from encampments to stem the lawlessness.[76]

These problems paled in Corse's eyes when compared with the challenges confronting him in early April. The previous November, he had written to his wife from Tennessee that he "had one of the hardest & most trying duties I think a soldier has to perform, I had to have 3 men shot, who had deserted our service & joined the enemy."[77] That situation now recurred twofold. The more notorious incident involved twenty-two U.S. prisoners of war who were identified as former Confederate soldiers, tried by court-martial, and hanged. Corse was later said to have been involved in two ways.

The general and his staff happened upon a group of these turncoats being taken back to camp by Confederate soldiers, also attired in the blue coats and tall hats worn by the Yankees, which they had acquired when storming a northern earthwork. Spotting the large party in Federal uniforms, Corse remarked, "We are in for it now." The guards did not challenge the riders, leading Corse to inquire, "Who are you?" "We are Southerners, General, with prisoners." "What are you doing with that blue uniform on?" he asked. "We captured it at the fort," they answered. "Get to the camp," said the Alexandrian, "and as soon as you reach there take it off."[78]

At a campsite on the way back to Kinston, the captives were huddled together outside the commanding general's tent when the flap flew open and out came Pickett, trailed by Corse and Hoke. In disgust, the division commander ordered the prisoners away, then, in an aside to his subordinates, he remarked, "We'll have to have a court-martial on these fellows pretty soon, and after some are shot the rest will stop deserting." Corse reportedly replied, "The sooner the better."[79] Was this just bravado, or did it reflect the Alexandrian's true feeling on this matter?

About the same time, six Confederate deserters were caught with weapons in their hands, although not wearing the uniform of the enemy. Corse served as president of the court-martial that determined their guilt and sentenced them to execution as well. The prisoners were tied to stakes in a kneeling position and shot in a single burst of fire.[80] Within a short space of time, Corse had twice been involved in the application of military discipline that troubled him deeply.

As Pickett's North Carolina expedition entered its third month of demonstrations without victory, it became clear that Lee's original objective of taking Newbern would not be achieved. Looking ahead to a spring offensive engineered by Lt. Gen. U. S. Grant, the beleaguered commanding general in Virginia wrote to the War Department on April 13, asking that Pickett's division be disengaged and sent to rejoin Longstreet. "If anything is to be done in North Carolina it should be done quickly," Lee concluded.[81] Within a matter of days, Hoke launched an attack on Plymouth, North Carolina, well north of Newbern on Albemarle Sound. Aided by the CSS *Albemarle,* the Confederates effected the surrender of the garrison of twenty-eight hundred men on April 20. Corse was once again employed with five regiments of Virginia troops to occupy the enemy at Newbern, thereby keeping reinforcements away from the rebels' real objective. It no doubt came as a disappointment to Corse when Hoke, his junior as a brigadier, was summarily promoted by Davis to the rank of major general immediately upon his triumph at Plymouth. Corse's command was reassigned to Hoke's division.[82]

After one last failed expedition against Newbern in early May, Richmond declared the campaign a success on the strength of Hoke's victory, the first by the Confederates along the Atlantic coast in a long time. The Virginians were recalled to help defend against a massive, multi-pronged Federal offensive. Corse's brigade left Kinston by train on May 10–11, at the same time Lee and Grant were squaring off at Spotsylvania Court House and Lt. Gen. J. E. B. Stuart was meeting his denouement at Yellow Tavern. To the west, cadets from the Virginia Military Institute were poised to resist the Yankee advance up the Shenandoah Valley at New Market. Corse and three of his regiments reached Petersburg to find it wild with rumors about the threat posed by Maj. Gen. Benjamin "Beast" Butler's 25,000 troops just eight miles away at City Point.

Marching in the direction of Richmond, Corse and his men were engaged in heavy skirmishing at Swift Creek. Meanwhile, Corse's other regiments, the Seventeenth and Thirtieth Virginia, were stopped in

Petersburg and sent westward by freight cars to protect bridges along the Danville road from Brig. Gen. A. V. Kautz and his raiders, which the Virginians did successfully at Flat Creek.[83] Meanwhile, the main body of Corse's brigade was roughly handled by Butler's troops when Hoke tried to contain the Federal Army of the James. In the dense fog of early morning on May 16, Corse's regiments were finally reunited at Drewry's Bluff overlooking the James River south of the Confederate capital. Beauregard, the senior leader on the field, had complained earlier about being assigned brigadiers found wanting by the War Department, and Douglas Southall Freeman has suggested that the Creole was once again saddled with a less-than-stellar collection of subordinates.[84] Whether Corse was considered in this class is conjectural.

The men of Corse's brigade were hungry, not having eaten for twenty-four hours. One former soldier recalled the general passing along the line, encouraging his soldiers with the prospect of bountiful rations in the Yankee campsite up ahead. When word came to move forward, the men bounded out of their trenches, sounding the rebel yell. Positioned in front of the line, Corse received a minor wound across the loins but did not let it stop him from leading the charge. The Virginians drove the enemy from the field, in the process capturing hundreds of prisoners, many of whom Lieutenant Colonel Herbert declared did not know enough English to surrender. The rush was so successful that the brigade became isolated ahead of the rest of the Confederate line and vulnerable to counterattack from its right flank. Corse quickly withdrew. At the conclusion of the engagement, his command was ordered to follow the retreating Federals, but no further action ensued.[85]

After the battle of Drewry's Bluff, Corse's men first went into the earthworks near the Howlett house and then marched into Richmond, where they camped on Capitol Square. On May 20, Corse and four other brigade commanders were ordered to report to the commanding general of the Army of Northern Virginia.[86] They would remain under Lee's command for the remainder of the war. On the way to Hanover Junction by rail, Corse's men were dropped off at Penola Station, ten miles south of Fredericksburg, and told to continue on foot. Four miles later, at a point called Poorhouse Field, the Alexandrian spotted the enemy up ahead and formed his men into a line of battle. They were about to charge when Corse was informed that he was facing the whole of Maj. Gen. Winfield Hancock's corps. Fortunately for Corse, his adversary misidentified his troops and those of another nearby unit as a formidable Southern force, and the two sides carefully separated.[87]

Assigned to Pickett's division once again, Corse's brigade was now a part of First Corps, commanded by Maj. Gen. Richard Anderson in the absence of the wounded Longstreet. During Grant's all-out assault at

Cold Harbor on June 3, Corse's men were only engaged in some heavy skirmishing, as the futile Yankee charge took place to their right. After the carnage, pickets from the two antagonists settled into a pattern of chatting and trading tobacco and coffee that would continue, with only brief interruptions, for many months.

On June 16, Grant's flanking movement across the James River caused Beauregard to abandon the defenses along Butler's front at Bermuda Hundred and move south to defend Petersburg. No longer confronted by rebels, Butler naturally moved forward to threaten the turnpike and rail line extending south from Richmond. Pickett's division was therefore sent to the south side of the James to block Butler's advance. Corse's brigade stopped opposite the Howlett house and threw out a picket line east of the pike. One of his regiments, the Fifteenth Virginia, was deployed to locate the enemy and report back to Corse. Discovering the Yankees relaxing several hundred yards in front of the former Confederate earthworks and unaware of its presence, the Fifteenth launched a bold attack that succeeded in driving the enemy back into the Butler fortifications at Bermuda Hundred. The Southerners sparsely occupied Beauregard's trenches and called for help from their brigade, located nearly a mile to the rear. Corse was reluctant, at first, to believe that the undersized regiment could achieve such success. The next morning, "our silver-haired old hero," as the regimental commander referred to Corse, strengthened the line, thereby reestablishing Confederate control at one of the most strategic points to guard against naval approaches.[88]

Pickett's units now occupied a three-mile stretch of breastworks reaching from the James River to the Appomattox River and known as the "Howlett Line" for the doctor's house at its north end. Fields of fire were enhanced by felled trees, and pickets were protected in rifle pits.[89] This perimeter would be home to Corse's brigade for most of the next nine months. Fortunately for the undermanned defenders, it would be a quiet sector of the Richmond-Petersburg fortifications.

Even Corse described the duty as "lazing in the trenches, sweltering in the sun." For a short while, he was hospitalized with an intestinal infection. The idle brigade commander soon began a series of regular letters to his wife, housed in Richmond with in-laws, in which he related his thoughts on what was transpiring, in addition to repeated expressions of love for her. "I have no fear of Gen. Lee not being able to controvert Grant in his strategic moves," Corse assured Lizzie. He worried about whom to appoint if authorized an assistant adjutant general, and he related that Pickett was promoting Harry Hough from Alexandria, a clerk at his headquarters for the past two years. Corse's comments indicated an awareness of military and political developments. He worried that Jubal Early would not escape safely from the Federal forces converging on him after his raid on Washington; he hoped that W. T. Sherman would be destroyed before reaching the Atlantic coast; and, when President Lincoln was reelected, the brigadier steeled himself for renewed struggle with the Yankees across the line. With the advent of the cool nights of autumn, the field commander asked his "dearest wife" to have two pairs of flannel drawers made for him.[90]

What Corse wanted most was for Lizzie to join him, but he knew that this was impossible. His yearning increased when Virginia Beverley, the first of four children, was born in November. Corse then became more practical, realizing that his new family would be housed some distance from the front lines, where he was required to remain on call almost continuously. Their vulnerability constituted for him "a constant state of anxiety," he confided to his wife. The tables had turned, however, for Lizzie was disconsolate at being unable to nurse her infant and pleaded to join her husband. "There is no chance of your getting milk down here," he replied. "I don't know of a cow in the neighbourhood."[91]

The love-struck husband might have spent less time thinking about his personal life and given more attention to his command. In an unusually harsh letter to Longstreet, Lee addressed the findings of a team of inspectors who had visited Pickett's division and the Alexandrian's command, in particular:

> In Corse's brigade, the 29th Va. regt. is reported to be unsoldierly & unmilitary, lax in discipline and loose in military instruction. In the whole brigade the officers & men are indifferently instructed in discipline and drill, & the former are said to be inefficient. Commanding officers know but little about the condition of their men & there is a great want of clothing.
>
> Prompt measures must be taken to bring inefficient officers before examining boards & get rid of them.[92]

When Corse applied for Christmas leave to see Lizzie and his daughter, he was denied. The army had other plans for him. He was sent to Gordonsville to take charge of two other brigades while their commanders enjoyed time away. Even his faithful adjutant, Capt. Phil Hooe from Alexandria, went off for ten days, leaving the disappointed general to confront the loneliness of command.[93]

Deserters crossed the lines in both directions, bringing information that was greeted with a healthy degree of skepticism. In the wake of the slaughter at Cold Harbor, Yankees claimed their former comrades were demoralized; Confederate defectors said the same thing. Corse was reluctant to place any confidence in reports brought by Northerners and regretted the loss of reliable soldiers from his own ranks.[94] His brigade was now suffering from ague and fever, ailments common along the

James River. The old brigadier avoided the malady, somehow, perhaps through immunity developed in Mexico or California.[95]

The last winter of the war was generally uneventful for Corse's brigade. Memories of the encampment were lighthearted. In addition to constructing log cabins for their own use, the soldiers built a meeting place, partially dug into the earth, which they dubbed "Corse's Chapel" in light of regular religious services held there. On November 1, Lee inspected the Howlett Line, much to the men's delight. A fellow officer later recalled a game of whist in Corse's tent, when a cannonball passed through its peak. The players dove for the exit, with Corse reaching the opening first and falling unceremoniously in a bucket of water.[96]

As winter drew to a close, redeployments and skirmishing became more common. Corse's brigade was sent north of the James River near Fort Gilmer for six weeks of suffering in tents in the wet, mud, and cold. Rumors abounded about being dispatched elsewhere in Virginia, or even to North Carolina. Lizzie Corse informed her husband of talk of evacuating Richmond, to which he replied, "do not write me any more sorrowful letters."[97] Returning to the Howlett Line, Corse found that skirmishing had picked up, along with the desertion rate. U.S. First Corps recorded 144 rebels coming across the lines to surrender from Corse's units alone during a ten-day period in mid-March. Clearly, the stage was set for an end to the four-year struggle.[98]

Corse's brigade participated in three final engagements before the surrender—at Dinwiddie Court House, Five Forks, and Sayler's Creek. Pickett's division was being assembled on March 28 and sent by rail to Sutherland Depot, where Corse's brigade disembarked and joined the extreme right of the Petersburg line three days later.[99] On the way, the Seventeenth Virginia became engaged in skirmishing. During the firing, women and children were observed rushing about in no-man's-land, about a hundred yards ahead, trying to find shelter from the projectiles whizzing about. When Corse was informed of the situation, he sent a courier to usher the refugees to the safety of his lines.[100]

On the morning of March 31, Pickett's retreat from the Richmond-Petersburg lines began through Five Forks toward Dinwiddie Court House. The enemy attacked at this point, inflicting severe casualties on Corse's brigade in particular. Pickett rallied his forces, however, and pushed the Federals back. Realizing they were outmanned, the Confederates quietly withdrew to Five Forks the following day.

The Yankees launched assault after assault against the rebels on April 1, eventually pouring through the left side of the defensive line. The men under Corse and Maj. Gen. "Rooney" Lee never gave way. Pickett reported, "We compelled a rally and stand on Corse's Brigade, which was still in perfect order, and had repelled, as had W. H. F. Lee's cavalry, every attempt of the enemy against them."[101] When the Confederate defense collapsed altogether, Corse's men moved smartly to the rear. Private Edgar Warfield and a comrade stopped to help an old school chum who had been shot in the leg. Riding up, Corse shouted to put the man down and save themselves.[102]

Corse was more composed by nightfall. A member of Crenshaw's Battery, which had supported Corse's brigade, related that the general organized a proper retreat at sunset. The butternut infantry marched alongside the artillery in full view of the enemy's cavalry. The lead driver of the first gun was urged by the wagoners behind him to drive faster or get out of the way. "I heard a voice at my side say: 'For God's sake don't let those horses trot,'" the driver related. Turning his head, he discovered the speaker to be General Corse. "Don't let your horses go out of a walk for much depends on you," he continued. Turning to the other teamsters who were crowding up, Corse spoke out in a loud voice, "Steady men, steady men, remember you are Virginians."[103]

Heading toward Amelia Court House, an enlisted soldier remembered Corse appealing once again to his brigade, providing the leadership needed to survive. "Men, it is necessary for the safety of this Command that we keep well together and we will probably encounter strong bodies of the enemy's cavalry along our route and we must brush them aside or fight our way through them in our effort to rejoin the main body of our army."[104]

The soldiers of Lee's army were now suffering terribly from weariness and lack of anything to eat. As they trudged westward, Corse's brigade was assigned as rear guard for the division wagon train, which had miraculously escaped capture. Soon, the entire army's wagon trains, eight to ten miles long, joined the retreat. The exhausted troops marched on, through severe rain, during the night of April 5. The following day, they were stopped by Federal cavalry at Sayler's Creek. The column was struck from both sides, and when the enemy began to overlap the rebels, Pickett ordered a retreat. Emerging into a large field on the Harper Farm, the Virginians spotted a dense woods a few hundred yards away that promised refuge. As they headed for cover, a trooper from the First New Jersey Cavalry rode down on Corse and his staff. The general threw up a white handkerchief, waving it above his head as a sign of surrender. The captives were then marched to the rear and turned over to the Federal provost marshal.[105]

Colonel Herbert, commander of the Seventeenth Regiment, took control of the brigade and pushed the survivors along the route of march. The next day, near Farmville, the starving soldiers broke into commissary stores aboard the wagons and helped themselves to flour and bacon. At Appomattox Court House on April 9, Lee surrendered 32 officers and 262 men from Corse's brigade.[106]

The brigade's captured commander was taken first to Petersburg, where he jotted a letter to Lizzie on April 12 encouraging her to write and, in his naïveté, even suggesting she might visit him. Along with other general officers captured at Sayler's Creek, however, Corse was quickly removed to Boston, where his uncle had been incarcerated three-quarters of a century earlier during the War of Independence. It was at Fort Warren in Boston Harbor that the prisoners learned of the assassination of Abraham Lincoln. Lt. Gen. Richard Stoddert Ewell immediately wrote to Grant, expressing the abhorrence, shared by the fourteen flag officers confined with him, of this act.[107]

Corse languished in detention for more than three months. His imprisonment was made more bearable by regular correspondence from Lizzie and Alexandria cohorts and by the benevolence of a Boston family he had befriended early in the war. The Cliffords sent fresh vegetables and reading material as thanks for Corse's assistance to their daughter when she attempted to pass through the Confederate lines to nurse her brother, lying wounded in a Southern hospital. George D. Fowle, a contemporary from that prominent Alexandria family, wrote from New York to assure Corse that he and Arthur Herbert had visited Lizzie in Richmond and found her to be well and comfortable. Corse also heard from his sister, Julia, who had sheltered Lizzie during the conflict.[108]

The defeated general did everything expected of him in an effort to be reunited with his wife and daughter. On June 16, he took the oath to "faithfully support and defend the constitution of the United States and the Union of States," along with the "laws and proclamations made during the existing rebellion, with reference to the emancipation of slaves." (Corse and many of his comrades in arms had gotten into trouble in the first place by standing up for the constitution, as they interpreted it.) At the same time, he appealed to President Andrew Johnson for restoration of his rights as a citizen under provisions of the Amnesty Proclamation of May 29. Finally, on July 24, upon swearing to remain on good behavior and not commit or encourage hostility against the United States, Corse was released from custody.[109]

Returning to his hometown, Corse proceeded to build upon his reputation as one of Alexandria's beloved city fathers. He rejoined his brother's banking firm and remained there until its closing in 1874, when he retired from business. The old general was in the state capitol in 1870 when the floor collapsed, dropping him onto the story below. "With remarkable presence of mind," the *Alexandria Gazette* reported, "when he felt himself descending, he pulled his hat down over his eyes and ears and kept his hands clenched upon the brim of his hat. He lighted upon his feet, and was almost the first one to emerge from the rubbish. He only received some slight scratches on the head."[110]

Corse was evidently close to Robert E. Lee, for he introduced the general at the reception held in his honor in Alexandria, served as a pallbearer at his brother's funeral, and spoke at the city's memorial service for the Confederate general in chief. When the reclining marble figure was unveiled on the icon's vault at the Washington and Lee Chapel in 1883, Corse was included on the platform of notables. He later made the rounds of Confederate memorial dedications, beginning with the ceremony in Alexandria in 1889 and continuing with Lee's statue in Richmond in 1890, Fairfax Court House in 1890, and Fredericksburg in 1891.[111] Corse was a vestryman at St. Paul's Episcopal Church, a member of the Virginia Military Institute's board of visitors, and a charter member of the Confederate veterans camp organized in Alexandria.[112]

The aging field commander was in the habit of making the rounds through his beloved hometown each day. He went to market before breakfast, accompanied by "Uncle Charles," a retainer loyal from days before the war. During different stages of his retirement, Corse's walk included daily visits with his longtime friends, Dr. Magnus Lewis and John B. Daingerfield, and stops at Edgar Warfield's drugstore and the Burke and Herbert Bank. At nightfall, the stroll would more likely lead the old Alexandrian to recall times and occurrences long forgotten on the city streets he traversed. It is said that during one saunter in the mid-1880s, a minié ball fell out of Corse's leg, having been lodged there since he was wounded at Second Manassas.[113]

At President Grant's second inaugural parade, Corse first realized his eyesight was failing. A slight haze seemed to obscure the troops marching by. A cataract operation left him blind in one eye, so he delayed trying to correct vision in his other eye until totally blind. As his seeing deteriorated, he amused himself by reciting Shakespeare and following a more limited route through the city's streets, using dark glasses and a cane. When he returned to his daily routine after surgery restored some perception to one eye, townspeople on every square flocked to greet him.[114]

Corse returned their love. As his sons grew up and spent most of their time pursuing careers away from home, they encouraged their father to move closer and see them more regularly. "I am too old to be transplanted," was his reply. "I wouldn't be happy anywhere else. My friends are here, my associations are here, the best people in the world are here. No, I must spend my remaining years in Alexandria!"[115]

On December 31, 1894, the beloved Lizzie passed away. Corse was disconsolate but seemed to sense that he would soon join her. During a terrible blizzard in February 1895, he fell ill. Drifting in and out of consciousness, his mind wandered like those of other Confederate chieftains in their last hours. Several times, in a clear voice, Corse gave commands and issued directions for the disposition of his troops. In the early hours of February 11, Corse breathed his last. "He was a brave man and a Southern gentleman, and was held in high respect and esteem by all who knew him," proclaimed the *Alexandria Gazette*. Perhaps the *Baltimore Sun* would be considered more objective about someone who was not a local resident. Its editor opined, "There was no more heroic or unselfish brigade commander in the Confederate Army of Northern Virginia than Gen. Montgomery D. Corse."[116]

Wrapped in the same Virginia flag presented to the Seventeenth Regiment by Governor Letcher, the casket was ushered to the grave by, among others, Colonels Marye and Herbert, Captains Hooe and Charles Williams (former aide-de-camp to Corse), and James Darchin, a Forty-niner who was with Corse in California. Attendees included a large contingent from the city's Grand Army of the Republic post, reflecting the respect of veterans from both sides in the conflict. A chapter of Alexandria history closed on February 13, 1895.[117]

The old soldier clearly won the affections of military subordinates and fellow Alexandrians, but how should Montgomery Corse be evaluated as a senior commander? During a war in which advancement was accelerated, Corse served two and a half years as a brigadier general. His son later claimed that promotion could have been obtained by transferring to another command but that Corse chose, instead, to remain with friends in his old brigade.[118]

It would be interesting to know if his Alexandria colleague, Robert E. Lee, gave special preference in assignments to Corse. The brigadier and his troops were sent away from the Army of Northern Virginia on missions to invest Suffolk, protect southwestern Virginia, reclaim Knoxville, capture Newbern, and, finally, man the Howlett Line for almost a year. None of these deployments brought distinction to Corse's service record. They were pursued at the expense of his participation in landmark battles at Chancellorsville, Gettysburg, and the Wilderness. Despite these omissions, which were not of his own choosing, Corse was constantly involved in the Southern war effort, from before First Manassas to Sayler's Creek. He led with consistency, if not always with brilliance, and avoided the kinds of missteps that took the lives or tarnished the reputations of a good many of his peers.

Taken as a whole, Montgomery Corse's life deserved the respect he received in Alexandria for his initiative in forming units to fight in two conflicts, for loyal service as a field commander during the Civil War, rising to the occasion when adversity struck, and for civic contributions over many years. It cannot be said, however, that his performance of duty ranked Corse in the upper echelon of general officers during the war of secession.

CHAPTER FOUR

PRESIDENTIAL AIDE
✯✯✯ G. W. CUSTIS LEE

ARLINGTON MANSION COMMANDS A RIDGE OVERLOOKING
the Potomac River and the capital city sprawling before it on the opposite
shore. The tripartite structure consists of two wings extending on either
side of a grand central hall. The portico, supported by eight massive
Doric columns, is patterned after the temple of Theseus in Athens. A
house museum and prominent national cemetery today, during the first
half of nineteenth-century Arlington was an eleven-hundred-acre estate
in the middle of Alexandria County.

Completed in 1804, the mansion was built by George Washington
Parke Custis, Martha Washington's grandson and her husband's adopted
son. During its first six decades, Arlington contained precious relics of
George Washington, along with other heirlooms and treasures from
Mount Vernon. The Marquis de Lafayette was entertained at Arlington in
1825.[1] Curious sightseers frequently stopped by to receive an informal
tour by the lord of the manor. Custis's will granted his daughter, Mary
Anna Randolph Custis Lee, a lifetime interest in the property, after
which the estate would pass to the patriarch's namesake, her son, George
Washington Custis Lee. The young heir's paternal side descended from
the Revolutionary War hero "Light Horse Harry" Lee. Inheriting the
mantle of three noble families, it is not surprising that Custis Lee was
extraordinary.

The greatest influence in Custis's life, however, was none of these forebears, but his father, Robert Edward Lee. Custis was born on September
16, 1832, at Fort Monroe, Virginia, where Lieutenant Lee was assigned
in the Corps of Engineers.[2] Custis was separated from his father for much
of his childhood, as Mary Lee preferred the comfort of her parents'
home to the more Spartan existence in army quarters.[3] Yet his father was

never far from Custis's thoughts. One snowy day, father and son went for a walk. The elder Lee looked behind to observe the little boy imitating his movement by stepping in his footprints left on the ground. "When I saw this," Lee shared with a friend, "I said to myself, 'it behooves me to walk very straight when this fellow is already following in my tracks.'"[4] As if to keep showing the path, a stream of letters from military posts sounded a drumroll on the importance of moral and mental development. Dignity and self-restraint, for which his father would become renowned, were qualities for Custis to emulate.

Mary Lee accompanied her husband to his posting at St. Louis in 1838 and began tutoring "Boo" (as Custis was known in the family) in reading and writing, under the watchful eye of now-Captain Lee. By the age of nine, the youngster had outgrown home schooling and was enrolled at the Fairfax Institute, Rev. George A. Smith's classical academy at Clarens next to the estate of Samuel Cooper on Quaker Hill outside Alexandria, convenient for spending weekends with the grandparents.[5] As the eldest son, Custis was expected to achieve top scholastic honors. His father kept a close eye on Custis's progress, taking particular note of his shortcomings in algebra. During this period, the youngster began to take seriously the responsibility of upholding his family's good name.[6]

The impressionable youth received a profound lesson in duty and honor when his father served twenty-two months away from home during the Mexican War. Letters from the front entreated the children to strive for excellence in everything they undertook. Somber in the wake of the engagement at Cerro Gordo, the captain wrote his son, "You have no idea what a horrible sight a field of battle is."[7] His father's outstanding record throughout the campaign led to his elevation to brevet colonel, once more inspiring the youngster to follow in his footsteps.

It was not surprising, therefore, that Custis expressed an interest in attending the U.S. Military Academy. His mother suggested he receive preparation at Benjamin Hallowell's school in Alexandria, as her husband had done. Lee was less than enthusiastic about the idea. In an incredibly graphic and candid reaction, especially for the reserved officer, he expressed an abhorrence of the Quaker's pacifist influence on his pupils. "I hope he will not become like 'Hallowell boys' as they were termed some years since. I would rather be pierced by a hundred Mexican balls than to see him so." The agitated father went on to question the value of Hallowell's course of study, which emphasized practical English subject matter.

> I have given you my opinion about Custis going to West Point. The difficulty I see to his going to Mr. Hallowell should he persist in his desire to go to W[est] P[oint] is that if he fails to obtain a cadets appt. I fear he will

lose much of his classics. It will also depend somewhat as to his advancement in Mathematics, whether it will be necessary to go to Mr. H. I had thought he was pretty well advanced. You must exercise your own judgement on the matter. If Mr. H's is as good a school now as you represent, & he can take drawing lessons, the change may be beneficial, especially if he could review his classics & study french. The latter will be necessary. I wish him also to take dancing lessons. . . . If he goes to W. P. he will have to study hard. There is no child's play there.[8]

Lee soon initiated a campaign on behalf of his son's admission to West Point, enlisting Maj. Gen. Winfield Scott, the army's commander in chief. Lee also imposed upon the adjutant general to obtain an endorsement from Maryland and Virginia lawmakers to help in the endeavor.[9] The nineteen members of the two states' congressional delegations signed a petition for an at-large appointment. Senators Robert M. T. Hunter and James Murray Mason of Virginia wrote first to President James K. Polk and then to President Zachary Taylor on Custis's behalf, including reference to "the great and acknowledged service rendered to the country by Col. Lee in the late war with Mexico." Lee's efforts paid off when Custis was admitted to the academy in June 1850.[10]

Custis proved to be a good student with an aptitude for mathematics, which was central to the institution's curriculum. Conversely, he found contemporary literature and poetry less appealing.[11] His closest rival academically was Oliver Otis Howard of Maine, a future corps commander in the Union army, who stood first in the class after one year. By conclusion of the 1852 term, however, Custis had moved into the top position, a ranking he never relinquished.

The one stain on his record at West Point occurred in June 1851, when an instructor unexpectedly entered Custis's room and found him holding a bottle of brandy. The mortified cadet insisted he had not brought the spirits onto the grounds and refused to divulge who had so violated the academy's regulations. He also declined to take advantage of the gratuitous pledge of his classmates to abide by the rules concerning liquor for one year if the charges against him were dismissed. Anguished over his son's plight, Colonel Lee wrote him letters of encouragement. Custis subsequently pleaded guilty to illegal possession before a court-martial, leaving no alternative but application of the prescribed punishment of dismissal. Seven of the court's eight members, however, urged remission of the sentence in light of the extenuating circumstances. Upon reviewing the case, the secretary of war rejected the formal recommendation and chose, instead, to issue a public reprimand. Retaining Custis in uniform may well have been influenced by the high esteem in which his father was held.[12]

Custis's family joined him at West Point in the fall of 1852. Over Colonel Lee's objections, he had been assigned to the position of superintendent.[13] He was soon worshiped by the corps of cadets for his dignity, integrity, and soldierly appearance. The pressure on Custis to emulate his father was now greater than ever. Whenever she could, Mrs. Lee pampered her son, but the cadet's visits to the superintendent's quarters were limited to a weekly call on Saturday afternoon. "It is the only time we see him," lamented his father.[14]

In combination with strong family influences during his formative years, the West Point experience completed the development of Custis's personality. His courtesy, reserve, and impeccable manners represented old Virginia gentility at its finest, reflecting favorably on his family's prestige. A classmate characterized Custis as "a singularly modest man, a close student, methodical, precise and quiet. In his physical and mental presentiment he strongly resembled his father, [Brevet] Colonel Robert E. Lee."[15]

Four years at the military academy constituted the one time in his life when Custis bested his role model, as he finished first academically, while his father had been second in the class of 1829. By graduation day, Custis also achieved the status of corps adjutant, the second highest cadet rank. Of the forty-six graduates in the class of 1854, thirty-seven would take part in the divisive conflict to come, twenty-three on the Federal side and fourteen as Confederates.[16] Included in the latter contingent were such stalwarts as J. E. B. Stuart, Fitzhugh Lee, Stephen Dill Lee, John Pegram, Dorsey Pender, and John Villepigue.

With facility in mathematics and his father's example, it was quite natural for Custis to begin his military career in the Corps of Engineers. His first posting was to the engineer headquarters in Washington, permitting him to live with his grandfather at Arlington. In March 1855 Lieutenant Lee was assigned to Amelia Island off the Florida/Georgia coast to make drawings for a proposed fort, survey its boundaries, and commence construction. Regular letters to family members referred to long hours, hordes of mosquitoes, and sweltering working conditions made less bearable by the absence of the gentility afforded by women. During this posting Lee grew the auburn beard that distinguished him for many years. It was also the first time he suffered from the rheumatoid arthritis that crippled his mother.

After two years, Lee requested and received a transfer to Fort Point, California. He stopped at Arlington to await the next available steamer embarking from New York. His doting mother was ecstatic at seeing Custis and wrote to the army's chief engineer to delay his departure. The young officer meekly accepted her interference with his orders, telling his superior that he was unwell.[17] Lee finally arrived at San Francisco in late

August 1855 and began work on a fortification sited to protect the harbor with seacoast artillery.[18] The lieutenant was responsible for overseeing a crew of more than two hundred masons, stonecutters, teamsters, and other civilian laborers. In addition, he maintained financial ledgers and submitted detailed monthly reports required of every supervising engineer officer. Lee soon encountered a familiar face, Lt. James McPherson, who graduated first in the West Point class of 1853 and would soon achieve prominence in the Union army. Another associate, Capt. Jeremy Gilmer, was destined to become chief of engineers for the Confederate army.

Lee's grandfather died on October 10, 1857. His father returned home from a cavalry regiment in Texas to execute the will and found Arlington to be long neglected and heavily in debt. When Custis learned of the estate's rundown condition, he offered to renounce his claim in favor of his father, who was saddled with responsibility for untangling its problems. The gesture was declined: "I cannot accept your offer. It is not from any unwillingness to receive from you a gift you may think proper to bestow, or to be indebted to you for any benefit great or small. But simply because it would not be right for me to do so. Your dear G[ran]d. father distributed his property as he thought best, & it is proper that it should remain as he bestowed it."[19]

The colonel was anxious to return to his command, however, and began a campaign to influence Custis to resign his commission or request a transfer to Washington so he could oversee the property and assist his mother and sisters. Custis's arthritis was aggravated by the San Francisco climate, providing another reason to insist that the young officer leave northern California.[20] To achieve his personal objective, Colonel Lee, like his wife earlier, intervened in his son's career, this time by ensuring that the secretary of war was presented a recommendation to order Custis to the engineer bureau.[21] The dutiful son eventually succumbed to family pressure and agreed to the reassignment.

Custis arrived at Arlington in October 1859 and began to learn about managing the estate from his father while at the same time settling into new duties at the headquarters in Washington. The colonel left for Texas in February 1860 and resumed a steady correspondence to pass along instructions and advice on business and personal matters.[22] In the spring, Custis escorted his mother and her companions to a Canadian spa and then returned to take the waters in New York State for his recurring arthritis. Along with the rest of the country, Custis endured the heat of the national political campaign in the summer, and, like the majority of his fellow Alexandrians, favored the Constitutional Unionist ticket in the November election.[23]

The year 1861 opened for Custis with reassignment from his desk job to nearby Fort Washington, where he supervised renovation of the masonry complex. His improvements included restoring bridges, clearing fields of fire, and preparing embrasures to mount howitzers for the marines stationed there.[24] The citadel's location across the river from Mount Vernon was just far enough away to preclude commuting from Arlington. By March, his father had returned home, as the prospect of armed hostilities became more eminent. Three days after the Virginia convention voted to secede, Colonel Lee resigned his commission in the U.S. Army. Surprisingly, Custis did not immediately follow suit.

The threat confronting the nation weighed heavily on the younger Lee. A majority of the Virginians who had graduated from West Point and were still on active duty were sticking with the Union.[25] A former West Point classmate remembered Custis agonizing over the decision: "[William] 'Averell, that Arlington estate over the river is mine. I would give it in a moment and all I have on earth if the Union could be preserved in peace, but I must go with my State,' and I left him leaning his elbows on the mantelpiece with his face buried in his hands, agitated with profound grief."[26] Two friends and fellow Virginians, Lieutenants Lunsford Lomax and John B. Magruder, quickly tendered their resignations, but Custis held on.[27]

For once, his father declined to instruct him what to do. Lee had earlier written to his son: "when I contemplate the condition of the Country, I feel as if I could easily lay down my life for its safety. But I also feel that would bring but little good."[28] Now, Lee was silent. "Tell Custis," he wrote his wife, "he must consult his own judgment, reason and conscience as to the course he may take. I do not wish him to be guided by my wishes or example. If I have done wrong, let him do better. The present is a momentous question which every man must settle for himself and upon principle."[29] Custis later recalled that the War Department asked him to complete his work at Fort Washington before leaving and, with a heightened sense of duty ingrained over twenty-eight years, he remained at that post until the job was done.[30] Finally, on April 27, eight days after his father's resignation, Lieutenant Lee withdrew. He wrote the chief of engineers of "the sad feelings with which I leave the army, particularly my own corps; and deeply regret the necessity which compels me to it."[31]

Custis faced one remaining task before he could share in the excitement erupting in Richmond. He had to help his mother close the mansion on Arlington Heights. His father anxiously implored her to secure the George Washington memorabilia. "War is inevitable," he exclaimed, "and there is no telling when it will burst around you."[32] He also wrote to tell Custis to bring his horse, tack, blankets, towels—anything of use for field service.[33] Little did any of them realize that the young officer would have little need for such accoutrements.

The mother and son sent some manuscripts and relics to Richmond; other family portraits and treasures from the first president went to the Fitzhugh cousins at nearby Ravensworth; and several chests of silver were shipped to Lexington, Virginia. The items locked in the house were subsequently stolen by the troops who occupied it during the war or confiscated by order of Secretary of War Edwin Stanton.[34] The last two private owners of Arlington finally fled on May 14, abandoning with regret the site of the nuptial rites of Robert Lee and Mary Custis thirty years earlier.

Arriving in Richmond, Custis was put to work on the city's defenses. He had been made a major in the Virginia state engineer corps before leaving Arlington. The Confederacy's hunger for engineering skills was evident when Brig. Gen. Philip St. George Cocke, writing from Alexandria while Custis still served with the U.S. Army, requested that he be assigned to construct Southern fortifications along the Potomac intended to interrupt transport with the Federal capital.[35]

On July 1, Lee received a Confederate commission as captain, one of only sixteen members of its regular army assigned to the Corps of Engineers. His experience in the old army was immediately put to use, as he was sent to North Carolina by stage and stern-wheel steamboat to inspect its coastal fortifications and batteries.[36] He was dispatched to North Carolina again in October, this time as task force commander of nineteen companies of Georgia volunteers with the mission of repelling a Federal invasion from the sea, which did not materialize.[37] This would be his only field duty for the next two years.

On August 31, 1861, Lee's rank was abruptly advanced to colonel to correspond with his selection as Jefferson Davis's aide-de-camp.[38] The appointment was ideal from the president's standpoint. Lee was dignified, diplomatic, and discreet, qualities indispensable to a confidant who would sit in the highest councils of war and convey personal messages of utmost importance to senior military leaders. Mrs. Lee seemed relieved that by serving on the president's personal staff her son would be safe from the dangers of war. From the perspective of a young officer anxious for the glory and exhilaration of combat, however, the assignment was terribly disappointing. Modesty and reserve prevented Custis from complaining about his steady diet of administrative tasks. Years later, a friend explained that "the position at best was a trying one, and no one but a soldier can fully understand what this enforced duty meant as the heroic years went by, to a man of high spirit and consummate military equipment."[39]

Once again, Custis's personal wants took second place to his duty. Mary Chesnut, the Richmond observer, seemed to understand the situation: "Custis Lee is A.D.C. to the president—they say because his father wishes it. If he prefers to be in active service, that matters not. He must stay where he can do most good."[40]

Carte de visite of George Washington Custis Lee in a Confederate colonel's uniform. Special Collections, Alexandria Library.

Lee settled into a routine of processing the president's communications, encoding and deciphering his messages, meeting with field commanders to transmit instructions and information back and forth, accompanying Davis on inspection tours, and attending social funtions.[41] His access to the president sometimes led friends, like J. E. B. Stuart, to use him to intervene on their behalf, not unlike the position in which Adj. Gen. Samuel Cooper often found himself. Lee's combination of propriety and military acumen was ideal for dealing with senior officers in the field. He consulted with the district commander about fortifications along the Rappahannock River. He commiserated with the major general at Norfolk over reassignment of naval artillerists relied upon to man the port's batteries. And, he reassured Gen. Joseph E. Johnston, protecting Richmond against a Federal advance from the southeast, about defenses on the James River. The president's high regard for the young colonel was reflected in introductions given his emissary, such as, "I sent Colonel Lee, my aide-de-camp, to converse with you freely and confidentially," "Colonel Lee will . . . bear to me any information and reply which you may intrust to him," and "Colonel Lee has no doubt . . . communicated more fully in relation to our condition and my views than it is prudent to write."[42]

With General Lee deployed to a succession of locations in Virginia, South Carolina, and Georgia, the eldest son inherited responsibility for caring for the family. The will of Custis's grandfather specified that his slaves be freed within five years of his death, and Custis was now tasked to locate the blacks scattered by the flight from Arlington and manumit them.[43] The arrival in Richmond of his mother and sisters in June 1862 required Custis to find quarters for them. When they returned in the fall of 1863, he turned over his own residence on Franklin Street, which had served as the mess for a lively group of staff officers.[44]

It was during this period that Custis had his closest brush with marriage. For a brief period in the late summer of 1863, Custis was engaged to Sally Magee Warwick, a beautiful and high-spirited friend of his sister Agnes but twelve years his junior.[45] His father was skeptical that the wedding would ever take place, and he was proved right when the betrothal was quickly terminated. The social circle in which he moved presented Custis with many potential mates, and, like his father, he engaged in regular correspondence with several women for many years. But never again, before or after, did a relationship become as serious as the one with "Miss Sally."

Custis was uniquely suited to convey personal messages between his father and the president. Confronted with the customary loneliness of command, General Lee now used his son as a sounding board and sought his views on military appointments, among other matters.[46] In one uncharacteristic outburst late in the war, the elder Lee complained to Custis that the Confederate Congress did "not seem to be able to do anything except to eat peanuts and chew tobacco, while my army is starving."[47] Custis's visits often brought his father relief and respite from the constant concerns of command. After the general injured both hands in an accident, he asked Custis to pen some personal correspondence for him, including a letter to Mrs. Lee.[48] When he went to Winchester in October 1862 on an assignment for the president, Custis was able to offer assurance that Robert, the youngest family member, had survived the battle at Sharpsburg after the general had last seen him returning to the thick of the fighting.[49] Appreciating Lee's hunger for news about his sons in uniform, Davis frequently included asides on Custis's health in correspondence to the general.[50] After the war, Davis was quoted as saying that if it had ever been necessary to transfer Gen. R. E. Lee away from Virginia, he knew of no one he would have preferred to entrust the command than Custis Lee. Davis confirmed the statement, adding, "The only defect I found in him was his extreme diffidence."[51]

Davis's high regard for his aide's judgment was indicated by a mission in the spring of 1863. On April 7, Federal warships steamed over the bar into Charleston Harbor and began shelling Fort Sumter. The attack was repulsed, but Davis wanted a knowledgeable and objective assessment of the situation. Consequently, he dispatched the senior officer on his personal staff to evaluate the threat.[52] Arriving in Charleston on April 11, Lee found six monitors, plus the *New Ironsides,* still inside the harbor entrance. Another fifty vessels and as many as fifteen thousand troops were in the immediate area, poised to strike. Colonel Lee recommended sending reinforcements from Wilmington, North Carolina, since the troops could, if needed, be quickly returned over the connecting rail line. Upon receiving this message, Davis directed the secretary of war to move a brigade to Charleston. Within a week, however, the danger dissipated when the ironclads steamed off to the south. Lee soon acknowledged that he was uncovering nothing beyond what the commanding general, P. G. T. Beauregard, was transmitting in daily dispatches to the War Department and quietly returned to Richmond.[53]

The previous December, Custis had accompanied the president on a trip to assess the leadership and esprit of the western army. The subaltern probably used the close access afforded by several weeks of travel to discuss his longing to serve in the field. In June 1863 Davis finally placated his restless subordinate. Maj. Gen. George Stoneman's cavalry raid had exposed the Confederate capital's vulnerability to Yankee attack, and a brigade of local defense troops was consequently organized. Lee was given command of the new unit with the rank of brevet brigadier general.[54] While pleased with an assignment that might test his fiber as a soldier, Custis was undoubtedly distressed by the politics that seemed to pervade the posting. Unfortunately for him, as the war's final outcome was being determined at Vicksburg and Gettysburg, Lee became entangled in a picayune war of words between Maj. Gen. Arnold Elzey, commander of the department of Richmond, and the petulant Maj. Gen. D. H. Hill, temporarily in charge of the capital's defenses. The disagreements concerned such relatively insignificant matters as chain of command, reliability of convalescents, and placement of troops outside the city.[55]

Lee's new command initially consisted of five battalions with approximately two thousand men present for duty.[56] Unit members were drawn from workers otherwise exempt from military service because of their employment in government offices and at the city's arsenal, armory, and iron works. Clerks, mechanics, artisans, machinists, and the like constituted a force of questionable dedication and reliability but capable of generating relentless political clout. Soon after these citizen soldiers were first mustered by Lee in reaction to reports of a Federal force gathering on the Peninsula, the secretary of war directed that they be returned to their various departments and workshops, where their services were deemed more valuable.[57]

With the discipline bred into a son of Robert E. Lee, as well as that instilled at West Point, Custis began the formidable task of organizing and training his reluctant "volunteers." One bureaucrat expressed sentiments shared by many:

> The clerks in the departments were startled to-day by having read to them an order from Brig.-Gen. Custis Lee (son of Gen. R. E. Lee), an order to the captains of companies to imprison or otherwise punish all who fail to be present at the drills. These young gentlemen, not being removable, according to the Constitution, and exempted from conscription by an act of Congress, volunteered some months ago for "local defense and special service," never supposing that regular drilling would be obligatory ... They are willing to fight, when the enemy comes (a probable thing); but they dislike being *forced* out to drill, under threats of "punishment." This measure will not add to the popularity of Col. (or Gen.) Lee.[58]

The same malcontent later complained that "Custis Lee's brigade of clerks . . . were assured, when volunteering, that they never would be called out except to defend the fortifications of the city, built by negroes!"[59]

During the remainder of 1863, after the Yankee threat subsided, Lee devoted the majority of his time to duties as presidential aide. He continued to use the rank of colonel when acting on the president's behalf, reserving his brevetted status for command of troops. In the autumn, he once again joined Davis on a trip to assess forces in the field, meeting with Gen. Braxton Bragg and his staff in Georgia and accompanying the president to Charleston to evaluate for himself the adequacy of Beauregard's defenses. When they required assistance in Richmond, Generals Bragg and R. E. Lee each called for the aide to come and consult with him.[60] Despite the press of military duties, the dutiful son was still not relieved of family responsibilities. He issued a pass through the lines to a former slave at Arlington, who returned the kindness by divulging to the bluecoats all that he saw and heard about the Southern defenders on his journey northward.[61]

The prospect of field duty surfaced again in the winter of 1864. Davis received a request from supporters in western Virginia to appoint his aide to command that department. The president's observations of Lee's performance over two and a half years had convinced him of the colonel's abilities, and he was offered the post. Another aide reportedly confided in Davis that Lee was concerned about his own preparedness for this position.[62] The assignment went instead to Maj. Gen. Robert Ransom. After the war, a senior officer serving in West Virginia stated that he went to the headquarters of the Army of Northern Virginia and spent several hours discussing the matter with Custis's father. The commanding general was reported to have observed: "General Custis Lee is my son, and whilst I think very well of his abilities, yet, in my opinion, he has not been sufficiently tried in the field, and because he is my son and because of his want of sufficient experience in the field, I cannot and I will not recommend him for the place."[63]

The following summer, when Ransom's poor health required him to be relieved, Davis concluded that Custis Lee's was "not physically equal to the duty," referring either to his continuing affliction with arthritis or to a severe case of typhoid fever contracted during the war. Another candidate was therefore chosen once again.[64]

General Lee did not completely dismiss the notion of his son's assignment to a field billet. Two months after the West Virginia opportunity arose, the senior Lee was reorganizing his army's engineer corps and identified Custis as one of three generals qualified to be its chief engineer. Ever mindful of his own subordinate position to the nation's chief executive, Lee refrained from requesting his son's assignment but left open the door if Custis could ever be spared from his "peculiar duties" as presidential aide. "I should like very much to have him," the senior Lee acknowledged.[65]

Custis's inclination was to join the Army of Northern Virginia as chief of staff, but his father would not hear of it: "This would be very agreeable to me, but more open to all the objections that could be brought against your holding the place of Chief of Engineers. I presume, therefore, it would not be favorably considered. It is a delicate matter to apply for any one on the staff of another. I am not certain that it is proper to ask for one, serving with the President. In addition it is more important that he should have the aid he desires than I should."[66] Custis's military career was once again caught in the dynamics between the Confederacy's president and its senior commander.

As the winter of 1864 abated, the Federals resumed their efforts to reach the Confederate capital. At the same time the man who would eventually capture Richmond, Ulysses S. Grant, was ascending to overall command of U.S. armies, an ambitious cavalry foray set out. Leading five hundred troopers in from the west, Col. Uric Dahlgren approached within a couple miles of the city, where he encountered the convalescents, factory hands, office workers, and home guards commanded by Custis Lee. The most colorful unit in Lee's defense was the "boy company" (Company G, Third Battalion Local Defense), whose members were not old enough for regular military service. The youngsters won lasting fame by firing two brisk volleys that blunted a charge by Michiganders at Hick's Farm.[67] The resistance held along the entire line, leading to Dahlgren's death and Lee's commendation for repelling the strike.

When Grant subsequently began his relentless movement south, Lee's route-step command was called to duty with increasing frequency. The aide's attention was drawn away from his ministerial duties as he established a field headquarters near Chaffin's Bluff, seven miles below Richmond on the James River, and concentrated on strengthening the city's defenses. Maj. Gen. Ben Butler threatened the capital from the Peninsula, generating repeated reports of infantry and cavalry appearing to the southeast, where Lee's troops were posted. Davis inspected the lines in early June and reported to Custis's father that his son was well.[68] Shortly after the president's visit, Custis received orders giving him command of all troops east of the earthen defenses.[69]

As Grant's army approached Richmond, Southern defenders frantically searched for reliable information on its whereabouts. Custis Lee relayed a series of intelligence briefs based upon reports from pickets, civilians, and stragglers. On June 21, Grant and President Lincoln felt comfortable conferring at City Point, just fifteen miles south of the capital. Their opponents were more nervous than ever. Gray-clad cavalry reported a Federal pontoon bridge spanning the James River, and Lee cited estimates ranging from 2,000 to 2,500 enemy troops digging in to his front. Learning that four regiments of Federal cavalry were moving westward to interdict communication between his outposts, the worried commander called for help. His father advised him to identify the essential points necessary to protect Richmond, then use all available forces to hold them. Concerned that he could not discern the enemy's intentions, Lee withdrew his troops behind prepared positions to await further developments.[70]

Federal pressure intensified in July. Confederate hopes of drawing the enemy away from Richmond rested on Lt. Gen. Jubal Early's incursion into Maryland to threaten the Federal capital from the northwest. Southern strategists also envisioned a right hook against Washington, delivered by rebel prisoners of war freed, armed, and led by a team of adventurers commanded by Custis Lee and John Taylor Wood, who simultaneously held ranks in both the Confederate army and navy. Among his other duties, Wood served as an aide to Davis and had socialized with Lee on occasion. The principals were poised at Wilmington, North Carolina, awaiting a shipment of rifles before steaming off to surprise the Yankee prison camp at Point Lookout, Maryland. A contingent of marines was aboard the CSS *Tallahassee,* which Wood captained, to overpower the guards and organize the prisoners.[71] A cavalry troop was already under way with orders to conduct a simultaneous attack on the enclosure.[72] To their disappointment, Davis telegraphed on July 10 that the enemy had learned of the expedition's objective. Indeed, the *New York Herald* reported that most of the prisoners had already been transferred out of reach of the operatives. Once again denied an opportunity to prove his mettle, Lee headed back to Virginia.[73]

Lee returned to find Petersburg under siege by Federal forces. Richmond and the Confederate hierarchy were threatened as well, and, throughout the fall, Lee's command was repeatedly called out in response to alarms of Yankees advancing on the capital. Lt. Gen. Richard S. Ewell, now in charge of the city's defenses, proposed utilizing the locals as a garrison unit to occupy the inner defensive line. Gen. R. E. Lee also recommended that these fortifications be manned. As military demands on civilian workers increased, however, pressure intensified within the government to utilize other troops for protection. Col. Josiah Gorgas, chief of the ordnance department, complained that ammunition could not be manufactured for heavy guns and mortars as long as workmen from the Richmond arsenal were kept under arms.[74]

Custis Lee faced another problem that added to Gorgas's woes. When sent to the field, mechanics, ironworkers, and other skilled laborers regularly deserted. Lee reported losing two or three men every night. When posted on the perimeter of the defense, the part-time soldiers ran across to the enemy. A later analysis concluded that as many as four hundred men defected or were absent for other causes. One brigade member described them as "foreigners & Yanks—mechanics who have hitherto been exempt. They should be withdrawn as they are useful to us as citizens."[75] "The men who desert are for the most part from that class which has no interest in our cause," Lee observed. Despite his orders not to interact with enemy pickets, irreplaceable assets were lost to the Confederate war effort.[76]

The local brigade could only be called out by the president. Enjoying a warm rapport with Davis, Lee did not appear unduly hampered by the requirement. Secretary of War James A. Seddon, however, questioned the repeated demands on the reserves. He raised the matter with Ewell:

In compliance with your request, the President has ordered out the local troops, and they will march at once to the points commanded. He apprehends, however, you may not exactly appreciate the character of these troops, who are composed of workmen, employes, detailed men, and clerks of the various departments, and, as they cannot be called out without entailing most serious delays and confusion in all branches of the Government business, are not kept as a force disposable for ordinary service, but only for an emergency involving the safety and actual defense of the City.[77]

Receiving intensified complaints when the brigade was mustered in December, the secretary of war suggested that local troops be recalled from their positions and the line held by extending the soldiers on either side. "The public service suffers much from their absence," he reiterated. Facing Grant's increasing numbers, Gen. R. E. Lee replied that he did not know where to obtain troops to replace the reserves under Custis's command.[78]

The complainants included the army's adjutant general, Samuel Cooper, who certified that C. B. Tebbs, his chief clerk, was "an expert and indispensable." In approving his transfer back to an office job, Lee took the opportunity to highlight the problem it represented:

This case is very similar to a great many in this command; and as it has become so much reduced in officers and men and constantly much disorganized.

I can recommend that after this no more details be made from this command. The men cannot perform their duties in Richmond and in the trenches at the same time. If they are indispensably necessary in Richmond, it is for the War Department to determine whether they should go in. We have only about 1,000 men in the field out of 3,000 on our rolls; and setting aside the dissatisfaction which these large details occasion we cannot spare the men from our lines unless other troops are sent to take their place.[79]

The final straw was calling out the brigade on Christmas Eve. "Gen. Custis Lee has mortally offended the clerks by putting them in the trenches yesterday, and some of them may desert," complained one reservist.[80] From the commander's perspective, the slackers had already been leaving and, if the defenders were not mobilized, the capital itself might be lost.

The beleaguered commander tried to simplify his own situation by being relieved of the responsibilities of presidential aide, but he was refused. Instead, Custis Lee received official recognition as a general officer on February 3, 1865, when the Confederate Congress confirmed his appointment to the permanent rank of major general, effective the previous October. He was now given command of a division consisting of two brigades, plus the local defense troops.[81]

In his role as special adviser to Davis, Braxton Bragg had proposed Lee's promotion to general officer almost a year earlier and Cooper had dutifully concurred.[82] When the opportunity first arose, the aide was as reticent as he had been about the western Virginia command. The Richmond diarist, Mary Chesnut, recorded Custis's concern: "It would not do for me to take a general's commission now, over the heads of men who have been in active service from the beginning while I was doing office work."[83] By the winter of 1865, however, Lee must have gained confidence and felt that his leadership in defending the capital warranted the higher rank. Cynics, of course, viewed the appointment differently:

> He is a West Pointer. That will gain him every advantage with the powers that be. West-Point-on-the-brain is, and will continue to be, the disease of the day with those who have military rank to seek or confer . . . Custis Lee being, I say, a West Pointer is bound to jump up from his ornamental staff appointment. West Point will have as much to do with his advancement as with the fact that he is R. E. Lee's son. For a gentleman and a show-soldier, he does very well: for a red-tapist, he does well, too. Men like him, women are bound to admire. But, why he was so soon made a major-general in the army, neither the likings of men nor the admiration of women could ever satisfactorily explain. . . . In that rank, he accomplished as much as he had previously credited to him—nothing. Rumor had it—how impertinent Rumor always is—that "the power behind the throne" smiled on him as on few. I doubt if he smiled very complacently in turn. What could be more desirable in that way than the gallant-looking son of the soldier's idol—Lee?[84]

After three and a half years as a presidential aide, Lee finally had a chance to show his worth as a real soldier. The opportunity would be short-lived, however, for the end of the war was in sight. On New Year's Day, 1865, Lt. Gen. James Longstreet, the First Corps commander in charge of the line east of the capital, had cited Custis Lee's unit as a prime example of the need to strengthen the organization of Confederate forces before the Federal offensive expected in the spring. Of 2,849 troops assigned to his two regiments and four battalions on January 1, Lee reported only 650 present for duty. Any mobilization of local defense troops in the absence of an outright attack continued to generate criticism. Robert G. H. Kean, chief of the bureau of war, protested the use of these men without a pressing emergency and suggested that G. W. C. Lee shared this opinion: "Nearly all of these men, except the artisans, are weak, delicate, or old," Kean contended, and "the inconveniences, delays, and neglect of public business caused by the removal of the clerks . . . is well known."[85]

Nevertheless, Longstreet persisted, directing Lee and the other sector commanders to alert their pickets to report immediately any enemy movement. Lee was instructed to build bombproofs along his line and implant a strong abatis in front. Provision was also to be made for fireballs to light up the terrain in front of the Southern defenses during a night attack. Longstreet was not hesitant to express his displeasure when the work was not performed quickly enough to suit him. As winter drew to a close, the soldiers in gray observed telltale signs of a Yankee initiative. Federal cavalry pickets were replaced with infantry; white pickets were relieved early, and Negro vedettes doubled. For weeks before the actual offensive, hasty messages from nervous superiors warned of impending battle. On March 29, these reports were no longer rumors, as Union forces, numbering about 125,000, began moving forward.[86]

On the first day of April, when the Federals crumpled the Confederate right and almost encircled Petersburg, the embattled commanding general called for evacuation of the capital. About ten o'clock the following evening, Custis Lee received orders to abandon the entrenchments and join the main body of the army on its withdrawal to the southwest. Lee led his division across a pontoon bridge over the James toward Manchester. Richmond could be seen burning in the distance.[87] A subordinate recalled that the reservists "melted away as fast as they were formed, mainly under orders from the heads of departments who needed all their employes in the transportation and guarding of the archives, etc., but partly, no doubt, from desertions."[88] Men fell by the wayside on the strenuous trek, due to exhaustion and having nothing to eat.

At Amelia Court House, a naval battalion and contingent of heavy artillerists from the James River defenses joined Lee's division, along with another battalion of light artillery, minus their field pieces. One of the subordinate units was the Alexandria Artillery from Lee's hometown. Midday on April 6, a mounted attack up ahead caused the column to halt. Lee's troops deployed until the rear element caught up and then moved forward across Sayler's Creek and onto the rise beyond, where they rested. At this point, enemy cavalry crashed into the rear of Maj. Gen. Joseph Kershaw's division following behind Lee. The two commanders formed a line of battle, Lee on the left, Kershaw to his right, as Yankee infantry arrived on the field. Cannonading announced an attack.[89] The Southerners had no artillery to answer, as their guns were with the trains. Nevertheless, the Confederates were initially able to drive their assailants back across the stream. Kershaw's right was soon turned, however, enabling the Federals to surround their prey. Savage hand-to-hand combat erupted all along the line until officers on both sides restored discipline.[90]

The battle of Sayler's Creek was over. Ewell's entire force was captured, along with its commander, Lee, Kershaw, and at least four other general officers. Of the 6,000 soldiers who were present for duty out-side Richmond, according to Ewell, only 2,800 were taken prisoner. An estimated 3,000 men had deserted or fallen out on the retreat, and the remainder were killed or wounded.[91] In their reports of the encounter, Federal commanders at the regiment, division, and corps levels vied for the recognition of having captured the son of Robert E. Lee. Ewell's account of the engagement was more flattering to the former aide. He noted that "the discipline preserved in camp and on the march by General G. W. C. Lee, and the manner in which he handled his troops in action, fully justified the request I had made for his promotion."[92] Custis's cousin, Fitzhugh Lee, a major general commanding the remnant of the army's cavalry corps, summarized the outcome: "Though portions of this force, particularly the command of General G. W. C. Lee, fought with a gallantry never surpassed, their defeat and surrender were inevitable."[93]

Custis Lee's first battle was his last. The senior officers were taken initially to Grant's headquarters and then to Petersburg. En route, a Union general told Lee that his mother had perished in the Richmond fire. The concerned son telegraphed Grant and received a parole to investigate the situation. Arriving home, Custis was relieved to find his mother safe in the house on Franklin Street. He therefore reported to the Federal provost marshal's office to be taken back to his division, now incarcerated in Washington, D.C., only to find that Grant had instructed that the Confederate notable remain free on his own recognizance. Lee was ashamed of receiving special treatment because of his family's prominence and made sincere but unsuccessful efforts to convince the authorities to return him to his men. Unlike earlier situations when he received preferential care, in this instance Lee had taken the initial step by using his special status to contact the commanding general of the conquering army and ask for an exception to normal processing in order to pursue a personal matter. He had no one to blame but himself.[94]

As the country began to sort through the ruins of its manmade national disaster, Custis shared the fate of his family, among the most visible symbols of the Lost Cause. The Lees stayed together, first in Richmond and then, briefly, in a modest farmhouse placed at their disposal fifty-five miles northwest of the city. "I had an idea of going to Mexico," Custis wrote to a friend, "but could not bear the idea of leaving the Old State, and have determined to remain as long as I can."[95] Once again, duty and loyalty outweighed all other considerations. Shortly after Washington College called the senior General Lee to be its president, Custis was pleased to be offered an appointment as professor of civil and military engineering at the Virginia Military Institute, also located in the hamlet of Lexington.[96] Custis approached the new assignment with characteristic humility, asking for advice in teaching civil engineering, with which he had only a passing acquaintance, and offering to resign if a more competent person could be engaged.[97]

During the summer, Custis had fallen into the familiar role of informal aide to his father. Custis became a personal secretary, answering correspondence, and a gatekeeper, limiting the public's access. In this latter role, he served as intermediary with Maj. Gen. George G. Meade, who sought to schedule an audience with the former Confederate chieftain.[98] When the family relocated from Richmond to the country by packet boat, Custis dutifully rode ahead on Traveller to prepare the way.[99] After father and son assumed their new duties at Lexington in the fall, they used the two months before the rest of the clan arrived to renew their close bond. Not long after being pulled into the village's social circle, Custis's legendary shyness surfaced in his response to a young lady's entreaty to sit down: "I am a modest man, and for a modest man to have his hands and feet on his mind at the same time is too much; when I stand my feet are off my mind and I have only my hands to attend to."[100]

Despite his reserve, Custis was the perfect choice for his new post at the Virginia Military Institute. He had graduated first in his class at the country's premier engineering school and possessed extensive field experience as a military engineer. His eagerness for this opportunity was evident in volunteering to teach classes in chemistry, geometry, and calculus that were beyond his normal course load, and by his willingness to develop an applied science curriculum and undertake a topographical survey of the institute's grounds.[101] During his first term, Custis faced the challenges of few cadets, no textbooks, and little technical equipment. He slept in the old treasurer's office and took meals with his parents and sisters, at a time when his two brothers were rebuilding their lives on properties inherited from their grandfather. Custis's performance as a competent, dedicated academic, in addition to his distinguished bearing and dignity, soon generated offers from other institutions of higher learning, but he chose to remain nearby his family and honor his commitment to the military school.[102]

The ties between father and son, evident in that snowy walk three decades earlier, remained strong. Custis continued to be his father's helper and confidant. When the elder Lee contemplated writing his observations of the war, the younger Lee aided in research for the proposed manuscript. He applied his engineering talents to help design and supervise construction of a chapel at Washington College and a suitable home for its president.[103] When General Lee acceded to having a bust made, he proposed that Custis sit in his stead, since the two were said to resemble each other in appearance.[104] On more than one trip, Custis helped his father shepherd the ladies and their entourage to the baths at

White Sulphur Springs. Custis also accompanied the aging general to Richmond on several occasions, including the Jefferson Davis trial in 1867 at the Federal circuit court. One contemporary observer recorded the warmth clearly evident in the relationship of father and eldest son: "Once, I was at the Lee home on the General's birthday, and was sitting with him when his son, General Custis Lee . . . entered the room. Memory of that meeting can never be effaced, the stately yet gracious greeting of the son and father, the familiar and fond aspiration that he might 'enjoy many happy returns of the day' brought tears to my eyes and brings them still."[105]

There was one matter on which Custis did not defer to his father, however. General Lee tried to lead Southerners back into the Union by signing an oath of allegiance to the victorious government and applying for a pardon.[106] Custis chose not to do so, thereby spending the remainder of his life with the legal status of a disenfranchised, unrepentant rebel.

Robert E. Lee died on October 12, 1870. It required only two weeks for the trustees of what would soon become Washington and Lee University to select as his successor George Washington Custis Lee, age thirty-eight. The selectors were undeterred by the candidate's relative youth and inexperience as an administrator. The new president's name embodied the two illustrious personages invaluable to a campaign to rebuild the institution. The obedient son was once again cast in his father's mold. Custis's diffidence was well known to the board of trustees, so there was little concern that he would usurp its authority in managing the school. Instead, Custis was relegated to representational appearances, disciplining students, answering correspondence, and teaching, to the extent he chose to do so. At the same time, the university perpetuated its association with the Lee name considered so important to fundraising.

Custis's twenty-six-year tenure as president continued the lifelong pattern of duty at the expense of personal preference. He stoically accepted his role as keeper of the family flame, all the while uncomfortable with what he perceived as his own record of underachievement during the war. An example of his long-suffering obligation to the past was burying Traveller, wrapped in horse blankets, under a large tree on the campus, assisted by four small girls and three blacks.[107] Custis's enthusiasm soon waned with the pressures and frustrations of his job. His depression was heightened in the fall of 1873, when his mother and sister Agnes died at home within the space of three weeks. Overwhelmed by troubles and disappointments, Custis submitted his resignation, effective at the end of the 1874 term. Thus began a series of episodes spanning two decades, during which Custis repeatedly sought to withdraw and the board of trustees insisted he remain as president to ensure the university's continued viability. A heightened sense of obligation prevented Custis from carrying through on his intentions, resulting, instead, in sporadic unpaid leaves of absence. Custis eventually became resigned to his fate, conceding in 1887 that it seemed to be intended that he should end his days at Washington and Lee, and possibly it was just as well as he was "too good for nothing . . . to undertake anything else."[108] During this period there were accounts of Custis Lee having a drinking problem. These rumors may well have been no more than malicious gossip, as there seems to be no hard evidence to confirm them.[109]

Custis repeatedly demonstrated his personal commitment and generosity by contributing money to various school projects, including new heating and plumbing systems for the president's house. Meanwhile, as he confided to West Point classmates, his health continued to deteriorate, for he was beset by rheumatism with swollen ankles and feet and crippled hands.[110] He was finally permitted to retire in 1897. His continuing interest in the institution was manifest over the succeeding decade in his establishing a $6,000 scholarship fund, donating five hundred books to the library, and loaning (and eventually bequeathing) to the university the incomparable family portraits of Washington and Lafayette by Charles Wilson Peale.[111]

The ailing veteran of military, government, and academic wars retreated to Ravensworth, the family estate just west of Alexandria, occupied at that time by the heirs of his deceased brother. Joining Rooney's widow, son, and sister-in-law, Custis made this his home for the remaining sixteen years of his life. He applied his engineering skills to projects on the grounds while seeking to relegate representational responsibilities to his siblings. Despite his objections, Custis was considered the living symbol of Robert E. Lee and repeatedly involved in efforts to perpetuate his name and fame. Custis was drawn into arguments that periodically flared up concerning General Lee's views—for example, whether or not he had described U. S. Grant as the greatest military genius the world ever knew. As the eldest son, Custis oversaw the custody and preservation of the few wartime records and papers retained by the family. When queried, he patiently provided background on the life-size painting of the commanding general astride Traveller.[112] Custis also authorized a campaign to erect a monument to his mother in Alexandria.[113] The work was never completed.

In December 1911 Custis slipped on a staircase and fractured his hip, confining him to bed and a wheelchair for the remainder of his life. His sole surviving sister, Mary, was at his side when Custis passed away on February 18, 1913. The body was taken to Lexington to be placed in the family mausoleum at the university chapel. Characterizing Custis Lee as "a familiar figure in our streets" during his youth, Alexandria's R. E. Lee

Camp of Confederate Veterans asked to escort their townsman to his final resting place. They were refused, however, in deference to the deceased's request for no public display after his death. In recognition of more than three decades of contributions to the academic community in Lexington, the funeral cortege proceeded in measured pace past a formation of Virginia Military Institute cadets and through a throng of assembled Washington and Lee students to lay to rest the remains of a soldier whose conduct and values served as positive examples for all to emulate.[114]

In a eulogy delivered the following year, the president of the Virginia Historical Society made note of potential not fully realized as a result of responsibilities imposed by family and country. "In the contemplation of [Custis Lee's] career, one cannot, indeed, escape the constant suggestion of the touch of tragedy, despite the lofty reflection . . . that the path of duty, firmly trod, is ever the way to real glory."[115] Custis's life was, in many ways, a sad life. Once, when counseling a student after some prank, the sixty-year-old university president had offered no reproof but advised instead, "Son, have all the fun you can. I have never had any fun in my life."[116]

As the eldest child of Robert and Mary Lee, Custis was held to a higher standard than his siblings or most children.[117] He dutifully accepted the extraordinary responsibilities placed on his shoulders as a youth and tried, to the best of his ability, to satisfy his family's aspirations for him. Like the offspring of other famous parents, as an adult, Custis received special treatment because of his surname. At the same time, his opportunities were constrained by the stature of his revered father and a respectful, diplomatic demeanor cultivated as a way of coping with the extraordinary pressures weighing on Robert E. Lee's oldest son. Foremost among these expectations was a duty to serve others. Custis strove to live up to this standard at West Point, in the armies of the United States and Confederate States, and, finally, in academic positions at Lexington. The life of George Washington Custis Lee was aptly summed up by the obituary writer for the *Richmond Times Dispatch:* "He served the nation that was and the nation that is, faithful through all to his State. He did his duty simply and quietly wherever he found it."[118]

While the war raged, Custis Lee's estate sat stoically overlooking affairs in Washington. Under provisions of an 1862 act of Congress, the U.S. government sold Arlington to itself for $26,800 in January 1864. (The property was valued at $80,000 in the 1860 census.) Mrs. Lee had arranged for a cousin in Alexandria to pay the $92.07 owed in taxes, but the money was refused because it did not come directly from the owner of record. The government proceeded to use the grounds as a cemetery for Union war dead and a reservation for freed slaves. Custis and his mother decided to ask the Senate for restitution in 1872 but received, instead, a firestorm of indignation from the Northern press. After his mother's death, Custis tried again, first unsuccessfully with the Congress and then reluctantly in a suit filed in state court in Alexandria. A verdict was rendered in his favor and upheld in December 1882, after appeal to the U.S. Supreme Court. The following March, Congress appropriated $150,000 to purchase the property. Custis immediately accepted the offer. After back taxes and fees, he realized only $100,000. Upon paying his sisters the legacies specified in their grandfather's will, settling expenses to bring the suit, and losing a sum invested with unscrupulous brokers, Custis was left with almost none of his financial inheritance.[119] He had instead the weighty burden of being heir to an idol.

CHAPTER FIVE

GENERAL STAFF OFFICER
✳✳✳ GEORGE BRENT

GEORGE WILLIAM BRENT'S EXPERIENCES IN THE 1860s were archetypal of many Alexandrians. At the outset of the decade, Brent was highly respected, both for professional competence and political acumen. His was a voice of reason calling for support of the Democratic Party in the election of November 1860. Several months later, he represented his fellow citizens' pro-Union sentiments in the state's secessionist convention. When their views were overruled by a majority of Virginians, Brent put on a gray uniform and served the South through the entire conflict. Returning home at its conclusion, he endured the Reconstruction that alienated communities supporting the defeated rebel government, as well as Alexandria, which had been occupied by Union troops during the entire war.

Brent was born in Alexandria in August 1821, the eldest of six children of George and Elizabeth Parsons Brent. His father engaged in the city's commerce, making him prosperous enough to own a few slaves and send his namesake to study law at the University of Virginia. Upon graduation in 1842, Brent moved to Warrenton, where he practiced for the next ten years, with one brief interlude. It was in Warrenton that Brent met and married Lucy Goode, daughter of the physician who developed Hot Springs into a famous sanitarium, and began a family that would grow to seven before the next census. Brent's contacts within the Democratic Party won him a seat in the state senate in the 1852–53 session, representing Fauquier and Rappahannock Counties. During this same period, Brent also served on the board of visitors at the Virginia Military Institute in Lexington. In 1853, he returned to Alexandria and entered a law partnership.[1]

The nation's political passions peaked in the presidential election of November 1860. As an elector for Stephen A. Douglas of Illinois, Brent spoke at public gatherings that heightened fervor throughout Alexandria. At the largest crowd to gather at Liberty Hall on Cameron Street up until that time, the electors each spoke for an hour about their respective candidates. Brent expressed astonishment that after a successful seventy-one-year experience, dissolution of the national government should be contemplated if the wrong party prevailed. As election day drew near, the governor appointed Brent as one of three commissioners to oversee balloting within the city. He, in turn, selected four officials to supervise polling within the first ward.[2]

A majority of Alexandria's electorate cast votes for the Constitutional Union candidates, John Bell of Tennessee and Edward Everett of Massachusetts, helping to secure Virginia's support for this ticket in the electoral college. Brent's candidate garnered only 8 percent of the 1,732 votes across Alexandria County.

As states to the south withdrew from the Union, anxiety mounted among Virginians. Consequently, in mid-January 1861, the legislature called for a convention to consider the question of secession. Only three weeks were available for selecting delegates before the opening session on February 13. The choice narrowed to Brent, a unionist, and another attorney, David Funsten, who favored secession. As the date set for balloting drew near, campaigning to represent Alexandria intensified.

Brent's views on the emerging crisis had been set forth in December, when his letter advocating a state convention was published in the *Alexandria Gazette*. This statement made salient points that Brent would express repeatedly over the next several months. The writer traced the underlying problem to the ascendancy of a Northern party organized around sectional views hostile to the South's rights and institutions. Virginia was caught between "abolitionism" to the north and the threat of "secession and disunion" if siding with her sister states farther south. "I am not one of those that believe that either the honor or the interests of the South demand a *secession* of one or all of the Southern States from the Union. I do not, however, deny the right of a State to secede, 'in a case of a deliberate, palpable, and dangerous exercise of powers,'" he wrote. "But the right is one thing, the propriety of exercising it, is another," he continued. " I cannot see how *secession* is a remedy for any wrong suffered or evil threatened." Brent made his position perfectly clear. "My own view is that our remedy is in the Union. The Constitution is ours—the Union is ours. We have rights, cherished rights, guaranteed and protected by them. Under their operation, we have exhibited a degree of success which has astonished the world and excited its admiration. . . . The choice then simply is between a brave, manly and loyal defence of our rights under the Constitution and in the Union or a weak and timid desertion and abandonment of those rights by a withdrawal from it. . . . *Secession,* under any such circumstances, would in my humble judgment be *national suicide.*"[3]

A series of debates took place across the city between proponents of the two positions. A large audience gathered at Liberty Hall on January 22 to hear one of the city's wealthiest residents, William H. Fowle, speak in measured terms on behalf of remaining in the Union. The fiery state senator from Alexandria and Fairfax, Henry W. Thomas, presented the opposing argument. Funsten had built his case on congressional adoption of the compromise offered by Sen. John J. Crittenden of Kentucky to restore the Missouri Compromise, an argument that Fowle rejected. The following evening, another local lawyer, Charles E. Stuart, supported Funsten's position, while Fowle continued as the stand-in for Brent.

The contest reached a boiling point on January 28 before a boisterous, pro-Union crowd of workingmen and mechanics. This time, William Massey served as the stalking horse for Brent, restating his view that certain Southern statesmen were executing a preconceived plan "to precipitate the Cotton States into a revolution." To jeers from some onlookers, Massey asked whether the city's considerable foreign-born population was protected by the Stars and Stripes or by South Carolina's palmetto flag. When Funsten attempted to reply, his answer was drowned out by voices that turned to three cheers, first for Massey and then for Brent. The unionist candidate himself finally stepped forward and appealed to the crowd to listen to the resolutions proposed in favor of the Southern states, but with no success. The introduction of band music was equally ineffective in calming an uproar described by the city newspaper as a "scene, the like of which was never before witnessed in the good old town of Alexandria." Shouting, cheering, and hissing soon led to fighting, and a Washington reporter observed that "all hands pitched in promiscuously." Frustrated by the throng's refusal to listen to Funsten and the melee which ensued, Brent gave up and moved that the meeting adjourn.[4]

At a gathering the following evening, Brent presented his arguments in opposition to dissolution of the Union. "To a large, remarkably attentive, and appreciative audience," the *Alexandria Gazette* reported, he gave a "speech which proved conclusively and beyond the shadow of a reasonable doubt the utter folly of supposing for an instant that secession is the remedy for our present difficulties."[5] On the eve of the election, pro-Union demonstrators, accompanied by a band, paraded through the streets by torchlight, stopping first at Fowle's house for a greeting and then proceeding to their candidate's home at Prince and Pitt Streets. Brent appeared on his porch and modestly acknowledged the crowd's enthusiastic support.

Election day featured a few fights, as usual, and more music and pro-cessions after the polls closed. When the ballots were tallied, Funsten had garnered 438 votes, far less than Brent's 1,119, representing a whopping 72 percent of the total.[6] Alexandrians had shown, once again, that they were solidly in favor of preserving the Union.

At the state secessionist convention, Brent joined a distinguished body of delegates, including an ex-president (John Tyler) and a pair of former cabinet members, plus current and former state executives, legislators, and judges. Two future generals in gray were present: Eppa Hunton, who was in favor of secession, and Jubal Early, who was opposed to it. One observer remarked, "I have never seen a nobler looking set of men, in consultation or debate, taken all in all. They were as much superior to the Congress which sat at Montgomery as . . . the British House of Lords is to the House of Commons."[7]

At the outset, between 40 and 60 of the 152 delegates (depending upon the account) were viewed as immediate secessionists. The *Alexandria Gazette* estimated that another 60 representatives favored delaying a decision until a convention of border states could meet. This bloc included Brent. In between these two positions were the conditional unionists, who favored working within the old system until it became untenable. Brent and the other unionists endured intimidation and abuse from galleries packed with secessionists, attacks by pro-Southern newspapers in Richmond, and pressure from representatives of the pro-visional national government in Montgomery.[8]

The Alexandria delegate submitted a single proposal, which was referred to the Committee on Federal Resolutions. It made two impor-tant points: first, "that in times like these it becomes the duty of every patriot to rise above party or sectional considerations, to make an earnest effort to save the Union"; and, second, "the employment of the army and navy ... will inevitably plunge the country into civil war. . . . We, therefore, invoke the Federal Government, as well as the seceding States, to with-hold and stay the arm of military power, and on no pretext whatever to bring on the country the horrors of civil war."[9] Otherwise, with one exception, Brent supported those members with whom he agreed. Brent firmly declined to be nominated as one of three commissioners to go to Washington and inquire what policy the president intended to pursue regarding the seceding states. The Alexandrian did agree to serve on the Committee on Taxation, however, when appointed by the convention president, John Janney of Loudoun County, another unionist.

Brent's reasoning was evident on March 8, when his turn came to address the convention. He spoke for over an hour on the views and pur-poses of the seceding states and the course Virginia should pursue. Brent attributed the disruption in the cotton states more to a desire for free trade than to protection of the institution of slavery. He identified three reasons being advocated for Virginia to secede—the election of a Republican president, exclusion of Southern slaveholders from the territories, and the North's refusal to surrender fugitive slaves—and dismissed each in turn. Brent pointed out that slavery would not flourish where it was unprofitable and, relying upon peaceful repose, would wither and die after the war tocsin sounded. Interestingly, he observed that the seceded states "have established a Government with means and armies sufficient to maintain in independence not only against the Government of the United States, but against the world." The Alexandrian would soon be involved in a bloody test of that assertion.

In presenting his vision of Virginia's role in this crisis, Brent expressed the sentiments of many citizens of his hometown.[10]

> Virginia is called upon to rescue this Union from peril. It is her ancient privilege so to do. She rescued it when at its last gasp in the great political revolution of 1798; she saved it by her peaceful mediation in 1833, and she rescued it in the compromise measures of 1850. . . . The duty of Virginia is to act in the present emergency with decision. Let her speak out. Let her demand a settlement of the issues pending between the two sections of the country, now and forever. . . . Let her . . . call a conference of the border States. Let them determine upon such amendments to the Constitution as may be deemed necessary for the protection of the South.[11]

Brent concluded, "My lot is cast with that of Virginia; come weal, come woe." While his characterization of Virginia's role in earlier Federal crises was somewhat exaggerated, Brent was correct that Virginians had rejected the lure of extremism at other crucial points in the young nation's history. Embellishment may be excused in this case in light of Brent's fervor for remaining in the Union.

The convention remained in session through March, reaching no decision. On April 4, a resolution providing for secession failed by a vote of eighty-eight to forty-five, with Brent in the majority. The tide shifted from April 12 to April 15, however, as Fort Sumter was fired upon and captured and President Lincoln called for 75,000 state militiamen to put down the insurrection. The delegates retired into secret session on April 16, and the following day an ordinance of secession passed by a vote of eighty-eight to fifty-five. This time, Alexandria's representative was counted in the minority.

As soon as the convention concluded its business, Brent sought to join the state's defense forces. On May 2, the day after adjournment sine die, the governor commissioned Brent as a major in the volunteers and assigned him to Alexandria's militia battalion, which would soon be designated the Seventeenth Virginia Infantry. He served on the headquarters staff, earning recognition by both his brigade and regimental commanders for exemplary performance in the skirmish at Blackburn's Ford that preceded the battle at Bull Run.[12] Brig. Gen. James Longstreet, leading the brigade, made note of Brent recognizing the need for staff officers and offering assistance.[13] By fall, Brent had assumed the duties of regimental inspector and mustering officer.[14]

As a member of the Virginia convention, former state legislator, and prominent attorney, Brent was not a typical regimental staff officer. During the encampment at Centreville, he became known to the commanding general, P. G. T. Beauregard. Thus, when "the Napoleon in gray" was posted to the west, Brent's name was included on the list of officers requested for assignment to his staff. Beauregard explained, "Major Brent has shown capacity for the important duties of the place, and has had experience that would make him valuable to me."[15] On March 17, 1862, as the Seventeenth Virginia moved south in response to the Federals' redeployment to the Peninsula, Brent parted from his fellow Alexandrians. A comrade regretted losing his "social companionship [that] had quickened the dragging hours of many a dreary march."[16]

Brent reported for duty with the Army of the Mississippi (the designation of the principal Confederate fighting force across the Appalachians) in time to be on the battlefield at Shiloh. With several brief interludes, he would serve in the western theater for the remainder of the war. His initial assignment was acting inspector general for Beauregard. The position entailed enforcing circulars issued in Richmond, general orders published by the army's headquarters, and specific directives from the commanding general. These policies addressed a wide variety of subjects very familiar to modern-day soldiers—musters, medical policy, subsistence, equipage and ammunition, sentries, seizure and destruction of private property, even the format for an inspection report. In addition to these Confederate documents, Brent's papers at the end of the war included more than fifty instructions, circulars, and general orders issued by the Federal army, indicating his interest in how the opposition was handling the same matters.[17]

During the seven weeks that the Southern army garrisoned at Corinth, Mississippi, recovering from its ordeal at Shiloh, Brent conducted investigations typical of any inspector general. The matters addressed by Brent's reports represent a sampling of common problems confronting the Confederate army at this time. A week after the battle, Brent was examining and analyzing papers on the evacuation of New Madrid, Missouri, on the Mississippi River. He advised Beauregard that, in his estimation, the works could have held out longer, insufficient transportation was available, and disorder and confusion prevailed, resulting in the guns being lost. He further studied stragglers withdrawing from the battlefield at Shiloh. As an attorney, the inspector general must have taken special interest in the question of whether a military commission had acted properly in prescribing flogging as the punishment for a Mississippi volunteer. He concluded that corporal punishment was legal under the articles of war and the regulations of his War Department. Brent inquired into a citizen's complaint that Southern soldiers had pillaged his fodder and stolen from his shops, and he recommended greater accountability by officers for disorder within their commands. He also registered opposition to the arrest of citizens who refused to accept Confederate money as legal tender, while conceding their infidelity to the Southern cause. In addition to inspecting the condition of soldiers, horses, and arms, Brent ensured general orders were followed that required units to arm all of their men with weapons of the same caliber and description. As he learned about diverse martial matters, Brent transitioned from the intricacies of the practice of law to the precision of the profession of arms. Until comfortable with a new set of military standards, the former attorney carefully weighed matters using common law principles familiar to him.[18]

As the Confederate army prepared to withdraw from Corinth, Brent assumed a more important role in which, with few interruptions, he would make his most significant contributions to the Southern cause—that of chief of staff. During an illness that incapacitated the incumbent, Brig. Gen. Thomas Jordan, Brent was appointed on May 19, 1862, as acting chief of staff by Beauregard, now commanding the western department. The Creole characterized his selection as "intelligent, gallant, and meritorious" and asked Richmond to promote Brent to lieutenant colonel in the adjutant general's department.[19] When Beauregard left his post due to poor health and Gen. Braxton Bragg succeeded him, Brent was utilized as chief of staff for long periods between the designation of three West Point graduates to occupy the billet. Brent also served as chief of staff for Beauregard in his later assignments.

A chief of staff directs and coordinates the work of the headquarters while at the same time serving as adviser and confidant to the commander. Although he does not make policy, in the course of overseeing the execution of orders and directions by the commanding general, the chief of staff provides substantive guidance, not only to the staff but also to subordinate commanders, on the details of implementing the commander's decisions. Thus, the chief of staff is a principal assistant to the commander, although the extent of his influence depends upon the leadership style of the superior officer.[20]

As the army withdrew southward in late May and June, Brent's signature was seen on general orders and letters conveying the commander's instructions. By the end of June, however, Brent became dissatisfied with the War Department's processing of his promotion. Relieved from his posting in Mississippi, he reported to the adjutant and inspector general in Richmond, where he wrote an explanation of his concern over his key role as a principal staff officer for Beauregard and Bragg, but without permanent status or appropriate rank.[21]

Brent's complaint was effective, for by the end of July he was commissioned a lieutenant colonel. Returning to Mississippi, he was appointed judge advocate on a court of inquiry into the conduct of a general officer. Jordan was once again functioning as Bragg's chief of staff, and Brent was without a formal slot. He was therefore assigned first to the inspector general's office and then to the Department of East Tennessee as the Confederates prepared to invade Kentucky. Maj. Gen. Edmund Kirby Smith made note of Brent's performance on the field at Richmond, Kentucky, where Southern forces achieved a decisive victory on August 30.[22]

After the battle, Brent returned to Bragg's headquarters in Bluegrass Kentucky and was announced as acting chief of staff on October 2. Jordan's primary loyalties were to Beauregard, and he had obtained reassignment to South Carolina to become his patron's chief of staff. Brent once again replaced Jordan. Bragg obviously appreciated an individual of Brent's stature, who by now, in addition to serving as Jordan's stand-in during his illness, had experience in the inspector general, legal, and administrative dimensions of staff work. Five days after his appointment, Brent was issuing orders on Bragg's behalf to the army's two wing commanders, positioning them for the battle at Perryville.[23]

In mid-October, Bragg received two communiqués from the secretary of war informing him that the Congress had authorized appointment of additional general officers and that the president wanted a brigadier general to act as adjutant and inspector general of the western army.[24] Brent was assigned on paper as chief of orders for Department No. 2, the geographic command under Bragg's direction. After the Army of Tennessee was created in November, Brent became chief of the department of orders in the field, reporting to Bragg's new chief of staff, Brig. Gen. Johnson K. Duncan. When the incumbent died unexpectedly the following month, Brent resumed functioning as acting chief of staff. It was May 1863 before Bragg once again obtained the permanent services of a general officer. Until then, Brent continued to sign correspondence as "Chief of Staff and Assistant Adjutant-General."[25]

The adjutant is a perplexing staff officer to assess. Much of the writing that bears his signature reflects the views of others, most notably the commander. It is often difficult, therefore, to separate the individual and his personal feelings from the formal products of his military assignment. Occasionally, an official letter conveys the views of its signatory. Other insights are provided by personal correspondence, of course. In the case of George Brent, scholars are fortunate to also have access to his remarkable private journal.

Brent's most lasting contribution to the history of the war is his diary from October 1, 1862, to December 2, 1863.[26] His entries are those of an educated observer at a strategic vantage point on the staff of the general commanding the primary Southern military force west of the Appalachians. Throughout the period covered by the diary, the Alexandrian traveled with the commanding general and his personal staff and was naturally privy to information at their disposal and aware of their private interpretations of matters as they unfolded.

The thoughts expressed are sometimes reminiscent of dialogue at the convention in Richmond before the war, as Brent comments upon the overall war effort in addition to the daily demands and events swirling about him. Lacking formal military training, Brent initially analyzed the immediate military situation in light of what he had read of Napoleon and his wars. While understandably judicious in recording criticisms of his superior, Brent was not reluctant to set forth his assessment of other senior general officers.

At the outset of their relationship, Brent perceived the army's commander as being "very distrustful of my experience." Part of this tension was undoubtedly due to Bragg's nature, as he was considered difficult to please. Indeed, Brent confided to his journal, "He told me, that he was exacting 'but tried to be just.'"[27] With some justification, Bragg was leery of the primary loyalties of staff officers, like Brent, whom he had inherited from Beauregard.

The extant diary begins when the Army of the Mississippi occupied Kentucky and Bragg was in Lexington, poised to inaugurate a pro-Southern governor to solidify Confederate hold on the state. After the invaders were pushed out of the capital at Frankfort by a Federal advance, Brent observed, "The enemy front seems extended & dispersed, a good opportunity to strike a blow."[28] Brent made note of his superior's order to Maj. Gen. Leonidas Polk, commander of the army's Left Wing. He was to reinforce his counterpart commanding the Right Wing, Maj. Gen. William J. Hardee, by attacking the enemy at Perryville, routing him, and then proceeding to support Maj. Gen. Edmund Kirby Smith and the Army of Kentucky, under Union pressure at Versailles.[29] It was all said so easily, as though the adversary would pose no opposition to the plan's execution.

What Bragg's command encountered on the battlefield at Perryville was clearly the most sobering military encounter of their lives up until that point. Brent described it as "the most hotly contested battle I ever saw took place. Genls. Bragg & Hardee & all the regulars pronounced it the severest struggle ever witnessed. Gen. Hardee said to me, on the field, that it was 'Nip & Tuck' & he once thought 'Nip' had it. . . . I visited the battle field at night. It was a fearful scene."[30]

Brent's explanation for Bragg's withdrawal from the Bluegrass State offers a credible basis for historians' subsequent interpretations. The army in gray was outnumbered and far removed from its base of supply, while the Federals could draw men and subsistence from nearby cities and depots along the rivers to the north. Kentucky had not furnished the men expected when Bragg decided to occupy it. The enemy was threatening to cut off the invaders' escape route through Cumberland Gap. Finally, word was received that Confederate forces had been defeated by the Federals at Corinth, Mississippi, thereby exposing the breadbasket of middle Tennessee, vital to provisioning Southern forces.[31] Brent offered an interesting assessment of the Confederacy's unsuccessful foray: "Kentucky is Surrendered & will prove a heavy blow—but politically it will be one obstacle removed in the settlement of issues between North & South."[32]

While further news from southwest Tennessee "demonstrated the propriety & absolute necessity of our retreat" to Brent, others throughout the South were less impressed by Bragg's strategic decisions and performance. It is noteworthy that, upon reaching safe haven in Knoxville, Brent simply entered the statement, "Gen. Bragg sent for to Richmond," when he was, in fact, being summoned to the political citadel to explain his actions to Davis and his detractors. Bragg returned in good spirits, according to the diarist, pleased that "his conduct in Kentucky had been approved by the President."[33] Neither commander or staff officer could be aware that this was just the first in a series of challenges to Bragg's authority over the next year that would prove debilitating to the western army's senior leadership.

Brent's maturing military acumen after a year in uniform is suggested by his recurring fears concerning the disposition of Southern forces. His apprehension was first expressed during the withdrawal from Kentucky, when he observed the long, heavy trains moving at an excruciatingly slow rate of speed.[34] Brent was baffled why the enemy did not strike a blow that, in his eyes, would be fatal.[35] Once the army arrived in middle Tennessee, Brent was worried again. "I do not feel quite at ease at the position of our troops," he wrote in November 1862. Two weeks later, he bemoaned, "If enemy were to press us vigorously, disaster would befall us," and, later, "Our line is not safe. The enemy might mass on either flank."[36] Whether these thoughts evolved from his own analysis of these situations or reflected concerns expressed by others at the army's headquarters is impossible to tell.

Like many of his contemporaries, careerists as well as citizen-soldiers, Brent looked to what were considered the classic military encounters in Europe for models of how to conduct a campaign. Consolidation of forces was one ironclad tenet, articulated, among other places, in the teachings of Henri Jomini and Count Carl von Clauswitz's nineteenth-century

George W. Brent in a Confederate officer's uniform. Valentine Richmond History Center.

primer, *On War*.[37] The importance of this rule of engagement may well have been imbedded in Brent's mind by Maj. Gen. William J. Hardee, the respected author of the U.S. Army's antebellum manual on tactics, when he wrote to Bragg on the eve of the clash at Perryville, "Do not scatter your forces. There is one rule in our profession which should never be forgotten; it is to throw the masses of your troops on the formation of the enemy."[38] Brent returned to this principle repeatedly in his journal, notably when he fretted about the bifurcated command structure west of the Appalachians in late 1862. "Unity of command will alone secure a triumph. How much Napoleon lost from divided command, & a want of concert amongst his Generals!"[39] Before the battle at Chickamauga, Brent worried, "We cannot hold Knoxville and this place [Chattanooga]"; afterwards, he fretted, "This distribution of forces seems hazardous."[40]

Brett's observations on tactics were not confined to troop placement. He was sensitive to the negative effect on morale caused by the commanding general's indecision on where to establish a defensive line when withdrawing from the encounter at Murfreesboro (known today as the Battle of Stones River). First, Bragg identified the Elk River as the rallying point. Then, he changed his mind to the Duck River, farther to the north and therefore closer to the enemy. Brent commented: "The policy of holding as much of Tennessee as we can, is good. It was unfortunate that on leaving Murfreesboro, the line of the Duck had not been determined on. The movement so far to the rear, has had a bad effect on the troops & the public mind."[41]

Nevertheless, Brent also appreciated the limitations of a static defense. When Bragg's army was centered at Tullahoma, the chief of staff disparaged a system of fortifications protecting the town to the north as "useless." He elaborated upon his conclusion by writing, "Field works, very light, have been thrown around Tullahoma. This place has no positive strategic value."[42] Perhaps he was merely repeating what he was told by Bragg. Later in the spring of 1863, Brent recorded, "The Engineers are busy in strengthening the field works around Tullahoma. Genl. Bragg has never shown much confidence in them, Murfreesboro for example."[43] It is also possible that Brent could have added this analysis to his diary after Federal forces simply bypassed Tullahoma on their way to Chattanooga in June.

Brent's comments on strategy transcended troop concentrations and field fortifications. In December 1862, shortly after hearing "news of a victory in Virginia [at Fredericksburg]," he reflected on its impact upon his own theater. "Now, that our victory in Virginia looms up in such splendor & proportions, I deem it more probable, that the Army of Potomac will go into winter quarters, & that the enemy will throw all his forces & energies in the South West. Mississippi & Middle Tennessee are now his legitimate field of operations."[44]

He was still mulling over this notion three months later.

> Tennessee occurs to me to be the true strategic centre of our military operations. On the Potomac & Mississippi we can not make any offensive movement. Here we can & with effect. Give the Army force enough & Rosecrans will be defenseless, Kentucky & Tennessee redeemed. And with

them a large accession of numerical strength, & immense resources for the Commissary & Qr. Masters Dept. Supply is now the pressing question of dread. The success of such a movement would relieve our armies on the Potomac & Mississippi. Force enough for defensive purposes might be kept at these points, but all over should be sent here at once.[45]

A final example of Brent's strategic awareness was provided in April 1863 when he expressed his appreciation for the essence of the inevitable Confederate defeat: "We can't afford to hazzard a battle unless a certain & decided victory is promised. A victory without results is to us defeat. The enemy can repair his losses of men. We can't lose them. They are our Jewels."[46]

Brent also understood the importance of good intelligence, or lack thereof.[47] One diary entry at Tullahoma in March 1863 lamented, "Telegraph from Dr. Shaw that the enemy was falling back!! [Maj. Gen. Joe] Wheeler telegraphs that he thought not!!! No certain intelligence yet received of the intentions & movements of the enemy."[48] When Bragg's army was stalled outside Chattanooga in late August, Brent again bemoaned the absence of reliable information. "Our Scouts bring in but little definite or reliable intelligence. Our Secret Service Corps gives us nothing tangible." And, the next day, "Nothing positive about the enemy is known." Later, "It seems truly wonderful that no reliable information can be had."[49] Historians writing about both sides' shortage of knowledge of the situation leading up to the clash at Chickamauga Creek generally begin with D. H. Hill's postwar assessment of the dearth of information available. The firsthand source, written at the time, is that of George Brent, who deserves greater credit.[50]

A notable sidelight to the record of events and strategic analysis at the army headquarters is Brent's account of a conversation over Easter dinner with Maj. Gen. John C. Breckinridge in 1863.

> Poetry, history, annecdote, war, & politics were the topics. Gen. Breckinridge alluded to his Presidential nomination. He did not wish it. He had instructed his friends accordingly. He was, with Senator Jeff Davis at the latter's house, when the announcement was made to him, of his nomination. He determined to decline it. Davis said he must not, & could not. Believing the defeat of the Democratic party inevitable if both he & Douglas should run, he sent a common friend to Douglas with a proposition that both should withdraw, or suggest some means by which the trouble could be healed. The proposition was not made by that friend, because he found Douglas & his friends in such a state of excitement & confident of success. Finding that his withdrawal would only increase the "fissure" already made, he reluctantly consented to remain a candidate.[51]

Among the most engaging aspects of Brent's journal are his personal feelings about the generals with whom he came into contact. When promotions were announced on December 14, 1862, his entries that day applauded the elevation of Patrick Cleburne to major general but despaired the same promotions of Lucius Polk, the bishop general's nephew; Edward C. Walthall, a wealthy cotton broker; Zachariah C. Deas of Alabama; and Kentuckian Roger W. Hanson. The arrival of Bragg's classmate Brig. Gen. William W. Mackall to occupy the position of chief of staff in April 1863 did not elicit resentment from Brent, who was once again being replaced by someone less knowledgeable of the command and staff. Brent simply described the addition as "a plain straight forward earnest officer."[52] When, at his own request, Mackall departed the following October, Brent added to his praise: "I part with him with great regret. An invaluable and faithful officer, a courteous soldier, an affable gentleman, and a true friend."[53] Mackall returned the compliment, later writing of Brent, "He was a most excellent & intelligent officer and we had served without anything unpleasant ever occurring."[54]

Brent's greatest accolades, however, were reserved for Nathan Bedford Forrest: "Forrest is the best of our Cavalry Commanders. He has been uniformly successful; kept his men in good order, & in an improving condition. He is brave & active, & a man of excellent judgment. Had he been educated & cultivated he would have made a higher reputation. He is honest zealous, & his heart is in the work in which he is engaged."[55]

The historical significance of Brent's diary is nowhere more evident than in his notations on the series of clashes between Bragg and his generals. During the invasion of Kentucky, continuing through the greatest victory of the Army of Tennessee at Chickamauga and, soon after, its most devastating defeat under Bragg at Missionary Ridge, the internecine warfare at the top of the command structure undermined the sacrifices of the officers and men in the ranks of the Confederacy's principal army in the West. Chroniclers of the Army of Tennessee and biographers of its generals have repeatedly turned to Brent's personal record to understand, from Bragg's perspective, what transpired and the reasoning behind it.

As criticism mounted of Bragg's failure to destroy Buell's army and his decisions to withdraw from the battlefield at Perryville and, soon thereafter, from Kentucky, the Southern commander looked to his subordinates to corroborate his actions or, if all else failed, to serve as scapegoats. The retreat from Murfreesboro after the engagement at Stones River added to the tension. In January 1863, Bragg asked his staff if he had lost the army's confidence and should resign. Not receiving the supportive response he anticipated, Bragg composed a similar query addressed to his corps and division commanders. Brent disliked the original draft and considered Bragg's revision to be scarcely better. "The letter, however, was still broad, & tended to open up controversy, which ought to be avoided," Brent confided to his diary.[56] While he disagreed with Bragg's reaction to the criticism, Brent saw the situation from his commander's point of view, and believed, "The administration at Richmond is answerable for many difficulties we labored under."[57] Later in the year, when Lieutenant General Longstreet's troops arrived from Virginia, Brent would write, "they come after the damage has been done, a lock and key on the stable after the horse has been stolen, such has been the action of Jeff Davis in the Western Campaign, always too late."[58]

As winter turned to spring, Brent's diary reflects Breckinridge demanding a court of inquiry into his alleged incompetence at Murfreesboro. A few weeks later, the commanding general reopened the dissension surrounding the leadership of Southern forces at Perryville by asking the generals whether they supported Polk in disregarding Bragg's order to attack at sunrise. Hardee, for one, refused to answer. The staff was further unsettled by the arrival of Gen. Joseph E. Johnston, who was expected to succeed Bragg as commander, although nothing concrete came of the visit.

In May 1863, at his own request, Brent was relieved from the position as the army's adjutant general due, in part, to his health. A week later, he was granted thirty days' leave of absence to visit his family in Richmond. The commanding general apparently believed the separation to be permanent, for his praise was uncharacteristic in describing Brent as one "who, by his intelligence, diligence, and urbanity, has won the confidence of his superiors and the respect of all." When his leave expired, Brent expressed a desire to continue in military service and was ordered to report back to Bragg, by this time at Chattanooga. The commanding general soon recommended him for promotion to colonel, which was approved on September 5, 1863.[59]

Matters deteriorated further after the bungled Chickamauga campaign that nonetheless resulted in a rare Confederate victory in the West. An obviously relieved Brent telegraphed from the battlefield, "The enemy are routed. I am safe."[60] In the wake of this triumph, Polk and Maj. Gen. Thomas C. Hindman were criticized for their reticence to attack at McLemore's Cove, despite specific orders to do so. When Bragg relieved them, Davis intervened on their behalf.[61] Bragg also replaced Forrest, who threatened to kill the commanding general. When Bragg asked Davis to remove Maj. Gen. Simon Bolivar Buckner and Brig. Gen. William Preston as well, there was little doubt in Brent's mind that "troubles are brewing in the command."[62]

As early as October 4, 1863, Brent knew of "an effort being made among the General Officers to have Genl. Bragg relieved of command. Genl. [D. H.] Hill is regarded as prominent in this movement. So also

Genl. Buckner."[63] Dissension at the top eroded discipline throughout the army, as Brent recognized when he recorded that Longstreet, deployed on Lookout Mountain, had not executed Bragg's order to dislodge the enemy that had crossed the Tennessee River. Two days later, Brent noted Bragg's telegram to Davis concerning Longstreet's disobedience and slowness in moving. During the same three-day period, Buckner filed with the War Department for a redress of grievances, and Bragg again asked the president to come to Tennessee and remove certain senior officers. Brent saw the situation more clearly than his commander: "Gen. Bragg will regret that he has not insisted on being relieved. It will not be in his power to suppress the jealousies & discontent which exist."[64]

Brent's prediction was accurate. First, Maj. Gen. B. Franklin Cheatham asked to be reassigned. As the month of November progressed, the journal records increases in desertions, rations becoming scarce, and more complaints expressed. Brent had earlier observed, "Hungry bellies are opposed to patriotism."[65] Once a superb organizer and provider, Bragg had become, instead, a harsh disciplinarian. "Gen. [Gideon] Pillow telegraphs asking for authority to offer an amnesty to deserters in Tennessee. Gen. Bragg instructed me [the chief of staff] to reply 'the only promise he could give deserters was to shoot them if caught.' Before it was sent it was modified, that no conditions could be promised."[66] By month's end, Cleburne and Hindman were transferred by the War Department. Bragg asked to be relieved from command, and, to his dismay, the request was granted. On December 2, the beleaguered commanding general publicly announced his departure and left the headquarters that night.

As the army's second-ranking officer, Lieutenant General Hardee assumed command. Brent continued to soldier on, functioning as both assistant adjutant general and de facto chief of staff. There is no indication he knew that Hardee turned down the offer to be appointed permanent commander of the Army of Tennessee. The acting commander was more than a caretaker, however, and made a concerted effort to restore the army's discipline and morale. More drills and parades, greater leniency on furloughs, and reorganization of the artillery were three of the corrective actions Hardee took.[67] Brent contributed his legal perspective by circulating general orders deploring leniency in addressing offenses, directing the prompt trial of cases and execution of sentences, and instructing inspectors general to oversee the carrying out of judgments. "Inadequate punishments for such offenses are neither just nor humane," he declared.[68] Brent was satisfied with the results of Hardee's policies, reporting, "The effective strength of the Army is now equal to what it was on the 25th of Nov. [the date of the demoralizing defeat on Missionary Ridge] The health of the men is good, and a fine spirit prevails."[69]

While Hardee received his full support, Brent's higher loyalty remained with Bragg. He stayed in touch with the unassigned general, recovering his health at Warm Springs, Georgia. The adjutant assembled copies of the departed commander's official records and correspondence for him, as requested. More significantly, Brent shared with Bragg his thoughts on the commander who succeeded him, soothing the general's ego in the process.

> Your absence is I think beginning to be seriously felt, & a most marked change is seen in the condition of things. Gen. Hardee is unquestionably a good soldier, but lacks that reach & expansiveness of thought & determination of purpose so necessary to constitute a general. He is easily impressed by those who surround him, & hence there is frequently uncertainty & indecision. I do not think I shall be able to remain with him, & as soon as it shall be determined by the powers at Richmond that he will be placed in command *en permanence* I shall ask to be relieved.[70]

Brent did not have long to wait, but the decision was not what he expected. Gen. Joseph E. Johnston took the reins on December 27, generating new concern. The incoming commander was accompanied by his own retinue and, although there were no immediate signs of staff changes, Brent confided to Bragg that if Col. Benjamin S. Ewell, Johnston's assistant adjutant general, remained, "I do not see how both of us can stay."[71] Nevertheless, Brent remained at his post with the Army of Tennessee for two more months before rejoining Bragg.

In early 1864, Davis summoned Bragg to Richmond and appointed him military adviser to the president, charged with "the conduct of military operations in the Armies of the Confederacy." The day after assignment orders were published on February 24, Bragg asked to have Brent report to him for duty as assistant adjutant general. Within a week, he was relieved from duty in Georgia and on his way to the capital.

As inspector general for Bragg, Brent's first task was to report on hospital care provided for the sick and wounded prisoners of war in Richmond's military prisons. Coauthored by a military surgeon, Brent's report contained sharp criticism. The wards held more than twice their capacity, in some cases with two patients in a single bunk. The mortality rate escalated every month and, at 200 per 1,000, was ten times worse than the comparable ratio for Confederate soldiers in Southern hospitals. Insufficiency of medicines and flour was cited as contributing to the deplorable situation.[72]

The Alexandrian's major undertaking for Bragg began on April 5, when he was sent back to the army in the West on an inspection tour of Polk's Department of Alabama, Mississippi, and East Louisiana.[73] Brent was one in a series of officers dispatched by the War Department in an attempt to coax the western army to take the offensive. The emissary's first stop was his former headquarters in Dalton, Georgia, where he observed "no indication of an advance on the part of Gen. Johnston." The army was "stuck on the defensive." Yet Brent assessed the soldiers as being in good spirits and eager for a fight. He concluded his communiqué to Bragg by assuring him that he possessed "the confidence & affection of the Army of Tennessee," thereby assuaging the general's bruised ego.[74]

The tour of inspection next went into Alabama and Mississippi as Brent turned his attention to the infrastructure providing logistics and troops to the Confederate war effort. He found excessive numbers of officers assigned to the quartermaster department, safe billets behind the lines. Regulations were ignored by civilians acting in official capacities without commissions, and quartermasters and commissaries frequently serving without being bonded. At Columbus, Brent discovered mismanagement on such a scale that the inventory of hides in that city could, in his estimation, supply the entire army with shoes. Corn was also in abundance, along with adequate transportation to move it to the army. The critical shortage was a lack of sacks.

For once, Polk was cast in a favorable light. Brent's dispatches reported that the commander had organized provost marshals to arrest absentees and deserters and break up bands of marauders and robbers preying upon the countryside. The bishop general obtained an agreement from the governor of Mississippi to muster two battalions of state troops into Confederate service. Polk was also working to rebuild the railroads that crisscrossed the state.[75]

Brent's most extensive report concerned the new cavalry command of Major General Forrest. It was addressed to Gen. Samuel Cooper, the army's adjutant and inspector general. While the irascible cavalier was a favorite of Brent's and gave the inspecting officer his full cooperation, the resulting report noted several abuses of power, including enrolling deserters from the infantry into the cavalry, impressing horses into service, and taking liberties with the authority to organize units. A few weeks before Brent's visit, Forrest's troopers had captured Fort Pillow, Tennessee, killing a large number of black soldiers in the process. Aware of the controversy already brewing over whether the Negroes had actually been massacred, Brent advised the cavalry leader to obtain a report from his aide-de-camp and dispatch a jurist to collect statements from Federal officers involved in the engagement while the details were still fresh in their minds.[76]

At the same time Brent was on tour, General Beauregard, newly designated the departmental commander for North Carolina and southern

Virginia, was asking for the Alexandrian to be assigned as his chief of staff. Returning to the capital in mid-June, Brent found Beauregard defending Richmond before a sizable force approaching from the south. Brent was not hesitant about returning to a field headquarters, especially one commanded by his champion. On July 15, the day Federals began attacking Petersburg, Brent asked to join Beauregard. Given the tactical exigencies, Bragg could hardly object, and orders were published two days later.[77]

When Brent arrived at Petersburg, Lee had just taken charge of the defenses there, and Beauregard was beginning the uncomfortable relationship of working for another four-star general. For the next three months, Brent functioned as the conduit for information flowing between Beauregard and his subordinate field commanders, even when the general left the immediate area to visit other parts of his department. Unbeknownst to the Confederates, a Federal signal station near the Richmond-Petersburg road was intercepting rebel signals directed to Brent.[78]

Beauregard escaped what he considered to be a demeaning command situation by being appointed commander of a new department for Georgia, Tennessee, Alabama, Mississippi, and East Louisiana, comprising Gen. John Bell Hood's army in the first two states and Lt. Gen. Richard Taylor's forces in the last three. The Creole's new area of responsibility was vast in size but without adequate military resources to defend it. General Orders No. 1 of the Headquarters, Division of the West, published October 17, designated Brent as the command's senior staff officer.[79]

Brent performed the duties of chief of staff, serving as the communications hub for Confederate forces in the west. Beauregard traveled around his area of responsibility, inspecting defenses in northeast Mississippi, conferring in Macon with Maj. Gen. Howell Cobb about the District of Georgia, and organizing defenses and planning the evacuation of Savannah and Charleston. Brent was left to mind the store at the division headquarters in Montgomery, passing information back and forth between subordinate commands, keeping his superior informed of both fact and rumor, relaying orders from the commanding general, and, when necessary, issuing directives on his own initiative. Taylor later recounted the chief of staff being present at a discussion with Beauregard concerning tactics to distract Maj. Gen. William T. Sherman. Brent "said all that was proper for a staff officer in favor of my views," Taylor recalled.[80] When a subordinate commander, such as Hood, refused to accept Brent's instructions as carrying the imprimatur of the commanding general, Beauregard was not adverse to following up with a written restatement directed to the recalcitrant.[81] Brent would often transmit information directly to Richmond, wisely sending copies to Beauregard and other interested commanders, as well. The cautious citizen-soldier had become a confident, trusted stand-in for an arrogant Southern legend.

Brent's communiqués addressed the full gamut of military matters— exercise of authority, command and control, courts-martial, assignment of units, conditions in hospitals, use of scouts, reaction to enemy threats, utilization of horses, provision of cattle, collection of rations, arms and ammunition, construction and placement of pontoons, repair of railroads, and even the question of whether the land or naval commander should control a torpedo boat on Mobile Bay. When confronted with the last issue, clearly outside his limited military experience, Brent asked Beauregard, "What must be done?"[82]

The frustration of trying to keep a widespread command functioning in the shadow of military defeat is well illustrated by one example. On December 18, Brent informed Beauregard of the desperate need for quartermaster funds, as, with the end of the Confederacy in sight, certificates of indebtedness were no longer being accepted by the local populace. The general forwarded the problem to the War Department, which, in turn, handed it to the quartermaster department. On January 7, the quartermaster general returned the correspondence, expressing his opinion that the army was not paralyzed for want of funds.[83] Bureaucratic nonresponsiveness could defeat the Confederate army faster than its enemy.

A chief of staff relies upon communication; when it failed, Brent was truly stymied. Telegraph was used to remain in contact with Beauregard and other headquarters whenever possible; otherwise, Brent depended upon couriers. On at least one occasion, Brent hand carried correspondence himself. Another time, he complained to Taylor that Beauregard had taken away all the staff, leaving no one to send on a mission. Could Taylor spare a staff officer, he inquired? Later, in desperation, Brent telegraphed a subordinate command asking for an inspector general to report to Montgomery.[84]

A noteworthy information failure concerned the fate of Hood's army when it invaded Tennessee. Hood's final situation report of 1864 was received by Brent on December 12; the last communiqué of any kind was dated December 15, the day of the Confederate army's decimation at Nashville. Nine days later, Brent began searching for information from subordinate commands. On Christmas Day, he telegraphed Beauregard a cryptic message from Lt. Gen. Stephen Dill Lee, one of Hood's corps commanders, asking for Beauregard's views on the recent events in Tennessee. Brent feared the worst but did not know what had happened. Neither did Cobb, who relayed the message, or Beauregard, who forwarded it on to Cooper. Richmond was also in the dark. In desperation, Brent wired his superior on December 27, "If you can be spared from your present duties, I think it important that you should come here as soon as practicable." It would be almost a week before Beauregard departed Charleston. While he waited, Brent tried to establish alternate lines of couriers to Hood and telegraphed inquiring of his plans. On New Year's Day, the chief of staff apprised Hood that Beauregard wanted a report of his operations since December 11. Two days later, Hood informed the secretary of war (with a copy to Beauregard) that "the army recrossed the Tennessee River without loss" since "the battle in front of Nashville" (in the message to Richmond) or "the battle of Franklin" (in Beauregard's version).[85]

Beauregard finally observed the condition of Hood's army at Tupelo in mid-January and accepted the defeated general's resignation. Taylor briefly replaced the Texan. As the month wound to a close, Beauregard was summoned back to Georgia to help meet the threat posed by Sherman's army. Brent left departmental staff behind in Montgomery and transferred the division headquarters first to Macon and then to join Beauregard at Augusta.

While Brent was painfully aware of the dire situation, the command around him continued a routine familiar to soldiers in every war. The heads of subordinate commands repeatedly asked for news related to them. Headquarters in Richmond issued orders to apply all available resources to completion of the Georgia and West Point Rail Road. The local engineer responded by asking for the impressment of Negroes and acquisition of twenty-four four-mule teams and wagons.[86] The defenses at Montgomery required one hundred thousand blacks, according to another correspondent. Subordinate headquarters sent in regular summaries of troop strength. Lt. Col. Alfred Roman, Beauregard's close Louisiana friend, filed a routine inspection report on the clothing, shoes, arms, etc. in Lt. Gen. Stephen Dill Lee's Corps. Brent himself had made these same kinds of investigations not many months before. General Taylor asked that the practice of issuing furloughs be terminated to help reconstitute units. He inquired whether valuable machinery and stores should be moved eastward as protection from the Yankees moving into Mississippi and Alabama. A call was issued to governors for collection of individual arms scattered throughout the countryside. Brent's representative in Macon wrote, saying he felt a little foolish back there in the rear awaiting orders, although he added a postscript that he did not object to staying in Georgia, as, in his view, he could be more useful there than in the Carolinas.[87] It was almost business as usual, in the face of national collapse.

Sherman's army was moving out of Savannah and Hilton Head toward a destination unknown to the defenders. On February 2, Beauregard conferred on the military situation with Hardee, now the departmental commander for South Carolina, Georgia, and Florida. Also present were D. H. Hill, in charge of Augusta defenses, and Maj. Gen. Gustavus W. Smith, commanding Georgia militia. Brent transcribed Beauregard's notes into a report transmitted to the War Department. Its gloomy conclusion was that the Federals' strength and independence from a line of communication permitted them to march to Charleston, Columbia, or wherever they chose in South Carolina.[88]

Once again, Beauregard did not stay in one place for long. He took his field staff and shifted between Columbia and Charleston. The situation deteriorated for the army in gray, and communications between Beauregard and Brent became less reliable. By necessity, the chief of staff became more assertive, making decisions to command and control the unit remnants passing through Augusta and to implement the general's wishes, as expressed in his directives or as Brent perceived them to be. At times, he was forced to provide Beauregard with a situation report based almost entirely on his own assessment. Relations with other general officers sometimes proved tricky: Wheeler moved toward Columbia without authority, and Hill wanted to join Beauregard but remained in Augusta while Brent anxiously requested his superior's instructions.

On February 17, Hardee abandoned Charleston, and Beauregard withdrew from Columbia. The need to reposition troops in response to other contingencies forced Brent to remain at Augusta, although he yearned to rejoin Beauregard in Charlotte. Brent continued to push elements northward to reinforce the defenders. The interposition of Sherman's army between the rebel commanding general and his headquarters made contact by telegraph or railroad even more irregular. Brent began to communicate in cipher. On March 2, he received a directive, dated February 13, to relocate the headquarters staff to be with the commanding general. The following night, however, orders arrived for Maj. Gen. P. M. B. Young to organize the Augusta resistance and for the chief of staff to remain in place.[89] Two weeks later, with the situation deteriorating to crisis proportions, Brent finally left for North Carolina.

After pausing at Henderson, Brent was summoned to Raleigh. He arrived just in time to receive the news on April 10 that Lee had surrendered his army at Appomattox Court House. Brent forwarded the message to Johnston's headquarters at Smithfield. Beauregard boarded a train to meet with Davis and Johnston, leaving Brent behind to take charge. He was specifically tasked to care for the Creole's personal belongings (not an insignificant responsibility in view of the uncertainty that lay ahead), pack up the headquarters in three boxcars, and catch up with the commander. Mindful of the magnitude of the crisis, Brent telegraphed his counterpart on Johnston's staff, asking to be "advised, in cipher, of any movements, so that I may act promptly and intelligently."[90]

Brent and the headquarters were reunited with Beauregard at Greensboro. At first, business continued as usual, arguing with what remained of the War Department and managing a string of couriers. On April 16, on behalf of Johnston, Brent directed Hardee's decimated corps of the Army of Tennessee to halt in place and report its position. Brent was being told that commanding officers were reporting mass desertions, leaving barely sufficient troops to guard stores.[91] Ten days later, Johnston surrendered his command to Sherman. As a member of Beauregard's staff, Brent was paroled the same day.

Brent's war was over. Beauregard composed a farewell to his staff, expressing gratitude for their service over four years, as several officers had followed the general throughout the entire course of the conflict. No one merited this thanks more than Brent. "You have served me, personally, with unvarying zeal, and officially, with intelligence, and advantage to the public service. I go from among you with profound regret. My good wishes will ever attend you, and your future careers will always be of interest to me."[92]

Brent returned to his family and the practice of law in Alexandria. He was readily accepted back into the local bar, as evidenced by his appointment the following year as commissioner of the circuit court for Alexandria County to convey property sold at public auction.[93] He also settled into the city's political life, being elected a member of the Common Council from the first ward for the 1866–67 term. A year later, by order of Bvt. Maj. Gen. John Schofield, serving as secretary of war for President Andrew Johnson, former Confederate soldiers became ineligible to hold public office. Consequently, the Republicans installed their own city government.

The former colonel could not completely sever ties with his Confederate past. He was drawn into the postwar controversy over treatment of prisoners in the wake of the execution of Confederate Capt. Henry Wirz, commandant of the camp at Andersonville, Georgia. Brent responded to a request for documents by recalling that in January 1865, while at his headquarters in Montgomery, Alabama, he wrote to Brig. Gen. John Winder, at the behest of Beauregard, asking for thirty Federal prisoners to remove "*sub-terra* shells and torpedoes from the cuts in the West Point and Atlanta railroad." Winder replied that this use of captives would violate War Department orders and the laws of war. Brent closed his letter in 1868 with the observation that "the present heated and embittered condition of political affairs would result in no practical use [of the information provided], and might possibly create unnecessary prejudice against those now living and to Southern interests."[94]

By 1870, when the full rights of citizenship were restored in Alexandria, Brent was no longer in physical condition to withstand the rigors of

civic service. In April the legal counselor was seriously injured in a catas-
trophe at the Virginia state capitol. A crowd of onlookers pressed into
the chambers of the court of appeals to hear the opinion announced in
a mayoralty case. The gallery gave way and spectators dropped onto the
main floor, which was already overloaded and, in turn, collapsed into the
hall of the House of Delegates below. Brent was seated in front of the rail-
ing surrounding the judges' bench and, when he felt the floor buckle,
sprang forward and clutched the rail. He did not fall until a timber from
the ceiling struck him, breaking a leg and sending him seven feet below
into the legislative chamber. Upwards of fifty Virginians were killed
almost instantly and hundreds hurt. Brent's throat was severely cut, and
he suffered bruises and abrasions to his head and body. It was several
weeks before he was brought back to Alexandria, but he was said never to
have fully recovered.[95]

The weather was cold and disagreeable in Alexandria as 1872
approached. The night before New Year's Eve, Brent contracted pneumonia as a complication of typhoid fever. His condition deteriorated
rapidly. On January 2, at the age of fifty, he died. His hometown newspaper reported a gloom over the community at the sudden passing of
one "esteemed, honored, and respected for his genuine worth, acknowledged ability, and the many excellent qualities which made up the
man."[96] Members of the city bar met and composed resolutions expressing their sorrow. It is somewhat ironic that Judge John C. Underwood,
a radical Republican hated by ex-Confederates, presided over eulogies
delivered in Alexandria's U.S. District Court.[97] Yet his participation symbolized the bridge between extreme political positions spanned by
Brent's statesmanship. Among the prominent attorneys who spoke affec-
tionately about Brent was Charles E. Stuart, a former Confederate colonel
and one of Brent's adversaries in the debate over secession in January
1861. George William Brent was then laid to rest in the cemetery of his St.
Mary's parish church.

Brent is believed to have been a convert to Catholicism. His will stated,
"I die in the faith of the Holy Roman Catholic Church. My children
have been baptized in that faith. I desire to be buried in the Catholic
church yard." While Catholics were targets of bigotry in other parts of the
South, there was no such stigma in the more cosmopolitan Alexandria.
Catholics constituted a formidable minority of the populace and were
respected citizens. In the 1860 election, Brent had led the city's Douglas
Democrats; another Catholic, William F. Carne, organized the party's
rival Breckinridge faction. Before the conflict, Brent served on the building committee that enlarged St. Mary's sanctuary to hold eight hundred
worshipers.[98] His Roman Catholicism stood in marked contrast to the
Episcopalianism of the Lees, Cooper, Corse, and many other Virginia

generals, the Presbyterian Stonewall Jackson being a notable exception. Brent's church membership undoubtedly smoothed relations with the Irish companies in his initial military assignment with the Seventeenth Virginia. Indeed, Brent's religion may have been instrumental in forging the bond with his closest wartime mentor, General Beauregard.

Brent's initial role in the division of the states was that of a dedicated unionist who tried to find a way for the country to avoid the bloodletting that accompanied secession. Once his home state was committed to the Confederacy, Brent contributed his talents to the Southern cause. His development as a general staff officer was evident as the war progressed and he was placed in positions of increasing responsibility and independence. Brent's experience as an attorney, requiring him to maintain a rapport with clients, regardless of how difficult or unreasonable, and to win their confidence apparently served him well in relations with the irritable Braxton Bragg. Like many of his peers in uniform, however, Brent preferred to serve with the magnetic Beauregard. His success with both generals in multiple assignments, plus short stints with Hardee and Joseph E. Johnston, was undoubtedly due to a combination of innate intelligence and an orderly, logical approach to problem solving developed in the practice of law. Whether investigating and reporting on a vexing military problem or representing a demanding general in gray, Brent exhibited professionalism that distinguished him from staff officers of lesser ability and dedication. At the same time, the war provided Brent an opportunity to grow beyond the adjudication of private torts to participation in decisions and operations of senior headquarters engaged in a war for national survival.

Brent's transformation from unionist to secessionist was evidenced during the euphoria following Lee's victory at Fredericksburg. He exclaimed, "Abolition papers admit a terrific defeat in Va. Will not such reverses counsel the North how idle & foolish their effort to subdue us." A twenty-first-century commentator described the 1860s conflict as the country's second civil war, after the War of Independence. Like many of his fellow Alexandrians, Brent saw it differently. On the last day of 1862, he wrote, "Would it could be the last of the Revolution."[99]

CHAPTER SIX

POLITICIAN

✶✶✶DAVID FUNSTEN

THE SECESSIONIST CANDIDATE DEFEATED BY GEORGE BRENT in the 1861 canvass for delegates to the state convention was David Funsten. The adopted son of Alexandria may be viewed as a surrogate for secessionists throughout the South in proudly proclaiming and defending the new nation, before suffering the pains and anguish of its long, slow demise. By the time Funsten reached the apex of his political career, representing Alexandria in the Confederate Congress, natives of that city fully appreciated the grim sacrifices attendant to the glorious notion of Southern independence. The fact that they embraced Funsten after the wartime suffering was over and a painful reconstruction under way is testament to the quality of the man who tried to plunge the city directly into the crisis.

Funsten was born on October 14, 1819, at the historic village of White Post in Clarke County, Virginia, where Lord Fairfax erected a pillar to direct travelers to his nearby manor house. David was the ninth of ten children sired by Oliver Funsten, a prosperous Irish immigrant. The patriarch died when David was seven. Formal education was obviously important to his widowed mother, for she sent him away from rural Shenandoah, first to Benjamin Hallowell's acclaimed boarding school in Alexandria and then to an academy at Winchester. Apparently instruction outside the South was respected as well. David's brother, Oliver, two years his senior, went north to Jefferson Medical College in Philadelphia. The youngest son was sent to Princeton, entering as a junior in 1836. It would not be the last time that David took the path of his elder sibling. Completing the curriculum two years later, the graduate returned to his native county to study law and enter private practice.

David soon followed his brother's example once again. Oliver married Mary Catherine Meade of Benvenue, an estate at the western base of the Blue Ridge. In turn, David wed Mary Catherine's younger sister, Susan, five years his junior, at Christ Church in Millwood in November 1844. Campaigning as a Democrat that year, David was elected to represent Clarke and Warren Counties in the legislature in Richmond, where his older brother was already serving in the state senate. Oliver constructed a handsome brick residence he named "The Highlands," one mile west of White Post. The year following his marriage, David built "Erin," a white clapboard house with classic antebellum columns, flanking wings, a circular hall, and a spiral staircase, on property inherited from his mother four miles southwest of the hamlet.[1]

The pattern faded in 1852, when David moved his legal practice and growing family to Alexandria. It was not long, however, before he was once again involved in public affairs. In June 1856, Funsten was the principal speaker at the dedication of Ivy Hill Cemetery, which would eventually contain his remains and those of many of his comrades in the conflict to come. In September, Funsten addressed a meeting of the city's

David Funsten and Susan Everard Meade Funsten. From *The Ancestors and Descendants of Colonel David Funsten and His Wife Susan Everard Meade*, compiled by Howard S. F. Randolph (New York: Knickerbocker Press, 1926).

Democrats at the Lyceum, speaking for nearly two hours.[2] He was undoubtedly pleased when the party's candidate, James Buchanan, won the presidency in November.

In August 1858, Funsten set off in a different direction. He sailed to England from New York aboard the Cunard steamer *Persia,* the largest ship of its day. The vessel was almost four hundred feet from stem to stern, with two paddle wheels to augment its canvas. The voyager visited London, Paris, Brussels, and the Hague, along with other nearby cities. Regular letters to his wife and children served to memorialize the trip and to reinforce Funsten's strong affection for his family. He commented on cuisine, art, religion, landscape, and folkways. In light of the fate ahead for the wayfarer and his country, some of his observations are of particular interest. Funsten witnessed large standing armies in training at each stop. He noted that the victorious Emperor Napoleon I had removed art treasures from Holland to enrich his own country's collections. A British veteran of Waterloo guided the American tourist over that battlefield. Reflecting on Europe's wars, Funsten praised the Lord for religion that could overcome divisions among peoples to unite them as one. A few years later, that point of view was absent from his personal correspondence.[3]

In 1860, as rhetoric rose to new heights in an American political campaign, Funsten spearheaded the debate in Alexandria. He invited the distinguished U.S. senator from Mississippi, Jefferson Davis, to address his party's faithful in July but was refused. Returning from their state convention in Charlottesville, Democrats urged unification behind electors pledged to John C. Breckinridge. In an effort to solidify support, the Democratic Association of Alexandria was formed in August with Funsten as its president. It inaugurated a series of rallies with flags, bands, flowers, colored lights, and, of course, the inevitable speeches. At one such event in front of the city courthouse, Funsten outlined the difficulties facing the Democratic Party, most likely concerning the other wing that supported Stephen A. Douglas of Illinois. Yet a platform perceived as hostile to the republic was indigestible to most Alexandrians. The city newspaper acknowledged Funsten's good intentions but allowed that his "eloquence and ability we could have wished had been enlisted in a better cause."[4]

After defeat at the polls in November, Funsten and the Breckinridge faction were clearly identified in the public's mind as pro-secession. It was not surprising, therefore, that Funsten stood as a candidate to represent the city at the state secession convention and that the electorate rejected him in favor of the unionist George Brent. Funsten's loss hardly dampened his enthusiasm for the course he deemed right for Virginia. As the confrontation escalated with the firing on and surrender of Fort Sumter,

Funsten made a special effort to be in Richmond when the convention voted to secede on April 17, 1861.

The following day, Gov. John Letcher sent Funsten back to Alexandria to inform Col. Robert E. Lee of the convention's action and ask him to lead the state's defense forces. As a fellow Alexandrian, Funsten was a natural selection for this task. Furthermore, his wife was related to the colonel through both the Lee and Custis families. The emissary was delayed by transportation difficulties, however. Receiving no word from Funsten, the governor dispatched a second emissary, Judge John Robertson, to interview Lee and other Virginians in uniform. This messenger was also held up, and by the time he reached the port city, it was learned that Lee had already resigned his commission. A delegation, which may or may not have included Funsten, waited down the street while Lee attended Christ Church in Alexandria on April 21. Returning with Cassius Lee to his cousin's house at the intersection of North Washington and Oronoco Streets, the future Confederate immortal was informed of the governor's intention to offer him command of Virginia's militia. Colonel Lee left by train for Richmond the following day.[5]

While the country paused to ascertain whether a statewide referendum on May 23 would uphold the convention's action, rumors abounded of an imminent Federal invasion of Northern Virginia. The Funstens closed their house in Alexandria and prepared for the worst. Susan sought refuge for her eight children at the Meade family home in Clarke County occupied by her brother, William Fitzhugh "Buck" Meade.[6] She wrote to him, "There is no alternative we must leave here immediately, and Benvenue is the only place I can think of where I could go *without* an *invitation*. A dispatch has just been received from Richmond saying that Alexandria will probably be attacked on Monday . . . I leave my dear home with a sad, sad heart."[7]

As his family joined the growing exodus, Funsten headed back to Richmond to arrange for a supply of weapons to arm the new rifle company being formed in the port city.[8] He also sought a field appointment in the state defense force. His selection as captain to lead a new volunteer company being organized in Alexandria was apparently insufficient to satisfy Funsten's fervor to contribute to the Southern cause.[9] On May 12, he wrote to reassure his wife: "In your letters . . . you say these are *sad* times. Truly they are, but the future, I trust, has a brightness to reveal that will repay all our present troubles. I hope and believe, my Darling, that we will yet rejoice over our national & social & domestic conditions —that we will reassemble at our home, in prosperity & safety & happiness. . . . I never felt more clearly that I was in the line of duty."[10] In the euphoria before the shooting started, this brand of optimism was prevalent among ardent secessionists across the South.

Funsten soon accomplished his personal objective. Rushing back to Alexandria, he enrolled in the Eleventh Virginia Infantry, a component of the state militia's Sixth Battalion. The following day, May 17, Funsten was appointed a lieutenant colonel. A week later, as Federal soldiers occupied the port, pro-Southern troops marched out of town and boarded cars bound for Manassas Junction. Funsten eventually caught up with his men after being cut off while reconnoitering on horseback, but, to his regret, the trunk with his clothes and other personal belongings was lost en route.[11]

Funsten's regiment was formed of militia units organized in Lynchburg and the surrounding counties. One company consisted of the town's merchants, another mostly of farmers, and a third of faculty and students from the local college. Funsten may well have known the regimental commander before the war, as Col. Samuel Garland was an attorney who had campaigned for Breckinridge in 1860. Garland suffered two personal tragedies in the summer of 1861, when his wife and young son died back home in Lynchburg. As the second-ranking officer, Funsten was given a brief taste of command by Garland's absence to attend to family matters.[12]

The Eleventh Virginia was assigned to the Fourth Brigade, along with the First Regiment from Richmond and the Seventeenth Virginia from Alexandria. The men sent to Camp Pickens, northwest of Manassas, soon learned how to soldier—drilling, erecting tents, and conducting armed reconnaissance as far as the outskirts of Alexandria.

At the outset of July, Brig. Gen. James Longstreet, a veteran of the Mexican War, assumed command of the brigade. Longstreet was charged with defending Blackburn's Ford across Bull Run. On July 17 he deployed his troops on the creek's south bank, with the Seventeenth Infantry southwest of the crossing, the First Virginia to the east, and the Eleventh Regiment behind in reserve. The Federals opened fire the next day and attempted to cross the stream. When they failed, two companies from the Eleventh Virginia were ordered to join the counterattack. After the engagement subsided, Funsten's entire regiment was moved forward to relieve their battle-weary comrades on the front line of defense.

Three days later, when a major battle erupted on the plains of Manassas, the Eleventh Virginia was left out. Elements of the regiment crossed Bull Run to take positions as skirmishers but soon withdrew. The wary men of the Fourth Brigade heard firing throughout the day and cries of "Victory!" at sunset. They stormed across the stream once again in pursuit of Yankees and over the next two days, in a pouring rain, salvaged equipment abandoned by the enemy.[13]

After it was all over and he had time to write home, Funsten marveled, "It is really wonderful how much I have endured." He went on to describe the cannonading with grape and canister and closed with the optimism overflowing throughout the Southern camp in the aftermath of a perceived triumph. "We will doubtless advance in a week or ten days & I would not be greatly surprised if the enemy should retire without a fight . . . with the equipment added by the late battle we will overwhelm everything before us."[14]

In mid-August, Longstreet's troops redeployed to Fairfax Court House, where they settled into a familiar routine of drill, inspections, and picket duty. As officer of the day, Funsten reported venturing as far as Annandale, eight miles from Alexandria, before returning to camp without incident. Taking an advanced position a few days later, he enjoyed a view of the Federal capital across the Potomac.[15] One Sunday in late September, the kindly colonel entertained the son of a prominent Alexandrian at dinner, and the young enlistee, Randolph Fairfax, reported hearing that "he [Funsten] is very popular with his regt."[16] In the third week of October, the Eleventh Virginia returned to Centreville to prepare for winter.

As Christmas approached, the lieutenant colonel was quartered in a hut, nine feet square, over which a tent was stretched. A fireplace and chimney at one end provided warmth. Funsten fervently wanted to be with his wife and children for the holidays and, despite a rigid policy on granting leaves, applied for a thirty-day absence. The request passed through the regiment, brigade, and division commanders before being approved by Gen. P. G. T. Beauregard.[17] On December 20, Funsten left for Benvenue, and with him when he returned were his two eldest sons, David (known as "Daisy") and Robert. The boys were helping soldiers complete a roof for the hut when the structure collapsed for lack of nails, pinning Daisy between the upper logs and rafters. The youth became delirious that night and lost his power of speech. For three months, including his tenth birthday, the boy remained in camp, where he could receive good medical attention. Finally, in April, the army began heading south. Funsten reluctantly sent his comatose son through the enemy lines back to his wife. Daisy died at Benvenue on Easter Sunday. It was the middle of May before his father learned of the loss. "I have heard at last of that woeful event which will stand out as the most anguishing in all my past life—the death of my brave, manly, noble boy."[18]

The Confederate army was reacting to the shift of Federal forces to the Virginia peninsula. The Eleventh Virginia joined the column of marchers heading south along muddy roads, climbed on slow-moving railcars taking them to Richmond, and boarded ships to steam down the James River to Yorktown. During the redeployment, the Fourth Brigade acquired a new commander, Brig. Gen. Ambrose Powell Hill. At the end of April, the strength of the regiment was reported as 750 men, although only 55 percent were present for duty.

On May 3 Hill's brigade retreated from Yorktown through Williamsburg. Two days later, it turned around, marched back through the old colonial capital, and formed a line of battle to confront the advancing Yankees. This time, the Eleventh Infantry was on the front line at the extreme right. Hill led his troops forward into a copse of trees. In the confusion caused by the firing, brigade discipline dissolved into regimental tactics. Despite being wounded, Colonel Garland was seen ordering a charge with his arm in a sling. The delaying action seemed a success, although the following day, when Garland's command resumed the withdrawal toward Richmond, one-quarter of its men were counted as lost in the bloody encounter. In his report on the battle at Williamsburg, Hill characterized Funsten and the brigade's other field officers as "brave, active, and energetic in the discharge of their duties."[19]

Hill and Garland received promotions after the engagement, and Col. James Kemper of the Seventh Virginia ascended to the brigade command. Funsten succeeded Garland as regimental commander, although his formal designation as full colonel was not dated until May 23. The move westward halted just a few miles outside Richmond, close enough for soldiers native to the city to go home. It was at the capital that Funsten learned the sad news about Daisy.

As the month of May drew to a close, Confederate defenders became concerned about the Federal pincers closing upon them, one prong halted along the Chickahominy River and the other moving toward them from the north. The only logical response seemed to be confronting the enemy piecemeal. The Eleventh Regiment was part of the gray-clad force sent back down the Williamsburg road to attack Yankee troops isolated on the south side of the river.

The offensive developed slowly on May 31. Under a heavy rain in late afternoon, Kemper formed his units into a column, with the Eleventh Infantry at its head. Entering a Federal camp in a locale called Seven Pines, the brigade came under deadly fire from the surrounding woods. At the front of the advance, Funsten's regiment received the full force of an ambush. Confusion enveloped the Virginians, as the brigade's close formation made it difficult to return fire. Men rushed among the tents before finally obtaining cover in breastworks dug earlier by enemy troops. In the melee, the Eleventh Virginia suffered 30 killed and 115 wounded, including Colonel Funsten, who was shot in the foot.[20] Funsten did not realize it at the time, but his war as a combatant was over.

The wounded colonel was carried to a dry patch of ground alongside the roadway. A doctor cut his boot away and cleaned the wound. Funsten then joined several other casualties in an ambulance headed into Richmond. He would undoubtedly have preferred to recuperate with his family in Clarke County, but the regular appearance there of Yankee patrols made this impractical. Instead, he was sent to a plantation near Charlottesville known as Mirador, owned by his brother in-law.[21]

As summer turned to autumn without his wound healing completely, Funsten became disconsolate. He journeyed to Richmond in December to see if his name had been offered as a judge for a military court. Learning that nothing was being done on his behalf, Funsten was advised to apply himself for one of the appointments. His letter to Jefferson Davis expressed his hopes and frustrations.

> I beg leave to present an application for a Judgeship in one of the military courts authorized by a recent act of Congress. . . . At the battle of "Seven Pines" I was wounded by a Minnie ball passing through my foot. . . . More than six months having passed, however, without my being restored, & it appearing that my disability will be much longer protracted if, indeed, it shall not prove permanent, I have thought it proper to make this application. I have all along been embarrassed with the reflection that I am a standing obstacle in the way of the promotion of those meritorious officers below me . . . I have acted with the advice of friends, but have sought the influence of no one in support of this application. I will, however, respectfully refer to my friend P. V. Daniel, Esq, who will deliver this to you, to Hon. R. M. T. Hunter [past Confederate Secretary of State], Lt. Genl. Longstreet, Judges [John J.] Allen, [Richard C.L.] Moncure, [William] Daniel & [William J.] Robertson of the Ct. of Appls. of Va & J. R. Tucker, Esq. Atty Genl of Va. as gentlemen acquainted with whatever qualifications I may have for the position named.[22]

Indeed, Funsten's professional colleagues added letters of endorsement, praising the candidate's character and temperament, exceptional legal background, military service, sacrifice of wealth and family, and disability in the line of duty. A quartermaster sergeant who had served with Funsten in the Eleventh Virginia, Robert G. H. Kean was now chief of the bureau of war, and he lauded Funsten as "one of the earliest & most earnest & eloquent advocates of the secession of Virginia." Davis could not be influenced, however. He replied that all the appointments had been made and there were no vacancies. P. V. Daniel responded by identifying a specific opening being created in a military court through a personnel reassignment. But, alas, Funsten was held at bay.[23]

When nothing materialized on this front, Funsten redirected his energies to politics. Brig. Gen. William "Extra Billy" Smith, an antebellum governor of Virginia, had been serving in the army in Northern Virginia while at the same time representing his state's ninth district in the Confederate Congress. Smith resigned from public office in early 1863 when he realized he could not function as a legislator during the important military campaign ahead.[24] Although his foot would not permit him to campaign as a soldier, Funsten was not completely immobile, and he undertook a two-week exploratory tour of the Shenandoah Valley to ascertain his prospects as an office seeker. Buoyed by what he found and how well his foot felt, Funsten announced his candidacy for the seat being vacated.

In addition to Alexandria, the district encompassed Fairfax, Loudoun, Prince William, Fauquier, Rappahannock, Page, and Warren Counties. Much of this area was under Federal control, circumscribing polling on May 28.[25] Most of the votes, therefore, were cast by soldiers and refugees from Northern Virginia. With strong legal, political, and military credentials, Funsten was elected.

Before being admitted to the national legislature, however, Funsten took steps to protect his family from the growing Federal threat to Clarke County. As Lee's army drew the Yankees northward in the summer of 1863, Funsten returned to Benvenue and evacuated Susan and the children to Greenwood, near Mirador in Albemarle County. Food was plentiful and schooling available, but it was a simple existence, as Funsten related to his brother-in-law. Boys' trousers were fashioned out of tent canvas, and folks rode to church in a farm wagon, not a carriage. But the husband and father was no longer separated from his loved ones, and, during the next two years, two more babies were added to the burgeoning family.[26]

Funsten resigned his commission as colonel in the Confederate army in a letter dated August 1, 1863. He was sworn in to fill Smith's unexpired term in the fourth session of the First Congress on December 7, 1863. In many ways, the representative from Alexandria was typical of his new colleagues. Like the majority of members, Funsten was middle-aged, an attorney, a Breckinridge Democrat, and a secessionist. Some of his fellow legislators had attended college, and two-thirds sat in state legislatures before the war, as Funsten had. He was also different in several important respects. The median wealth of the membership was $47,335, whereas the 1860 census reported the value of Funsten's estate to be $6,400. The median number of slaves held by congressmen from the Upper South was twelve (far fewer than members from the cotton states), but Funsten reported only six chattel. Most significant to his performance as a solon, Funsten had actually served in the Confederate army, in contrast to most of the other politicians.[27]

As an unproven member joining the House of Representatives in the final weeks of the First Congress, Funsten received a perfunctory appointment to the printing committee. His background was well suited, however, for an additional assignment to the special committee inquiring into illegal arrests. When the Second Congress convened in May 1864, the Alexandrian received more prestigious seats on the standing committees on naval affairs and the flag and seal. In addition, he served on a special committee on illegal seizures and, in the closing months of the war, on the delegation concerned with exchange of prisoners.[28]

Funsten's own experience in uniform was an obvious influence on his legislative behavior. His most notable accomplishment during three sessions was sponsorship of legislation creating an invalid corps of disabled service members who would be available for assignment to other, less-strenuous duty. As units became decimated by casualties, he offered a resolution, which was approved, to inquire into the expediency of consolidating regiments and companies. He introduced a bill to organize a military court for armies in the field and a resolution, which was adopted, to instruct the Committee on Ways and Means to look into increasing the pay and rank of judge advocates in military courts. (Could Funsten have been preparing for his own return to military service?) He was also a proponent of increasing the pay of enlisted personnel. Funsten's novel idea of permitting officers to purchase a ration a day for each family member was soundly defeated in the First Congress, however. He believed that officers should be authorized to draw army rations and be allowed to buy clothing from the quartermaster, proposals that were also rejected. Funsten supported the formal organization of a general staff, despite the concern expressed during the legislative debate that it could become a collection of officers avoiding duty with line units. His interest in expanding opportunities in the logistics field is puzzling, as supply billets were notorious as safe assignments for gentlemen officers. Funsten voted to authorize the appointment of quartermaster and commissary officers with field grade ranks at the army, corps, and division levels. He also proposed increasing the pay of certain officers in the quartermaster office in Richmond.[29]

Funsten's legislative behavior frequently reflected the special interests of the counties he represented. Despite its support by the revered Gen. R. E. Lee, Funsten voted against a proposal to break up the partisan ranger corps, which would have destroyed Mosby's Rangers in the northern and western part of his district. Funsten also worked on behalf of a concept to mitigate the taxes of property owners whose holdings were damaged or destroyed by the enemy or who had been prevented from raising crops by the intrusions of war. Nor was Funsten reluctant to introduce personal relief bills. For example, he requested that the secretary of the Treasury afford special treatment to a widow and asked the Congress for payment to a constituent whose fuel and forage had been consumed by the Southern army. In one instance, the presiding officer appointed a special committee of five, including Funsten, to examine the merits of his case and determine an appropriate remedy. Despite his efforts, none of these personal relief initiatives was enacted into law.[30]

With the war winding to a close, the strongest determinant of a legislator's position on any issue was whether his district was occupied by Federal troops. This was true for Funsten from the outset of his service in the Congress, and, as months passed, more and more of his colleagues found themselves representing areas external to Confederate control. Their constituents were no longer susceptible to the sacrifices required by drastic measures under consideration in the Congress, so these members often became more extreme in their positions. Indeed, when dissatisfaction with Jefferson Davis mounted in some parts of the South, as an outgrowth of reversals on the battlefield, legislators from occupied districts provided the majorities needed for the president to maintain control of the Congress.[31]

The use of conscription was one of the best indices of a politician's support for the Confederate cause.[32] The challenge of refilling ranks thinned by adversity and the necessity arising from military clashes moving closer to the capital caused the last session of the Congress to consider seriously a measure unthinkable in earlier times—employing blacks as soldiers. Funsten supported the broadest possible conscription, so he exhibited no hesitation in voting for free Negroes and slaves to serve in uniform.[33]

While the racial dimension made this the most volatile issue, it was by no means the only conscription question faced by Funsten during his time in office. In his view, no one should be excused from military service unless absolutely necessary to produce subsistence for the army.[34] He voted against employing substitutes and agreed that no person eligible for military service in the field should be appointed to audit the claims of deceased soldiers. By late 1864, the Congress was willing to declare a citizen guilty of a misdemeanor for leaving the country to avoid military service, with Funsten included in the majority.[35]

Some of his legislative initiatives are, quite frankly, difficult to understand. For example, Funsten introduced a resolution in December 1864, which was passed, respecting the payment of real estate taxes on one side of the Mississippi River by citizens residing on the other side. He twice proposed measures to require all matters regarding negotiations for peace to be referred directly, without debate, to the Committee on Foreign Affairs. And, a week before the Congress adjourned forever, Funsten made a special point of adding assessors in the city of Petersburg to a bill providing a 50 percent pay raise for their counterparts in Richmond.[36]

One characteristic that was not a determining factor in voting patterns was a legislator's former party affiliation. By the time the war broke out, Democrats and Whigs in the South held basically similar views; what divided politicians below the Mason-Dixon line was their position on secession.[37] Consequently, there were no political parties in the Confederate

Congress. The absence of a loyal opposition denied the members an organized alternative to those policies of the executive branch that they opposed. This void was never more evident than on the question of suspending the right of habeas corpus.

President Lincoln had done it up North, but the idea was contrary to everything Southern idealists thought their new nation stood for. The government had experimented with martial law and habeas corpus suspension in 1862 and found them to be politically unpalatable. Yet habeas corpus was a major barrier to effective conscription, which became more urgent in the South as news from the battlefields grew more dire. The lame duck session of the First Congress finally responded to the request by President Davis for permission to suspend the writ by removing the legal impediment to raising manpower until July 31, 1864. Thus, the question was thrown into the lap of the new Congress when it convened on May 2. Funsten repeatedly supported the suspension in multiple ballots. Only after Davis characterized the measure as "not simply advisable and expedient, but almost indispensable to the successful conduct of the war," did the House act, with Funsten once again backing his president.[38] By then, it was mid-March 1865, and nothing could avert the pending disaster.

While he navigated political crosscurrents in the national legislature, Funsten also attended to constituent services within the executive branch. He naturally endorsed requests of citizens hailing from Alexandria but was mindful, as well, of the special interests of supplicants from other jurisdictions in the ninth district. Not surprisingly, soldiers whose problems resembled his own in the Eleventh Virginia received Funsten's wholehearted support. The inventory of special pleadings provides a human dimension to the bureaucratic machinations of the Confederate war effort, while, at the same time, revealing another side of Funsten's political persona.

The Stuart family of Alexandria was very familiar to Funsten. Charles E. Stuart, a lawyer, spoke in support of Funsten's position before the Breckinridge wing of the Democratic Party in the 1860 campaign. Before the war, a younger Stuart, Henry, had been an accountant in a large commercial house in the city. Funsten must have taken special pleasure, therefore, in presenting a petition in favor of a patent sought by Charles Stuart for a device to sight cannon that had been adopted by the ordnance department. The representative could also endorse with enthusiasm Henry's application for a commission as a captain in the quartermaster corps, especially in light of his unblemished service as a clerk in the quartermaster department. Neither request was granted, however.[39]

Funsten may well have known William H. Dulany, as well, as he was an attorney in northern Virginia in the 1850s. Representing Fairfax County at the state convention, he voted in opposition to secession, yet Funsten did not seem to hold this opinion against Dulany. As the first commander of Company D, Seventeenth Virginia, the Fairfax Riflemen, Dulany was seriously wounded at Blackburn's Ford. He was subsequently elected to the state senate to represent Alexandria and Fairfax. Dissatisfied at no longer having an active role in the war effort, in 1864 he sought a position as a claims agent for property impressed by the army. In his letter to the secretary of war endorsing the appointment, Funsten noted Dulany's inability to take the field again, analogous to his own disability. The assignment was soon made.[40]

Another case that Funsten could relate to and support was that of Pvt. E. W. Hamilton of Alexandria's Seventeenth Infantry. Three weeks after Hamilton enlisted, Funsten asked the secretary of war to detail him to care for three families—his own, one of his officer's, and a third clan—who were all living together under a single roof and were dependent upon Hamilton for protection and support. By month's end, the soldier was back home.[41]

Funsten succeeded, as well, in having an Alexandrian transferred to the city's regiment from a Missouri unit he had precipitously joined in the wave of patriotism at the outset of hostilities.[42] The legislator also obtained an extension to the furloughs of two Seventeenth Virginia soldiers recovering from the effects of illness and confinement in the Federal prison at Point Lookout, Maryland.[43] Funsten's political powers were not as persuasive when seeking authorization for a Brentsville taverner to raise a cavalry unit in Prince William County or acquiring an appointment for a constituent's son to serve as a cadet in a field unit until he attained the age and gained the experience to be commissioned an officer.[44]

One last case in early 1865 suggests that Funsten and Brent maintained contact with each other after they went their separate ways to serve the Confederacy. Captains Jerome B. Norvell and Chancellor A. Nelson were sworn into the Forty-ninth Virginia Infantry ("Extra Billy's" unit from the western portion of Funsten's district) in July 1861 by Maj. George Brent. Absent a regimental commander for a long period, Norvell nevertheless failed to obtain a promotion to field grade rank to lead the unit because of a technicality concerning his relative seniority compared with Nelson, who had been incarcerated since mid-1863 at Johnson's Island, Ohio. Reassigned to Richmond in the spring of 1864 to assist Gen. Braxton Bragg, Brent offered an affidavit to help resolve the question of command. Funsten relied heavily on this statement to substantiate Norvell's case and, in obtaining it, must have met with his old colleague from the small world of Northern Virginia law and politics. The former adversaries were unsuccessful, however, when they finally took the same side on an issue and tried to convince the War Department.[45]

These seven special interest cases all related to the war effort, which perhaps is not surprising in the closing months of the conflict. Funsten's willingness to become involved stemmed from a desire to help a deserving constituent or to correct an apparent injustice, requiring an exception to regulations or special sensitivity by government bureaucrats to remedy. A genuine concern for others was a hallmark of Funsten's personality and seemed to be appreciated by his contemporaries.

As the noose drew tighter around Richmond, on March 18, 1865, the Confederate Congress adjourned into history, sine die, and its members scattered. The denouement at Appomattox soon followed. Funsten initially retired to his family's wartime refuge at Greenwood. Unfortunately for his sagging spirits, Susan and the children returned to Benvenue, so he was alone once more. His failure to obtain a pardon from the government in Washington and the poor prospects of an early settlement of the matter added to his discouragement. Yet he was determined to go back to Alexandria and practice law again.[46]

When Funsten returned, what he found was not all bad. A considerable portion of the library and furniture were safe in his old law office in Washington, D.C., although virtually everything at his house in Virginia was gone. While staying with Rev. G. H. Norton, rector of St. Paul's Episcopal Church in Alexandria, the refugee was fortunate to find a comfortable five-room house at Howard, about a quarter mile from the seminary. He was pleased with its fertile garden encompassing several acres. Funsten also boasted that the elevation commanded an excellent view of Washington City, Alexandria, and miles of the Potomac River. The problem was furniture: there was very little, other than a bedstead, wardrobes, and some miscellaneous items. He soon heard where sundry pieces were available and took steps to acquire them.[47] Susan was unwell for a time, but she and the children eventually joined him in the fall. When she did arrive, Susan was pleased that her old acquaintances did not think she had changed in appearance, despite the four hard years behind her.[48]

The practice of law was even more uplifting. Opening his office at the beginning of September, prospects seemed bright, and Funsten began paying off some personal loans, as it was through the generosity of his friends that he was able to reestablish himself so quickly. It would be another month before he could send money to his children at Benvenue, but by 1866 it was possible to enroll the boys at nearby Episcopal High School.[49]

The problem that could not be solved was Funsten's health. A bout of illness prevented him from getting out of the house for a full week in October. By the end of the year, he was having so much trouble with one of his eyes that he returned to Mr. Norton's parsonage in town to avoid exposure to daylight during his commute. The patient was confined to a dark room for a time but eventually the suffering eased. His health continued to deteriorate, however. On the morning of April 6, 1866, David Funsten passed away at Howard. The popular explanation was that he died as a result of wounds suffered at Seven Pines, but a more analytical diagnosis attributed his death to typhoid pneumonia. His friend, Reverend Norton, performed the funeral service, after which a long cortege of mourners followed the popular Alexandrian's casket to Ivy Hill Cemetery for last rites.[50]

The *Alexandria Gazette* was unusually glowing in its praise of the city's fallen leader, citing "the traits of gentleness, truthfulness, honor, integrity, virtue, and true piety, [which] won for him the love and esteem of the whole community. . . . He was warm and decided in all his political opinions, and never hesitated to express them with freedom and independence. But he was at the same time so courteous and urbane, that no personal feeling of hostility was ever engendered in the breasts of those who were opposed to him. They respected him none the less for differing from them."[51]

It is possible that Funsten would have been proudest of the eloquence of his old political adversary, George Brent, who paid his respects to the deceased at a special meeting of the bench and bar of Alexandria. They were two of a kind, Funsten and Brent—lawyers, politicians, civic leaders —cut from the same mold but opposites in how they viewed the best interests of their city and state as the nation split in two and then went about the deadly business of deciding whether to reunite. Funsten was incorrect in assessing the situation and wrong in trying to lead Alexandria away from the Union. In an age of radical abolitionists and fire-eaters espousing Southern nationalism, Funsten exhibited the qualities of a statesman by the manner in which he expressed his views and conducted himself. Decency in politics was not an insignificant legacy to leave to a citizenry that did not always agree with him but never lost their respect for David Funsten.

CHAPTER SEVEN

NAVAL OFFICERS

⁕⁕⁕FRENCH AND DOUGLAS FORREST

IN 1861 A MAGNIFICENT MANSION KNOWN AS CLERMONT SAT astride a wooded ridge four miles west of Alexandria city. "It is a large, fine-looking wooden building," wrote one visitor, "stuccoed, with an ample porch leading into a spacious hall, standing on a gentle eminence in an inclosure of some ten acres, the grounds fringed with cedars and beautifully laid out in graveled drives and walks."[1] One-third of the estate's 300 acres was wooded, another 160 acres consisted of bottomland along Cameron Run, and the remainder was cultivated in corn, oats, and wheat. The large house encompassed eleven chambers on three floors, with two parlors, a large library and an office. The outbuildings included summer and winter kitchens, servants' quarters, a barn and blacksmith's shop, and assorted sheds for carriages and farming equipment, drying and storage, and animals.[2]

Sydney Smith Lee, the Confederate chieftain's brother, had lived at Clermont. It was the birthplace of his son, Fitzhugh, destined to become a Southern cavalry leader. At the outset of the Civil War, the property belonged to French Forrest, Lee's cohort in the U.S. Navy. Forrest was named for and descended from Daniel French, who owned the plantation before the War for Independence. The 1860 census valued the estate at $30,000, including nine slaves in the inventory.

Forrest bought Clermont at auction for $10,020 in May 1851. The new owner was a naval officer of considerable distinction. The third son of an army major, he was born on October 4, 1796, in St. Marys County in southern Maryland. Short of his fifteenth birthday, Forrest was appointed a midshipman in the navy. During the War of 1812, he served briefly aboard the frigate *Constitution,* until being assigned to the brig *Hornet,* on which he spent most of the conflict with England. In February

1813, Forrest was present for the capture of HMS *Peacock* off British Guiana, and he claimed to have also participated in the Battle of Lake Erie. His orders to report to the sloop *Argus,* under construction at the Washington Navy Yard, were revoked after the vessel burned, along with the capital, in August 1814. Before abandoning the city, however, the midshipman commanded a battery defending the White House. The young veteran was commissioned a lieutenant in March 1817.[3]

Over the next twenty-seven years, as he climbed the ladder to the rank of captain, Forrest served aboard a number of vessels, interspersed with recruiting duty in Washington, Baltimore, and Norfolk, most notably for the South Seas Exploring Expedition. He fought pirates in the West Indies, patrolled the Mediterranean, and in 1839 commanded the first U.S. warship to enter San Francisco Bay, where he earned the gratitude of the British and Americans under arrest by Spanish officials.[4] As a consequence of his many and varied experiences, by the outbreak of hostilities with Mexico in 1846 Forrest was one of the navy's leading ship captains.[5]

Some of his most dramatic experiences in over a half century in naval uniform occurred during the Mexican War. Forrest captained the *Cumberland,* flagship of Commodore David Conner's Home Squadron, as it established a blockade along Mexico's Gulf Coast. Forrest's participation began inauspiciously when his frigate ran aground while leaving its anchorage in late July 1846, interrupting Conner's attack on Alvarado. Recurring problems caused by shallow waters and sudden storms convinced the invaders to employ a ground expedition in conjunction with their naval assets. In October, Forrest led a landing force of 253 sailors and marines as part of a coordinated attack on the city of Tabasco.[6] He carefully positioned his men according to a preconceived plan, only to have the task force commander decide not to send the party beyond the cover of his squadron's guns. A subordinate at the time recalled Forrest as "a man who literally did not know the meaning of the word fear," so he must have been terribly disappointed by the reversal.[7]

Forrest's role the following March was far more successful. A recent arrival in the theater, Maj. Gen. Winfield Scott, commanding general of the entire U.S. Army, prepared to open a new offensive against Veracruz. Forrest was assigned responsibility for landing 8,600 men on Collado Beach, two and a half miles south of the city. At one critical juncture, Forrest used regimental colors and hawsers to organize landing craft that had been thrown into confusion by strong currents swirling off the beach. The captain accomplished the mission in less than five hours without a single loss of life, the first major amphibious operation conducted by the U.S. Navy and one that remains a model to this day.[8]

Forrest's other important antebellum assignment began in 1856, after serving for a year as commandant of the Washington Navy Yard. He was appointed commander in chief of U.S. naval forces along the coast of Brazil. As a captain commanding a naval squadron, Forrest was entitled to be addressed as "Commodore." During the first week of October, he hoisted his pennant on the USS *St. Lawrence*, a frigate being outfitted at Norfolk for her maiden voyage.[9] Forrest found the vessel unsatisfactory for the task ahead. As he explained to the Navy Department, his cabin was not furnished to properly represent the United States in foreign ports. His quarters failed to present a "respectable appearance" appropriate for entertaining foreign officers and dignitaries of high rank. Receiving little satisfaction, the flag officer set sail later that month, arriving at Rio de Janeiro in forty-seven days.[10]

The Brazil squadron was one of several naval forces deployed to protect American trading interests. Although it was one of the busiest in the navy, Forrest was disappointed by not being selected for the Mediterranean squadron. His new command consisted of only a flagship and sloop. The former alternated between Buenos Aires and Rio de Janeiro, the squadron's headquarters; the companion ship anchored mainly at Rio de la Plata because of continual unrest nearby. Forrest echoed the complaints of the squadrons' earlier commanders that additional hulls were needed to accomplish their mission, especially vessels with shallow drafts to navigate the silt-filled entrances to harbors. With just two ships, Forrest could not be expected, for example, to suppress slave trading by Americans violating U.S. law.[11]

Because the flagship spent a large portion of its time in port, many of Forrest's concerns related to personnel and administration. Epidemics of yellow fever were common, and he was especially worried that the disease would erupt aboard ship. Fortunately, hospitalization for sick and disabled seamen was available on shore. There were the usual problems with drunk and disorderly seamen, although Forrest also had to deal with local authorities regarding a sailor charged with murder in Uruguay.[12] As squadron commander, he supervised ordering food and naval stores from home, as well as purchasing items on station. Boring worms indigenous to the South Atlantic were a constant problem for the wooden vessels. In view of the region's harsh conditions and the monotony of the mission, Forrest urged Washington to assign a finer flagship (the *Minnesota*) to uplift the officers' spirits and a band to raise the crew's morale.

The high point of Forrest's three years on station occurred in late 1858, when President James Buchanan temporarily enlarged the Brazil squadron to fifteen ships and twenty-two hundred sailors and marines to respond to a challenge from Paraguay. Its dictator was notorious for confiscating property from successful foreign businessmen. Relations with the United States reached a boiling point when one of its ships was fired upon while charting the Parana River. The subsequent U.S.

naval demonstration, in which Forrest led one division, succeeded in forcing Asunción to sign new treaties guaranteeing commercial rights to Americans.[13]

Forrest returned home in May 1859, received three months' leave, and was then added to the growing number of senior naval officers from Virginia listed as "awaiting orders." The Navy Department may have already become concerned about its warships falling into the wrong hands if bellicose Southern states carried out their threat to withdraw from the Union. In the 1860 presidential election, however, Forrest's loyalist sentiments reflected those of his community. He recalled (referring to himself in the third person) that "he attended the polls, and took with him five freeholders & voted the Union ticket and did then & there openly declare before the assembled crowd his opposition to the Secession of the State of Virginia."[14]

The following spring, when the state convention in Richmond voted to secede, a stream of resignations flowed into the Navy Department. The correspondents included French Forrest, now among the senior 25 percent of the service's seventy-nine captains. He offered no reason, simply stating: "I have the honor to tender to you my resignation as a Captain in the Navy. I deeply regret the necessity of leaving a service which has ever been dear to me from associations which you can well understand and which severs me from many of my old companions in arms."[15] The letter originated from Richmond and was dated April 19, 1861. It was a daring decision that must have been difficult for the sixty-four-year-old veteran of fifty years in the U.S. Navy. Forrest later explained that after the ordinance of secession was passed, he had been invited to the state capital by the governor and offered a commission in the Virginia navy. He accepted "with the belief that he owed his first allegiance to the State, and this was the generally received opinion."[16]

In its last months in office, the Buchanan administration had graciously honored declarations of this kind. The inauguration of Abraham Lincoln, the arrival of Gideon Welles as secretary of the navy, and the firing on Fort Sumter now cast these actions in an entirely different light. Welles refused to accept Forrest's resignation and instead dismissed him from Federal service, a distinction of considerable importance at the time, akin to a dishonorable discharge.[17]

Forrest was one of 373 departures during 1861, representing almost one-quarter of the naval officer corps. The defectors anticipated receiving ranks equal to or higher than those held in the old navy. There were far more candidates available, however, than positions aboard the twelve small hulls that constituted the Southern sea service in March 1861. Even after individual states folded their provisional navies into the Confederate equivalent, requirements never equaled the number of officers on duty at any one time, peaking at 727 in April 1864.[18]

During the captain's tours of duty in the 1850s, his wife, the former Emily Douglas Simms, had remained at Clermont. The one exception occurred during his year at the Washington Navy Yard, when Emily moved into the commandant's quarters. Now, as Forrest joined his state's navy, rumors abounded of Federal troops about to invade Northern Virginia. Clermont was filled with objects of art and other memorabilia collected on innumerable visits to exotic ports of call. The Forrests' only daughter had died at Clermont in 1853, and her clothes remained undisturbed in one bedroom. A friend noted that although wagonloads of possessions were packed and sent away, when Yankee soldiers marched into Alexandria in late May 1861, Mrs. Forrest fled with only a few articles of apparel.[19]

French Forrest's contributions to the Southern navy were made in three billets: commandant of the Gosport shipyard, chief of the bureau of orders and detail, and commander of the James River Squadron. The assignments each lasted approximately one year but bore no similarity in duties and experiences.

Immediately upon commissioning him a captain in the navy of Virginia on April 19, Gov. John Letcher dispatched Forrest on an important mission.[20] The old warrior was sent to Norfolk, where the following night the Federals abandoned the dockyard at Gosport, just outside Portsmouth on the south branch of the Elizabeth River. Protected by a high brick wall, the Gosport Navy Yard was one of the finest shipyards on the continent, with property and inventory valued at $6.5 million. The departing Yankees hurriedly scuttled vessels, burned buildings, and made a half-hearted effort to destroy the yard's equipment and supplies. Forrest crossed the river in an open boat the following day, accompanied by a Yankee prisoner who begged him to turn back. "Do not enter that yard—it is mined," he pleaded. "My country calls and I will go at every hazard," Forrest was said to have replied, according to a nineteenth-century chronicle.[21] Displaying the fearlessness he had shown in Mexico, Forrest proceeded to seize the prize. On April 22, while Robert E. Lee was being confirmed by the Richmond convention as commander of Virginia military and naval forces, French Forrest took command at Gosport, organizing control of the waterways around Norfolk.

Within his first month as commandant of the shipyard, Forrest was confronted with myriad problems, which he efficiently addressed. He quickly guaranteed safe conduct to commercial vessels in the vicinity, furnishing tugs to assist them when required. He directed that funds held by the naval agent of the United States be seized for the state and then ensured passage for the custodian back to "the Northern Confederacy." He offered safe conduct, as well, for families wishing "to return to their Northern friends." An officer was sent down river to Hampton Roads to observe enemy ships, and a system of signals was established to

French Forrest in the naval uniform of a Confederate flag officer. Library of Congress.

exchange information and instructions. Obstructions were emplaced in channels to hinder navigation. Forrest also took charge of existing naval batteries, ordered construction of new defenses, and supplied them all with ordnance.[22]

The new occupants found a large, undamaged store of seasoned timber and planking for ships, along with a considerable stock of naval guns, carriages, and other ordnance.[23] Forrest set about restoring buildings, returning repair shops to working order, and developing a capability to make fuses for shells. The yard was soon manufacturing a variety of products, from steam engines to light boats, tents, barrels, and shot and shell. Forrest shipped cannon to defenses being erected in Virginia and across the Southeast. At the same time, the commandant began mandatory training for employees of the yard in manning its guns, thereby developing a capability that would later argue against surrendering the dockyard. He also supported the build-up of naval defenses along the North Carolina coastline, and, on one occasion, hospitably received the officers of a French man-of-war that ran aground on the beach below Hatteras.[24]

More important, workmen began raising and reclaiming vessels only partially destroyed by the Federals in their haste to leave Gosport. On May 30, Forrest transmitted to Lee what an enthusiastic historian has characterized as "one of the most significant messages to go over the wires during the war": "We have the Merrimack up and just pulling her in the dry dock."[25] Stephen R. Mallory, secretary of the Confederate States Navy, to whom Forrest reported after Governor Letcher transferred control of Virginia forces on June 8, subsequently approved the concept of reconfiguring the screw steamer for harbor defense by adding an iron shield and heavy guns to her salvaged hull. Mallory directed the shipyard's commander to "proceed with all practicable dispatch to make the changes in the form of the *Merrimac* [*sic*], and to build, equip and fit her in all respects according to the design and plans of the constructor and engineer, Messrs. [John L.] Porter and [William P.] Williamson. As time is of the first importance in the matter, you will see that the work progresses without delay in completion."[26]

Forrest's outstanding achievement as a Confederate naval officer took place over the following nine months. He effectively organized men and materials to construct a prototype ironclad ram. Appeals were made to send scrap iron to Tredegar Iron Works in Richmond, charged with manufacturing the warship's two-inch plating. As many as fifteen hundred workmen were employed around the clock to accelerate production. Work proceeded in the wake of a stream of communications from Mallory urging speed, promising financial support, and directing that every other project be delayed, if necessary, to finish the new combatant as soon as possible.

As the conversion drew to completion, Forrest became concerned with the public attention being focused on the *Merrimack*. The commandant's apprehension grew when an employee defected to the enemy, despite having taken the oath of allegiance to the Confederacy required of all workers in the dockyard. A pass system was instituted for visitors.[27] Furthermore, Forrest asked that contact under flag of truce with Fort Monroe be suspended until "the great experiment we have in contemplation has been submitted to the test."[28] He worried that Union sympathizers in Norfolk and Portsmouth would communicate the ironclad's departure to the enemy by means of rockets or lights. Therefore, he suggested to the army commander of the Department of Norfolk that signal officers be furnished similar devices to be used in confusing the Yankees. Forrest's fears were not unfounded, for Secretary Welles subsequently received a secondhand report from several French Zouaves who visited Gosport and related what they saw to a Federal naval officer in New York.[29]

While Forrest proved to be a capable manager of a vibrant shipyard, Mallory was not convinced of his aptitude to command what he termed "a novelty in naval construction." Consequently, the Confederate secretary turned to the chief of his department's Office of Orders and Detail, Capt. Franklin Buchanan. Only four years younger than Forrest and one of his friends from the old navy, the new commander was hardly representative of the service's new breed of ambitious, aggressive young officers. He benefited, however, from having the secretary's ear. Assisted by Lt. John Taylor Wood in identifying soldiers with experience as seamen or gunners, Buchanan went to considerable lengths to assign a first-rate crew to the ironclad before formally being given command. There is reason to believe that Forrest expected to become commander of the ironclad, and, if so, he was sorely disappointed.[30] Mallory sidestepped the delicate question of seniority by separating Buchanan from Forrest's chain of command and appointing him as flag officer in charge of naval approaches to the James River, a direct water route to the Southern capital.[31]

On February 17, 1862, the *Merrimack* was formally commissioned the CSS *Virginia* and received its complement of officers and men. It then waited to take on coal and powder before getting under way. Finally, on March 8, the ram moved slowly away from the dock. Forrest and his staff boarded the steam tug *Harmony* and joined a flotilla of small craft headed for the mouth of the Elizabeth River to witness the ironclad's combat with the Union squadron in Hampton Roads.[32]

On its second day at war, after an engagement with the ironclad USS *Monitor,* the *Virginia* returned to Gosport badly in need of repairs. Forrest transferred the officers and crew to a receiving ship and began work on the ram. At the same time, he was concerned with the Federal army's advance up the Peninsula and dispatched a ship-of-war on the James River to protect the Confederate right flank. Mallory soon grew impatient with what he regarded as Forrest's unresponsiveness. On March 20, the secretary exclaimed, "The work of getting the *Virginia* and the iron-plated gunboat in course of construction at Norfolk ready for sea at the earliest possible moment is the most important duty . . . and yet this Department is ignorant of what progress is being made upon either. I am not advised that a day's work has been done upon the *Virginia* since

she went into dock." Three days later, he telegraphed, "Report the condition of your vessel. Is she ready for service? If not, when will she be?"
Forrest reacted by tasking Porter to send the secretary a daily progress
report. Dissatisfied at not receiving an acceptable reply, Mallory ordered
Capt. Sydney Smith Lee to relieve Forrest, who was summoned to Richmond to occupy Buchanan's former billet.[33]

The Navy Department had not heard the last from Forrest on matters
at Norfolk. Shortly after arriving at his new post in the Office of Orders
and Detail, he was appointed president of a court of inquiry to look into
destruction of the *Virginia* by Southerners when the Federals arrived at
Norfolk en masse under Maj. Gen. George B. McClellan. The board concluded that the sacrifice was unnecessary, as the warship could have
escaped up the James River. Forrest assigned much of the blame to the
army's hasty evacuation of Norfolk.[34] The following winter, Forrest was
called to appear before the Confederate Congress investigating the loss
of the navy yard. His relationship with Mallory undoubtedly suffered
when Forrest testified that the shipyard could have been saved and that
he had asked to return to Gosport to defend it with the employees he had
trained and the considerable weaponry available. The secretary reportedly declined Forrest's offer, claiming it was "a military necessity" to destroy the facility and retreat.[35]

The Office of Orders and Detail was the most important of the four
bureaus comprising the Confederate Navy Department. Its primary
responsibility was the administration of paperwork related to five thousand officers and enlisted personnel. This encompassed the negative
tasks associated with deaths, discharges, desertions, and courts-martial,
along with a steady stream of assignments and transfers. Forrest issued
orders, exchanged correspondence with elected representatives, and
organized boards of inquiry. The most notable of these panels examined
the actions of Comdr. John K. Mitchell in trying to prevent the enemy
from ascending the Mississippi River to New Orleans. Mitchell's conduct
was upheld.[36]

For young naval officers, the most controversial issue on Forrest's
watch was the matter of promotions. In the spring of 1862, Congress
authorized a fixed number of officer billets to be filled "solely for gallant or meritorious conduct during the war."[37] Forrest had resented
Buchanan's selection to command the squadron at Norfolk, an assignment he felt entitled to based upon seniority. After all, only one Southern officer could boast of longer service in the old navy than Forrest.[38]
Lieutenant Wood, who would make his mark as a commando, applauded
the opportunities promised by the legislation but worried about the reaction of a group he characterized as "the old, infirm, drones, etc." "A party
consisting of Commodore Forrest, [Comdr. Arthur] Sinclair, [Flag Officer Ebenezer] Farrand, [Comdr. Robert B.] Pegram, and others are

endeavoring to have the law repealed and a stop put to further advancement except by the old system of stagnation [seniority]."[39] The statute was not overturned, although the following year Congress established a provisional navy, which was implemented in a way that resulted in little appreciable change in the officer corps or its morale.[40]

Forrest's service in the naval headquarters gave him visibility and, to some degree, notoriety. He was a prominent member of a generation that included Alexandrians Samuel Cooper and Smith Lee, who had exchanged a lifetime of service to the United States for the opportunity to defend Southern nationalism. To some, Commodore Forrest appeared a "fine, white-headed old blusterer, of the real old-tar school."[41] A Richmond newspaper painted a more sympathetic portrait: "In person he is the very type of the sailor, his expression is frank and pleasing, and the mingled firmness and amenity of his character renders him at once fitted for any circle, the deck and the drawing room, the council chamber and the theatre of combat." The reporter also admired "the polished urbanity of his manners and the charm of his varied expression."[42]

To some naval observers, such as Buchanan, Forrest's impact was far less positive, if not outright malicious. When the Confederate navy's official Register of Officers was issued on Forrest's watch, it listed Buchanan's name under three dotted lines in the section for "Admirals," implying that there would be flag officers appointed superior to him. Buchanan castigated Forrest for his pettiness, concluding, "You have never given any evidence, by applying for orders where there was a prospect of danger, that you wished to serve your country, or to display gallantry to secure *your* promotion" to admiral.[43] The old sea dog was not going to be drawn into a protracted quarrel with his mate of many years and dismissed the matter as a misunderstanding.[44]

As a senior officer with daily access to Mallory, Forrest surely had influence on naval matters transcending the narrow focus of his bureau. One way in which he and the others who held this office, to include Buchanan, utilized entree to the secretary was to secure an operational command for themselves, coveted as an alternative to a desk job in the bureaucracy. Forrest succeeded in being reassigned in March 1863. A contemporary observer noted, "Then there was old Forrest: he got an indoor berth and held his peace until he insisted on getting a squadron, and he got that of the James River, after much waiting."[45]

Perhaps not surprisingly, Buchanan saw it differently. He wrote to Forrest's successor, John K. Mitchell: "We have wanted for some time a man of method and system there; old Forrest with his selfishness would have ruined the Navy had he continued there much longer. He used to give some queer orders showing an utter ignorance of his duties."[46] Buchanan's biographer even suggests that the transfer to the James River emanated from his subject's gibes.[47]

Forrest assumed command of warships with the mission of protecting the capital from naval incursion. His new squadron consisted of eight hulls: the flagship, CSS *Richmond*, an ironclad sloop; four steam gunboats, each with only two guns; a steamer to lay torpedoes (or submarine mines); CSS *Patrick Henry*, a side-wheel former packet refitted with four guns and an iron shield; and a tender.[48] Two additional ironclads— *Fredericksburg* and *Virginia II*—were under construction but would not be fully outfitted for combat during Forrest's tenure.

Forrest divided his time between the flagship, Drewry's Bluff where part of the squadron was anchored, and the office of the Richmond station, which he also commanded. Although he did not appreciate it at the time, his stewardship took place during a quiet period well suited to prepare for a Federal offensive. The defenders may have derived a sense of security from obstructions placed to impede navigation on the James River. Two Federal forays up the waterway were attempted during Forrest's first months in command, neither posing a serious threat.[49]

In the summer of 1863, Forrest and his staff began periodic examinations of engines, machinery, and ordnance.[50] The squadron commander's time was also occupied by such diverse matters as inspections of Marine guards, the threat of ice to the river's pontoon bridge, army deserters on-board ship, distribution of prize money for capture of Federal gunboats, and the discipline of sailors on liberty in Richmond.[51] Forrest later reported that a French warship had been steered up the river by a pilot who had taken an oath of allegiance to the Yankee government. The concerned captain urged that, in the future, pilots be provided from Richmond to prevent the enemy from obtaining intelligence on river navigation.[52]

As autumn turned into winter, the squadron received two new missions. The *Patrick Henry* was converted into a school ship and began receiving the first of fifty midshipmen assigned to acquire the skills necessary to become commissioned officers. Second, in late January 1864, the Navy Department tasked Forrest to support now-Commander Wood with men, weapons, equipment, and clothing for an unspecified mission that later was learned to be a foray to Newbern, North Carolina. The raiders ultimately failed in their attack against the Federal flotilla on the Neuse River.

On May 5, 1864, the day on which the Battle of the Wilderness began, ten Federal gunboats accompanied fifty-nine transports up the James River. Maj. Gen. Benjamin Butler was moving against the Confederate capital as part of Lt. Gen. U. S. Grant's campaign to end the war in the East. The Richmond station would no longer be primarily concerned with shipbuilding; the James River Squadron could hide behind maritime obstructions no more. The Navy Department concluded once again that the aged commodore was the wrong man to direct combatants. Secretary

Mallory moved quickly to appoint Commander Mitchell, now chief of the Office of Orders and Detail, to take charge of the river's defenses.

The following day, Forrest received orders removing him from the naval force on the James River, as well as from the Richmond station. Being relieved by Mitchell certainly grated on Forrest, for his successor was of lesser rank, fifteen years his junior in age, and therefore less experienced in the old and new navies. Furthermore, Mitchell's reputation had been stained by his defeat outside New Orleans at the hands of Adm. David Farragut. Forrest pressed Mallory to ascertain his reasons for the decision, but the secretary declined to be candid. His reply lauded Forrest's zeal and patriotism before attributing the replacement to technicalities in the organization of the regular and provisional navies.[53]

Whatever contributions to the war effort Forrest may have made after that time are now shrouded in mystery. Later in May, he was reported among the pallbearers at funeral services in Richmond for Lt. Gen. J. E. B. Stuart. Unspecified claims filed by Forrest were considered by the Second Congress the following month, and, still later, his endorsement was cited to help legitimize the third national flag adopted by the Confederacy.[54] In the fall, his son noted that the commodore had been assigned to a billet once more and had moved out of the Spotswood Hotel, where the Forrests had lived in the capital, and into a residence with a garden. The following spring, the flag officer apparently joined the exodus of high-ranking officials out of Richmond, as he was included on the list of Confederate naval officers paroled at Greensboro, North Carolina, on April 28, 1865, in accordance with the military convention agreed to by Gen. Joseph E. Johnston and Maj. Gen. William T. Sherman.[55]

During the war years, Commodore Forrest had not been the only member of his family to wear the uniform of the Confederacy. His son, Douglas French Forrest, spent twenty-one months assigned to the would-be commerce raider *Rappahannock*. The military career of the younger Forrest began like many other Southerners in the euphoric spring of 1861, as he hastened to join the infantry regiment being formed in his hometown of Alexandria. Once he donned the gray, however, Douglas took a path through the conflict that diverged from most of his peers.

In his military pursuits, Douglas had the advantage of being the sole surviving child of French Forrest. He was born on August 17, 1837, in Baltimore, Maryland, where the elder Forrest was on recruiting duty. Douglas began formal schooling at the Abbotts' Georgetown Classical and Mathematical Academy during the period when his father served, first on the navy staff and then in the Mexican War. The academy's principal complimented the youngster for scholarship and "his bright, sunny temper, his fine social qualities, and striking purity of character," characteristics presaging his calling later in life.[56] When the family acquired

Clermont and moved to Northern Virginia, Douglas attended Benjamin Hallowell's school in Alexandria. Again, the headmaster praised the pupil's integrity, noting a positive influence on his peers. Young Forrest went on to receive private instruction from Dr. William Sparrow, a professor at the nearby Episcopal Theological Seminary, before matriculating to Yale College in 1854. Graduating after three years with both a B.A. and M.A., he next studied law at home and at the University of Virginia, 1859–60, where he was commended for academic excellence. His tutor in Charlottesville, Prof. John B. Minor, once more cited his student's integrity and conscientiousness. Forrest was a practicing attorney in Alexandria when war clouds began to gather in 1861.[57]

Maj. Montgomery Corse swore Forrest into one of the city's militia companies, the Old Dominion Rifles, on the same day the state's convention decided to leave the Union.[58] Forrest voted in favor of the ordinance of secession when the decision was placed before the Virginia electorate on May 23. Within a matter of days, another prominent Alexandrian, Maj. George Brent, mustered Forrest onto active duty as a second lieutenant in Company F, Seventeenth Virginia Infantry. He consequently led his men in the July engagements at Blackburn's Ford. Pvt. Edgar Warfield related that at the conclusion of the skirmish a bewildered man dressed in gray appeared on the bank opposite the unit. Forrest ordered the men to hold their fire while he ascertained the stranger's identity. "Who are you, where are you from?" Forrest inquired. "Union, Massachusetts, from Washington," came the reply. They were his last words as a volley of shots rang out.[59]

The green lieutenant had two narrow escapes three days later, when the Battle of First Manassas erupted. Ordered across Bull Run as scouts, Forrest's party narrowly missed being victims of a shell that exploded in front of them. Repositioned to observe the movement of enemy batteries, Forrest had succumbed to the peacefulness of his immediate surroundings when a comrade startled him from his reverie by shouting that Yankee skirmishers had approached thirty yards to his front. Once again, the novice avoided harm.[60]

In September, Forrest was ordered to serve as aide-de-camp to Brig. Gen. Isaac Trimble at Evansport, one of a series of fortifications constructed along the western shore of the Potomac River south of Alexandria in an effort to blockade Washington, D.C.[61] The young officer's recklessness, as well as his patriotism, was shown by his offer to infiltrate U.S. Brig. Gen. Daniel Sickles's camp as a spy to gather intelligence for an incursion into southern Maryland.[62] Nothing came of the idea, but Forrest's fervor remained undiminished.

In early 1862, while on three months' leave in Norfolk, where his father commanded the Gosport naval yard, Douglas volunteered to assist

Flag Officer Franklin Buchanan on board the ironclad *Virginia.* The old skipper immediately informed Captain Forrest of the request, expressing qualms about the idea in light of crowded conditions aboard ship and "knowing what an idol [Douglas] is" to his mother. Reluctantly, Buchanan consented.[63]

While waiting for the ram to be placed into service, young Forrest wrote a confidential letter to President Jefferson Davis, proposing an ambitious mission for the novel warship. The exuberant patriot advocated steaming up the Potomac to Washington to attract the world's attention as Confederate ground forces closed on the capital. His hope was that Marylanders would be drawn to the Southern cause, and the Federal government toppled by a coordinated attack from land and water. At the very least, Forrest foresaw the destruction of the Washington Navy Yard, formerly commanded by his father, along with the city's arsenal and the president's house, which his father had defended in 1814. What must the addressee have thought when reading Douglas's closing, which credited the plan to Flag Officer Forrest?[64]

The Confederate ironclad finally got under way on March 8, attacking wooden warships blockading Hampton Roads. Lieutenant Forrest later recalled that he "did not enjoy it although I was perfectly safe because I felt I was of very little use, carrying orders."[65] Buchanan later commended Forrest's service as aide and clerk.[66] As soon as the Confederate armorclad returned to port, Forrest and Lt. John Taylor Wood were sent to Richmond to report the triumph over the USS *Congress* and USS *Cumberland.* Forrest delivered the dispatches, and Wood carried flags captured from the enemy vessels. Forrest later recorded that Davis flattered him by stating, "That young man is one of the most talented & elegant gentlemen I ever knew."[67] The somewhat embarrassed officer returned directly to the Seventeenth Virginia, thereby missing the historic encounter the following day between the USS *Monitor* and the CSS *Virginia,* née *Merrimack.*

Lieutenant Forrest rejoined his regiment in time for the journey from Orange Court House back through Richmond to the Peninsula, in response to General McClellan's 1862 offensive on the Confederate capital. The Alexandrians then settled into rain-filled earthworks at Yorktown to await the advance of the Yankees. Forrest had been tasked to lead his unit, a selection endorsed by the men of Company H when they elected him to be their commander. To his regret, he would be denied the opportunity.

Forrest's enthusiasm for field duty placed him in greater danger than his parents could endure, it seems, for his father began lobbying the president for a naval billet for his son. Davis first offered a lieutenant's commission in the navy, which the senior officer declined. "I [should]

Douglas French Forrest
in a Confederate naval
paymaster's uniform.
Museum of the Confederacy,
Richmond, Virginia.

not have had as much sense," Douglas later wrote. "I was entirely unqual-
ified for such a position."[68] As an attorney, however, he was well suited to
the business of war. Consequently, Forrest received orders as an assistant
paymaster, a designation not considered an officer of the line. He initially ignored the appointment in the excitement to protect Richmond
from the threat massing to its southeast. Eventually turning his attention
to the matter, Forrest insisted that it was not something he sought and
pleaded to remain in the army. The concerned infantry officer once
again wrote directly to President Davis, signing his letter, "Your young
friend."

> I pray you, therefore, Sir, to indulge me in my wishes. If I cannot get some
> field commission for the war, & thus obtain command & responsibility,
> could you not give me some provisional commission, suitable to my cause

and order me upon some staff duty with the army that is to go into Maryland? I am well mounted, fond of a soldier's life, inured to privation & fatigue, cheerfully subordinate, as willing to *command,* & anxious to be useful.[69]

When he was turned down, Forrest saw no alternative to accepting the transfer, given his father's intervention on his behalf. The parallel to Robert E. Lee and his son, Custis, is all too apparent. On May 6, 1862, the lieutenant's resignation from the Seventeenth Virginia was accepted, and he was commissioned in the Confederate navy.[70] His initial assignment was to Wilmington, North Carolina. Once yellow fever erupted in the port, however, Flag Officer Forrest, now chief of the Navy Office of Orders and Detail, quickly transferred his son back to the Southern capital, where he remained until the spring of 1863. On May 20, he received orders to proceed to Charleston, South Carolina, and report for duty abroad.[71]

At midnight one week later, Forrest departed for Europe aboard a blockade runner, *Margaret and Jessie,* and barely reached the Bahamas ahead of a fast Federal side-wheeler in pursuit. Seasickness during his first three days on the open sea did not bode well for a mariner, but Forrest was unaware that his naval career would be spent entirely on shore. Transferring to larger, seagoing vessels, Douglas and his companions finally docked in southern England on July 29, after intermediate stops in Havana and St. Thomas.

Forrest's adventures abroad are memorialized in the journal he maintained from the night he sailed out of Charleston until his return to North America in 1865. The entries have been published in the late twentieth century under the title *Odyssey in Gray.* In addition to recording a Southern officer's wartime service, the volume is full of colorful descriptions of the places he visited, accounts of frustrations in dealing with French officials, and observations of the people he met. Of particular interest to the young American was the European female. Although there is no reason to conclude from the narrative that he engaged in improper liaisons, it is clear that Forrest enjoyed the company of women and was, in turn, attractive to the opposite gender. A diary notation upon arriving in Southampton illustrated this fascination: "Walked by myself about the town, saw a great many pretty women. Exquisite complexions, very fine specimens, many of them, of my favorite style of beauty—the blonde."[72]

Flag Officer Forrest had succeeded in removing his only living child from the crossfire of America at war and placing him in an idyllic setting thousands of miles away. Before continuing on to his duty station in France, Douglas became acquainted with the British Isles. He traveled by railway coach to London and absorbed the sights familiar to every tourist. Next, he took a boat to Edinburgh, where he celebrated his twenty-sixth birthday. Forrest may have visited Ireland, as well. It was a full two months after arriving in England before he finally went to France and first met Lt. William P. A. Campbell, commanding officer of the *Rappahannock,* which was to be his assigned ship.

Originally built for the Royal Navy and launched as HMS *Victor* in 1856, the *Rappahannock* was intended by Southern agents to be a tri-masted, bark-rigged gunboat with steam propulsion. In November 1863, the *Victor* was one of a number of "despatch-boats" offered for sale at public auction. The purchase was made by a commercial firm, acting for an agent appointed by Comdr. Matthew Fontaine Maury, the renowned hydrographer who had been sent abroad to acquire ships for the Confederate navy. With neither masts nor rigging on board, the vessel was quickly placed in dry dock to be refitted for active service. When concern arose that the British government was about to interfere, the *Victor* was towed into the English Channel, where she was able to proceed under her own power to Calais. During the crossing, the ship was commissioned the CSS *Rappahannock.*[73]

The *Journal de Calais* observed that for two months prior to the appearance of the Confederate vessel, thirteen well-behaved young Americans, many of them former members of the U.S. Navy, had waited at the port under the guise of being students.[74] Included among this group was Douglas Forrest. The *Rappahannock* docked on November 27 in deplorable condition, and the French government agreed that she could be repaired before putting back out to sea. In light of persistent objections by the U.S. minister, however, French authorities determined that the ship could not be provided armament, outfitted with equipment of war, or leave port with more men on board than when she arrived.[75]

The assistant paymaster was traveling to London to arrange financing with Maury when the *Rappahannock* docked at Calais. Two days later, Forrest was dispatched to Paris for the same purpose. He first located Capt. Samuel Barron, commander of Confederate naval forces in Europe, and then went to a banker with John Slidell, Richmond's commissioner to France.[76] This was by no means the first in a series of visits that Forrest made to these capitals, nor was it his only contact with prominent figures like the former U.S. senator from Alexandria, James Murray Mason.

Forrest's fiduciary responsibilities, along with the ship's small complement, afforded him social opportunities unusual for a young man. On one occasion, the handsome junior officer was proud to escort the famed Confederate spy, Rose O'Neal Greenhow, from the wharf in Calais to its depot.[77] Forrest was a frequent guest in Parisian salons, enjoying the company of the upper crust of French and British society, often accompanied by daughters whose charms he never seemed to overlook.[78]

By the first of December, the novelty of a Southern vessel in a French port had apparently worn off. Forrest noted that the ship's officers openly paced the decks in Confederate uniform and that residents of Calais no longer flocked to the quay to watch them. Confidence abounded about converting the craft into a commerce raider and taking to sea, as repairs proceeded apace and applications poured in for positions on the ship's crew.[79] While work was under way, the Confederates began using the *Rappahannock* as a receiving ship for seamen assigned to other vessels in European waters. The *Florida* and the *Stonewall* were two of the Southern warships manned by employing the *Rappahannock* as a way station.[80]

Forrest and his shipmates were ready objects of praise and ridicule. In response to admiring inquiries, he denied any kinship to Nathan Bedford Forrest, whose cavalry exploits were making the surname famous across Europe. Conversely, on at least one occasion, the Alexandrian was accosted by "a drunken blackguard," crying "Vive! Emancipation des negroes!" Forrest believed the belligerent was recruited by Northern sympathizers to provoke an ugly incident, which failed to materialize.[81]

By mid-February 1864, the ship's captain announced that the *Rappahannock* would be ready to get under way once it finished taking on coal.[82] Forrest's diary entries indicated his confidence that the steamboat would finally put to sea, an opinion at odds with other contemporary views. The strong assertion of righteousness reflects his characteristic idealism.

> The ship is now under sailing orders, and I & [T. A. Miller, Forrest's clerk and interpreter] are the only officers allowed to go ashore for any purpose, we solely on the ground that we have business to transact . . . . We are now perfectly ready to go to sea, for the Engineers say that they can fix the Condenser at sea and meanwhile our supply of water will meet our wants. We now only await the permission of the French Government to go upon our cruizings. I will not doubt that it will be granted. It would be too perfidious, too high-handed perfidy to detain us without a shadow of right or justice.[83]

Forrest was so convinced of an imminent departure that he moved on board the *Rappahannock* for the first time. Until then, he had resided in a hotel in Calais, being required to report each morning for a muster on deck. Now, he went ashore each day to purchase articles of clothing, apples and oranges, and incidentals for the crew.

As weeks passed without permission to sail, the quiet became depressing. Three assistant engineers deserted one night, further demoralizing the waiting mariners. Forrest attributed the treachery, along with the ship's continued detention, to the Yankee secret service, which, in his analysis, would spare no expense to undermine the Confederates.[84] Campbell was soon relieved as the ship's captain. In the eyes of his superiors, he had allowed the one brief window of opportunity opened by French officials in early February to close without leaving port.[85] Forrest worried that his relationship with the new commander, Lt. Charles M. Fauntleroy Jr., would fall far short of his rapport with Campbell.[86]

Upon his arrival, Fauntleroy conducted an inspection of the *Rappahannock* and found her to be unseaworthy. He assessed storage space as minimal, the design of the vessel's interior to be impractical, and the ship seriously in need of sails and caulking. He concluded that she was ill-suited as a combatant.[87] Having made personal commitments to Richmond to launch more commerce raiders, however, Barron was not prepared to scuttle the steamship in detention at Calais.[88] The French government permitted the vessel to remain in port flying a Confederate flag but prevented her from being outfitted as a ship of war. Boredom weighed heavily on the cruiser's officers and men.

Forrest's melancholy was accentuated by news from Virginia. He learned that his home was being ravaged by its Yankee occupants. At one point, he exclaimed, "Upon my honor, it is only the desecration of Clermont that annoys me." His worries were reinforced by a letter from George D. Fowle, an Alexandrian waiting out the war in England, who enclosed a receipt for furniture from Clermont that had been taken to an Alexandria firm for safekeeping. "I should have secured much more, but the Yankee soldiers commenced its destruction when they saw me engaged in removing it, & used every exertion to prevent the removal of any portion of it." Not long afterward, Fowle passed through Calais and further updated Forrest.

> [Fowle] said that when he secured a guard & permission from General [John] Sedgwick to remove the more valuable property from Clermont to a place of safety, it seemed to be a signal for a general demolition, that as he entered the parlor, a soldier was in the act of smashing one of the mirrors with the butt of his musket, he threw up his hands, & supported by the guard, succeeded in saving them, that the whole country is a wilderness, Clermont a small pox hospital for negroes after being first despoiled of everything.[89]

The spring and summer of 1864 dragged by with no word from the host government. Letters from Fauntleroy and Slidell to the French minister of marine produced no results.[90] On June 19, Forrest proudly noted that word had been received that the CSS *Alabama* was about to leave port and give battle to the USS *Kearsarge*, awaiting her in the Channel. Heartbroken the following day, he wrote, "Dreadful news! The Alabama went gallantly out of Cherbourg at 10 am yesterday morning and in seventy minutes was a shattered & sunken wreck. Her losses in men & officers are not exactly ascertained . . . This event has filled every heart among us with sorrow."[91]

As summer wore on, Forrest amused himself with picnics, regattas, and fetes, interrupted by an occasional rumor that the government in Paris was about to free the imprisoned ship. Fauntleroy finally met with Barron and James D. Bulloch and concluded that the *Rappahannock* could not put to sea with only the thirty-five officers and men acknowledged by port authorities when she entered Calais. The assistant paymaster settled accounts with the crew, reducing the ship's complement to twenty men. He sadly watched forty sailors depart on the boat for Dover and confided, "I begin to fear we shall never leave this port."[92]

Encouraged by his mother's letters and by shipmates returning from holiday in Germany, Forrest set off for a six-week tour of the Continent on October 4. He began in Brussels, continued down the Rhine Valley to Switzerland, and then entered Italy, where he remained for a full month. He marveled at grottoes filled with plantings from every clime, solid construction in hotels, art of the Old Masters, basilicas and frescoes, crusty breads and surprising liquid concoctions, and, always, people of every nationality, class, and walk of life. Forrest returned with renewed spirits for the final chapter in the saga of the *Rappahannock* and his own genteel service abroad.

Very little of note occurred at Calais over the winter of 1864–65, as reflected by the terse entries in Forrest's diary. He seemed content with lunches, parties, concerts, and balls. Unbeknownst to him, Secretary Mallory instructed Bulloch to discontinue the expense of maintaining the steamboat without reasonable hope of freeing her. Bulloch commissioned one final survey, which failed to justify additional resources for the project. Consequently, he ordered the cruiser abandoned.[93]

Weary of waiting and being repeatedly disappointed, Forrest seemed relieved:

> The poor Rappahannock is to be put out of commission & either dismantled or sold. The crew will be discharged & the officers detached about the 25th [of March]. I am overjoyed to learn that we are to return Home about the middle of April. I long to be once more with my precious ones there, and then I crave to renew the soldier life I once led with such a satisfying consciousness that I was doing my duty to my beloved country . . . Oh! How I shall fight those fellows! I *must* be in the army when I return. I am ashamed to be a Paymaster at a time like this. I shall hold the President to his promise & get a staff appointment.[94]

On March 30, 1865, Forrest left Calais for the last time, sailing to Dover, where he boarded a train to London. At Liverpool, he turned over his vouchers to Bulloch. Among the passengers on the return voyage across the Atlantic was his superior, Samuel Barron.

After intermediate stops at St. Thomas and Havana once again, Forrest arrived in Galveston on May 3. Continuing on to Houston, he was accepted on the staff of Maj. Gen. John G. Walker, whom the naval officer understood to be the most popular general in the Trans-Mississippi. The Alexandrian was soon concerned about lawless bands taking advantage of the power void between collapse of the Confederate government and restoration of Federal control. Quartermaster stores of the defeated army were prime targets for predators. In the sparse remnants of the South's fighting force, Forrest took his regular turn on guard duty. At the same time, he and the other diehards were subjected to recurring rumors of demoralization and dissension in the North and various fates said to have befallen military elements and political leaders in the South.

The Department of Trans-Mississippi formally surrendered at the end of May. Undaunted, Walker collected a small band of soldiers willing to emigrate to Mexico. The exhausting summer trek across the Texas prairie soon caused Forrest to fall ill with fever. He left the party at San Antonio, taking a room at Menger's Hotel to recover. During his convalescence, he had a change of heart and decided to turn back and rejoin his parents in Virginia. Forrest first returned to Houston, where he was paroled. The long journey home took him through Galveston and New Orleans, up the Mississippi to Cairo, and then to Cincinnati, Washington, and Alexandria. In July, he was finally reunited with his parents in Richmond.

By this time, the Forrest family was well aware of the fate of their home outside Alexandria. During the first months of the conflict, it served as headquarters and accommodations for troops from Maine, Vermont, New York, and New Jersey. In July 1861, the residence became a hospital for the Union wounded from Bull Run. As smallpox and typhoid became more prevalent in the town, ambulances began transporting the sick to Clermont. Soon, its rooms were filled with as many as two hundred patients. By then, the Forrests' possessions had disappeared. Other than the few items packed up by Mrs. Forrest and those sent into storage by Fowle, the majority of their belongings had been carried off by pilferers. A nurse acknowledged having some articles of clothing and commented upon seeing a number of "beautiful" letters at the residence that Douglas had sent to his mother from college.

At the end of May 1865, Commodore Forrest wrote to his neighbor at Wilton Hill, Anne Frobel, declaring that he was completely ruined by the war and inquiring about "very humble quarters" for himself and his wife. Any thought of moving back into Clermont vanished in September, when the house burned to the ground. The fire started in one of the rooms, quite possibly caused by burning clothing and other items contaminated by smallpox victims.[95]

Undoubtedly with an eye to recovering his property, French Forrest launched a campaign to recover his United States citizenship. On June 1, 1865, he wrote to President Andrew Johnson, soliciting clemency and restoration "of all his just rights & privileges as an American citizen, which under the proclamation of date the 29th ultimo he is denied."[96] Forrest referred to the amnesty decree that returned property rights to persons supporting the Southern war effort, with certain noted exceptions. Unfortunately for Forrest, he was disqualified on several accounts —ownership of taxable property over $20,000, service above the rank of lieutenant in the U.S. Navy, and resignation "to evade duty in resisting the rebellion." There was a proviso, however, for individuals in excepted classes to apply for a pardon directly to the president.[97]

On June 17, the supplicant appeared before the provost marshal in Richmond and swore allegiance to the United States. He then wrote to Secretary of State William H. Seward, asking his intercession, and again to the president. Forrest's final efforts in the fall of 1866 emanated from Georgetown, D.C., where he had taken refuge at the home of his brother. The Alexandrian was now concerned not only for Clermont but also for his property near Nineteenth and I Streets in the District of Columbia, for which he was still obligated to pay taxes even though the holding had been confiscated for use by the Federal government. "The fact of my not being pardoned appears in a great degree to prevent action in this instance in my favor," he complained.[98] Forrest followed a personal call on the president with additional communications with Johnson and the Freedmen's Bureau. The aged mariner did not live to see the conclusion of his last battle, however, as he died of typhoid fever, at age seventy, on November 22, 1866.[99]

As the sole descendant, Douglas inherited his father's estate. He immediately set out to regain Clermont. A surgeon with the Sixty-first New York Volunteers when the mansion was their regimental hospital, Dr. John Bigelow had acquired the Forrest home and acreage for $1,900 at a public sale for nonpayment of taxes in the summer of 1865. As an attorney, the younger Forrest had no hesitancy in filing suit to recover possession. The Virginia Supreme Court of Appeals upheld a lower court ruling that Bigelow had acquired only the former owner's lifetime interest in the property. As the rightful heir, Douglas Forrest was declared the legal owner. This decision was upheld by the U.S. Supreme Court in 1869.[100]

Meanwhile, Douglas had moved to Baltimore, where he formed a law partnership. A commitment to religion soon began to overshadow his interest in jurisprudence, however. In 1870, he was ordained a deacon, working for the church while continuing his practice of law. On a trip to Europe and the Holy Land the following year, he decided upon a full-time ministry. Forrest enrolled in the Episcopal Theological Seminary outside Alexandria and in 1873 formally entered the clergy. His wedding to Sallie Rutherfoord of Richmond also took place that year. For the remainder of the nineteenth century, Reverend Forrest served parishes in the states of Virginia, Maryland, Washington, Ohio, California, West Virginia, and Florida, plus the District of Columbia. Suffering increasingly bad health, in his sixty-fifth year Forrest died on May 3, 1902, at the home of his sister-in-law in Ashland, Virginia. Clermont passed to his widow, then to her nephew, and finally in 1939 to a buyer outside the family. Today, this legendary plantation is obliterated by suburban housing and an expressway, leaving nothing tangible to remember the extraordinary personalities who dwelt there.[101]

The contributions of the two Forrests to the Southern cause fall short of major significance. Flag Officer Forrest's skills in managing the Gosport shipyard and organizing and provisioning the James River Squadron for the final battle for Richmond represent their greatest accomplishments. In this sense, Forrest might be compared to Braxton Bragg or Joseph E. Johnston, more adept in preparing for combat than in actually conducting it. Their service is of value, however, in illustrating several facets of the Southern naval experience during the war.

Forrest's bravery before the war indicates that he would have gladly led his command into conflict if the caution often attendant to old age did not dim his courage. Douglas Forrest seemed to have inherited this boldness, at least as shown by his volunteering for hazardous duty early in the conflict. The subsequent posting in France denied him the opportunity of carrying through on his inclinations. Perhaps, like Custis Lee, he was a pawn of his family's prominence. What both Forrests represented was the determination of many Alexandrians to serve the new nation that their state had decided to join, even at the cost of having to leave home. Thus, it was patriotism and commitment at considerable financial sacrifice, and not specific accomplishments, for which these Virginians are remembered.

CHAPTER EIGHT

SPY

✷✷✷ ORTON WILLIAMS

LIKE MANY AMERICAN COMMUNITIES THAT SENT MEN OFF TO the Civil War, Alexandria later erected a statue in memory of those who lost their lives in the conflict. The senior officer of the one hundred names inscribed on the base of the solitary Southern sentinel standing on Washington Street is "Col. Wm. Orton Williams, C.S.A." He was a month shy of his twenty-fourth birthday when he suffered the death of a spy while in military service of the Confederacy.

"Orton," as he was known later in life, was born on July 7, 1839, in Buffalo, New York, where his father, William George Williams, supervised triangulation of Lake Erie as a captain in the Corps of Topographical Engineers. Orton was the great-great-grandson of Martha Washington, which made him first cousin, once removed, to Mary Anna Randolph Custis, who married Robert E. Lee. Orton's mother, America Pinkney Peter Williams, died when he was just four years of age. His father perished three years later of wounds suffered in the capture of Monterrey during the Mexican War.[1] This left "Bunny," as he was called in family circles during childhood, to be raised by his sister, Martha Custis Williams, or "Markie," at Tudor Place, the home of their maternal grandparents in Georgetown, D.C.

Markie maintained close contact with Mrs. Lee, both while her cousin was in residence at Arlington House across the Potomac in Alexandria County and when she was away from home with her husband. As he had known her since childhood, Lee assumed the role of surrogate father, corresponding with Markie for the rest of his life, and, in one early letter, ironically referring to Orton as "the young hero." Bunny frequently visited the Lee family, at one point seemingly taking a shine to Lee's niece, "pretty Annette Carter."[2] The attention paid to his cousin, Agnes Lee, was longer and more serious. He was reported to have chatted with her for three hours one evening at West Point, when Brevet Colonel Lee was serving as superintendent.[3]

Orton had his mind set on attending the military academy. His father had graduated there in 1824, and his older brother was a member of the class of 1852. Unsure as to which direction to point her younger sibling, Markie wrote to Lee for advice. He replied on September 16, 1853, discouraging her about Orton's prospects for attending the school, in light of the difficulty of obtaining another appointment for a family that had already sent a son there. After discussing a school at Sing Sing, New York, St. James College in Western Maryland, Virginia Military Institute, and William and Mary, Lee recommended an academic institution in Northern Virginia.

> My friends in Alexn. Mr. Dana especially, give me favourable accounts of the [Episcopal] High school near that place. I know nothing of it personally, except from what I can judge from the scholars themselves. I believe it to be a good school in every respect. Dr. Maguire [sic], is less rigid than Mr. Dalrymple, & is therefore more popular with the scholars. He has good teachers & the principles of the pupils are attended to with care. All things being equal I prefer a school in the country . . . What more can I say Markie, except that the nature & disposition of the boy himself ought to be considered with other circumstances by which he is surrounded, in the choice of a school.[4]

It was in this context that Lee offered the often-repeated indictment, "I can advise no young man to enter the Army."[5]

Orton consequently attended the 1853–54 session at Episcopal High School, where he received a certificate for scholarship and deportment signed by the principal, Rev. John P. McGuire, and members of the faculty. The orphan did not give up hope of matriculating to West Point, however. In 1857 Markie wrote from Arlington to seek an appointment for her brother as a cadet, as did Benjamin Hallowell, the prominent Quaker educator who was instructing Orton at his Alexandria Boarding School. At Markie's urging, Bvt. Lt. Gen. Winfield Scott, the army's general in chief, also endorsed the nomination.[6] For whatever reason, Orton was not admitted.

The young man's tenacity was again shown by his persistence in seeking a position with the U.S. Coast Survey. His candidacy was firmly dismissed in November 1858 by its superintendent, Alexander Dallas Bache.[7] Undeterred, in 1859 Williams signed on with a surveying expedition to Minnesota as part of the Great Lakes mapping project under direction of Capt. George G. Meade of the army's Corps of Topographical Engineers.[8] A talent for drawing, along with his surveying experience, led to Williams being employed as a draftsman with the hydrographic drawing division at the Coast Survey headquarters in 1860. The survey was the premier scientific agency in antebellum America. Besieged with applicants, it could afford to be very selective in hiring employees. It was not by chance, certainly, that the trainee's new supervisor was Lee's brother, Comdr. Sydney Smith Lee, on detail from the U.S. Navy.

Undaunted by his failure to be admitted to West Point, Williams continued to pursue a direct commission in the army. Now commanding the Second U.S. Cavalry, Brevet Colonel Lee wrote a letter of recommendation for Williams to Secretary of War John B. Floyd in 1860. While Williams waited during the following winter, he sometimes spent the night at Arlington in the role of protector for the Lee ladies left alone by their men in uniform. At the same time, new opportunities for military service were being created with the formation of a new national government by the seceding states. Lee reported that his nephew and son, Custis, were seeking captaincies in the army of the Southern republic.[9] On March 30, 1861, however, Williams achieved his original objective of being commissioned in the U.S. Army and accepted appointment as second lieutenant in Lee's regiment. He was assigned, however, as an aide to General Scott, not surprising in light of Markie's influence. At the time of his selection, Williams listed Alexandria County as his residence, no doubt referring to Arlington, where he was devoting a great deal of time to his Lee cousins. The new subaltern wore the uniform with panache, as noted by an observer in Georgetown, who was attracted "by the sight of a dashing young cavalry officer showing off the paces of his handsome black charger."[10] Williams was promoted to first lieutenant on April 25, although his mentor, Colonel Lee, had already resigned from the U.S. Army to cast his fortunes with his beloved Virginia.[11] It is even said that Williams delivered Lee's letter of resignation to General Scott.[12]

As the Union dissolved and Lee became identified with the rebellious South, Williams rashly continued to make trips across the river to court Agnes, despite being told by his military superiors to cease visiting Arlington. In light of the old general's expressed fondness for her husband, Mary Lee wrote Scott on May 5 to ask his protection so that she could remain in her family home. She received no direct reply, but Lieutenant Williams rode over to warn her that Arlington Heights would soon be occupied by Federal troops. Mrs. Lee consequently sent away those family possessions of special value.[13]

Visits by Williams to the Lees aroused enough suspicion among the Federal high command that he was arrested on May 7. Mary Lee gave her impression of the situation to her husband, noting the role played by their son Custis.

I begin now to think tho, it is all suspicion that Orton was made the tool of some of the authorities in Washington to alarm us, either to bring us out to defend our home, or get us out of the House . . . I do not mean to intimate that Orton lent himself to the deception but was himself deceived. Poor fellow he appeared here very early a few mornings since, said he could stand it no longer, had intimated his intentions of resigning to his friends Capt. [E. D.] Townsend and Col. [Lorenzo] Thomas who had demonstrated with him in the most unfair manner, told him, he would be branded as a traitor of the deepest dye & no one would believe that he had not done so to betray, all their plan of operations of which he had been made confidant. He went to the general [Scott] who sent word he was sick & would not see him. Custis advised him to return boldly to Washington and write to the General or see him. He did so & was placed immediately under arrest.[14]

Williams was subsequently detained on Governor's Island, New York. He was taken into the home of the post commander, and the impetuous youth was later reported to have fallen in love with his jailer's daughter, who considered herself engaged to Williams when he eventually went south.[15] During confinement, he resigned his commission and wrote a seven-page letter to Scott explaining the underlying reasons and special circumstances. Williams insisted that Lee had not advised him to defect. He also foresaw that "the North must necessarily, & will *ultimately* conquer the South," due to a disparity in numbers. Nonetheless, Williams stated his desire to share the fate of the seceding states.[16] "I cannot fight against my relations & friends," his sister recalled him saying.[17]

By early June, the former aide's knowledge of Union war plans was no longer considered current and of value to the rebel mobilization. The army thus accepted Williams's resignation and released him on June 10.[18] He promptly made his way to Richmond, where he met with now-Brigadier General Lee, C.S.A., and, according to one contemporary, served for a short period as the Virginian's aide-de-camp.[19] In July, Williams was commissioned a first lieutenant and appointed aide to Maj. Gen. Leonidas Polk, commanding Southern forces in a vast area along the Mississippi River.[20]

Lee is said to have regretted that he could not retain Williams on his staff, believing he could help curb the young man's rashness, "but I knew it would have reopened the batteries of the Northern Press, reviving their scandalous assertions."[21] Lee was not the only one to recognize this foolhardiness. One comrade cited a "fearlessness and a daring that was hard to distinguish from the reckless."[22] Underlying some of Williams's behavior may have been an over-fondness for drink. The young officer was described as being quite dashing. "He was tall, blonde, erect, scrupulously groomed, strikingly handsome, except for harsh features," wrote one comrade in arms. "He wore a kepi, hussar jacket, duck trousers, Wellington boots, rattling saber. He was militarism embodied."[23]

That brash militarism would soon cause Williams serious trouble. By October, he was promoted to captain and placed in command of what became known as Williams's Company of Tennessee Light Artillery.[24] At Columbus, Kentucky, in early 1862, Williams encountered a private who failed to salute him during an inspection of the artillery stable. The soldier explained that he had given a salute when the captain first entered the area but refused to render honors repeatedly, whereupon Williams drew his sword and killed the subordinate. The captain later explained the incident: "For his ignorance, I pitied him; for his insolence, I forgave him; for his insubordination, I slew him."[25] An inquiry into the matter was superceded by Confederate withdrawal to the south soon thereafter.

When Secretary of War Judah Benjamin approved the evacuation of Columbus, Williams was conferring with the War Department about circumstances leading to the fall of Fort Donelson. Polk had sent the captain as a courier to Richmond on February 12, presumably to distance him from the uproar caused by his violent act.[26]

Williams had been joined in his new unit by his first cousin, once removed, Walter "Gip" Peter, who secured an appointment as first lieutenant on February 1, 1862. Peter and Williams would be an inseparable duo during their remaining service to the South. The Marylander was born on October 18, 1842, to Maj. George Peter, son of Georgetown's first mayor, a light artillery officer in the War of 1812 and commander of a battalion of militia at the Battle of Bladensburg. Gip was described by a friend as "a generous, warm-hearted, gallant man, six feet in height, straight as an arrow, a splendid horseman and every inch a soldier."[27]

Saddened by the death of his revered father in June 1861, Gip crossed the Potomac to offer his services to the Southern cause. He resided temporarily with a cousin's family in Leesburg and volunteered to serve as civilian aide to Col. Walter Hanson Jenifer, commander of cavalry for Col. Nathan G. "Shanks" Evans's force defending Loudoun County. Peter's performance on the battlefield at Ball's Bluff in October was evident by the five bullet holes he proudly displayed in his hat and coat upon returning to his kinfolk following the engagement. Soon afterward, Peter joined Capt. Elijah White's new company of couriers and was elected a lieutenant and commander of its outpost at Winchester. Peter's ambition, however, was to wear the star of a major, the same rank as his father. He left Virginia at the turn of the year to follow Williams to the Confederate army in the West. His eldest sister was aghast when she heard the news. She warned Gip to beware, as "he [Orton] is so foolhardy and rash."[28]

The month after Peter's assignment to his artillery company, Williams was transferred to the staff of Maj. Gen. Braxton Bragg, Second Corps commander in the Army of the Mississippi, presumably because of the slain enlistee. Williams was designated assistant to the chief of Bragg's artillery.[29] At the battle of Shiloh in early April, Williams distinguished himself by scouting for the general and, at one point, providing his large sorrel as a replacement for the horse shot out from beneath Bragg. One participant later wrote, "I saw Orton continually throughout this memorable Sunday. He was a fearless and daring officer, and Gen. Bragg appeared to rely more on him than any member of his staff in the execution of important orders."[30] Brig. Gen. Charles Clark added, "Captain Williams . . . was conspicuous for his courageous bearing, waving his sword in front and being the first person upon the hill in our second charge." Williams continued to distinguish himself the following month during a skirmish at Farmington, Mississippi.[31]

While the Confederate army regrouped after Shiloh, Williams initiated legal action to change his name to "Lawrence William Orton." The choice is interesting, as his brother's name was Laurence. It is easy to speculate that his given name had been irreparably sullied by the killing in Kentucky, impeding his prospects for military advancement. The alteration was consequently effected by an act of the Mississippi legislature.[32]

Orton served as commander of General Bragg's headquarters escort during the Confederate invasion of Kentucky in the summer and fall of 1862. Later that year, the captain also published a book on military tactics.[33] By the end of 1862, however, the ambitious officer had grander intentions. He wrote to Col. George Brent, the army's chief of staff, asking to be relieved from duty as escort officer.[34] Once he obtained his release, Orton carried letters advocating his promotion from Bragg to Richmond. Maj. Gen. John B. Magruder proposed that Orton be made a brigadier general, Bragg recommended a colonelcy, and Polk simply endorsed further advancement for the officer he referred to as "Major Williams."[35]

Bragg's request was quickly approved, and Orton proceeded twenty miles north of the Confederate capital to spend Christmas with Agnes Lee and her mother at Hickory Hill. For gifts, Orton brought his sweetheart a riding whip and pair of gauntlets, as they were both accomplished equestrians. The suitor proposed marriage but was refused.[36]

Orton nevertheless returned as a colonel to Tennessee, where he was ordered to report to Maj. Gen. Joseph Wheeler at Tullahoma. On April 2, Orton was assigned command of a cavalry regiment in the second brigade of Martin's cavalry division, as part of a new consolidation of mounted regiments under Maj. Gen. Earl Van Dorn.[37]

At Columbia, Tennessee, the bachelor had met a young, attractive woman who represented herself as the widow of a Colonel Lamb of South Carolina. On the rebound from his rejection by Agnes, Orton soon fancied himself in love and proposed marriage. Orton is reported to have told friends that they were wedded. Whether a ceremony was indeed performed depends upon the source, and it was also rumored that the "bride" did not attain true status as a widow until some time *after* Orton's execution, when her first husband died.[38]

Peter accompanied Orton to Columbia as his adjutant, for the lieutenant had been relieved from the light artillery company for the stated purpose of being attached for duty with his cousin.[39] Orton was itching for a fight, as indicated by his request for two regiments of infantry to help ambush a foraging party expected to emerge from the Federal lines.[40] He was not well received by the cavalry regiment, however, presumably due to his reputation as a martinet and because the officers and men believed they should be led by one of their own. Learning of the dissension, Bragg rescinded the assignment order, leaving the cousins in limbo. Orton was "mortified by this state of affairs," in the words of a comrade in arms, and set out to make his mark on the war in the West.[41]

In early June 1863, Orton and Peter stopped at an outpost in Bell Buckle and obtained some stationery from the assistant adjutant general's tent.[42] Their whereabouts are next known on June 8, when they crossed through the lines on the Murfreesboro Road. Orton Williams and Gip Peter were about to become legendary names in the annals of the Civil War.

In the estimation of the contemporary *Richmond Whig,* "On[e] of the strangest and most tragic events of the Revolution took place at Franklin, Tennessee, on the 9th inst."[43] It all began the previous evening. Col. J. P. Baird, commanding Fort Granger on a bluff overlooking the Big Harpeth River, reported, "Two men came in camp about dark dressed in our uniforms, with horses and equipments to correspond, saying that they were Colonel Orton [or "Auton"], inspector-general, and Major Dunlap [*sic*], assistant."[44] They carried sidearms and were attired in civilian overcoats and Federal-regulation trousers and caps, with the addition of white flannel havelocks, a cape cover protecting the neck. The latter was an accoutrement rarely seen on Civil War soldiers, especially in the western theater. The strangers introduced themselves as being sent from Washington to inspect troops in the West. They claimed to have been accosted the previous day by rebel pickets who captured their orderly and took their coats and purses before the travelers could escape.[45]

Four documents verified their identity. Special Orders No. 140, published by the War Department and signed by E. D. Townsend, assistant adjutant general, relieved Col. Lawrence W. Auton and Maj. George Dunlop from duty in Washington, D.C., and directed them to "inspect the Department of the Ohio and the Department of the Cumberland." A letter signed by Brig. Gen. James A. Garfield, future president of the United States, communicated the request of Maj. Gen. William S.

William Orton Williams *(seated)* in a Confederate colonel's uniform and Walter Gibson Peter in a Confederate officer's uniform. Tudor Place Foundation, Washington, D.C.

Rosecrans that the visitors examine his outposts before drawing up their report. The commanding general of the Department of the Cumberland asked all subordinate commanders to assist the special inspectors. Two additional letters with the signatures of Garfield and an assistant adjutant general in Nashville directed guards and outposts to pass the officers without delay and provide all possible assistance.[46]

Once Baird was satisfied with their papers, the strangers expressed a desire to continue on to Nashville, and the Federal commander provided them with the necessary passes. One account described Orton pulling out a map that was clearly not drawn for the Union army. When questioned, he explained that it was a captured document, preferable for his purposes because of its fuller representation of rebel-held territory.[47] Baird divulged the countersign and lent "Colonel Auton" fifty dollars, taking the inspector's note in exchange. Orton even had the audacity to ask for and pocket some cigars from his host.[48]

After the strangers departed, Baird began to have doubts about their authenticity. His apprehension was shared by fellow officers who observed the travelers. Consequently, Col. Louis Watkins, Sixth Kentucky Cavalry, was dispatched to retrieve the two men. He overtook them about a third of a mile from Franklin and insisted that they return to Baird's camp. Watkins led them to his own tent, where they were placed under guard. It was only in attempting to pass outside the enclosure that Orton and Peter realized they were prisoners.[49]

Baird attempted to obtain verification of the inspectors' identity from higher headquarters. He first tried using flares to wigwag his superior officer, Brig. Gen. Gordon Granger at Triune, where the riders claimed to have stopped. He was unsuccessful. Baird then telegraphed Brig. Gen. Robert S. Granger at Nashville seeking information. Baird next asked Garfield if there were inspectors general named Orton and Dunlop, and, if so, to describe their personal appearances. Receiving no response to any of these inquiries, Baird telegraphed further explanation to Garfield at 11:30 P.M. "The one representing himself as Colonel Orton is probably a regular officer of old army, but Colonel Watkins, commanding cavalry here, in whom I have the utmost confidence, is of opinion that they are spies, who have either forged or captured their orders. They can give no consistent account of their conduct." Just after sending this message, Baird received Garfield's reply to his first communiqué. "There are no such men as Insp. Gen. Lawrence Orton, colonel U.S. Army, and assistant, Major Dunlop, in this army, nor in any army, so far as we know. Why do you ask?"[50]

Upon receipt of Garfield's telegram, Baird undertook a closer inspection of the suspects. The major consented reluctantly to a search; the colonel protested, even placing a hand upon his hilt, but submitted in light of the overwhelming numbers against them. When Dunlop's sword was drawn from its scabbard, etched into it was found the identification "Lt. W. G. Peter, C.S.A." Each man had his real name and Confederate rank in the band of his headgear, which, in Dunlop's case, was a gray cap obscured under the havelock.[51] Lt. Henry Wharton arrived from Triune and declared the signatures on the documents to be forgeries.

With these discoveries, Baird remarked, almost in admiration, "Gentlemen, you have played this very well." To which Peter replied, "Yes, and it came near being a perfect success."[52] The captives proceeded to confess their deception but denied being spies or having any intention of obtaining military intelligence. Perhaps to prove his honorable character, Orton reminded Watkins that they had served together in the same regiment in Washington, when he was known as "Lt. Williams." Watkins had not recognized the stranger, but Orton claimed to have immediately remembered the cavalryman and resisted the temptation to shoot him, as he could not kill an old friend.[53] Baird reported his findings to Garfield, adding with chagrin over being hoodwinked, "My bile is stirred, and some hanging would do me good."[54]

At midnight came Garfield's directions. "The two men are no doubt spies. Call a drum-head court-martial to-night, and if they are found to be spies, hang them before morning, without fail. No such men have been accredited from these headquarters."[55] At 3:00 A.M., a court of commission was convened, consisting of four officers and Wharton as judge advocate. It found the defendants guilty of the charge of being spies.[56]

After the trial ended, one member of the court, Capt. William T. Crawford of the Eighty-fifth Indiana, notified the defendants of the verdict. He later remembered that Orton beckoned him to one side and confided, "I am engaged to be married to Miss . . . . Will you be kind enough to have this Gold watch and chain and message (briefly penned) showing their fate sent to her." Crawford assured Orton that he would do so. The captain also claimed to have encouraged Baird to telegraph General Garfield to have the prisoners sent to Nashville for punishment. Baird's request included the information that "Colonel Watkins says Colonel Williams is a first cousin of General Robert E. Lee [actually, Lee's wife], and he says so."[57] Orton added his own plaintiff cry in a separate message. "Will you not have any clemency for the son of Captain Williams, who fell at Monterey, [sic] Mexico? As my dying speech, I protest our innocence as spies. Save also my friend." Word came back almost immediately, "The general commanding directs that the two spies, if found guilty, be hung at once, thus placing it beyond the possibility of Forrest's profiting by the information they have gained."[58] Baird consequently approved the court-martial's finding and ordered the prisoners to be executed, as directed by Rosecrans.[59]

The specter of Nathan Bedford Forrest hovered over the entire affair. The Southern scourge had threatened Franklin just the preceding week. The thought that the mysterious inspectors might have been acquiring information about Federal outposts played on the fears of the Union defenders. Eager to learn what Rosecrans's headquarters knew about Auton and Dunlop, Baird activated this paranoia by concluding his second message to Garfield: "If these men are spies, it seems to me that it is important that I should know it, because Forrest must be awaiting their progress."[60] The death of the two Confederates would preclude any advantage that might be gained by the rebel raider.

Once the sentence was decreed, the accused did not want their punishment delayed, but asked that the execution be changed from hanging to shooting. The petition could not be granted by Colonel Baird.[61] At daybreak, soldiers began constructing a scaffold beside a wild cherry tree in a public place near the railroad depot. Meanwhile, the chaplain of the Seventy-eighth Illinois visited with the condemned at their request. Both men wrote some final letters.

At 9:00, the garrison was assembled around the gallows and two poplar coffins. A crowd of civilians gathered. Twenty minutes later, the prisoners were brought forth, accompanied by guards marching with arms reversed. The condemned officers took their places on the platform of a cart, and the provost marshal, Capt. Julius H. Alexander, tied a linen handkerchief over each face. Orton requested that their hands not be tied, which was granted. Being given permission for one last farewell, the two men tenderly embraced. One witness later wrote to Orton's sister that Peter sobbed, "Oh Colonel, have we come to this!" To which Orton was said to have replied, "Let us die like men."[62] The cart moved out from under them at 9:30.

Newspaper accounts report that Peter ceased to struggle after two minutes. Orton, however, grabbed the rope with both hands and strangled for a full five minutes or longer. At last, after twenty minutes, a physician examined the bodies. All signs of life had ceased. The corpses were cut down and placed in the coffins in full military dress. Orton was buried wearing a gold chain and locket containing the portrait and a braid of hair of his wife (or intended wife). Her image was also placed in his vest pocket. Both caskets were buried in the same grave.[63]

Several notable postscripts accentuated the tragedy. The following year, the shock of Orton's death was said to have killed his sister, Kate, and the responsibility for raising her four children once again fell to the long-suffering Markie. The Peters succeeded in having the bodies returned to Georgetown, where they were reinterred in the family plot on a slope at Oak Hill Cemetery.[64] A short time before, in an engagement at La Fayette, Georgia, a rebel officer captured a sword bearing the inscription "W. Orton Williams, C.S.A., chief of artillery. Shiloh, April 6, 1862."[65] The blade of the condemned man had been given to Orton's former comrade in the old army, Colonel Watkins.[66] Two decades later, General Lee's daughter, Mildred, noted in her journal that her dying sister, Agnes, declared, "Perhaps Cousin Markie had better have my *Bible*— you know *Orton* gave it to me."[67]

Lee learned of Orton's death from a news account. He wrote to his wife, "I can hardly believe [it]; & yet it is given with such circumstances, & is in such accordance with the spirit of our enemies, I fear it is [so]. If he did go into Franklin as is stated, his life was forfeited under the laws of war, & yet even under those circumstances I see no necessity for his death except to gratify the evil passions of those whom he offended by leaving Genl. Scott."[68] Three years later, Lee was still upset. "My own grief . . . is as poignant now as on the day of its occurrence, & my blood boils at the thought of the atrocious outrage against every manly & christian sentiment which the Great God alone is able to forgive. I cannot trust my pen or tongue to utter my feelings." [69]

For what purpose did Orton Williams and Gip Peter pass behind Federal lines, wearing uniforms assuring them, if discovered, treatment as spies? Long after the war, Captain Crawford wrote, "I was present on their entrance to Fort Granger, witnessed their inspection of Fort Granger—Cannon, Small Arms & Commissary Stores."[70] This is the popular explanation of their mission—to gather intelligence on the Federal defenses, perhaps to aid Forrest.

The senior officer at Franklin, Colonel Baird, told a different story in his official report to Garfield:

> The officers I executed this morning, in my opinion, were not ordinary spies, and had some mission more important than finding out my situation. They came near dark, asked no questions about forces, and did not attempt to inspect works, and after they confessed, insisted they were not spies in the ordinary sense, and that they wanted no information about this place. Said they were going to Canada and something about Europe; not clear. We found on them memorandum of commanding officers and their assistant adjutant generals in Northern States. Though they admitted the justice of the sentence and died like soldiers, they would not disclose their true object. Their conduct was very singular, indeed; I can make nothing of it.[71]

The woman Orton was planning to marry (or may have already wed) received one of his final letters. "When this reaches you, I will be no more. Had I succeeded I would have been able to marry you in Europe in a month. The fate of war has decided against us. I have been condemned as a spy—You know I am not."[72] Orton wrote to his sister, Markie, "Do not believe that I am a spy—with my dying breath I deny the charge. I hope you will not grieve too much for me. . . . Although I die a horrid death, I will meet my fate with the fortitude becoming to the son of a man whose last words to his children were, 'Tell them I died at the head of the column.'"[73]

Peter's cousin in Leesburg, with whom he had stayed in 1861, reported receiving a final letter from the Marylander saying he was going into Kentucky.[74] The complete story will never be known. What is certain is that, in an ironic twist of fate, Peter achieved his lifelong ambition of wearing the uniform of a major, just as his father had done so proudly in the War of 1812.

The impetuous nature displayed by Orton in this tragic episode was consistent with his spoiled upbringing and repeated irrational behavior in early adult life.[75] Despite his protestations to the contrary, it would certainly have been in keeping with the Alexandrian's personality to undertake some grand attempt at espionage. Perhaps the most insightful explanation into Orton Williams and his mission on June 8, 1863, is contained in a letter to the governor of Tennessee from former Maj. Joseph Vaulx, inspector general on the staff of Maj. Gen. B. Franklin Cheatham at the time of the incident. "The general belief about the man was that he was out of balance, erratic, full of conceit, personal vanity and distorted views of his military importance and dignity. To sum up—he was not entirely sane." Vaulx continues, "I never heard at any time in our army a single man express the opinion that Williams' actions in this matter was known to any officer in authority over him." The writer concludes, "Neither the army nor its generals wanted him; his commission and orders were procured by some influences at Richmond; he was chagrined, and reckless— he was not a sound man, and there is no accounting for the freaks such an one [sic] will take."[76]

CHAPTER NINE

SCOUT

⁜⁜⁜FRANK STRINGFELLOW

BENJAMIN FRANKLIN STRINGFELLOW, "LEE'S SCOUT," AS HE was proud to be called, or a common spy? What is the difference between a scout and a spy? Wearing a uniform may be considered one distinction. As his army's eyes and ears out beyond the picket posts, a scout might be expected to exhibit his troops' colors. The visual difference between the adversaries became blurred as the Civil War progressed, however. When the South was unable to adequately clothe and equip its troops, it became common for Confederate soldiers to wear apparel and carry weapons acquired from Federals in the field. Consequently, a Southerner's attire might consist of a hybrid of what he brought from home, the meager quartermaster issue, and items obtained from his counterparts in blue. In inclement weather, this hodgepodge could be further confused by a somewhat nondescript slicker. Stringfellow was certainly known to go forward in such garb. In Washington, D.C., and Alexandria, Virginia, he also donned civilian apparel to facilitate his movement and acceptance by knowledgeable individuals, military and civilian, in order to obtain information.

Time spent behind enemy lines can be viewed as another discriminator between scout and spy. The stereotypical scout would be expected to ride out to ascertain the lay of the land and disposition of opposing forces and then return to report to his superiors. A classic spy, on the other hand, remains among the adversary to ingratiate himself (or herself, as some of the most successful and notorious spies utilized feminine charms) to persons with access to information of military value. Stringfellow pretended to be a dental assistant in Alexandria in 1862 to maintain extended access to war news reported in Northern newspapers, and was said to have used the same ruse in the Federal capital in 1865 in order to travel freely about southern Maryland. On these occasions, Stringfellow seems to have crossed the line between scout and spy.

A third distinction might be drawn as to whether a network of agents was in place to convey the intelligence gathered to friendly forces. Scouts are thought to carry back news themselves to the leaders who deploy them; spies are part of a clandestine network complete with couriers to ensure speedy transmittal of information that is often time sensitive. On those occasions when Stringfellow set up operations north of the battle lines, he took with him or inherited agents to transmit his findings to Richmond.

After the war, Stringfellow acknowledged being equally engaged in "scouting, secret service, and partisan warfare."[1] He drew the distinctions this way in describing his own role.

> From the many detailed for special duty Col. John Mosby was appointed by Genl. [J. E. B.] Stuart as a Partizan, [Capt. Redmond] Burk[e] as a Spy, & I was chosen as a scout. I have frequently been asked the difference between a Spy, a Partizan [sic] and a Scout. A Spy is one who goes within the lines of the enemy in citizen's dress, or in the uniform of the enemy, and never fights if he can avoid it. A Partizan generally goes between the two Armies, and wears his own uniform. A Scout occupies the middle ground, sometimes acting in one capacity, sometimes in the other. Generally I used my own uniform *in part,* and the rest I made of such a questionable character that I might be taken for a soldier of either Army. So that I was as often suspected and arrested by my own men as by the Federals.[2]

In carrying out assignments, Stringfellow was, in the words of a comrade in arms, "Modest, unassuming, self-sacrificing and patriotic, he sought no reward but the approbation of his officers, and the consciousness of duty performed. General Lee knew him well, and valued him most highly. General Stuart was his friend, his inspiration."[3] Stringfellow's survival was repeatedly dependent upon his assessment of human nature. He claimed never to shy away from seeking the refuge of a Union woman, for example. On one winter foray, he stopped at the house of someone known to be sympathetic to the North and asked for supper, which he received. When he turned to go outside to sleep, she insisted that he spend the night by the fire.[4] On another occasion, he asked for food and lodging from an Irish widow with four sons in the Federal army. At first she refused but, seeing his weariness, eventually relented. "Weren't you afraid to place your life in the hands of a woman who was hostile to the South?" Stringfellow was once asked. "No," he replied, "I knew women, when you place yourself wholly [sic] in their hands."[5]

Stringfellow was born on June 18, 1840, in Culpeper County, Virginia. When he was only two years old, his father, Rittenhouse, died of yellow fever contracted while conducting business in Mississippi. Consequently, his mother, the former Anne Slaughter, took her three sons—Frank and his older brothers, Martin and Robert (known by his middle name, Stanton)—to live at the Stringfellow family home, "The Retreat," a rambling structure near Raccoon Falls on the Rapidan River. His mother was from another family of local distinction in Orange and had friends in Alexandria.[6]

Although not an Alexandrian in the usual sense, Stringfellow's ties with the city were strong and continual throughout his long life. As a youngster, Frank was described as playing soldiers and Indians through the same Alexandria streets and alleyways he would so carefully tread as a Confederate agent. This could well have been when his uncle, Horace, was attending the Episcopal Theological Seminary, just outside the county line at Howard, while his wife and children boarded in Alexandria.[7] While Frank was between the ages of six and nine, his brother Stanton attended Episcopal High School, also at Howard. Stanton courted a local lass, Eliza Green, daughter of the English-born owner of a prospering furniture factory three blocks from the Potomac wharves. The Green family resided in the historic Carlyle House, the port's largest eighteenth-century residence. During the antebellum years after their marriage, Stanton apparently helped manage the city's elegant Mansion House, billed as one of the nation's best hotels and built and owned by Eliza's father, James.[8]

Frank received his primary schooling in Albemarle County, near his home, but by 1858 his widowed mother must have wanted to introduce her sensitive, religious son to cultural and educational opportunities not found in rural Virginia. Given the family ties with Alexandria, it is not surprising, therefore, that she sent him to Episcopal High School. In addition to his brother, this institution had educated five of Frank's cousins, the sons of Rev. Horace Stringfellow. Frank attended Episcopal for two years, earning silver medals for exceptional proficiency in biblical studies and deportment.[9] One teacher, Henry G. Stribling, graded him a superior student in Greek and Latin, although less accomplished in mathematics.[10] During this period, Frank also fell in love with Eliza's sister, Emma, and, consequently, was repeatedly drawn to Alexandria throughout the war to court her.

Upon graduation in 1860, Frank's facility in classical languages was sufficient to secure a teaching position at Stanton School in Shoqualak, Noxubee County, Mississippi. As the educator taught primarily children from families named Slaughter and Stanton, his mother's cognomen and brother Robert's middle name, Frank was no doubt drawn to the Magnolia State through kinship.[11] In April 1861, however, Frank left abruptly to return home amidst the excitement generated by formation of a Southern confederacy.

Frank Stringfellow. From *Confederate Scout: Virginia's Frank Stringfellow,* compiled by James Dudley Peavey (Onancock, Va.: Eastern Shore Publishing Co., 1956).

As the result of a chronic cough, the young scholar came back a gaunt ninety-five-pounder, standing five feet eight inches tall with fair complexion, light, curly hair, and blue eyes. He was apparently turned away by several Confederate units as being too slight for the rigors of cavalry service. Consequently, he set about building up his weight and strength. He had added fifteen pounds by the time Virginia voters ratified its secession from the Union. Four days later, on May 27, 1861, Stringfellow left home to join Company E of the Fourth Virginia Cavalry, known as the Powhatan Troop. The unit was bivouacked at Culpeper Court House, just more than ten miles northwest of the Retreat.

Stringfellow's remarkable career in uniform spanned the entire war. As a Southern scout, his service differed from that of regular soldiers. His encounters with the enemy were on a personal basis, often behind enemy lines, rather than as part of a formation of troops aligned against the enemy and accompanied by artillery and cavalry support. Consequently, fighting for Stringfellow was man to man. His wits were tested when attempting to deceive; quick thinking could mean the difference between escape and capture. Coolness and shrewdness, along with good judgment and discretion, enabled Stringfellow to collect information and avoid detection. Use of disguise, on occasion, helped create an image of mystery and omnipresence.

Agents dispatched on important missions by senior military and civilian leaders rarely carry papers explaining their role or customarily leave written records of their deeds and findings for posterity. Stringfellow's service for the South is further obfuscated by decades of discourses delivered across the former Confederacy. The speaker left an incomplete written record of his remarks. Sketchy coverage in the press and imperfect recollection by those in attendance do little to provide an authoritative account of the scout's contributions and adventures. Almost fifty years of listening to the Stringfellow story from his own lips created for Southerners a veteran of heroic proportions, a persona further magnified by legend and lore. The challenge for the twenty-first-century admirer is to separate fact from fiction.

After four years of conflict and controversy in the early 1860s, Stringfellow restored a balance to his life by devoting the postwar years to helping others as a member of the Episcopal clergy. Given this credential, it seems reasonable to have confidence in those recollections known to emanate directly from him, in his own hand or in print with his personal imprimatur. At the same time, prudence suggests considering with a grain of salt those other stories retold by well-meaning admirers but, nonetheless, susceptible to embellishment.

The story of Stringfellow's enlistment is an example of the borderline apocryphal. Stringfellow is said to have surprised a solitary picket on duty outside the Powhatan Troop's camp and ushered the embarrassed soldier, along with two of his comrades, back to the headquarters tent of their commander, Capt. John F. Lay. The officer readily accepted the volunteer after the aspirant said he had performed the feat to prove his worthiness for cavalry duty. The following day, Stringfellow was sworn in as a private, a rank he would claim for four years. That designation, like so much of his military service, remains subject to debate even to this day, as, at different times, he was offered commissions as a lieutenant and as a colonel.

As Federal and Confederate forces gathered on either side of Bull Run on July 17, Lay's unit reported to Gen. P. G. T. Beauregard at Manassas. Not unexpectedly, Stringfellow's initial assignments were relatively straightforward and performed under the supervision of others. His squadron escorted the commanding general to the Southern lines at the stream, and Stringfellow was said to have guided Brig. Gen. Thomas J. Jackson's brigade into position behind Mitchell's Ford two days later.[12] When fighting erupted on July 21, Stringfellow acted as a courier between Beauregard and his subordinate commanders, rallied stragglers, accompanied a staff officer around the battlefield, and guarded prisoners on their way back to Manassas Junction.

In September, newly promoted Brig. Gen. J. E. B. Stuart asked Stringfellow to join his staff as an aide. The cavalry commander apparently made the offer based not only on the young soldier's solid performance at Bull Run, but also upon hearing of his unique introduction to Captain Lay and his success in acquiring intelligence on the movement of Union forces before the fighting began. Allegedly, the new recruit had slipped into Alexandria and obtained the Federal order of battle, as well as intelligence on when Brig. Gen. Irvin McDowell would lead his troops out of their defensive positions toward Manassas. Stringfellow later recounted that his sweetheart, Emma Green, and her servant, Belinda, had crisscrossed the city at night, contacting Southern sympathizers to gather the information for him.[13]

Not long thereafter, Stuart again recruited Stringfellow for a special assignment, this time for extended operations in Alexandria. He was to peruse Washington newspapers for announcements of troop arrivals and unit assignments. The agent was expected to send regular synopses to Richmond by special messenger. Before starting out, Stringfellow was briefed by a signal corps officer and given documents identifying the bearer as Edward Delcher, a dentist's apprentice from Baltimore. The real Delcher had gone to Vicksburg, Mississippi, to serve alongside his brother in the Confederate army. In undertaking this assignment, Stringfellow was clearly assuming the role of spy.

With the assistance of a family that had lost a son at Bull Run, Stringfellow had no difficulty making his way through the Union lines and into Alexandria. He went directly to a building that served as residence and office for a dentist who was a Southern collaborator. During the day, Stringfellow assisted and learned dentistry from his benefactor; at night he pored through the Northern press, copying pertinent information and leaving it for a courier to pick up sometime after midnight. Only once, by chance, did he see Emma, as he did not want to place her in danger through association with him. His main concern was being detected and reported by the dentist's wife, a Union sympathizer. When betrayal seemed imminent, Stringfellow bolted, escaping through the Federal defenses and rejoining Stuart near Yorktown in mid-April 1862.[14]

Stringfellow reportedly made at least two more visits to Alexandria during the conflict. The better documented originated with a request from Stuart in February 1863 for information on Yankee troop movements, and was related by Stringfellow in a letter to Jefferson Davis after the war. The scout undertook to establish a network of agents and messengers. This involvement again transformed him from scout to spy. Stringfellow headed north to meet and evaluate the individuals upon whom he would rely. One was the father of a guide in Fairfax County; another was an old man who regularly went into Alexandria to deliver wood. Crawling on hands and knees between Union picket posts, commandeering a sutler's wagon and passes to ride through the lines, and using bravado when necessary, Stringfellow made his way into the city. He spent six weeks in Alexandria, this time notifying his intended of his presence and enjoying her companionship.

One day Stringfellow reputedly escaped from a pursuer on the city streets by bursting into a house and encountering its owner, an elderly lady who turned out to be an old friend of his mother. She directed him to hide under her hoopskirt, thereby preventing discovery and capture.[15] This was a deception recounted after the war by other Confederate veterans, as well, raising a question as to whether it also happened to Stringfellow. When time came to leave Alexandria, the scout masqueraded as a buggy driver and transported two conspirators, apparently Emma and a friend, through the lines, freeing him to return to the Army of Northern Virginia.[16]

The other recorded visit seems more apocryphal. The partisan leader, John Singleton Mosby, allegedly expressed curiosity about a play being presented to large audiences in Alexandria, entitled "The Guerilla, or Mosby in 500 Sutler Wagons." Mixing business with pleasure, Stringfellow rode to the city, chatted with Federal soldiers to gain important information, and attended a performance. He also reportedly brought back several copies of the drama to its protagonist.[17]

Much of his service throughout the war is captured in Stringfellow's own postwar description of his exploits.

> My *business* was to get information, but my *taste* and tempting opportunities frequently led me to assume the character of a Partizan, and I often indulged in capturing Picket Posts, raiding parties and wagon trains; in delaying the march of any advancing column; or in seeking to surprise Generals not too heavily guarded, while safely sleeping in their own encampments.
>
> Once within the Yankee lines numberless opportunities present themselves both for gaining information, and for attacking exposed points.[18]

As the war wore on, Stringfellow's attention seemed drawn more and more to the challenge of seizing a senior Union officer. It all began when the Federals captured Brig. Gen. William Henry Fitzhugh Lee, the commanding general's second son, "Rooney," who was recuperating from wounds suffered at Brandy Station in June 1863. Stringfellow later related to Davis that he approached Gen. R. E. Lee about trying to obtain a Yankee of equivalent rank for exchange. Lee reportedly referred him to Stuart, who specifically requested the apprehension of Maj. Gen. John Sedgwick, with whom he had served in the First U.S. Cavalry on the Kansas frontier. Stringfellow set out to reconnoiter Sedgwick's headquarters near Warrenton.

This is one of several instances when Stringfellow posed as a woman. He was able to play this role successfully because, in the words of a fellow trooper, he "was a beardless youth with a waist like a girl's."[19] Recruiting cousins of the commanding general to go with him, Stringfellow and the two ladies passed through the Federal lines in a buggy driven by an unsuspecting boy. They spotted Sedgwick reclining in front of his tent with "a robe or blanket over him . . . the nicest thing I had seen in the army on either side up to that time."[20] Completing their survey of the camp, Stringfellow's party rode through Warrenton, determining the locations of five other headquarters. Before the raid could be organized, however, Sedgwick's command redeployed away from the Southern cavalry's area of operation.[21]

Undeterred, Stringfellow set his mind on capturing Brig. Gen. Joseph J. Bartlett, camped at New Baltimore, Virginia.[22] Stuart had "learned from various sources General Bartlett was so much exposed as to make his capture practicable." Eleven men were selected to accompany Stringfellow. The reliability of their horses was just as carefully scrutinized. Moving along a little mountain road in the middle of the night, the small party was challenged by a Northern picket to identify itself. "The Third," replied Stringfellow, giving an offhand designation for the Third Pennsylvania, operating in the locale. Riding closer, they were halted again by a guard just twenty feet from the camp. This time Stringfellow could not silence the guard and shooting erupted. The raiders fired into two tents, but the general had moved from the encampment to sleep in a nearby farmhouse. Bartlett thus was able to make a precipitous escape in his bedclothes. The would-be kidnappers left as quickly as they had come, driving some horses tethered nearby through an adjacent headquarters camp to confuse the defenders. While disappointed in not accomplishing the mission, Stuart proudly sent Bartlett's headquarters flag to General Lee.[23]

Stringfellow was involved in one other cavalry operation targeted against a general officer, Stuart's celebrated raid on Maj. Gen. John Pope's supply trains at Catlett's Station in August 1862. Lee and Jackson were maneuvering to attack Pope's army before it was joined by Maj. Gen. George B. McClellan's troops from the Peninsula. Stringfellow was directed to scout Fauquier County to ascertain the position of Pope's right wing. He rode into Warrenton wearing a Federal officer's coat over his gray uniform, which was sufficient identification to elicit the location of Pope's wagon train from a group of bluecoats relaxing on the hotel porch. After inquiring about the security around Pope's headquarters from a family of Southern sympathizers, Stringfellow returned to his lines to tell Stuart what he had learned.[24]

Lee quickly gave his consent to a cavalry raid, and Stuart's troopers moved out across the Rappahannock River and took possession of Warrenton. Between them and their objective, however, was Cedar Run, swollen by a steady rain and growing worse. Stuart pushed his men and horses through the rushing water and then sent a regiment ahead to subdue pickets ringing the Federal encampment. He directed

Stringfellow to remain at the stream to watch for movement by the opposing cavalry. The Confederate troopers surprised the Federals, capturing more than three hundred officers and men, along with the commanding general's official papers and personal baggage. Stringfellow later contended that these documents provided the intelligence necessary to conduct the Battle of Second Manassas. Pope, however, had departed earlier in the day to oversee an engagement on the Rappahannock. Meanwhile, Stringfellow was surprised by Yankee horsemen, who confiscated his mount, saddle, and bridle but missed seizing the rebel scout. He was therefore delayed in reporting back to Stuart.[25]

Nothing seemed to delight the Confederate scout more than capturing and confounding a high-ranking officer in blue. In one oft-told episode, Stringfellow came suddenly upon a Yankee colonel, accompanied by two orderlies who were quickly scared away. Taking the officer as his prisoner, the captor was soon threatened by approaching Federal cavalry. He chose to escape by boldly accompanying the colonel at a gallop through his own camp of Pennsylvanians. "That was a daring act," the admiring colonel was said to have admitted afterward.[26]

Some other tales about Stringfellow have been told and retold so often that they border on legend. Undoubtedly, the inclusion of these vignettes in his lectures across the South helped build Stringfellow's image as invincible, for in each case capture appeared certain and yet he escaped. These incidents are recorded by several contemporary sources and, in the first instance, are documented in Stringfellow's own hand in the text of a lecture given to the Richmond Howitzers in February 1890.

In the summer of 1863, when the lines were drawn at the Rapidan River, Stringfellow and a compatriot were enjoying a pleasant evening with the daughters of a kinsman in their home in Yankee-occupied Fauquier County. During a bountiful supper, the scout heard someone inquire if he was in the house. "I knew that voice. It came from north of the Potomac," he recalled. The little girl who greeted the caller was too innocent to respond with anything but the truth. The trapped visitor quickly ascertained that the house was surrounded and, in desperation, raced to the second floor. At the top of the stairs, he encountered a black woman he had never seen before, who announced that she would hide him. Federal cavalrymen were yelling as they tried to force their way through the front door, but the servant calmly led the Southern soldier into the attic, where she concealed him behind some planks under the eaves. Lying in this position, Stringfellow heard her greet the searchers on the second floor and claim that the stranger had fled into the garden. When they insisted on examining the garret, the housekeeper held the lamp so as to throw a shadow on the opening where the fugitive waited to be discovered. Stringfellow said that the intruders remained in the house for six hours, so long that he eventually said his prayers and went to sleep.

He was awakened at two o'clock by the servant, who was sent by the young ladies to discover if their cousin was indeed safe. As he was enjoying the remainder of his meal, the Mosby Ranger with whom he had been dining emerged from another hiding place, which had also been pointed out by the black Samaritan. Stringfellow concluded his account by saying that after the war he founded the Martha Skinker School for colored girls, named for his protector.[27]

A second episode of legendary proportions occurred in November 1863 when the Federal army in Virginia was concentrated in the vicinity of Culpeper Court House. Stringfellow was dispatched to ascertain the number and position of the enemy forces. Depending upon the account, he was accompanied by companions numbering from two to six. After a long and stressful day, moving carefully around the Northern encampments, the small party of scouts prepared a dry place with pine boughs under a large tree and, warming themselves with blankets, fell sound asleep. They were awakened by Federal soldiers who pulled the covers back and loudly addressed them as "Johnny Rebs." Stringfellow apparently assessed the situation in an instant. Placing the blankets over his face, he reputedly exclaimed, "Oh, go away and let me sleep!" In the act of apparently returning to rest, he rolled over, drawing his pistol under the blanket. A comrade did the same, and when the aggressors finished their laugh and reached down to drag away the cover once more, the Confederates opened fire. Two of the Yankees were killed, along with one of Stringfellow's party. In the confusion, the surviving scouts escaped and hid before a search party unsuccessfully scoured the area.[28] Stringfellow's audacity in the face of what seemed like certain defeat undoubtedly captured the imagination of Southern audiences, instilling pride in a region recovering from Reconstruction.

A third tale comes close to defying belief as well. In the spring of 1864, exchange of fire across the Rapidan wounded Stringfellow's mother, who suffered a minié ball through her foot. She was evacuated to a house behind the river that was used as a Northern regimental headquarters. The worried son was determined to see her. Receiving permission from a reluctant Stuart, Stringfellow started on his way. As he was fording the Rapidan, the scout was surprised by a Yankee patrol and ran off to escape, losing everything, including a biography of Stonewall Jackson, inscribed to him by its author, John Esten Cooke, a friend on Stuart's staff.

After nearly being captured twice, once in the camp of Maj. Gen. Silas Casey, where Stringfellow was searching for documents with intelligence value, he finally reached the site of his mother's confinement. Enlisting the aid of the family servants, Stringfellow donned "an old wrapper and sunbonnet" and accompanied the black nurse past the sentry, up the stairs, and into his mother's bedroom. He stayed with her several days, hiding in a closet when outsiders entered the room. During that time, he overheard a Federal physician sadly inform his patient that her son had been killed, based upon recovery by the bluecoats of the autographed volume. When he was satisfied that his mother was being cared for satisfactorily, he jumped out a window into a pigsty one rainy night and made his way back to Confederate lines.[29]

The scout was not always so successful. He was captured by the Yankees more than once, managing to escape before incarceration in all but one instance.[30] That was on June 12, 1863, when Stringfellow was taken prisoner by the Fifth New York Cavalry, searching houses for Mosby's Rangers outside Middleburg, Virginia.[31] Transported to Washington, D.C., the captive was confined in Old Capitol Prison.[32] At first, Stringfellow was grilled for information on rebel forces. As Lee's army moved north toward Pennsylvania, however, the Federals became less interested in what seemed to be outdated intelligence. He was paroled on June 25 and exchanged on June 30 at City Point, Virginia, south of Richmond and far from the forces converging at Gettysburg.[33]

Another adverse outcome emanated from one of the two known occasions when Stringfellow rode with Mosby and was involved in a stinging defeat for the partisans.[34] In early 1864 he informed Mosby that Maj. Henry A. Cole and his battalion of Maryland cavalry, numbering 175–200 men, were camped on Loudoun Heights, overlooking Harpers Ferry, without infantry support and therefore vulnerable to attack. On the bitter cold night of January 9, Mosby and 80 or so of his riders approached the encampment. Stringfellow and 10 men went ahead to get in position to capture Cole and his staff at their headquarters in a house about one hundred yards from the campsite. Everyone was asleep, not even a sentinel awake. According to one participant, some of Mosby's troopers began firing into the tents, causing the inhabitants to emerge in their nightclothes, begging for mercy. Once the Yankees assessed the situation, however, they realized the size of the party attacking them and began firing on anyone astride a horse. At this point, Stringfellow's squad came dashing over a hill in front of the main body of Mosby's men, who mistakenly identified them as the enemy. Gunshots erupted in every direction. One account reported that a partisan emptied his revolver at Stringfellow, barely missing him with each shot. As the fiasco worsened, Mosby was forced to withdraw his troopers. Left behind were 7 killed, 4 wounded, and 1 captured, including some of the bravest Rangers. When an emissary returned later to retrieve the fallen comrades, Cole replied defiantly that to do so the rebels would have to surprise the camp again.[35]

By springtime, Stringfellow was back doing what he did best, gathering strategic intelligence for Stuart and the Confederate high command. Lt. Gen. U. S. Grant had arrived to lead the Federal campaign in the East, and Richmond was desperate for information on his intentions.

Mosby had reported troop movement along the rail line from Culpeper north to Alexandria, portending a redeployment, and Stuart instructed Stringfellow to determine the enemy's real design.[36] On April 11, the scout sent a dispatch relating his observations from the area around Alexandria. He dismissed the notion that entire units were being relocated and instead described the troops being shuffled as raw recruits and old men used to man fortifications surrounding the capital and logistics base at Alexandria. The report went on to dispel the rumor that the Eleventh and Twelfth Corps had left the West and passed through the port city in Northern Virginia. Stringfellow closed by declaring that he was heading into Maryland to gather intelligence at Relay House, a major rail junction outside Baltimore.[37]

Stuart remained in touch with Stringfellow via courier. Two weeks later, just back from Maryland, the agent reported through Maj. Gen. Fitzhugh Lee at Fredericksburg the troop strengths for Maj. Gen. Ambrose Burnside's corps and Maj. Gen. George G. Meade's army. The dispatch stated that "six steamers loaded with troops" had sailed down the Potomac from Alexandria. The following day, April 29, Lee informed Davis of this movement to what he described as "the Rappahannock frontier," adding that the Yankees would have to be met north of the James River. By that time, Davis was apparently aware of Stringfellow and the accuracy of his intelligence, as Lee made a special point of attributing the information to the perceptive scout.[38]

Not long thereafter, Stuart was dead, mortally wounded in fighting at Yellow Tavern. Stringfellow consequently reported to higher headquarters through Fitzhugh Lee or, as on May 30, directly to R. E. Lee himself.[39] By this time the scout was positioned with a string of lookouts on the Peninsula, tracking Grant's concentration of forces before the overwhelming casualties inflicted on his troops at Cold Harbor.

By the fall, Richmond was seriously threatened by Grant's offensive. With an eye to interrupting the Yankee momentum, Stringfellow returned to his idea of capturing a Northern general. This time, he focused on Brig. Gen. August V. Kautz, who had led various raids against Confederate supply lines into the Southern capital while commanding a division of cavalry in the Army of the James. Stringfellow constructed a plan for the operation, which R. E. Lee endorsed as "well devised." Its execution was stymied, however, by the repositioning of Federal mounted units resulting from Maj. Gen. Wade Hampton's cattle raid in September.[40] Undeterred, Stringfellow later proposed to Lee that he kidnap Grant, but, again, nothing came of the idea.[41]

At year's end, Stringfellow was being utilized more as a partisan than a scout. He was supporting Maj. Gen. Lunsford L. Lomax, who commanded Lt. Gen. Jubal Early's cavalry in the Shenandoah Valley. Lomax expected Stringfellow to perform scouting functions, signaling him at the opportune time for a strike.[42] But the general also wanted Stringfellow's help in obtaining a variety of items in short supply—from cattle, carbines, and ammunition to cooking utensils, overcoats, blankets, spades and picks. The commander was willing to pay for his acquisitions in tobacco or cotton.[43]

The relationship between Lomax and Stringfellow was not always smooth. In early December, the general sent his superiors a proposed plan of action that he identified as his own. Learning about what he considered to be a misrepresentation, Stringfellow protested to Lomax, "I think it is a pretty cold trick in you to appropriate my plan and get Genl. Early's approval. 'Give the Devil his dues.'"[44] On another occasion, Stringfellow complained that Lomax had not sent the gold promised in exchange for cattle obtained from Southern sympathizers.[45]

As the noose began to tighten around the Southern capital the previous October, Stringfellow had been ordered to report to President Davis, for what specific reason is now unknown.[46] A relationship was established, however, that would lead to a final episode in Stringfellow's service to the Confederacy that remains controversial.[47]

It began on March 1, 1865, when "Lee's Scout" was transformed into "Davis's Agent" as he left the president's office on a mission to Washington, D.C. Stringfellow intended to reach the Northern capital in time for Lincoln's second inauguration but was delayed en route and arrived the following day, March 5. He expressed his visceral commitment to the Southern cause when, upon reaching the city, he climbed the steps of the Capitol and spit on the building. That accomplished, he delivered papers to an unspecified embassy, according to a later report.[48]

Stringfellow's primary contact to obtain information was "an officer occupying an important position about Mr. Lincoln." They discussed a proposition of some sort, but the traitor was reluctant to make a final commitment, especially when Davis's representative had the audacity to come to his office one morning. Frustrated at this dead end, Stringfellow began to collect intelligence by listening to the chatter at his lodging among clerks working at the War and Treasury Departments.

The spy took up residence at the Kirkwood House, where Vice President Andrew Johnson was staying. As other guests began inquiring about the seemingly unemployed man asking all the questions, Stringfellow moved to other hotels and, then, to boardinghouses where government functionaries were known to live. On one notable occasion, a "lady detective" at a hostelry posed a toast to Abraham Lincoln. Stringfellow refused to join in, citing his abstinence from alcohol. When pressed to raise a glass of water, Stringfellow later said he responded by proposing a salute to Jefferson Davis and then made a quick departure to another inn.

During five weeks in Washington, Stringfellow pursued studies at a school of dentistry, the same discipline he had used so successfully as a ruse in Alexandria earlier in the war. He was pleased to receive occasional visits from his sweetheart from across the river. After taking the examination and graduating, the Southern operative received permission to practice his new profession throughout Maryland. When preparing to leave the city on April 8, Stringfellow was assisted by someone, now believed to be Mary Surratt, whom he mysteriously identified only as "a person whose name is linked in the history of those last dark days."[49]

A dozen miles from the city, the dentist's carriage was stopped by Yankee soldiers, who appeared to be on the lookout for the traveler and placed him under arrest. As they escorted him to their picket post, Stringfellow ate three documents he did not want discovered in a search. He forgot, however, to destroy a fourth letter, addressed to someone in the Confederate army, which, when found, strengthened his captors' suspicions. Reaching the confinement facility beyond Port Tobacco, Stringfellow was held with blockade runners, deserters, and the like. The next morning, orders came to transfer them to Washington. Stringfellow was informed by the lieutenant in command, "To be candid with you Dr. I believe that you will not be kept in Prison over one night, and then you will be hung." During his remaining day at Port Tobacco, the desperate scout tried to bribe his jailers with five hundred dollars in gold, but to no avail. One sympathetic guard offered assistance if Stringfellow demonstrated that he was a Mason. Alas, he was not, but "I have always desired to be," he weakly replied. His intentions were insufficient. The prisoner did eventually succeed in making his escape using an unsecured door late at night.

In a country alive with men searching for John Wilkes Booth and his accomplices, it took twenty-one days for Stringfellow to cross the Potomac, a period when, at times, he teetered on the brink of starvation. At last, he stole a boat and paddled across using a single oar. The fugitive first returned to the Retreat, where in the fall he worked like a common field hand, putting in a crop of wheat. His thoughts were full of his former exploits in uniform, which now acquired a romantic quality in his mind. "I should be happier now than I have ever been," he wrote Emma, "except during the time that I was a soldier. Ah! There is nothing like soldiering in this life. We support the cause wh[ich] we believe is right, defend the weak, and have as much or more praise than we are entitled to."[50]

Emma occasionally made the trip from Alexandria to see him. Despite her attentiveness, the former scout was uncomfortable in Virginia. The prospect of having to take "that hateful oath" of allegiance to the Union was abhorrent to him. Whether he was fearful of repercussions from the wartime bounty of ten thousand dollars on his head or allegations of his involvement in the Lincoln assassination is unknown. What is certain is that in the winter of 1866, Stringfellow journeyed to New York City and then up the Hudson Valley through Albany and into Canada. His Uncle Horace was serving as rector of a church in Hamilton, Ontario, and so that is where the traveler sought refuge.[51]

Stringfellow immediately inaugurated a campaign to entice Emma to join him, even suggesting marriage "in the best Confederate style" at Niagara Falls, where two former generals in gray were in residence. Although Emma resisted these entreaties, Stringfellow remained in her family's good graces, for Mr. Green loaned the expatriate money to resume his schooling in Hamilton. The next year, the cautious scout finally felt safe returning to Virginia. He married Emma and moved to Wakefield in Fairfax County near Alexandria, where he took up farming.[52]

It was not long, however, before Stringfellow was headed in a new direction, enrolling at Alexandria's Episcopal Seminary. By the time he graduated and was ordained in 1876, the new clergyman was father of the first two of six children eventually born to Emma. Over the succeeding decades carrying into the twentieth century, Stringfellow not only spread the word of God but also became a popular figure on the lecture circuit throughout the South. The *Washington Post* characterized his standard presentation as an "inoffensively partisan discourse"; the *Louisville Post* found him "very pronounced in his views and statements—possibly a little too much so for a general audience."[53] Time in the pulpit and advancing years failed to soften the old scout's views of what had happened in the 1860s and why. "The North forced the South to fire the first shot of the war, and she has been trying ever since that shot was fired to make the world, even the Southern people, believe that we began the war, when the truth is very different," he proclaimed.[54] Stringfellow never accepted remuneration for his presentations on "Scout Life," donating the receipts to churches and charities with which he was affiliated.[55]

The rector's days in uniform were not all behind him, however. In February 1898, the *Maine* exploded in Havana harbor, and America was suddenly alive with patriotism. Young men rushed to the colors. Cashing in a chit given him by U. S. Grant years before, Stringfellow obtained permission from President William McKinley to be inducted into the army. On May 28, 1898, the thirty-seventh anniversary of his enlistment in the Confederate army, fifty-seven-year-old Frank Stringfellow was sworn in as a captain in the Fourth Infantry Regiment, Virginia Volunteers. Entering military service at the same time was his son Martin.[56]

Stringfellow served as a chaplain, accompanying his state's citizen soldiers to Florida and Georgia before finally being deployed to Cuba at the end of the year. The volunteers were led by Fitzhugh Lee, who had obtained a commission as major general of volunteers, after an earlier appointment as counsel general in Havana. Stringfellow was now apprehensive about serving under his former comrade in gray. In August, he wrote from "Camp Cuba Libre," near Jacksonville, Florida, "Genl. Lee is to go to Cuba. He is a dangerous man to have here just now."[57] This sentiment may well have reflected a concern that Fitz Lee's long absence from the army could lead to disastrous results for the troops about whom Stringfellow cared so deeply.[58]

Stringfellow approached these final months of soldiering with the same energy and enthusiasm that distinguished his service almost four decades earlier. The scout-turned-chaplain preached in a gospel tent, but his ministry was far more extensive. He spent many hours each day visiting long rows of hospital tents, where young Virginians battled malaria, typhoid, yellow fever, and lockjaw. Suffering from rheumatism and chills himself, Stringfellow assured his wife that he did not stay overnight on the typhoid cots. He proudly wrote home that the surgeon in charge told him, "You are the most faithful chaplain in this Army."[59]

Stringfellow's ministry extended beyond comforting the sick. Every payday resulted in a full guardhouse, drawing the chaplain to counsel those confined. He attributed much of the discipline problem to alcohol. "Drink is the one thing which gets all of our men in trouble. It is the best thing in the world to let alone."[60] Consequently, he prided himself on never having taken a drop. At times, local girls visited his tent to confide their romantic attachments to soldiers. Conversely, when the volunteers reached Havana, "hundreds of boys" came to tell him of their love affairs with that city's senoritas. Stringfellow was more concerned about the starving Cuban children and was impressed by his countrymen sharing their rations with the youngsters.[61]

By the time the Fourth Infantry reached Cuba, Martin and hundreds of other Virginians had been mustered out of service, many due to ill health, some out of disillusionment with the drudgery of military life. As one would expect of the venerable campaigner, Stringfellow stayed until the end, ministering to his troops until they returned home.

Before his last hurrah in uniform, Stringfellow had been recruited as the first chaplain of the Woodberry Forest School for Boys, an Episcopal college preparatory institution founded by his first cousin in Orange, Virginia. Over thirty-six years of ordained service, he served as general missionary for the Diocese of Virginia and as rector in Powhatan, Mathews, Middlesex, Henry, Nelson, Mecklenburg, and Princess Anne Counties. His final parish was in Lindsay, Virginia, where, on June 8, 1913, the seemingly indestructible cavalryman succumbed to a heart attack.[62] His body was taken to Alexandria, where the funeral was conducted from the Green family home, now at 123 North Washington Street. Benjamin Franklin Stringfellow was buried at Ivy Hill Cemetery on a ridge overlooking the city. He was joined in 1929 by his beloved Emma, the magnet that repeatedly attracted "Lee's Scout" to Alexandria, during and after the war and throughout his entire life.[63]

CHAPTER TEN

ENGINEER

✬✬✬ WILSON PRESSTMAN

THE ACCOUNT OF THE ALEXANDRIAN TO ACHIEVE GREATEST prominence as an engineer during the Civil War is replete with twists of fortune. Periodically, when his course appeared to be set, fortune intervened to change the direction of his life, with fatal consequences at the end.

Stephen Wilson Presstman Jr., known throughout his life as "Wilson" to distinguish him from his father, was born in 1830. At eighteen years of age, the elder Presstman had clamored to take part in his generation's war which began in 1812, and succeeded in obtaining a lieutenant's commission in the army. Among other engagements, he participated in the American expedition to Sackett's Harbour that captured two English warships. The stresses of wartime evolved into the peace of the ministry, and he was serving as rector of Immanuel Episcopal Church in New Castle, Delaware, when his only son was born. In addition to being inspired by his father's military exploits, young Wilson derived self-esteem from earlier generations of Presstmans who prospered as shipping merchants, a heritage that would stand him in good stead in later life.[1]

Wilson's father died in 1843 in the twentieth year of his pastorship.[2] Quite naturally, the young man looked for a benefactor to help make his way. It is quite likely that he turned to Baltimore, where his father's family was centered. His older sister had married Isaac Ridgeway Trimble, an 1822 graduate of West Point who had resigned from the army and was engaged in the construction of eastern and southern railroads from his home base in Maryland. Presstman was working as an engineer for a rail line serving Alexandria when his fortunes took a dramatic turn for the better.

Presstman married Frances Lewis Fowle, several years his senior, at St. Paul's Church in Alexandria on November 6, 1856.[3] The bride was the daughter of one of the city's leading citizens and wealthiest residents. William H. Fowle was a large stockholder and director in the Orange and Alexandria Railroad, owner of the track connecting Alexandria with Washington, D.C., and president of the Chesapeake and Ohio Canal Company. He founded a financial house, which led to his presidency of the Bank of the Old Dominion. As a prosperous shipping merchant, the wharf at the foot of Prince Street bore his name. The family home at what is now 711 Prince Street is a charming flounder house expanded to an ell shape and marked by a grand entrance crowned with a Palladian window. It is situated on property between Washington and Columbus Streets acquired by the entrepreneur's father, William, in 1811. W. H. Fowle resided at 811 Prince Street.

It is long forgotten—if indeed anyone ever knew—what persuaded Fowle to give his youngest daughter's hand in marriage to the Delawarean. Was it Presstman's family connections to a successful Baltimore trading firm, the young man's promise as an engineer, or simply the earnest pleadings of his spinster daughter? Whatever the reason, with the patrician's consent, Presstman's future now appeared secure, and he settled into life as an Alexandrian.

Presstman's luck went bad just as quickly as his prospects had appeared to improve. On October 28, 1857, one year after their wedding, Frances died in childbirth.[4] The railroad engineer was alone once again, but that, too, would soon change.

In the spring of 1861, as external events pushed Virginia toward secession, militia activity quickened in Alexandria. The pace accelerated with the vote in Richmond on April 17 to withdraw from the Union and the subsequent appearance of the Federal gunboat *Pawnee* in the Potomac opposite the port city. A regiment with units organized in Alexandria began forming. One of these companies was an outfit composed mainly of railroad workers. This band of Irishmen was named for Daniel O'Connell, a folk hero whose resistance to British intolerance had resulted in Parliament passing the Catholic Emancipation Act of 1829. The O'Connell Guards were organized on May 18 and enrolled at Alexandria on May 23, with Capt. S. W. Presstman as their commander. The unit soon became Company I of the Seventeenth Virginia Infantry.

Presstman and his men joined the militia's flight from the city on May 24 as Yankees took control of the port. The retreating column scrambled aboard cars of the Orange and Alexandria Railroad and rode twenty-seven miles to Manassas Junction, where they set about learning the school of the soldier. Company I and the other outfit of Irishmen, the Emmett Guards, were left along the tracks to burn the railway bridges.[5] Presstman soon requisitioned tents and began the process of transforming his men into soldiers, but a band of railroad workers was far more valuable performing other tasks for the new Southern army. Presstman's troops were soon excused from training to interrupt the rail line between Alexandria and Manassas by tearing up track on W. H. Fowle's railway at Fairfax Station.[6] The company's first test as a fighting force took place on July 18 at Blackburn's Ford on Bull Run, where the regiment repelled an advance by Federals probing the rebel army assembled at Manassas. Presstman was reported "severely wounded" when his unit was rushed forward to stiffen the resistance to an attempted Yankee incursion.[7] It took several months for him to recover from this setback and return to duty.

In the aftermath of their subsequent victory at what they called the Battle of Manassas, the Confederates began solidifying their position at nearby Centreville. In November, December, and January 1862, Presstman was detached from his company to complete the rail connection between Manassas and Centreville and to supervise repair of nearby roadways.[8] In January 1862, Presstman was reported as commanding the "James Detached Corps," a nebulous designation in all likelihood denoting a separate work party in existence for no more than a few days.[9] His contributions during the early winter of 1862 set him apart from the relative obscurity of being just another line officer in a state regiment. Consequently, he came to the attention of the commanding general at Manassas. When transferred to the army in the West, Gen. P. G. T. Beauregard recommended that certain officers whose engineering expertise he found valuable in Northern Virginia be commissioned in the Confederate Corps of Engineers and assigned to his new command. The foursome included Wilson Presstman.

Presstman was one of sixteen captains on the first list of thirty-nine company-grade engineer officers appointed to the Provisional Army of the Confederate States on February 15, 1862. Ten days later, he was ordered to report to Gen. Joseph E. Johnston at Centreville. Beauregard persisted in requesting the services of the railroad engineer, however, and, in the wake of the engagement at Shiloh, Presstman was dispatched to the Army of the Mississippi. He arrived at Corinth on May 16.

As a stranger in an army consisting mainly of westerners, Presstman naturally looked for familiar faces from Virginia. One of these was Capt. John Morris Wampler, another engineer mentored by Beauregard and a drinking chum of Presstman's from the Manassas encampment. Shortly after reporting in, Presstman was sent with Wampler to an outpost outside Farmington to observe the enemy's breastworks about one thousand yards away. The two staff officers quickly came under fire from Yankee pickets, one ball missing the Alexandrian by only six inches and lodging in the fence rail on which they were leaning.[10]

Presstman worked on the army's engineer staff as Southern forces pulled back from Corinth and eventually redeployed to Chattanooga.

When Gen. Braxton Bragg, Beauregard's successor as commanding general, led his troops into Kentucky, Presstman was assigned as senior engineer of the left wing under Maj. Gen. William J. Hardee. Presstman's engineers prepared the way for passage by Hardee's troops and trains, and the Alexandrian was often sent in front of the column to conduct reconnaissance of what lay ahead. After the rebels returned to Tennessee, Presstman continued to enjoy the company of Wampler, his engineer counterpart with the right wing. Discouraged by the disappointing expedition into Kentucky, the two officers shared a yearning to return to duty with the messianic Beauregard and asked for his help in being reassigned to his staff.[11]

In November, Bragg appointed Wampler to head the engineer staff of the reorganized Army of Tennessee. When Beauregard asked that Wampler and Presstman be transferred to his new command at Charleston, Bragg easily deflected the request by pointing out that Wampler was acting as his chief engineer and Presstman was "engaged in important work for the protection of a Rail Road Bridge over Tenn. River at Bridgeport Ala. I have no available officers to replace them."[12] After a month as Bragg's senior engineer, illness and fatigue caused Wampler to be evacuated to Georgia to recover. Wampler's misfortune presented an opportunity for Presstman.

Wampler was returning by train to the army headquarters at Tullahoma, Tennessee, on February 8, 1863, when Presstman boarded the cars at Bridgeport. The Alexandrian had been at the river reassigning property to his successor, as he was now to assume the duties of chief engineer. Undoubtedly, Presstman's staff support to Hardee during the recent clash at Stones River had enhanced the stature of the railroad engineer in Bragg's eyes.[13]

The two friends maintained their strong comradeship, despite the reversal in their roles. Wampler now worked for Presstman, yet his predecessor's presence did not seem to make Presstman uncomfortable. The twosome reported together to Bragg on February 9. The chief engineer could not perform his duties simply sitting behind a desk, and during Presstman's frequent trips to the field, Wampler filled in for him at headquarters. When Wampler was sent off on an assignment, he regularly telegraphed or wrote to his cohort, who did the same when he was away from Tullahoma. The chums rode around the defensive lines, consulting on where to add positions and examining potential sites for bridges needed to shift troops rapidly in the event of a Yankee attack. They even lent money to one another and shared a common mess.[14]

A mutual concern was the army's commanding general. Braxton Bragg had a well-deserved reputation for being irascible. He focused excessively on details and was untrusting and ill tempered. Presstman's

Railroad bridge at Bridgeport, Alabama, protected by Wilson Presstman as a military engineer. From Francis Trevelyan Miller, ed., *The Photographic History of the Civil War*, vol. 5 (New York: Review of Reviews Co., 1911).

ability to work with Bragg over an extended period speaks well for his own patience, courtesy, and commitment to duty.

Another shared concern was promotion. A couple of years into the war, the two engineers were still captains, while other officers, less deserving in their opinion, had risen two or more ranks. Enlisting the aid of their benefactor in Charleston, they launched a joint campaign for advancement. Beauregard immediately responded by writing on their behalf to the engineer bureau in Richmond. Hardee also endorsed Presstman's candidacy for a majority, characterizing him as faithful, able, and efficient. Bragg was initially reluctant to become involved but eventually recommended his two subordinates.[15] Nothing, however, came of their initiative. Presstman's frustrations poured out in a letter to Wampler.

> Gen. Beauregard . . . has acted very handsomely toward us, but as you say it has not brot the Commissions. If others are promoted over us after such recommendations, I will as soon as I can without spiting myself, leave the [Engineer] Corps. . . . I recd a letter this morning from Virginia. Genl. Trimble [his patron earlier] has applied to have me report to him. I would be very glad to return to my friends, and feel sure that I could render good service in that section of the country, having been on a survey up the Valley as far as Harrisonburg, but I am afraid the [Engineer] Dept will refuse to make the change. I would love to get back to Old Virginia again and would make personal sacrifices to do so.[16]

Throughout the spring of 1863, Presstman addressed the engineer challenges confronting Bragg's army and effectively managed his small staff. He dispatched Wampler to Columbia in response to a request from Maj. Gen. Earl Van Dorn for bridging over the Duck River and, on two occasions, sent his assistant to McMinnville to rebuild the railroad bridge destroyed twice by Yankee raiders. Maps were always in short supply, and Presstman asked engineer officers throughout the command to make copies of hand-drawn field sketches for his use and that of the engineer headquarters in Richmond. Similarly, tools were scarce and had to be shared among multiple units in constructing defenses, frequently requiring intercession by the engineer office. Presstman and his cohorts also faced recurring difficulties obtaining work details of soldiers and hiring slaves from plantation owners.

Financial and resource accountability was an integral part of nineteenth-century engineering, so it is not surprising that Presstman's attention was also directed to receipts and ledgers. Presstman signed vouchers for sums ranging as high as fifty thousand dollars to purchase materials and hire labor needed for works projects. At the other end of the spectrum, he authenticated invoices for items considered expendable in modern times, such as envelopes, sheets of drawing paper, blotting pads, lead pencils, pieces of India rubber, and even a box of watercolors.

The careers of Presstman and Wampler diverged during the summer of 1863. In June, Bragg sent Wampler to Chattanooga to oversee engineering services throughout his geographic area of responsibility. In early July, Wampler turned from digging earthworks for the river city's defense to throwing pontoons across the Tennessee River to enable the Army of Tennessee to reach Chattanooga at the conclusion of the Tullahoma campaign. Later that month, Presstman reassigned his friend to strengthen the defenses at Atlanta. By summer's end, Wampler had been transferred again, this time to Charleston, where he perished answering Beauregard's call one final time.[17]

As the Federals closed in on Chattanooga, Presstman worked with Bragg's chief of staff to try to assist their uninspired commanding general in confronting or combating an enemy whose exact whereabouts was unknown. Support was provided by the engineer staff when possible. Presstman met with commanders at Bragg's behest. He sent instructions to engineers in subordinate headquarters to facilitate the movement of personnel and supplies. Engineering was inconsequential, however, in the Confederates' victory at Chickamauga and in their inability to maintain a foothold in southeastern Tennessee.

Presstman was finally promoted in late 1863, when he accepted command of engineer troops assigned to the Army of Tennessee. At the start of the war, the importance of military engineering had been unappreciated by the Confederate government. Engineers in the old army focused primarily on topography and coastal defenses. It was not until 1863 that decision makers in Richmond realized that plantation slaves and soldiers detailed from line units were insufficient to satisfy the burgeoning requirement for field construction. Consequently, the Confederate Congress authorized formation of four regiments of engineer troops to support military operations. Like many of his counterparts, Presstman was initially reluctant to leave the mainstream Corps of Engineers to raise, organize, and lead a route-step collection of mechanics, carpenters, carriage makers, and pontoniers. It was precisely Presstman's proven competence in working with these kinds of laborers, however, that convinced the War Department he could effectively command engineer troops in the West.

Presstman may have agreed to the transfer because of Bragg's selection of Brig. Gen. Danville Leadbetter as his permanent chief of engineers. Leadbetter and Presstman were appointed to their new positions by special orders dated October 23, 1863. Presstman accepted a major's commission on December 1. Returns for the Army of Tennessee that winter show Presstman's Third Regiment of Engineer Troops with seven companies, including one initially designated as pioneers and later reported to be sappers and miners. Their strength remained at approximately twenty officers and four hundred men present for duty. Within five months, the regimental commander was promoted to the rank of lieutenant colonel, this time with a strong endorsement from Bragg, who by then was no longer in command of the army.[18]

Bragg had been succeeded in December by General Johnston, who served briefly as a topographical engineer in the old army and understood the value of Presstman's skills. The Alexandrian's talents were soon in great demand. Johnston's number-one mission was to protect Atlanta —a vital military, transportation, industrial, and logistical center, as well as a symbol of Southern independence—and to do so, he would rely on an extensive network of trenches, parapets, and other earthworks designed by Presstman and his fellow engineers. As the war progressed, soldiers on both sides of the lines had learned that their chances for survival improved when protected by even a simple ditch. Reliance upon fortifications by Atlanta's defenders increased as they faced a growing disadvantage in numbers.

Johnston dispatched Presstman to lay out defensive works to be prepared by line troops under supervision of their unit officers. Companies designated as pioneers were committed to construction under engineer direction. As the defenders were pushed back by the weight of Federal forces under Maj. Gen. William T. Sherman, Johnston utilized Presstman to mark off new positions, modify roadways for transit by the army and its

trains, and, where necessary, erect pontoon bridging. Meanwhile, engineer troops labored with soldiers assigned to the Department of Georgia
to strengthen the defenses already in place outside Atlanta.[19]

By the summer of 1864, Leadbetter departed and Presstman once
again became the army's chief engineer while continuing to serve as
commander of engineer troops. The Federals repeatedly applied pressure by shifting their forces around the flanks, and on July 16 they
crossed the Chattahoochee River to threaten Decatur. The defenders
withdrew to positions on high ground overlooking Peach Tree Creek,
pre-designated by Johnston, and awaited the Yankees' next move. At
10:00 P.M. on July 17, Johnston and his chief of staff were seated at
a table with Presstman, examining a map of the locale and discussing instructions for the next day, when a telegram arrived from Richmond. It announced that Johnston was being relieved of command and
directed him to turn over leadership of the army to Bvt. Gen. John Bell
Hood.[20] The exchange of responsibility took place the following day.

Hood appeared to appreciate the importance of engineer support
to the defense of Atlanta. He quickly tasked conscription authorities
in nearby Macon to recruit two hundred men with skills needed by
Presstman to fill vacancies in the engineer regiment. Presstman was
again utilized to stake off fallback positions behind the existing lines and
directed to coordinate their preparation and use with the senior commander in each salient.[21]

When the final clash of the Atlanta campaign took place, however, it
was the rebels who took the offensive. On August 31, Hardee led two
corps in an attack against entrenched Yankee positions near Jonesboro.
Just before the line advanced, Presstman reported with his engineer
troops to Brig. Gen. Hiram B. Granbury in Maj. Gen. Patrick Cleburne's
division and was positioned 150 paces to the rear and left of the echelon. The Texans charged across an open field under artillery fire, engaging an enemy fighting behind barricades consisting of fence rails. When
the bluecoats were routed, they attempted to rally opposite Granbury's
left flank. The commander ordered Presstman and his men to pursue
at double-quick time, which the engineers did, scattering the defenders
once more.[22] Despite the success of Granbury's reinforced brigade,
however, the Confederates' last effort to save the Georgia citadel was
repulsed, and Hood began evacuating Atlanta the following afternoon.

The opposing armies now paused to recover and reorganize. Hood
quickly called for Presstman and his regiment to be relieved on the line
so they could return to engineering tasks.[23] With the advent of October,
Hood moved north into the Federal army's rear area to reclaim the initiative from Sherman and draw him away from Atlanta. Hood's forces
started toward Chattanooga along the Union supply line, then turned

westward into northern Alabama. In mid-November, when Hood finally
marched into middle Tennessee, his strategic objectives were unclear,
except, perhaps, for the lingering Confederate dream of reaching the
Ohio River and hoping that, somehow, their presence would cause the
war-weary Northern public to sue for peace.[24]

As chief engineer, Presstman's primary responsibility was to ensure
that bridging was available when needed. When Hood's army paused at
Tuscumbia, Alabama, before crossing the Tennessee River, Presstman
was directed to inspect the existing bridge to ensure its adequacy and
coordinate with local commanders to obtain pontoon boats as soon as
possible. Lt. Gen. Stephen Dill Lee had earlier been tasked to provide
any assistance necessary for engineer troops to lay pontoons at another
crossing point. Col. George Brent, chief of staff for Beauregard's new
command, the Military Division of the West, asked Presstman to furnish
the dimensions of planks and timbers needed to construct pontoons
so they could be manufactured in Alabama or Mississippi. The departmental engineer reported transferring twenty hulls to Presstman and
ordering another one hundred pontoon boats to be constructed as a
reserve train.[25]

Presstman and his men laid pontoons for the invading army to cross
over the Duck River outside Columbia, Tennessee, during the night of
November 28.[26] Two days later, when Hood's forces engaged the enemy
at Franklin, Presstman was once again thrown into the fighting, directing
a battery in support of Maj. Gen. William Bate's division. After first standing off to engage the town's defenses, Presstman eventually moved closer
to duel Yankee artillery on the Confederates' immediate front. When the
battle was over, the chief engineer returned to functioning as a general
staff officer to implement the commanding general's imprecise concept
of the operation. The subsequent clash at Nashville with Federal forces
commanded by Brig. Gen. George Thomas was disastrous. His army decimated, Presstman applied his waning strength to assisting its survivors'
escape to the sanctuary offered at supply bases in northeastern Mississippi. He worked with another engineer on the rail connection between
Pulaski, Tennessee, and Decatur, Alabama. Presstman then moved into
the van of the column of despair, relaying information on routes and
fords back to the commanding general. Wood stripped from buildings
along the way was utilized for decking on bridges by pioneers laboring
under engineer supervision.[27]

The retreat from Nashville was brutal. Wagons and baggage had been
abandoned outside the Tennessee capital, along with artillery and small
arms. The defeated army trudged over a hundred miles in the earliest
and coldest winter in decades. Soldiers wrapped themselves in blankets,
for many were without hats, coats, shoes, or shelter on the trek southward.

Exposure, suffering, disappointment, and defeat took a heavy toll on these veterans of so many losing campaigns in the West.

At the end of the retreat, Presstman was exhausted from the physical demands of almost four full years of soldiering. He obtained a surgeon's certificate on January 5, 1865, for sixty days leave of absence to recover his strength in Virginia. On his way home, the convalescent stopped at the engineer office of Beauregard's headquarters in Macon, Georgia, to pick up hand-drawn maps for delivery to the Confederate War Department. When he continued on his way north, destiny intervened one final, fatal time.[28]

On January 30, Presstman was traveling on the Piedmont Railroad in North Carolina, just below the Virginia line, when the cars ran off the track. While the derailed rolling stock was being righted and reconnected, the engine and tender proceeded to a nearby water tank. Presstman attempted to run across the track as they were returning to the cars. He fell and was caught and crushed by the ash box of the tender. After thirty minutes, he was dead.[29] The bitter irony in Presstman's life is that the railroad engineer was killed by a locomotive as he was reentering his adopted state of Virginia.

Wilson Presstman served the South well, contributing his engineering skills to a new nation hungry for men of accomplishment in its armed services. Like many of his peers, Presstman's training was acquired not at the school that produced the country's military engineers—West Point—but in a civilian capacity, working on the nation's expanding rail system. During three years of service in the western theater, he learned and supervised military applications for engineering while at the same time employing his own specialized expertise to address railroad problems facing the Confederate army. Presstman conducted reconnaissance, led road marches, laid out and erected defenses in the field, built and repaired bridging, threw pontoons across rivers, and, when called upon, executed the secondary mission of all military engineers, serving as a combatant. For more than a year, Presstman performed as chief engineer for the Army of Tennessee. His competence is evidenced by his having successfully worked for five of the Confederacy's senior and most demanding general officers—P. G. T. Beauregard, William Hardee, Braxton Bragg, Joseph E. Johnston, and John Bell Hood.

Like so many other soldiers in wartime, Presstman's end came from a twist of fate, the last turn in a life that seemed driven by powers that defied the engineer's methodical reasoning. Had it been otherwise, Presstman was the breed of principled, concerned citizen who would have helped restore Alexandria during the difficult Reconstruction that lay ahead.

CHAPTER ELEVEN

FLOWER OF THE SOUTH
✵✵✵ RANDOLPH FAIRFAX

UNLIKE THE TRAGIC DEMISE OF WILSON PRESSTMAN, WHICH received scant notice, Randolph Fairfax's death in combat in December 1862 generated an outpouring of grief from those who had known him during a life of twenty years and twenty days. In a letter to the family, extraordinary in light of the junior grade of the deceased, Gen. Robert E. Lee expressed his personal sorrow: "I have grieved most deeply at the death of your noble son." J. E. B. Stuart declared, "It is very desirable to place the example of Private Randolph Fairfax before every soldier in the army ... How invincible would an army of such men be!—men who never murmur and who never flinch!" A cousin remembered Randolph as "this youth, handsome and gifted, serious and purposeful beyond his years, the flower of his school and college, in all things worthy the traditions of his warlike ancestry." Countless wellborn young men perished in the national conflagration, yet, to many, this native of Alexandria symbolized the flower of the South that was sacrificed in a cause its proponents considered the second American Revolution. Who was this Byronic figure whose passing evoked such emotion?[1]

Randolph Fairfax was descended from a long line of nobility. His father, Orlando, a renowned and beloved physician in antebellum Alexandria, was the third son of Thomas, the ninth Lord Fairfax. The British Parliament conveyed the title to their forefather, Rev. Bryan Fairfax, even though he was an American citizen. The youth's mother was a daughter of two distinguished Virginia families, her parents being Jefferson Cary and Virginia Randolph. As a girl, young Randolph's great-aunt sang melodies at the request of George Washington. One uncle, a captain of volunteers, died of exhaustion while marching with the American army through Mexico; another uncle served as an officer in both the

United States and Confederate navies. An Alexandria doyen in a later time observed that their "mansion was one of the social and cultural centers of the town; the Fairfaxes were the important noble family of the 'upper reaches of the Potomac.' They intermarried with the Carlyles, Washingtons, Herberts, and Carys. Their contribution to Alexandria cannot be overrated, for in their personal lives and public service, they set an example of chivalry and courage."[2] The importance of his lineage was not lost on the heir to this eminence. When a politician complimented his surname, the boy was said to have replied, "It is the name of my ancestors; and if they have made it famous, I at least will try to do nothing to impair its brightness."[3]

The family home, just east of Washington Street, was a magnificent example of Federal architecture. A brick, three-story mansion in the Georgian style, Fairfax House faced onto Cameron Street with semicircular front steps and a walled garden. It was here that Randolph was born on November 23, 1842, one of nine children.[4]

Throughout his brief life, the concept of beauty was repeatedly used to describe both Randolph's physical appearance and his spiritual self.

> From his infancy he was remarkable for an almost womanly beauty. His eyes were hazel and his hair of a golden brown, his features regular and his complexion brilliant. These soft beauties as he grew in stature were developed into a manly form, which, though not tall, was distinguished for a noble and graceful bearing. His outward form was the fair index of inward purity. Even in his childhood there was an absence of the waywardness and fits of passion which generally characterize that age. From his earliest years it was said of him by those who knew him best, "Randolph is actuated by a desire to do his duty; his conduct seems to be governed by principle."[5]

Gentle temperament, graceful demeanor, and conscientious comportment characterized Randolph's personality. His first instructor was the famed Alexandria educator, Benjamin Hallowell, who described his pupil as "a little gentleman."[6] When next entering Episcopal High School, Randolph took honors in every class.[7] During this time, he was confirmed at St. Paul's Episcopal Church. A lieutenant in Kemper's Brigade later recalled, "My acquaintance with Randolph Fairfax commenced at the High School, in the fall of 1857, where his modest manners and unselfish disposition endeared him to all around him."[8] The school's principal, Rev. J. P. McGuire, provided an exceptionally glowing testament:

> As a pupil in the High School, as a student, a Christian, there was a uniform consistency—making one day of singular excellence but the representative of all the rest, and giving to the whole a completeness rarely equalled in its strength and loveliness. Intellectually he was undoubtedly

one of the first young men of his day. His mind was strong and clear, understanding promptly and thoroughly whatever he studied. A first-rate student, he acquired knowledge rapidly and accurately, promising real success and high rank in whatever department of intellectual labor he might select. Morally, I have not known his superior . . . However retiring and unassuming in his general bearing, he was, nevertheless, constitutionally brave; richly gifted with that moral courage, the want of which is often the great defect of men of genius and even of gallant soldiers. Not the slightest timidity was there; no hesitancy or avoiding of responsibility where duty was concerned.[9]

Randolph studied for a year with William Dinwiddie at his academy in Albemarle County before matriculating to the University of Virginia in October 1860. Randolph's record there conformed to his earlier academic success, as he earned distinction in mathematics, Latin, and French. In addition, he was active in the student Christian Association, a Bible study class, prayer meetings, and a mission station.[10] Randolph's mental and spiritual development soon fell under the shadow of the political storm engulfing the country. One professor reported even the oldest and wisest students being "carried away" by this "secession *feeling*."[11] Immersed in this groundswell of Southern patriotism, the impressionable student enlisted in a militia company in nearby Lynchburg. When the "Southern Guard" marched off to Harpers Ferry, however, Private Fairfax remained in Charlottesville in deference to his parents' wishes. Their apprehension did not preclude his participation in a six-week camp of military instruction conducted on the university grounds during the early summer.[12]

The clash at Bull Run ignited another surge of nationalism throughout Virginia, and this time Fairfax would not be denied. Nursing wounded combatants carried back to the campus did not satisfy him. On a hot, dusty day, Fairfax began the journey by rail to Manassas Junction, where on August 10 he enlisted in the artillery unit from Rockbridge County to the west of Charlottesville. The Rockbridge battery was attractive to refined young men from well-to-do families. First Company boasted of having on its rolls four masters of arts, twenty graduates of Washington College in Lexington, and at least forty students enrolled at that institution or at the University of Virginia.[13] Parents were reassured that their sons were being led by William N. Pendleton, a pastor in Lexington and the first principal of Episcopal High School. Pendleton had been promoted out of command, however, by the time Fairfax arrived, and the company reorganized with William McLaughlin as its captain. The battery was bivouacked at Camp Harman in a grove of oak trees just north of Centreville. Recurring false alarms that the Federals were advancing precipitated orders to march to Fairfax Court House that

Randolph Fairfax in a Confederate private's uniform. Museum of the
Confederacy, Richmond, Virginia.

were, in each instance, eventually countermanded. Artillerists engaged
in two-a-day drills on six guns—a twelve-pounder howitzer, two ten-
pounder Parrotts captured from the Yankees at Bull Run, and three six-
pounders, also trophies of war.

It was at Centreville that Fairfax began a series of letters to family
members that are the best extant insights into his personality. His glowing portrayal by others, drawn in the ornate style of the nineteenth century, is brought to earth by these firsthand documents. A contemporary
memorial to slain alumni of the University of Virginia credits the correspondence as displaying "a vein of strong common sense unusual in one
so young, and . . . [of such] uncommon sagacity."[14] In his letters, one
encounters a sensitive young man discovering the harsh realities of soldiering and learning that military life is only made bearable by friendships with comrades in arms. As a physician's son, the commentator
made note of his own state of health, which was invariably excellent.
The letters show Fairfax repulsed by senseless vandalism in the wake of
an invading army, longing for the homemade food and clothing taken
for granted during his formative years, and comforted by encouragement from the pulpit, fellowship with a former schoolmate, and support
expressed by someone from home.

At Centreville, Fairfax once again received spiritual reassurance
from the messages of familiar clergymen, Bishop John Johns and Rev.
Cornelius Walker. He was also afforded an opportunity to enjoy the company of old friends in the Seventeenth Virginia and chums from Charlottesville. A University of Virginia graduate, Lt. Douglas Forrest, assigned
to the regiment, was among those visited by the youth.[15]

On September 16, the battery relocated to the vicinity of Fairfax Court
House. It was here that Fairfax first began hearing the sounds of war
—skirmishing between pickets and firing of cannon. He also observed
the desolation caused by fighting. Imagining the changes taking place
in his hometown, Fairfax despaired, "Poor old Alexandria, I am afraid
it is done for. I'm afraid she will never raise her head again."[16] Once more,
however, there was a familiar face from his hometown to reassure him.
David Funsten, an Alexandria attorney serving as a lieutenant colonel in
the Eleventh Virginia, invited the raw recruit to dine with him.

Life in uniform did not appear so bad at this point. In response to his
requests, a stream of packages brought comforts from home that were
otherwise only available at the sutler's wagon at outrageous prices—an
overcoat, pies and cakes, even sweet potatoes. The weather was mild and
dry. The private slept on a frame eighteen inches above the ground in a
Crimean tent with five comrades. He bragged that "we are much more
healthy & as comfortable as we could wish" and "healthier than those

who do not lead as active lives." Fairfax was perfectly willing to rely upon
"our Generals—all we can do is to trust implicitly in them." In his innocence, he was content with his lot.

> I think I can sincerely say that I have not the least desire to be an officer,
> as long as I remain as agreeably situated as at present. With the exception
> of the pay, which perhaps is a considerable item, I believe my present situ-
> ation is the more desirable of the two. I have none of the cares & responsi-
> bilities of an officer, have as agreeable companions as I have ever had at
> school & college. The additional honor is very little, in my opinion, as my
> experience has shown me that epaulets are by no means criterions of
> merit. Now an artillery officer has a horse to ride, that I confess is a con-
> siderable advantage.[17]

Fairfax wrote home for personal toiletries and asked, especially, for
books and magazines. In an outfit with a disproportionate share of former students, Fairfax noted, "Reading is our chief amusement in camp &
books of all sorts are in demand."[18] Time was growing short to enjoy
them, however. The Confederates pulled back permanently from Fairfax
to Centreville in mid-October. At the end of the month, the Rockbridge
Artillery participated in a grand review before Generals Joseph E.
Johnston and P. G. T. Beauregard, at which Gov. John Letcher presented
Virginia flags to the state's regiments. On November 4, Maj. Gen.
Thomas J. Jackson was assigned command of the Valley District and delivered a stirring farewell to the "Stonewall Brigade" before galloping off
the parade grounds. Three days later, Captain McLaughlin was ordered
to proceed with Jackson's former troops to join him in the Shenandoah
Valley, his battery thereby acquiring the sobriquet of the "Stonewall
Artillery."[19]

The march to Winchester provided Fairfax with another dimension
of soldier life. The unit covered twenty-five miles during an eleven-
hour trek before stopping for the night at an old barn near a distillery.
Sleeping was futile, however, as the men found some whiskey and were
boisterous until dawn. The next day, the company struggled over the
Blue Ridge in a drenching rain, with the drivers drunk and the horses
exhausted.[20] The young enlistee complained, "It was certainly the most
disagreeable experience of war that I have yet had and I could hardly
realize that this was the same battery that Johnston had called the best in
his army."[21] But Fairfax had not yet known winter in the field or been
tested under fire.

Early in December, a section of four guns was sent to support Col.
Turner Ashby's cavalry near Martinsburg. Fairfax regretted that his piece
was not included, as the ensuing contest was the only one the battery had
been engaged in since he joined. "I am not, 'spoiling for a fight,' in fact,

I don't know a more peacefully disposed set of men, than soldiers are generally, but if there is fighting to be done, I should like to be there and I shouldn't like to go through the war without seeing a live Yankee."[22] Again, the neophyte was tempting fate. Instead, he had to be content with contriving an invitation for dinner at a home where Mildred Lee would be present. The youngest daughter of Virginia's illustrious general was attending a school with rules prohibiting gentleman callers, so it was necessary for Fairfax to use his wiles to see Mildred and talk about old times and mutual friends.

As 1862 opened, Jackson began a campaign to drive the Federals out of western Virginia and interdict the Baltimore and Ohio Railroad and Chesapeake and Ohio Canal. New Year's Day was sunny and balmy, so warm that the men marching out of Winchester in their woolen uniforms and coats complained about the heat. By late afternoon, however, the wind had picked up and the temperature dropped. After covering sixteen miles, the soldiers of the Rockbridge artillery slept as best they could on the frozen ground without tents. The weather continued excessively cold, and each successive day the distance traveled diminished. By the time the column reached Bath on January 4, snow covered the earth and the chill was intense.[23]

The Southerners easily pushed the Federals out of Bath. A band of artillerymen broke into a Yankee sutler's store and helped themselves to merchandise. Fairfax wrote that the pipes, tobacco, and cigars offered no appeal to him and denied taking anything, which is interesting in light of a later declaration that he owned some pipes.[24] Following the bluecoats to the Potomac, the Rockbridge battery set up on a hill overlooking Hancock on the opposite bank and began bombarding the village and engaging the enemy's guns. Fairfax worried, "It seemed to me very barbarous to be firing away indiscriminately at the town."[25] In addition to his first exposure to fire, Fairfax obtained a glimpse of the disparity between the logistics supporting the two sides: "Right opposite Hancock there was a deserted Yankee encampment, and I tell you they must have been fixed up nicely. Their tents were improved Sibley's of the best material and each one had a stove in it & every appliance for comfort. Besides this, we took a large warehouse full of Yankee Quarter-Master supplies, but these were disposed of by our Quarter Master."[26]

Despite superior numbers, Jackson's force was unable to dislodge its adversaries and began to withdraw on the afternoon of January 6. The horses' shoes had worn smooth on the trek northward, and the roads were slick with snow. Consequently, the men had to help drag the guns and caissons up every hill and steady the heavy carriages going down the reverse slopes. Horses fell and had to be assisted to their feet.[27] By the time the Rockbridge Artillery caught up with its baggage two days later, Fairfax's enthusiasm for a soldier's life was sorely lagging. "During this trip my patriotism has at times been put to very severe tests," he admitted to his mother, "& I am sorry to say has sometimes been at a very low ebb."[28]

When Jackson learned that the Yankees had evacuated Romney, he led his troops there, arriving on January 15. Again, the soldiers suffered along the way, as the ground had thawed and the caravan trudged along soft, slushy roads. After ten days of sleeping in a Methodist church, where the men were infested with vermin, the Rockbridge battery was finally ordered back to Winchester. On January 29, it moved into winter quarters at Camp Zollicoffer, four miles northwest of the town, and remained there until March.[29]

Fairfax's perceptions were, once again, somewhat different than might be expected. While acknowledging "the horribly disagreeable weather," he assured his mother that newspaper accounts of the army's suffering were exaggerated. His concerns were directed at the soldier's plight. "Really it seems to me that every obstacle is thrown in the way of the enjoyment of the poor private and the few privileges they have seem to be surrounded with every possible difficulty." The hurdles to be cleared in obtaining a pass made a jaunt into Winchester seem almost impossible. Yet he did not intend to quit military service when his enlistment expired, for several chums were trying "to get up a select artillery company to enlist for two years and to be made up of as many nice fellows from this Company as we can get." "The great object to be secured in a company," Fairfax acknowledged, "is congenial companions."[30]

On February 7, he was off to Richmond with thirty members of his unit after receiving a furlough of thirty-four days and a fifty-dollar bounty for extending his military obligation by two years.[31] Dr. and Mrs. Fairfax joyfully welcomed home a student in the science of warfare. They were now living in the Clifton House, a tired old structure where the physician had taken refuge as he attempted to rebuild a practice disrupted by the hostilities.[32]

When the soldier returned by stagecoach to military duty on March 14, his unit had moved to Cedar Creek, near Strasburg. The respite had restored his vision of the harshness of military life in the field.

> Well, I am at last back at camp, and the idea is not very pleasant, I tell you. I feel like I had just passed from the regions of civilization to those of barbarism. As soon as I got into camp I was surrounded by a crowd of dirty looking men, and a corresponding number of not very clean paws were extended to me to shake. I could hardly realize that these men were my former companions at college, and that I once looked as dirty and rough as any of them. I believe my furlough has merely had the effect of making me appreciate still more the blessings of home and friends.[33]

More recruits were now joining the unit, among them the youngest son of Gen. Robert E. Lee, an acquaintance from Alexandria. Two eight-pounder iron rifles, manufactured by the Tredegar works in Richmond, were added to the battery's inventory as well, bringing the totals to 225 men present and eight field pieces.

On March 23, the company began moving northward, leaving the valley pike about four miles below Winchester, near Kernstown, and turning to the west. Soldiers entering battle for the first time eased their consciences by throwing away decks of cards and taking Bibles out of their pockets. Under fire from the enemy's rifled artillery, the battery marched in column across a meadow and into position on a hill commanding the old valley road. As the men reached the crest, a well-directed shell passed through one of the wheel horses and into another animal, where it exploded, tearing off a driver's leg.[34] "It was a horrible sight to see the mangled horses and men, lying helpless on the ground," Fairfax recounted, sobered by his initial exposure to combat.[35]

In midafternoon, a section with four pieces, including Fairfax's gun, was ordered farther to the left to protect the flank. Before long, enemy regiments were pressing all along the line and Southern infantry began falling back. The rebels fired two rounds of canister into the bluecoats emerging from the woods on their left, amid growing concern about being cut off from the main body. The guns were ordered to withdraw, but, according to Fairfax, the scared new recruits serving as drivers took longer than usual to limber up, resulting in two men and a pair of horses being hit by incoming rounds. When the section struggled down into a hollow, one of the wounded horses died, leaving the gun stranded. Fearful of being trapped, the lieutenant ordered the men to take the remaining horses out of the traces and ride to safety as best they could. Fairfax escaped with a bullet hole through the skirt of his coat. "I hated mightily to leave our old piece," he lamented. "It was one taken at Manassas & one of the best of our six pounders." The brass gun was once again U.S. government property.[36]

The young Alexandrian suffered additional loss the next day. As Jackson's force retreated up the valley, the Rockbridge Artillery stopped at Cedar Creek to prepare dinner. Before the Virginians finished eating, Yankees appeared on the nearby hills, causing a scramble to pack up and move out before coming under fire. In the confusion, Fairfax was separated from his haversack with a pistol and ammunition, Bible, and toilet case. A dejected but wiser soldier lamented, "I have come to the conclusion that it is useless to provide yourself with little luxuries of civilized life in camp; for sure as you do you will lose them, or have them stolen."[37]

In many respects, Fairfax's letters from the valley are representative of the patriotism, optimism, and rumor found in writings by other Southern soldiers throughout the war. "We could have whipped them, if we had had but 3 regiments more," is a typical complaint from Fairfax. Initial reports of Confederate victories far away were later found to be false, but subsequent letters fail to mention the actual outcome. Here is what Fairfax first heard of the encounter at Shiloh: "Grant's army routed. Buell killed and his army defeated." The correspondent goes on to observe, "I hear that our fight of Kernstown is considered rather in the light of a victory in Richmond," when he knew it to have been a defeat for Southern forces. Conversely, Fairfax expressed indignation at what he considered "the greatest pack of lies," deceitful characterizations of battles being reported in the Northern press. "But no correct estimate of their [the Federals'] loss can be formed as they are so well provided with ambulances that they were able to carry off all their wounded, and probably some of their dead to hide them afterwards in the mountains." Fairfax was continuing to recognize the enemy's considerable advantage in resources: "of all kinds of fighting, artillery duels, though not the most dangerous, are I think the most disagreeable, especially when the enemy has so much better guns and ammunition. Besides nothing is gained by it, but possibly the killing of a few men."[38]

As the month of March wound to a close, Jackson withdrew up the valley in a series of short moves. In mid-April, a lull in the fighting permitted the Rockbridge Artillery to reorganize into a battalion with three companies. Fairfax's unit was reduced to 150 men, with priority given to soldiers who had already reenlisted. Many of the new recruits were forced into other organizations. With the loss of Fairfax's gun and another disabled at Kernstown, his company was once again servicing six barrels. In accordance with an act of the Confederate Congress, an election of company officers took place, and Lt. William T. Poague was selected as commander.

At the end of April, Jackson began moving northward once again, determined to drive the Yankees from the Shenandoah Valley. Spring rains produced mud as deep as thirty inches, causing the men to work hard to keep the guns, caissons, and wagons from becoming bogged down. When the opposing sides clashed at McDowell on May 8, no good position could be found for the Southern field pieces, so the Rockbridge unit was ordered back into camp. The artillery company crossed the mountain the following morning, passing dead soldiers lying on either side of the road. Catching up with the retreating Federals at Franklin several days later, two Parrotts engaged them in a skirmish before the unit resumed its march.[39]

The Rockbridge Artillery had been constantly on the move for over two weeks when Fairfax wrote to "Pa" boasting of its toughness. "I believe we have gradually arrived at the condition of veterans. We have no tents, carry our knapsacks & blankets, never ride on caissons, as we used to, obey orders implicitly, without enquiring the why or wherefore, and in case of necessity can live on half rations and not think it anything remarkable."[40] In the same letter, the young soldier repeated a commonly held explanation for the South's suffering that he had heard in a sermon.

"Dr. Dabneys view of the war was, that it was a visitation upon us for our sins and that it would not cease until the purposes of God were accomplished in it; i.e. until our people repent and turn to Him."[41]

The marching was far from over. Continuing down the valley, Jackson routed the Federals at Front Royal on May 23, although Fairfax's battery was not involved. Two days later, the unit participated in the battle at Winchester. The artillerymen were subjected to fire from enemy field pieces and sharpshooters arrayed behind a stone wall. The fighting raged for more than two hours before the Yankees fled, pursued by their opponents. For the first time, Fairfax reveled in the glory of victory: "Our passage through Winchester was perfectly glorious. The pavements were crowded with women & children & old men waving their handkerchiefs and weeping for joy and shouting to us as we passed by at a double quick."[42]

The cost of conquest was high, however. The Rockbridge company suffered its heaviest casualties of the campaign, losing twenty-one soldiers killed and wounded. Fairfax mourned the death of his Charlottesville chum, "Poor Bob McKim." He acknowledged, though, "It was only through the blessing of God, that more of us were not hurt."[43] "We are now completely broken down with fatigue. After marching for 30 days with only 4 days rest, and getting only 5 hours sleep at night, we made a forced march of 25 miles from Luray to Front Royal, and from there we marched all day yesterday & all last night, without the least rest, fought a battle this morning, and pursued the enemy, 5 miles."[44]

Despite his troops' fatigue, Jackson was not finished maneuvering. From Winchester he marched to Charlestown and skirmished near Harpers Ferry before heading back up the valley through Strasburg to Port Republic, where on June 7 the Rockbridge Artillery camped about a mile north of town. Fairfax had time to write a long letter to his sister Jenny. In his account of the past five weeks, he made special mention of capturing baggage trains abandoned by the Yankees. Fairfax recounted his delight in gathering as many ginger cakes as possible, along with some sticks of delicious cream chocolate. Despite the uniform on his back, he was still a boy at heart: "If you only knew how completely like a child a soldier is, in his eagerness for sweet things you might perhaps form some idea of the promiscuous scramble that ensued upon the discovery of anything good to eat. . . . Just to think of those Yankees having access to all these luxuries, good clothes and every convenience that can be devised and then complaining of the hardships of war."[45]

The following day was a Sunday, and the soldiers looked forward to a respite from the marching and fighting. They were astounded, therefore, to hear the roar of cannon coming from Port Republic. The Rockbridge company was immediately sent forward. Jackson personally placed one gun, which drove the enemy off a bridge and away from the river, and now-Captain Poague's other four field pieces were set up on a hill commanding Port Republic. From this vantage point, Fairfax's gun and other rebel artillery were able to disrupt a Federal column proceeding toward the front.[46] The young Alexandrian was pleased to have the advantage for once. "Our position was such that they could not bring any cannon to bear upon us, so that all the firing was on our side, a kind of fighting which we all agreed was decidedly the most pleasant we had ever tried."[47]

The next day, the unit was ordered to support the offensive of the Stonewall Brigade. The battery unlimbered in a field, where Fairfax and his comrades could see and hear balls cutting through the wheat on every side. Yet they escaped injury.[48] The cannoneers engaged in a hot exchange with enemy infantry and artillery until exhausting their ammunition and withdrawing. One brass six-pounder was lost during the repositioning. Three guns again moved forward late in the contest and assisted in dislodging the defenders.[49]

The rigors of Jackson's Valley Campaign had gradually worn down the unit from Rockbridge County. Of the 150 men on the rolls at the time of the reorganization, barely 70 were present for duty after the engagement at Port Republic. The vent pieces of the ten-pounders had burned out from frequent use, and the two Parrotts had been sent to Richmond for repair. Another piece was unfit, and a fourth had been captured by the Federals, leaving only two guns in service, a twelve-pounder and the six-pounder manned by Fairfax's detachment. Consequently, the company was sent to Staunton to rest, refit, and recruit. No sooner had it arrived, however, then orders were received to accompany Jackson eastward toward Richmond, their final destination known only to the eccentric commander. Fairfax was pleased to receive permission to stop along the way in Charlottesville and spend a pleasant evening with friends at the university.[50]

As he approached one full year of campaigning, a new strain began to appear in Fairfax's commentaries. As a raw recruit, he had relied entirely on the judgment of his superiors; however, the more seasoned soldier now began to second-guess decisions made on the battlefield. After the fighting at Port Republic, he questioned whether the advance had not been made too soon. Fairfax attributed his army's successful extraction from the field of combat in the face of greater numbers to the good fortune of finding an old mountain logging road. Now confident to comment on tactics, he told his mother, "No general I think ought ever to go into battle without providing a means of retreat in case of defeat." The one figure who retained his undying confidence, however, was Jackson. The stern Presbyterian had arranged for communion to be offered to troops in the field. Fairfax glowed with praise. "It is such a comfort and I think a great cause for thankfulness to have such a Christian man as Jackson for our general."[51]

Jackson's command joined Southern forces, now under Lee's leadership, deployed in defense of Richmond. The Rockbridge Artillery was held in reserve until July 1, when Poague's unit was ordered to a position in a wheat field near Malvern Hill. The firing was intense, and Fairfax was wounded. "For about an hour we were exposed to the hottest artillery fire I ever saw. Shell & shot seemed to pour over us in one incessant stream and burst right in our midst. We lost 2 killed & some 10 or 12 wounded most of them slightly. I was struck by a piece of shell on the collar bone but fortunately received from it only a bruise which put me on the disabled list yesterday. It was only through God's mercy that our loss was not greater."[52]

The shell fragment was nearly spent when it struck Fairfax. He did not try to use the injury as an excuse to be relieved from duty, although the thought occurred to him. Reporting the wound to his mother on July 3, he acknowledged wishing it would send him home. The following day, the Stonewall Artillery marched through Richmond and pitched camp a few miles outside the city. Fairfax's hopes were realized when he and a comrade were granted three days' leave. The Alexandrian found his parents now living on Franklin Street, "in a delightful situation," and enjoyed his time with them. "[I] was only sorry I could not 'get up a sick,' myself & remain at home, a few days longer."[53] When he returned to duty, the Rockbridge unit was still bivouacked outside the capital, but, over the next several weeks, it moved north in a series of marches.

Fairfax's service with an outfit organized far from Alexandria did not cause him to forget his old childhood chums, many of them members of the regiment raised in his hometown. The Seventeenth Virginia Regiment had been on Fairfax's mind throughout the spring fighting. In late May, he told his sister Jenny of hearing from a messmate that Cousin Carlyle Fairfax and Willie Fowle, son of the prominent businessman, were listed among the wounded in the Seventeenth Virginia during the fighting around Richmond. Fairfax asked his brother Bert to convey his love to his injured relative and send word of any other friends in the army defending the capital. In turn, Fairfax reported that, to his knowledge, the only casualty among their acquaintances in Jackson's army was Arthur Arnold, son of the Alexandria hatter and a fellow student at the university, now serving as a lieutenant in the Fifth Virginia. After the Seven Days battles, he was concerned once more. Word reached Fairfax that the Seventeenth Virginia had "suffered severely" and that among the Alexandrians lost as prisoners were a couple of friends and Lt. Col. Morton Marye.[54]

On August 7, Fairfax wrote another reflective letter to his mother. He renewed a dialogue with her concerning the likelihood of England declaring itself on the contest in America. Fairfax referred to the debate in Parliament and Lord Palmerston's stated position before concluding that the British would be "bullied" by the Yankee government not to support the Confederacy. The son also replied to his mother's suggestion that he transfer to a staff assignment. "I some times feel very much discontented with my position of private and have often thought of making some endeavor to better it, but I believe I have at last come to the conclusion that it is better for me to remain as I am. I don't think I would feel right, in accepting a position which would take [me] out of active service."[55] The young man's maturity belied his nineteen years, although time was running out on his fatal commitment to serve his new country on the front lines.

The next engagement for the Rockbridge Artillery occurred in early August at Cedar Mountain, where the brigade commander, Brig. Gen. Charles Sidney Winder, was mortally wounded while standing near one of the battery's guns, talking to the cannoneer, and looking through a spyglass.[56] Fairfax's crew was not involved in this battle due to the short range of their six-pounder. The Rockbridge men subsequently maneuvered with Jackson's troops in the foothills of central Virginia, eventually arriving at Manassas Junction. His unit's tactics and the timing of its mission to disperse a Yankee brigade headed for the second major engagement in that locale drew criticism once again from the now-judgmental private. "This affair was managed badly by our Generals if I may presume to criticise." Fairfax was enthusiastic about the outcome on August 29, however. "We had a splendid view of the battle, from a hill where our battery was in position. It was the grandest sight I ever saw."[57]

Fairfax raved that "nothing but the excitement and exhilaration of our unwonted success kept us up" in the Manassas campaign, in spite of the long marches and shortage of sleep.[58] That enthusiasm continued as the Army of Northern Virginia crossed the Potomac during the first week of September.[59] To the Southerners, many ragged and barefoot, Maryland's rich farms and well-stocked stores seemed like paradise. "We all think it a land of plenty," Fairfax wrote to his homefolks, "and since reaching Frederick City have been feasting on the productions of Yankee confectioners & providing ourselves with clothes etc. My only drawback in fitting myself out, is the want of money, which I don't see any chance of getting until they pay us off."[60] The fact that Fairfax was buying and not pillaging says a great deal about his self-control, as well as about his unit's discipline. The invading army was on its best behavior as Confederate generals were intent on converting Marylanders to their cause.

The cannoneers were not in the Free State for long, for they waded back across the Potomac at Williamsport when Jackson's corps was sent to capture Harpers Ferry on September 11. The company camped west of Martinsburg. The next day, Fairfax's gun, under command of Lt. John Baxter McCorkle, accompanied Maj. Gen. J. E. B. Stuart's cavalry and the

Tenth Virginia to burn a railroad bridge ten miles away near North Mountain Station. Hearing that Yankees were in some woods nearby, the six-pounder went forward to fire twenty or so rounds into the trees. The rebels were disappointed to find no sign of the enemy. They proceeded to tear up the track but retreated to Martinsburg when a large Federal force was reported to be advancing toward them.[61]

McCorkle's detail remained as provost guard in western Virginia when the remainder of the Rockbridge Artillery returned to Maryland and was placed in position near the Dunkard Church outside Sharpsburg. Fairfax therefore missed the ensuing battle at Antietam Creek, although he heard cannonading from that direction early on the morning of September 17. Despite a growing skepticism, he believed the boasts that his comrades had won a great victory.

The Southern army paused to recover and regroup. The battery was reunited at a camp near Bunker Hill outside Winchester. With the arrival of October, the Rockbridge unit was transferred from the First Brigade to Col. Thompson Brown's reserve artillery regiment of Jackson's Corps. "We are all sorry to part with old friends and break off connexions which have existed since the beginning of the war," Fairfax wrote.[62] He was pleased, however, with receipt of ordnance captured at Harpers Ferry. The battery was now armed with two ten-pounder Parrotts and two twenty-pounders, one of which was to be served by Fairfax.

With winter approaching, Fairfax's thoughts naturally turned to how best to prepare for cold weather. Tending first to immediate needs, he acquired the overcoat of a man who had been wounded and was no longer with the army, as his own garment had been lost when the unit baggage was left at the Rapidan River.[63] The idea of being detailed out of the field had not died. Campaigning was slowly wearing down the well-intentioned volunteer, and he was succumbing to the promise of an easier existence in service to his country. He confided his thoughts to "Dear Mama."

> You seem to be very anxious for me to get detailed this winter. I would very gladly accept a position bettering my present condition for the winter, if I could get one. But unfortunately all details from the ranks have been stopped, and though I entertained some hopes of getting a position in the Ordinance [sic] Dept through the examinations that are held for the purpose, there seem to be so many candidates, and only 70 to be appointed, that I am disposed to give that up too. Besides my age would exclude me from a commission.[64]

Another possibility was the signal corps, which seemed especially appealing. Fairfax figured that it was not as arduous or dangerous as the artillery, and its soldiers traveled by horse, remained with their baggage, rarely came under fire, and received extra pay of seventy-five cents a day.

His sister, Jenny, was working on a reassignment and had consulted with Lt. Lewis Randolph, a chum from the university and a staff officer in the First Virginia Battalion who was himself awaiting orders to be transferred to the corps. Fairfax advised that Captain Poague would not consent to losing anyone from his company, so the decision would have to be made at higher headquarters. The thought of leaving his companions in the Rockbridge unit did not seem as disloyal as it once had, for "Bob Lee" had just received an appointment as lieutenant of cavalry on the staff of his brother, "Rooney." Fairfax was not resentful. On the contrary, he lauded the general's youngest son as "a capital soldier" who deserved the commission as much as anyone.[65]

In November, Poague's company accompanied Jackson eastward on a fourteen-day march to the Rappahannock River. The unit camped above Port Royal, upriver from Fredericksburg, in woods a half mile from the water. The battery's mission was to employ its twenty-pounders against Federal gunboats cruising the river. The Confederates planned to set up an ambush along the banks and drive a combatant into it. They fired some rounds but failed to trap a vessel. "The whole thing was a perfect farce," Fairfax concluded with disgust.[66]

The cold was now intense, and Fairfax worried about the suffering of soldiers less warmly clad than he was. On December 7, he wrote to his mother, "O how I wish this cruel war would cease! I think when peace is declared, I shall feel somewhat like a man just released from prison or perhaps a condemned criminal just receiving his pardon."[67] For Fairfax, the fighting was about to end.

On Friday evening, December 12, Poague received orders from Colonel Brown to bring his battery immediately to Fredericksburg, as the Yankees were crossing the Rappahannock. Using a local guide, the men covered the distance overnight, earning special praise from Jackson. The next morning, the corps artillery was ordered to a ridge on the far right of Jackson's line near the Hamilton House. About 2:00, Brown sent Poague's two twenty-pounders to relieve another unit short of men and ammunition. The Rockbridge guns were entangled in a heated artillery duel while at the same time engaging the enemy infantry. Maj. John Pelham of Stuart's Horse Artillery remarked to Lt. Archibald Graham, the section commander, "Your men stand killing better than any I know."[68]

Berkeley Minor, one of Fairfax's closest friends and his mate in serving the Parrott, remembered that after about two hours Jackson rode up and ordered all the guns to fire simultaneously, as fast as possible. This barrage quickly drew a response from enemy cannon. After the exchange of rounds all day, the exact distance of the hill occupied by Jackson's pieces from the Yankee artillery was known to both sides. "Such a shower of shot and shell I never saw before and hope never to see again," Minor later exclaimed.[69] The intensity of the incoming rounds soon became so heavy that, near dusk, Lt. Col. Lewis Minor Coleman, the battalion's second in command and a former Latin professor at the University of Virginia, rode up and directed Poague to cease firing and take cover.[70]

Shortly afterward, an incoming shell exploded, fragments striking Fairfax in the forehead and fatally wounding Coleman and another private. A piece of iron entered the corner of Fairfax's left eye, killing him instantly. A few minutes later, Lieutenant McCorkle died near the same gun. Minor and Thomas McCorkle, another artilleryman serving the twenty-pounder, carried the Alexandrian's body off the field. Fairfax was buried with the young officer by their weeping comrades not far from where they fell.[71] Captain Poague later referred to the casualties as "two of the finest soldiers in the battery." He added, "If I were expected to select representatives of the two types of men composing our battery, I would name Fairfax and McCorkle—the former the cavalier element, the latter the Scotch Irish—each the perfect flower of his type."[72]

On Fairfax's body was found a letter addressed to his mother, composed the day before he perished.

> Dear mama, Remembering your injunction to write immediately after every engagement in which I might be supposed to have taken part, I hasten to obey it, and relieve you all of any anxiety on my account that may have been occasioned by the news of the engagement yesterday at Fredericksburg. We were here at the time on picket within about 1 mile of Port Royal, and though at least 15 miles from Fredericksburg, we distinctly heard the cannonade. It was the most continuous & rapid I ever heard lasting almost without interruption from 4 o'clock A M, until sunset.[73]

On December 16, General Lee stopped at the camp of the Rockbridge Artillery and inquired about Fairfax.[74] His body was subsequently unearthed and, still wrapped in a soldier's blanket, taken to Richmond, where it was placed on a bier in front of the altar at St. James Church. A mourner recalled seeing a mark on the temple made by the piece of shell and the golden curls matted with clay from his crude grave. Fairfax still wore the coarse flannel shirt, stained with battle smoke, in which he fell. He might have been simply sleeping. Dr. Fairfax was asked if the body should be dressed and was reported to reply, "No. Let my son sleep his long sleep as he fell at the post of duty."[75] When the lamentation concluded, the remains were placed in a coffin draped with the Confederate flag and interred in the city's Hollywood Cemetery.

The number of condolences, the intensity of sorrow, characterizations of the deceased—taken together they paint a portrait of Randolph Fairfax as truly an extraordinary young man. A fellow member of the

Rockbridge company, Joseph Packard, observed that "it was in the bearing more than in the daring of the soldier's life that his lovely character displayed itself." Packard went on to state that Fairfax displayed no signs of selfishness and never tried to avoid the unpleasant duties of a soldier's life. The comrade in arms specifically pointed out that nine out of ten men would have used the wound Fairfax received at Malvern Hill as an excuse to leave the battlefield, but the Alexandrian stayed at his post and seemed to work harder than ever.[76]

In writing to Fairfax's father, Captain Poague went beyond the customary sympathies expected from a commanding officer.

> In simple justice to your son I desire to express my high appreciation of his noble character as a soldier, a Christian and a gentleman. Modest and courteous in his deportment, charitable and unselfish in his disposition, cheerful and conscientious in his performance of duty, upright and consistent in his walk and conversation, he was a universal favourite in the company and greatly beloved by his friends. I do not think I have ever known a young man whose life was so free from the frailties of human nature and whose character, in all its aspects, formed so faultless a model for the imitation of others.[77]

Young Bob Lee sounded these same notes when informing his mother of the death. "Poor Ranny Fairfax; he will be a great loss both to his parents, friends & to the world. For a young man of more promise as regards this world & the next, I don't think can be found anywhere."[78] Tributes to the deceased are loving by nature, but third-party communication is not always so glowing.

In a time of chivalry, Randolph Fairfax seemed to stand out as a role model. Against the background of lavish praise flowing from his passing in the flower of youth, with full potential yet to be realized, Fairfax is made more human by personal revelations to his mother in private correspondence. He began the war as an innocent who never murmured discontent, as J. E. B. Stuart saw him, but gradually began to distinguish good leadership from bad and hard times from better possibilities. His joy at serving in uniform with peers who quickly became close friends was tempered by long months surviving in the field and under fire. Had he lived longer, like so many other enlistees and officers, Fairfax would have migrated, in all likelihood, to a softer assignment on a headquarters staff or with a support service. His noble principles and sentiments seem familiar, for they were recognized in a few of his peers as well. Where Fairfax seemed to rise above the others was in consistent adherence to these high ideals.

If the example of Randolph Fairfax inspired others to better their lives, he was someone to be remembered almost a century and a half later. A eulogy delivered at Christ Church in Alexandria in 1874 supports the conclusion that he was, indeed, a model for his generation, and, perhaps, for others.

> Among the stars that gild the night
> Of our deep humiliation,
> Young Randolph Fairfax lends his light
> To the lustrous constellation
> Of heroes, statesmen, saints and sages,
> Who will be known to after ages
> As the glorious Southern Cross.[79]

CHAPTER TWELVE

IMMIGRANT
✳✳✳ PATRICK O'GORMAN

AS THE 1860S UNFOLDED, THE IRISH WERE THE LARGEST ethnic group of the 1,246 foreign-born residents of Alexandria, as well as the most populous throughout the South.[1] Sons of Eire congregated on Sundays at St. Mary's Catholic Church, at quarterly meetings of the Hibernian Society, and, of course, in tumultuous celebrations each St. Patrick's Day.[2] Irish laborers gravitated to the city as a transportation hub that provided jobs working on the wharves and constructing the canal and railroads. When Virginia began to pull away from the Union, foreign-born members of work gangs were attracted to military service as a way of gaining greater acceptance in their new country.[3] Alexandria's militia battalion quickly added two companies of Irish Americans—the Irish Volunteers, an artillery battery organized on April 22, and the Emmett Guards, formed up on April 25. A third Irish unit, the O'Connell Guards, composed primarily of railroad workers, mustered into service on May 18.

As an immigrant, Patrick O'Gorman's military service represents a dimension of the Southern war effort that is underappreciated. The 1860 census reported 35,058 foreigners in Virginia, including 16,501 individuals born in Ireland and 10,512 from Germany. The greatest concentration of Germans was in Richmond, but Norfolk, Petersburg, and Lynchburg, in addition to Alexandria, had considerable numbers of German and Irish mechanics and laborers.[4] The Irish were drawn to military service by a zeal for Southern independence, pride in being a part of America, and a natural inclination to take part in any political agitation. The old cliché was "an Irishman loves a fight." Like other enlistees, the volunteer from Eire also exhibited an eagerness for adventure and a desire to join his fellows in the ranks. Once in uniform, they seemed to exhibit unusual devotion to a good leader, indifference to danger and discomfort, and a welcome cheer and wit.[5]

Interestingly, O'Gorman did not choose to go to war with his countrymen from the Old World, as most of the Irishmen in gray were inclined to do.[6] He served, instead, with the city's oldest military unit, the Alexandria Artillery. The other choices were not yet available to him when he enlisted, but there is no indication that he attempted to transfer once they coalesced. O'Gorman was on a track to becoming accepted as an American, without qualification, and restricting himself to immigrants would not have enhanced the new image he was striving to cultivate. O'Gorman spent the entire war with the Alexandria Artillery. The story of his service in uniform, therefore, is the history of their campaigning.

Patrick Francis O'Gorman was born in County Kilkenny, Ireland, in 1842. He was a Valentine's Day gift to his parents, Bridget Whitchew and Edward O'Gorman, who brought him to the New World in 1847. They first settled in Massachusetts and then, after two years, moved to Baltimore. In late 1850 the family relocated once again, this time to Alexandria County, outside the port city where Patrick's father worked as a laborer. The boy received some education there, quite possibly at the school for indigent children at St. Mary's, where Patrick would worship throughout his life. When he became of age, Patrick was indentured for four years as an apprentice cabinetmaker at Green's furniture factory on the southeast corner of Prince and Fairfax Streets. The young man was engaged in this craft as the national government began to unravel in 1861.

As a son of the Emerald Isle, O'Gorman was a natural-born storyteller, a trait that enhances the appeal of his journals. In recalling his entry into the military, he wrote:

> I did not know how the Mr. Greens stood in regards to the war, or whether they would consent to let me enlist or not, so one day, when Mr. John W. Green [the owner's son] came through the main shop where I was at work, I asked his permission to join the Alexandria Light Artillery, better known as Kempers Battery during the war. He did not answer me just then. He looked around at the men and boys who were all looking at me, then turned and went back to the office down stairs. I felt a little uneasy about the matter, as I thought I would have to go anyhow, but would like to have his consent. After a little while, Mr. Green came up again and standing near my bench, he looked around at the men and turning to me said, Pat, you have asked my permission to join the Artillery and I now give you my consent, and I am very glad there is one boy in our factory that is willing to fight for the South.[7]

O'Gorman's military records show that he enlisted on April 17, 1861, the day that the Richmond convention passed an ordinance of secession.[8] The next evening, the Alexandria Artillery met at the Friendship Fire Company and selected Delaware Kemper as its commanding officer. It was an inspired choice, as the candidate had no military experience other than serving as second lieutenant in a new militia company formed the previous December, known later as the Old Dominion Rifles.

What Kemper possessed was a fine reputation as an educator. He was born in Warrenton on August 24, 1833, and attended the University of Virginia, where his father was the proctor. Upon graduation, Kemper established a school for boys at Gordonsville. In 1858, he and his brother, William Kosciusko Kemper, came to Northern Virginia and took charge of the Alexandria Academy, succeeding Benjamin Hallowell.[9] The new commander's appearance reminded many Alexandrians of the South's current hero, the conqueror of Fort Sumter, Brig. Gen. P. G. T. Beauregard. Captain Kemper would command the city's artillery unit for little more than a year, but his stewardship was so extraordinary that the company would thereafter be referred to as Kemper's Battery.

Kemper's first impression of his new command was perceptive. He looked at the collection of volunteers and remarked, "Well, nearly all boys, but no matter, very often boys make the best soldiers."[10] The outfit needed ordnance and found some in a building at the corner of Columbus and Queen Streets. The city had borrowed four six-pounder brass cannon from the navy yard in the nation's capital to fire salutes on George Washington's birthday and had not returned them.[11] The company now appropriated the guns for its own purposes.

During the rest of April and into May, the new recruits began to learn close order drill and practice with the howitzers. The unit did not remain at home for long, however. Repeated rumors that the Federals were about to invade the city unnerved the militiamen to the point that the battery abandoned Alexandria on the evening of May 2. It was the last time O'Gorman and many of his mates would see their families until after the war. The company took the cars to Culpeper Court House, where they trained some more before moving to Manassas Junction on May 20. Over the next two months, the Alexandria Artillery was joined by a growing number of units from across the South. Once again, their regimen was interrupted repeatedly by long rolls of the drum announcing the approach of the enemy, which usually turned out to be false alarms.[12]

The battery's first engagement occurred on June 17, although the Irishman was not involved. According to O'Gorman, the men of Col. Maxcy Gregg's First South Carolina Infantry were embarrassed to return home at the end of their three-month enlistment without having fired their weapons. Gregg asked Kemper for help finding some Yankees.[13] A section of two howitzers accompanied the Carolinians to Vienna, where Federals had been reported. Late in the day a train appeared, carrying Ohio troops to repair and guard the Alexandria, Loudoun, and Hampshire Railroad. Kemper opened fire, scattering the soldiers and producing a dozen casualties. After burning six cars, the victors returned triumphant to Fairfax Court House.[14] O'Gorman dryly inventoried the spoils of war: "one prisoner, a wagon, an officer's sword, a lot of carpenters tools, blankets, guns, etc."[15]

Cannoneers and teamsters spent the next few weeks pulling guard duty and digging earthworks while awaiting the Yankees' response. It came on July 17, when the Federals advanced toward Falls Church. Kemper sent two guns to within a mile and a half of the aggressors before being ordered to fall back to Centreville. The Confederates alternately walked and ran; when the South Carolinians rested, Kemper's men lobbed shells at the pursuit. As night fell, the Southerners formed a line of battle, daring their tormentors to approach. With the repeated halts, it was almost daybreak before Brig. Gen. Milledge Bonham's command finally reached its destination and established itself at Mitchell's Ford across Bull Run.[16]

Two of the battery's guns stayed on high ground behind the stream with most of the South Carolina brigade. Kemper placed his other two six-pounders alongside two infantry companies on the east side and fired at the bluecoats when they approached later in the day. The Yankees, in turn, set up an artillery position beyond the range of Kemper's pieces and shelled the forward element, while the Federals' main thrust tested the mettle of Alexandria's Seventeenth Regiment and the other defenders at Blackburn's Ford, a half mile to the south. Kemper soon withdrew his men to safety, but late in the afternoon returned to fire five rounds at the enemy's infantry and cavalry, putting them to flight. "They ran like a flock of sheep," O'Gorman set down, although his gun was not involved.[17]

Three days later, on July 21, the principal engagement erupted. The Alexandria Artillery was left out of the action until afternoon, when it was ordered to join Col. Joseph B. Kershaw's South Carolinians as part of the reserve near the stone bridge over Bull Run. The Alexandrians were soon summoned again, this time to the Confederate field headquarters. Along with the Second and Eighth South Carolina, the cannoneers double-quicked to the Lewis House. O'Gorman recounted that his comrades were armed with long sabers to defend themselves at close quarters, but as the swords were heavy and clumsy to retain during the run, the troops dropped them by the wayside. "I was scared," he admitted, "and I thought to myself—oh, if I was only back in Old Alexandria, I would not ask Mr. Green for permission to join the Artillery. I felt ashamed of myself when this feeling came over me and looking around to see if anyone noticed it, I saw the other boys looked just like I felt."[18]

The reinforcements were directed to the left flank to support Confederates struggling to hold Henry Hill. As they moved behind the lines, the Alexandrians encountered scared and wounded men fleeing the battlefield. Most told the fresh troops to turn back, that the Southerners were being cut to pieces. O'Gorman stopped to listen to one bloody soldier who was trying to say something that could not be understood. He had a hole in the side of his face from a shell fragment that prevented him from speaking plainly. Frustrated, the wounded combatant at last put a hand to his cheek, covering the gap, and yelled out, "Go in boys. We are giving them Hell!"[19] The reassured artillerymen burst forth with lively cheering.

Kemper led his unit through heavy timber toward Sudley Road in thick smoke that disguised friend and foe. Riding out in front, the commander stumbled into a band of Yankees who briefly took him prisoner before they, in turn, encountered a party of rebels who freed the captain. At a gallop, the battery finally arrived at the fighting and unlimbered its guns. Kemper directed fire to the west, onto Chinn Hill, helping scatter the enemy's last organized initiative. In the process, his position was the objective of repeated attempts to capture the guns, but the Federal assaults were repulsed.

As their opponents dispersed, the weary defenders were urged to chase and destroy them. Kemper acquired a rifled Parrott taken from the enemy and joined the South Carolinians in pursuit. Crossing the stone bridge on the Warrenton Turnpike, the Alexandrians came upon abandoned wagons loaded with food and liquor. O'Gorman reported that, for a while, most of his chums began drinking champagne and having a good time. "I did not drink anything," he stated, and "had all I could do minding the horses of my gun, as the lead driver got off his horse before we reached the road and we did not see him again until after the war was over."[20]

The battery commander soon restored discipline, and the Alexandrians, along with their South Carolina comrades, ascended the heights overlooking the next valley and unlimbered their guns. Stretched out below was a stream of soldiers and horses, cannon, caissons, ambulances, and buggies—all fleeing toward Washington. The captain turned to Edmund Ruffin, the celebrated Southern secessionist who had fired the first shot at Fort Sumter, and invited him to pull the lanyard for the first round. The third shell struck a wagon, blocking the suspension bridge. Pandemonium ensued as the vanquished panicked and ran. Kemper's gunners enjoyed the rare opportunity to engage defenseless targets, sending shell after shell into the scrambling morass. By dusk, the frantic Federals were out of range, and the victors began collecting the stores left behind. To O'Gorman, it was all due to one "Lucky Shot."[21]

In its antipersonnel role on Henry Hill and its decimation of the retreat across Cub Run, the Alexandria Artillery had inflicted untold damage and suffering at the expense of one killed and two slightly wounded. At this point, O'Gorman's talent as a raconteur surfaced once again. He recalled:

> Before Kempers Battery left Bull Run for the new Battleground we realized that some of our men would be killed or wounded . . . Dick Owens of number four gun gathered up 14 straws, 13 long and 1 short one. He then went after each man of his squad, asking him to draw one straw, telling him that the man getting the short one would be the first man killed. He was a long time getting the men to draw, some said to him go away, Dick Owens, don't act like a fool etc. At last he succeeded, the 13 straws were all drawn leaving the short one in his own hands. This did not seem to disturb him much, he just said quitly [sic], I will be the first man of our squad to die.[22]

The battery's sole loss by gunfire was Dick Owens, a twenty-four-year-old stonecutter who was buried in an unmarked grave on the battlefield.

"After this battle we considered ourselves veterans," O'Gorman proudly declared.[23] The men were pleased to be issued a rifled twelve-pounder taken from the Yankees, and Captain Kemper began searching for new caissons to go with it. Orders arrived sending them back to Vienna, tantalizingly close to their homes behind Federal lines in Alexandria. This was the first in a series of campsites occupied by the unit that included Flint Hill, Union Mills, Piney Hill, Rocky Run, and, finally, Centreville for the winter.

The same subjects appear and reappear in O'Gorman's diary during that period. Initially, the Yankees are rumored to be fighting among themselves, and, later, they are thought to be advancing on the rebels. Individuals are arrested as spies at various times. Federal soldiers occasionally come over to the Confederates, well worth noting to the diarist, whose optimism is reminiscent of Randolph Fairfax in the early months of the war. After a Northern sympathizer threatens to shoot some rebel soldiers, his barn is burned. The capture of prisoners is also noteworthy for O'Gorman, especially when they are identified as "Negroes." It is not surprising that, as an artilleryman, O'Gorman routinely records cannonading and its sources. A favorite and increasingly familiar sighting for the intrigued Southerners is a Yankee observation balloon. O'Gorman watches his comrades get drunk and land in the guard house, grieves for two Louisiana "Tigers" of Irish extraction who are executed by a firing squad for attacking an officer, and delights in the accuracy of the new field piece when it is tested. It is natural to wonder if O'Gorman made note of Brig. Gen. Milledge Bonham's boast that it would only be a short time before Kemper's battery was back home in Alexandria, because the diarist really believed it.[24]

On March 8, 1862, the artillery battery joined the migration of Southern forces to the peninsula southeast of Richmond in reaction to the
repositioning of the Northern army. By April 13, Kemper and his men
were on the Warwick River, within easy earshot of Yankee drums. For
weeks the men listened to musketry and cannon from the direction of
Yorktown, until, on May 2, the outfit began moving north, through Williamsburg and New Kent Court House, as part of a general withdrawal.
The unit finally settled into the Richmond defenses. Over the succeeding
six weeks, O'Gorman recorded heavy firing almost every day, at times signaling a pitched battle, but the Alexandria Artillery was not directly
involved. Other than occasionally exchanging rounds with an enemy
battery that launched some shells in its direction or shooting at a Yankee
balloon with the rifled gun, his company's ordnance remained silent.
Finally, on June 29, the Alexandrians were summoned to action.

The Northern army was retreating, and Kemper's unit was ordered
to join in the pursuit. The men left camp at 6:00 A.M. and followed
Kershaw's South Carolina brigade, slowed only by firing from the enemy's
rear guard. Approaching Savage Station on the Richmond and York
River Railroad, the Confederates encountered opposition from Federal
artillery. The Alexandrians were called forward and, Kershaw reported,
they directed fire upon the enemy "with such rapidity and effect as to disperse them without the aid of the infantry."[25]

The column moved forward before being stopped once more, this
time opposite the left side of the Federal line. The Alexandrians unlimbered just off the Williamsburg Road and resumed firing. Visibility was
obscured, so the battery commander crept ahead to obtain a better look.
O'Gorman wrote that "Captain Kemper went through some woods on
our right to get a position nearer the Yankee guns, but finding an opening on the edge of the woods he could see the Yankee batteries better
than we could, and he directed our firing by signs."[26] The commander's
brother, Lieutenant Kemper, remained behind to manage the battery.[27]

The improved accuracy through use of a forward observer attracted
concentrated fire from their adversaries. After five minutes, O'Gorman
and his mates were forced to withdraw several hundred yards, where they
set up again and went back to work. This time the Federals attempted to
silence the guns with an infantry assault. The Twenty-first Mississippi was
dispatched for protection. O'Gorman said that it was a new regiment,
never tested under fire, and became demoralized by the firestorm
exploding all around. Lieutenant Kemper tried to lead the Mississippi-
ans into combat, with no success. Fighting for their lives, the Alexandrians poured canister at their attackers as fast as possible. "The Yankees
were now very close to us, we had two men killed, one mortally wounded,
who died in several days, and it looked like the battery would be taken
in a short time. Now this was a position where nine out of ten Artillery

Companies would have retreated and tried to save the men and guns, but not one man in our Company showed any signs of giving up."[28] With the help of the South Carolinians, the battery finally drove the Federals back.

The action at Savage Station was the only fighting by the Alexandria Artillery during the Seven Days battles. The unit's performance, albeit limited, earned plaudits from senior commanders. Maj. Gen. J. Bankhead Magruder commended the artillerymen and their commander for being "intrepid, tenacious, and skillful in the management of his guns." Another senior officer observed that the battery "opened fire with extraordinary rapidity and great effect." Kershaw summarized that "Captain Kemper and the officers and men under his command maintained the high reputation they established at Vienna, Bull Run, and Manassas."[29]

The accolades led to Kemper's promotion to major and his reassignment to an artillery battalion. His successor was a twenty-seven-year-old attorney from Alexandria, David L. Smoot, who would command the outfit for the remainder of the war. With the change in commander came the battery's transfer out of the Army of Northern Virginia and into the Richmond defenses, where the unit stayed for most of its remaining service to the Confederacy. The battery began the slow conversion to heavy artillery by surrendering its old brass howitzers to other companies and receiving larger ordnance. O'Gorman noted the addition of three twenty-pounder Parrotts and a rifled thirty-pounder in November. The downside was the manual labor required to construct defensive works and build roadways. Declining morale was evident as a group of privates were disrespectful to the orderly sergeant and consequently taken under arrest to Castle Thunder.[30] The rank and file was probably elated when relieved from garrison duty and sent to assist in the defense of Fredericksburg in December. The battery shelled the enemy for one full day, although little more is known about its brief deployment away from the capital.[31]

In early 1863, O'Gorman's journal records transfers of artillery pieces and caissons, culminating in the company being equipped with a pair of rifled thirty-pounder Parrotts. For the first time, the battery also began to receive conscripts, diluting the unit's integrity as representatives of Northern Virginia. On March 23, the Irishman was accidentally shot and wounded by an eighteen-year-old battery mate from Alexandria. Apparently, the injury was not serious, for on April 7, O'Gorman marched off with his comrades toward the Virginia Tidewater.[32]

Lt. Gen. James Longstreet had been dispatched to southeast Virginia to gather provisions for the Confederate army and to deny access to Richmond to Federal forces assembling once again on the Peninsula. Utilizing rail for the guns, the artillerymen took a week to travel by foot to the outskirts of Suffolk, where Longstreet had established siege lines north and west of the city. The Alexandria Artillery was sent to the extreme left flank, where the Western Branch empties into the Nansemond River. A sunken position was selected behind Hill's Point to hold Smoot's two guns, the largest ordnance available to Longstreet. O'Gorman wrote that the going was slow, as the Parrotts repeatedly became stuck in the mud. The men were also needed to help dig earthworks on the riverbank. Consequently, it was after dark on April 18 before the cannoneers and their pieces were finally in place.[33]

The Confederates intended to ambush Union gunboats patrolling the Nansemond. Smoot was specifically instructed not to fire at anything but a gunboat and not to unmask his guns until the target was within short range. On the morning of April 19, there were four gunboats above Hill's Point, near Suffolk, and three in the lower river. At 10:00, a staff officer from higher headquarters appeared at Smoot's position and directed him to open fire on vessels drifting into effective range as well as on two of the enemy's land batteries. The cannonade was returned, and a general exchange continued until midafternoon. O'Gorman recorded the Alexandrians firing thirty-eight shells without suffering a casualty, except for five men buried in dirt by an incoming eleven-inch round. The thirty-pounders scored several hits on the USS *Stepping Stones,* flagship of the Upper Nansemond Flotilla. O'Gorman subsequently heard from some Yankee sailors taken prisoner that several of the steamship's crew were wounded.[34]

The Federals struck back that afternoon. Three boats loaded with troops moved across the river and landed near the battery manned by the Fauquier Artillery on Hill's Point. As dusk settled in, the Yankees stormed the earthwork, capturing five field pieces and the entire complement of defenders. Located just two-thirds of a mile away, the Alexandria Artillery was vulnerable as well. By 10:00 P.M., O'Gorman recorded, his comrades had taken the precious Parrotts out of their pit and were moving them back to safety. The following day, the teamsters returned to retrieve the caissons and ammunition. The outfit withdrew three and a half miles to Providence Church. Even though the big thirty-pounders were gone from the Nansemond and would not return, the threat of a formidable masked battery continued to worry the admiral commanding the North Atlantic Blockading Squadron.[35]

The Alexandria Artillery made one final contribution to the Confederates' siege of Suffolk. On May 1 the unit received marching orders for South Quay on the Blackwater River, the location of a pontoon bridge used to reposition Southern forces. The hulls and planking that constituted the structure had been taken from the Yankees at Seven Pines and were precious to an army with a paucity of engineering equipment.

Arriving at suppertime, the cannoneers unlimbered and positioned their guns to protect against attack by land and to prevent gunboats from threatening the bridging. O'Gorman made special note of the arrival of the Seventeenth Virginia Regiment from his hometown. Once the pontoons were no longer needed, the Alexandria company provided drivers and horses to assist in moving the train to the rear. On May 22, the artillerymen loaded their guns aboard the Seaboard and Roanoke Railroad, the wagoners headed westward down the plank road, and O'Gorman and his mates began tramping back to the defenses of the Southern capital.[36]

The Alexandria Artillery was now assigned to the Department of Richmond. Its members were first sent to Battery No. 9, on the northwest side of the city. Over succeeding weeks, the men were dispatched via the York River Railroad to White House Station on the Pamunkey River, to a camp near Marion Hill outside Richmond, and to the strategic Meadow Bridge just west of Mechanicsville. Static defense was hard on morale, as O'Gorman cited unit members deserting, being court-martialed for disobedience of orders, and landing in Castle Thunder. The company finally settled in for the winter at Chaffin's Farm on the James River, seven miles south of the city.[37]

The battery was subjected to a major organizational change in January 1864. Orders from the War Department assigned the unit to the Eighteenth Virginia Heavy Artillery Battalion, a composite of units from across the state that were deployed around the capital's inner defensive line. As simply Company E of the Eighteenth Heavy Artillery, Smoot's battery lost the special identity that connected it with Alexandria. Perhaps just as distasteful, the unit was dismounted, surrendering horses, caissons, wagons, and drivers to other outfits.

Throughout 1864, the battalion shuffled from place to place in response to alarms of Federal threats. The scare turned out to be real in the case of the Kilpatrick/Dahlgren raid on the city in late February and early March. An inspection of the heavy artillery battalions in late May offered insight into the condition of the Alexandria unit. The one positive finding was that the men were well clothed with serviceable footwear. On the negative side, few noncommissioned officers were knowledgeable about firing the ordnance. Repeated details for guard duty in Richmond demoralized the troops and reduced their competence in servicing the guns by preempting training time. Most of the individual arms were antiquated smoothbore, and many were rusty. O'Gorman could take pride, however, in his promotion from private to corporal on June 1, becoming one of the company's four noncommissioned officers. By September, the strength of Company E had dwindled to three officers and forty-four enlisted personnel.[38]

On January 1, 1865, the Alexandrians were at Fort Gilmer, eight miles east of Richmond.[39] Company E had been stationed at this prominent salient on the intermediate line since September and would remain there into the spring. It was not a pleasant experience, according to O'Gorman: "The Company is now in a miserable condition; the men are treated worse than slaves, being half-clothed, half fed and no pay. Presuming officials are ruining the country very fast. Nearly all the Company have gone home and all will go very soon. They are willing to undergo any suffering, but will not be treated as slaves."[40] The Irishman went on to list the men remaining in uniform, twenty-six in number including four conscripts.

The denouement for the Alexandria Artillery, along with the rest of the Confederate forces in Virginia, came in April. The Eighteenth Battalion was now part of an artillery brigade assigned to Maj. Gen. Custis Lee's makeshift division of government clerks, naval gunners, and heavy artillerists. Smoot received orders to abandon his position on the evening of April 2. Moving westward in the column commanded by Lt. Gen. Richard S. Ewell, the Alexandrians were without food and slept in the open when time permitted. Furthermore, they had been separated from their cannon. Closely followed by Federal troops, on the afternoon of April 6, the rebels crossed Sayler's Creek and formed a line of defense on the ridge west of the stream. With O'Gorman serving as color guard, Smoot's few remaining men formed up on the left, along with the rest of Lee's division.

The defenders were successful in repulsing the initial Union assault. The combination of incoming artillery fire and successive waves of Federals soon overwhelmed the Southerners, however. The adversaries rushed together in hand-to-hand fighting along the entire line. Ewell quickly capitulated to save the lives of his few remaining troops. O'Gorman counted only nine members of his company left to surrender, six Alexandrians and three recruits.[41]

O'Gorman was wounded during the fray. He was unaware of the injury at first, but after the surrender he realized he had been shot when he suddenly fell to the ground. A musket ball had hit him in the left thigh near the knee. His boot was full of blood. While a comrade was trying to stop the bleeding, a Yankee rode up, put a pistol to the Irishman's face, and directed him to surrender. Being told that O'Gorman was wounded, the captor ordered his prisoner to climb aboard his horse to be taken to a hospital.

> I was put up behing the yankee, he started off saying now mind I shot you and captured you, it don matter to you now just keep your moth shut, he then said now Johnie if you have any greenbacks you might as well fork

them over as they will go through you anyhow when you get to the hospital. I told him I had none, just then another yankee rode up along side of us and said hello Grady what you got. Grady told him I was his prisoner, that he captured me right out of the rank the other yankee said my my Grady he looks very bad he may fall off here Johnie take a little of this, he held up his canteen and gave me a little whiskey. I thanked him and he started off. Grady called after him and said give me a taste of that, he rode off saying no Grady you have got enough. Grady then cursed him saying you ——— Dutchman you gave it to a rebel, but wont give me any. As I found Grady was an Irishman I felt of him to see if he would treat me a little better. I said Grady if things were changed and you were the wounded man instead of me and I found you were a countryman of mine I would treat you a little better, he turned his head around, looked me in the face and said that's played out.[42]

O'Gorman was first taken to a headquarters where Brig. Gen. George A. Custer and his staff were conducting business. Grady tried to receive credit for a furlough by bringing in the prisoner but was refused. The twosome continued on to a house near a small mill where other wounded Confederates were being held. The captive was given an "ash cake," dough put in the fire and covered with hot coals. After dark, Union troopers rode up and shouted threats to scare the detainees. Finally, another Irishman dismounted and asked O'Gorman if his wound had been treated. The benevolent Yankee called a doctor and, before he arrived, told O'Gorman to identify himself as a member of his Union cavalry troop. The physician made a record of the injury, but it was not until the next morning that the patient was carried to a barn filled with rebel and Yankee casualties.

Five days later, a group of wounded was sent to Port Walthall Junction, where O'Gorman was put on the floor of a freight car bound for City Point. He lost consciousness and awoke in a Federal hospital amidst casualties of the U.S. Sixth Corps. O'Gorman was later told that he had been identified as a Union soldier by the overcoat wrapped around him on the train. The Alexandrian was at City Point when news arrived of Lincoln's assassination. The Yankees became irate, talking about killing some rebels. His sense of humor still intact, O'Gorman said that he felt safe, as he was "a yankee pro-tem."

The Confederate wounded were soon shipped to Baltimore aboard a hospital steamer. Those who refused to take the oath of allegiance to the U.S. government were sent to Fort McHenry. Implying that he would not agree to swear loyalty to his former adversary, O'Gorman said that he was treated well at the fort but suffered terribly from gangrene. At one point, a doctor even stopped dressing his leg, rationalizing that the patient would never get well. Finally, on June 22, O'Gorman was freed in accordance with a War Department directive that required the oath to be taken as a precondition for release. The following day, his father came from Alexandria to take him home. It was two years before the former corporal fully recovered.[43]

While recuperating, O'Gorman sought to make up for deficiencies in his earlier schooling by attending St. John's Academy in Alexandria at the same time he worked as a night watchman. Years later, he sent a gift of one hundred dollars to the priest who headed the program as thanks for the kindness extended to him.[44]

It was also during this period that the Confederate veteran became known in Alexandria as "Gorman," rather than "O'Gorman." The Americanization of his name had come about during the war, as the Irish immigrant sought to be accepted as an equal by his fellow soldiers. He had enlisted as "P. F. O'Gorman" and referred to himself as such in his diary early in the conflict. At the war's end, however, he appeared on the prisoner of war rolls as "Gorman" and never went back to the original spelling.

By 1870, Jacob Germond and P. F. Gorman were established as boilermakers in the industrial section of Alexandria beside the wharves on South Union Street. Ten years later, he had a new partner, James L. Pettit, and was the senior member of a firm advertised as boiler manufacturers. Gorman achieved full acceptance as a citizen of his adopted country in 1889, when he was elected city tax collector. He continued to operate his boiler shop as well.

After recovering from his wound in 1867, Gorman married Anna M. Germond, daughter of the man who taught him to be a metalworker. Their residence on South Lee Street eventually housed eight children, plus his mother and an Irish maid. When he died of pneumonia on January 3, 1921, the *Alexandria Gazette* speculated, "Perhaps there never was a

Patrick Gorman as city tax collector early in the nineteenth century. From Alexander J. Wedderburn, *Wedderburn's Souvenir Virginia Tercentennial, 1607–1907: Historic Alexandria, Virginia* (Alexandria: n.p., 1907). Special Collections, Alexandria Library.

city official more honored and loved than P. F. Gorman." That statement could be considered standard fare for a eulogy, or it might have credence considering that he only had opposition once during three decades in elected office. The last rites were held at Gorman's parish church, St. Mary's, with Edgar Warfield as one of the honorary pallbearers.[45]

The Alexandria Artillery and Patrick Francis O'Gorman were fortunate to survive four years of armed conflict without greater loss. The battery suffered four men killed, another four wounded, and eleven captured, plus eight soldiers who died of disease.[46] O'Gorman was wounded twice, once seriously, but returned home to live a long and productive life, dying at the age of seventy-eight years. The company fought on four battlefields—First Manassas, Savage Station, Suffolk, and Sayler's Creek —in addition to less well-defined engagements at Fredericksburg and in defense of Richmond. Manning artillery pieces, especially in stationary defensive positions for long periods of time, was far less arduous duty than the continuous campaigning endured by many soldiers. The unit established a good name for itself at the outset of the war and carried that reputation proudly throughout the conflict, enabling it to return home with honor after peace was restored.

O'Gorman appeared to achieve his own personal objective, establishing a solid, if undistinguished, record as a soldier in defense of his chosen country. His reliability as an artilleryman was eventually recognized and rewarded with elevation to senior enlisted grade. Perhaps his greatest contribution to the cause he served, as well as to posterity, was the personal account he left behind of the experiences of a common volunteer—an Irish immigrant—enlisting, training, fighting, and, in the end, surrendering.

CHAPTER THIRTEEN

SOUTHERN SYMPATHIZER

✶✶✶ ANNE FROBEL

THE DIARY OF ANNE FROBEL PROVIDES A BRIDGE BETWEEN the war years and the Reconstruction that followed. This account of the Civil War era was first published in 1986, complemented by a couple dozen entries from 1873 to 1879. A third part of the volume consists of five letters at the end of the nineteenth century concerning the Frobels' claim for compensation from the U.S. government for property taken or destroyed by its army during and after the conflict.[1]

In the record for the day after Federal troops occupied Alexandria, Anne stated her purpose in keeping the journal: "This day I thought of, and determined to keep a daily account of all that occurs, or that we know anything of, hoping, that if either, or both of us die before these troubles are over, or if we are destined never to see any of our relatives again, this book may by some lucky chance find its way to the hands of some one who may feel an interest in our fate, and for the whole four years not a day passed without my writing something on it."[2] Women across the South were beginning diaries from an emotional need to express their feelings about the radical changes intruding on their lives.[3]

Unfortunately, Anne's account fell into the wrong hands, and most of it was destroyed. Only entries for September 17, 1862, through June 13, 1863, appear to be the actual comments jotted down on those days. The remaining passages are summaries of happenings and themes reconstructed by the author sometime after the war. Anne's reflections during the last two years of fighting are collected under two headings, the winters of 1863–64 and 1864–65, and equate to less than 6 percent of the material composed until then. Nevertheless, Anne's reports and observations are important as a chronicle memorializing the lives, fears, and fate of Southern sympathizers who remained at home in Alexandria.

Wilton Hill, home of Anne Frobel, almost twenty years after she lived there. Washington *Sunday Star,* February 7, 1915.

Anne Frobel spent the war years with her sister, Elizabeth (or "Lizzie"), at Wilton Hill outside Alexandria in Fairfax County. This was Anne's birthplace and home for virtually her entire life. More than 110 acres in size, the plantation included an eighteen-by-twenty-six-foot, two-story, brick and frame house with a traditional front porch, large barn, green-house, privy, and various other outbuildings. The acreage included culti-vated fields, pastureland, timber, a large garden, and ornamental box-wood. Upon the death of their parents in the 1850s, the sisters inherited the holdings at Wilton, including nineteen slaves, of which there were three males and five females above the age of twenty-one.[4]

The Frobels were members of the landed gentry who looked to nearby Alexandria as the center of their religious, social, and business lives—the Coopers, Forrests, Carys, and Cassius Lees being other examples. Anne was born in 1816 and confirmed at Christ Church, where her father was organist, and she attended services there most of her life. During the war, she rode or walked into the city regularly to stay abreast of local news. The seaport was visible from the second-story windows of Wilton Hill, and Anne made note of ships docked at the wharves or sailing on the Potomac. Before and after the war, Anne was a regular reader of the *Alex-andria Gazette,* and after she moved to Alabama late in life, she kept in touch with the city's progress through friends.[5]

Wilton was about two and a half miles from the seaport. Starting west on Duke Street, a traveler turned left onto Telegraph Road at the old toll-gate on Little River Turnpike. Crossing the stone bridge over Hunting Creek, one continued to the Old Fairfax Road coming in from the right. It was necessary to take this thoroughfare and ascend past the white Sharon Chapel situated on a corner of the estate. At the top of the hill, a lane to the left led less than a hundred yards to the house, now the site of the former Wilton Woods school.

The two maiden sisters shared a close relationship. Their bonding under the constant tension of military occupation fulfilled the need, identified by historian Catherine Clinton, among nineteenth-century plantation women for "one particular female friendship of special inti-macy and mutual trust."[6] Two years junior to her sister, Lizzie was always in the forefront. Anne played Boswell to Lizzie's Samuel Johnson. Lizzie's assertiveness was evident in their father's last days, when she helped him attend to family business. It was not surprising, therefore, that his widow and Lizzie, not Anne or one of the brothers, were named co-executrices of Mr. Frobel's will. Once the sisters became isolated behind Federal lines, Lizzie took the lead in dealing with problems. She would go into town, complain to the provost marshal, confront soldiers threatening the homestead, and make final decisions on what to do. Anne only stepped forward when Lizzie was away from the house or indisposed due to illness. On the rare occasion when their elder brother wrote home, the letter would be addressed to Lizzie with a parting perfunctory "love" to "my sister." It was all very strange.

By 1861 there were only two surviving male members of the family. After attending Episcopal High School, the elder sibling, Bushrod Wash-ington Frobel, had served two separate tours as a third lieutenant with the Revenue Marine Service, predecessor to the U.S. Coast Guard.[7] His expulsion in 1845 for "neglect of duty, repeated breaches of discipline, and general habits" offers a clue to his personality.[8] Despite these infrac-tions, Frobel had been reappointed in 1858 and was stationed at Wilm-ington, North Carolina, when Virginia seceded. Attempting to resign his commission, he was instead "*Dishonorably Dismissed* from the United States service." The Frobels did not recoil at his termination, as it was hardly a new experience.[9] Career naval officers, like Commodore French Forrest, who were treated the same way felt victimized by the new admin-istration's policies intended to disgrace disloyal Southerners.

Frobel proceeded to obtain a commission in the navy of Virginia. He was assigned to command the Cockpit Point batteries at the mouth of the Occoquan River, not far south of Wilton, one link in the chain of South-ern fortifications designed to control traffic on the Potomac. In an inci-dent consistent with what his sisters were confronting outside Alexan-dria, a loyal Southern property owner two miles up the river was outraged in December to discover his house and outbuildings dismantled so the wood could be used by Frobel to erect winter quarters for his men.[10] By 1862, Frobel had transferred to the Confederate army. When the rebels pulled in their defenses around Richmond, he became an aide-de-camp to Brig. Gen. William H. C. Whiting and later served as his commander of artillery, again at Wilmington. Frobel was performing duty in Georgia as an engineer officer in the rank of lieutenant colonel when the conflict ended.[11]

Bushrod seemed special in Anne's eyes if for no other reason than her poor opinion of her younger brother. "David is a poor erratic, thoughtless being," she commiserated at one point. Already married in 1861, he was probably concerned more for his wife's well-being than for his sisters'. David was twenty-one years junior to Anne, making her relationship to him almost maternal in nature. His military service was primarily in the Richmond defenses as an artillery and ordnance officer.[12]

The departure of white men to serve in the war had a devastating effect on the social and business structure of Southern households.[13] The outbreak of hostilities did not affect the Frobel sisters in the same way as many families, because they were already managing their estate's real property and slaves. The worries were often the same, however, as they expressed constant concern for their brothers' well-being. Anne's references to Bushrod reflected special warmth. Perhaps because he remained unmarried until after the war, Bushrod stayed in touch with and was closer, emotionally, to his maiden sisters.

On May 24, 1861, the women began the drive into town when they were stopped by some excited local men who informed them that Alexandria had been occupied by soldiers in blue. Anne took note of the railroad bridges on fire, no doubt the handiwork of Wilson Presstman's company of Irishmen. Roadways clogged with refugees confirmed that most folks who could possibly avoid the conflict on the horizon were escaping. "I believe every body from both town and country that could possibly get away left at this time . . . O what a feeling of loneliness and utter despair came over us when we thought of every friend and acquaintance gone and poor Lizzie and me being left entirely alone to battle it by ourselves. O how little we knew, or dreamed of what was going to befall."[14]

Why did the Frobel sisters not flee as well? Bushrod had joined the ranks of the rebels. David stopped to say good-bye before heading south with his family. The widow Mrs. Monimia Cary gathered up her children and abandoned their home across Cameron Run. Gen. Samuel Cooper's wife, Maria, whose estate was visible across Cameron Valley, sent messages imploring the sisters to collect their valuables and servants and come stay with her in Richmond. Anne said they reasoned that the servants would "hoot at the idea" and might take off across the river to Washington.

"Indeed we were so inexperienced as to suppose in being at home would be a protection to them and keep every thing intact."[15] This rationale was not so faulty regarding the contents of their house, as they would soon come to realize.

The sisters' naïveté was by no means unique at this early stage of the conflict. A little farther away, another Southern sympathizer, Judith Brockenbrough McGuire, was blissfully ignorant of what lay ahead. She declared: "We have determined, if we are obliged to go from home, to leave every thing in the care of the servants. They have promised to be faithful, and I believe they will be . . . I have no idea that officers would allow them [soldiers] to break locks, or that they would allow our furniture to be interfered with."[16]

This diarist was the daughter of a Virginia Supreme Court justice and wife of the principal at Episcopal High School. Her strong opinions were undoubtedly heated up by exposure to the fire radiating from secessionist leaders of Virginia society.[17] At Menokin, across Braddock Road from the school, was the country estate of Cassius Lee and his wife, Annie. Although her husband was known to be a unionist, Annie eventually became quite open in defending Virginia's action. In correspondence with her friend, Mrs. Samuel F. du Pont, wife of the prominent admiral in the U.S. Navy, Annie wrote, "The once Union men of the South are now the most decided in resisting the 'force' measures of the North."[18] Interestingly, the McGuires fled as soon as Northern Virginia was invaded, while Mrs. Lee, great with child, resisted her husband's pleadings to retreat to safety and chose instead to stay beside him in Alexandria. In 1863, Cassius was imprisoned and eventually permitted to move to Long Island. Not long thereafter, he and his family fled to Canada to avoid further arrest.[19]

In contrast, Anne Frobel's journal is silent on things political. Her views must be gleaned from between the lines. After the war, when she reworked her account of the early weeks and months of the conflict, the hollowness of her earlier hopes and the misplacement of her patriotism may have become all too apparent to her. The sisters' primary concern was the welfare of their two brothers, and they were especially frustrated during the eighteen months that elapsed without hearing a word from Bushrod. Anne's reactions to reports from the battlefield certainly revealed her Southern sympathies. Much of their news during the first half of the war was learned from the Northern press, obtained by sending Charles, their loyal servant, into town for newspapers.[20] "We had never heard the name of Beauregard until the yankees informed us he with his army was at Fairfax courthouse."[21] Reconstructing the timeframe from October 1861 to February 1862, the diarist recalled that no news of General Lee reached them, perhaps surprising to modern readers fully informed of the Southern hero's entire war record, but understandable considering his peripheral assignments and minor contributions early in the fighting.

In their isolation at Wilton Hill, the sisters were often traumatized by widely conflicting accounts of battles and political events. Subsequent recurring reports that the Federals were in Richmond or that Lee had surrendered proved false, making the women naturally suspicious about other reputed happenings. The announcement that Earl Van Dorn and "Stonewall" Jackson had been killed was viewed with suspicion at first. "The papers have given vague reports of the death of our Gen. T. J. Jackson. But he has been killed so often in yankee imagination that very little credence is given to the report."[22] The reconstructed portion of the diary is strangely silent about what happened at Gettysburg, which initially generated the premier example of misinformation for women throughout the South.[23] The gulf between what Northern papers and soldiers represented and conflicting accounts shared by civilian friends made separation from other Southern sympathizers almost unbearable at times. The unexpected appearance of women companions from town, armed with stories of recent happenings, therefore produced incredible joy at Wilton Hill.

From the outset, Union soldiers viewed the sisters with suspicion as Southern loyalists or even informers. For some bluecoats, every dwelling around Alexandria was thought to be the home of a friend or spy of the rebels.[24] At the beginning of the occupation, Northern soldiers repeatedly confronted the isolated women, insisting that they must have husbands off fighting for the enemy. The spinsters repeatedly denied the allegation and were careful only to mention their brothers to the most trusted friends. On one occasion, two disreputable women were dispatched to try to entice the sisters into admitting they were secessionists, so the schemers who sent them, in league with the guard stationed at the garden gate, could justifiably enter and plunder the house.[25]

The high ground on which Wilton stood was soon occupied by the Federals. It remained in Union hands throughout the entire war, although much of the rest of Fairfax County initially came under control of rebel forces. The Confederates' grip on Northern Virginia was strengthened by the Battle of Bull Run, and they maintained a strong presence in Fairfax until late 1861. Historian Noel G. Harrison has pointed out striking similarities in the two armies' treatment of civilians. During the first year of hostilities, the occupying forces in Alexandria and Fairfax Counties intentionally and unconsciously terrorized citizens, devastated property, and drove residents from their homes. At the same time, neighbors exploited one another and collaborated with soldiers, thereby obscuring the roles of the military and civilians.[26]

Anne was introduced to the harshness of military occupation on May 26, 1861, when left alone while Lizzie ran an errand. Into the dining room walked three Northern officers with pistols tucked in their belts and swords clanking. Stunned by the invasion of her privacy, the terrified woman sat silently as the intruders conducted a search. Pulling open drawers, a lieutenant remarked, "This is disagreeable business," to which Anne was able to reply, "not only disagreeable but very degrading."[27] Anne was consequently thrown into a state of fear familiar to other Southern women being baptized in unconventional warfare. Marauders might give her a day's rest, "But still I was kept in the greatest state of anxiety and excitement, could not eat or rest—walking—walking—all day long, not knowing what moment I would be pounced upon, upstairs and down stairs, in the kitchen, in the garden down to the road."[28]

The search for plunder continued almost daily, causing the sisters to keep the lower part of the house locked while they stationed themselves at an upstairs window. During one especially humiliating encounter, the insolence of the would-be intruder caused Anne to ask if he were not ashamed to speak to a lady with such rudeness. He responded with contempt, "I would like to know who in the h—— made you a lady," an example of what historian Michael Fellman calls "symbolic rape."[29]

The isolated women agreed that they must inform Bushrod of their plight. In order to ensure the letter reached him, Lizzie was dispatched to mail it at Fairfax Court House, under control of the rebels. She went to the home of two old friends, Rev. Templeton Brown and his wife. The diary reflects that Lizzie encountered many Alexandrians fleeing the occupation.[30] No doubt these included the Carys and McGuires, who had gone to the Browns to seek the succor of relatives. Mrs. McGuire noticed the carriage of Commodore Forrest, indicating that his wife may have also made Fairfax the first stop on her flight south.[31]

One common question was what to do with the family silver. Many Virginia women came up with the same answer—bury it. Constance Cary, who lived at Vaucluse, just southwest from the Episcopal Seminary, recalled her mother holding a lantern while a cousin and an old Negro gardener worked half the night digging pits for two large traveling trunks filled with a candelabra, urn, tea set, tankards, and much more. Four years later, after the house had been destroyed and the grounds used for a Union camp, the Carys unearthed the treasure.[32] Judith McGuire also advocated burying the silver. Others sent it away for safekeeping. To the extent she could, Mary Custis Lee carted off the heirlooms at Arlington House. Upon the outbreak of hostilities, the Frobels accepted the elegant Canton china of their cousin, Mary Foote, in Alexandria city and stowed it in their corn house. At the same time, they packed off a lot of their own possessions. The etiquette of the times, reinforced by their own personal pride, caused them to retain sufficient pieces to set a respectable table for the Yankee officers forced upon them for room and board. As soon as the boarders left, the nervous owners hid silverware up the chimney, then underground, and finally in the greenhouse stove.[33]

In secreting away their valuables, like their sisters across the South, the Frobels were unsure how much to reveal to their servants.[34] "We were afraid of the negroes treachery," Anne admitted. "We never know how far to trust them."[35] By unhinging Southern society, the war opened up opportunities for many blacks to play roles previously denied them. Most of the slaves left the Frobels' plantation when war broke out. Of those who remained, the hardest for the sisters to decipher was thirty-three-year-old Milly, the chambermaid.

Milly was protective of Lizzie and Anne. Yet she was also drawn to the bluecoats camped all over the hillsides, and at least one of them, the aide to Brig. Gen. Francis Patterson, was smitten with her. The bondwoman soon spent considerable time with new friends at Fort Lyon, which was beneficial for the Frobels when she brought back news of how the war was going. By the latter part of 1863, however, Anne concluded that Milly was keeping vigil at Wilton Hill and reporting what she saw and heard to the Yankees.[36] Yet Anne was sad to return home from a neighbor's on Christmas Eve in 1864 to find Milly gone. The old mammy was in tears, exclaiming, "A yankee man who keeps dat counterban hole in town come an took her away."[37]

It would have been difficult for the sisters to remain at Wilton without the help of two blacks, Charles and Mammy. Charles was in his mid-thirties and had a wife in Washington, whom he went to see on Saturday nights, returning on Mondays. As a male figure, he could protect his mistresses and be sent on errands into town. Before the carriage was confiscated, he frequently drove them to Alexandria. The traditional mammy was Agnes, forty-eight years old in 1861, who had faithfully served the family her entire life and felt a part of it. Her commitment was evident in many ways. For example, she recruited her nephew, John Allen, to come in on weekends to fill the void created by Charles's absence.

Both servants kept the Frobels alert to potential danger, such as the imminent approach of Yankees. At times, Anne and Lizzie learned about events from blacks passing it by word of mouth. "The negroes have practiced all their lives in communicating with each other," Anne observed, and now she and Lizzie were beneficiaries of these sub rosa transmissions.[38]

Southern women trying to survive on their own also relied upon the benevolence of neighbors. After their horses were stolen and the carriage appropriated by the Yankees to help build a barricade, John Fairfax, whose property was adjacent, lent the sisters a nag to ride to church. George D. Fowle, whose estate, Burgundy, was across the road, looked in from time to time.[39] Another neighbor, William Reid, brought them flour and extended other kindnesses. In return, despite the scarcity of their own provisions, the two ladies would send part of their meal to a poor old man nearby when they could. With this kind of mutual support, when Rev. Henry Wall came out from Alexandria midway through the war to urge the Frobels to move into town, they did not seem to be tempted.[40]

From their first appearance on Wilton Hill, Union soldiers came begging for something to eat. When they were denied or the opportunity presented itself by the owners' absence, troops helped themselves to whatever was unprotected in the yard and garden. Hens and milk were the first targets. Soon Muscovy ducks, beehives, pears, melons, even rye standing in the fields had been purloined. The most devastating loss was from the woodlands of Wilton Hill, as the incoming army felled all the trees for their quarters, barricades, and fortifications.

At the beginning, it seemed like a game. The little Negro children at Wilton yelled, "Yankee dogs coming," when spotting the glitter of a gun barrel on the drive.[41] Anne recorded that the adult servants referred to the soldiers as "dem people," reminiscent of Gen. R. E. Lee's characterization of "those people," which he sometimes used to refer to the enemy. By the end of the war, pilferage was no longer common because just about everything worth stealing was gone. Despite careful attention, the two old maids had even lost their last cows, all stolen or sold to buy provisions.

The Frobels saw that abandoned houses were irresistible to scavengers and vandals, civilian as well as military. When the Yankees moved out in September 1862, the local commander offered Lizzie and Anne what could not be taken along, but their neighbors were quick to collect everything, including the logs that came out of the Frobels' woods. "O save me from my *friends*," lamented Anne. Within the year, nearby residents became more brazen, taking furniture, bedding, and clothes from deserted houses. If they did not gather the loot themselves, Anne was told, they bribed Union soldiers to grab it for them.[42]

Isolation behind Federal lines in no way sentenced the Frobels to uncommon treatment by soldiers. Women in the no-man's-land that shifted back and forth between Yankee and rebel control experienced the same thievery. Historian Harrison found that by the spring of 1862 there was little to differentiate those areas of Alexandria and Fairfax Counties that had housed garrisons vis-à-vis the contested areas.[43] In between the lines in nearby Loudoun County, Kate Wampler complained that stragglers and deserters from both armies stole her chickens. What made Kate furious was when they used her own fence rails to roast the fowl.[44] The irritant in the Frobels' situation was that many of the skulkers were soldiers assigned to nearby units with ready access to plentiful army rations. These thieves and beggars were by no means starving.

The occupying armies quickly became insensitive as to who was sympathetic to their side and who was not. Even in the first year of the war, Confederate soldiers regarded all property—public and private—as their own.[45] The Federals encountered by the Frobels also did not always seem to differentiate between Northerners and Southerners. In one instance, the spinsters seemed to be the benefactors. The women must have been apprehensive in September 1861 when the Yankees began constructing a huge defensive complex, soon named Fort Lyon, on the high ground between their home and the river. They were certainly apoplectic when discovering shortly thereafter that a major fortification was to be built on their own property. Without much hope, Lizzie wrote to the new commander of the Army of the Potomac, Maj. Gen. George B. McClellan, begging him not to inflict this installation on two harmless women. According to Anne, McClellan rode with his staff over the terrain, viewing it from various perspectives, and decided to turn the position into a simple redoubt.[46] More than likely, as his memoirs reflect, McClellan's trip to Wilton Hill was to identify a position to cover Alexandria should the Confederates advance on the transportation hub.[47]

By the war's end, the Federals had constructed thirty-three forts, twenty-five batteries, and seven blockhouses south of the Potomac.[48] The impact on the countryside outside Alexandria city was devastating—hills denuded of trees, crops destroyed, private homes dismantled, trench lines and roads carved into the terrain.

Surrounded by this destruction, Anne saw far more negatives than positives in their separation from family and friends in town. Her commentary is filled with commiseration concerning their unique plight as two helpless souls alone behind Federal lines. "Towns people do not suffer as much as the country people do," she remarked soon after the county was occupied.[49] When the Yankees poured back into Alexandria to lick their wounds after a defeat on the battlefield, Anne complained, "We always get the worst of every battle, we poor insiders."[50]

Women in areas that swung back and forth with the winds of war would have heartily disagreed. Susan Caldwell in Warrenton repeatedly wrote to her husband in Richmond, complaining that groceries and dry goods were selling at reasonable prices in Alexandria, while the steady devaluation of Confederate money made the purchase of staples increasingly prohibitive for Virginians behind Southern lines. Furthermore, hucksters coming from Alexandria asked to be paid in gold or silver, if not U.S. government greenbacks. The local stores had few items on the shelves, forcing Mrs. Caldwell to trade with the out-of-town shysters for shoes, jeans, and other staples.[51] The Frobels, on the other hand, had ready access to consumer goods, but they, too, often lacked the hard currency demanded by vendors. Their most ready source of Yankee dollars was one they abhorred.

As it became apparent in the autumn of 1861 that the presence of Union troops would not be as brief as originally predicted, the Frobels' friends worried about their vulnerability to Northern soldiers. George Fowle appeared after breakfast one morning and mentioned that a Federal officer was looking for quarters for himself and his wife. Fowle advised the ladies to consent, as the supplicant was a respectable gentleman, recent graduate of West Point (Class of 1861), and staff officer for Brig. Gen. John Sedgwick, commander of the brigade camped around them. To the horror of Lizzie and Anne, Sedgwick had expressed a desire to commandeer Wilton Hill as his headquarters. The presence of a subaltern and his bride might deter him.[52]

The thought of sharing their family home with anyone, especially Yankees, was loathsome to the Frobel sisters. But the women acknowledged the added protection that would be afforded by having a Union officer in residence. Reluctantly, they consented. Lt. Eugene B. Beaumont and his wife turned out to be the perfect couple to introduce the Frobels to a living arrangement that would continue on and off with other boarders throughout the remainder of the military occupation. Anne described Mrs. Beaumont as "a perfect lady, cultivated and refined," and said the couple treated them like their older sisters.[53] The attachment formed with these young Pennsylvanians was so strong that they stayed in contact for years after the war. More important, whenever Lizzie and Anne faced a seemingly insurmountable problem, they did not hesitate to ask Beaumont for help, even after he was transferred to another theater of operations. Yet, despite the sisters' faith and reliance in the Beaumonts during the nearly five months they lived together under the same roof, Lizzie and Anne never said a word about Bushrod or David.

Another considerable benefit to housing officers was the income they provided. After their own garden was ravaged, the Frobels had to buy food to feed their lodgers, and doing so required prepayment by them. Charles was regularly dispatched to the market in Alexandria to acquire the ingredients needed by Mammy to prepare meals. Anne complained that "it takes nearly every cent they pay us for board to supply the table while they are here," and there was precious little left over to live on.[54] Having any source of food was a blessing in those difficult days, however. Counterparts behind Confederate lines did not have ready access to the wealth of produce available in Alexandria, and women trying to hold a household together between the opposing armies would rarely have been compensated by vagabonds who wandered in to be fed.

A second, though relatively minor, income stream opened up in 1863 when an old Irishman approached the Frobels about renting one of their townhouses in Alexandria. This was another source of hard currency generally unavailable to Southern sympathizers behind Confederate lines. When all else failed, later in the struggle, a neighbor lady kindly sold the cream from Wilton, providing money to buy a few indispensable items.[55] Most boarders were not as easy to live with as the Beaumonts. Women seemed to present the most problems. Mrs. Staples, the new wife of a colonel in the Third Maine, proved to be an exacting woman who demanded a great deal and expected to be waited upon by the servants. An officer in the Seventh New Jersey appeared at the door one day with a woman he said he intended to marry and her sister. One of them had a lap dog that joined her at the table. "I thought it degradation enough to sit down with yankees. But I never did imagine I would come to eat with dogs," Anne complained. The shady guests left several days later without having been induced to reveal their names. Even a sutler insisted in placing some "ladies" at Wilton Hill. Anne observed that every house in the neighborhood was filled with such women. The worst came later, after the surrender, when Northern women flocked to the army to be with their spouses and seemed to stay at Wilton forever.[56]

At least Lizzie and Anne were in their own home, and it was still standing. A nurse came to attend to Mrs. Staples one day and bragged about taking away the dresses of Mrs. French Forrest, a close friend of Anne's, from nearby Clermont, which had been converted into a smallpox sanatorium. Looking through their glass, the sisters could observe Cameron, the former estate of the Samuel Coopers, being piled high with embankments of yellow earth as the property was transformed into a major fortification.

By early 1863 the garrisons manning these bastions were intent on practicing with their heavy artillery. One of the first targets was set up in the field of "old Mr. Smith," the Frobels' cantankerous Yankee neighbor. Soon shells were whizzing overhead from Fort Ellsworth across Hunting Creek to the northeast.[57] It was not long before men, women, children, horses, and cows, irrespective of political persuasion, were casualties from the firing at this and other objects erected for gunnery training.[58]

When Southern partisans succeeded in a spectacular way, embarrassing the army of occupation, retribution was taken on the local citizenry. After John Singleton Mosby captured Brig. Gen. Edwin Stoughton in March 1863, Anne noted that folks thought to be Confederate sympathizers were being arrested and imprisoned. "L[izzie] saw as she came home two ambulances filled with them."[59] After raids by Mosby, Frank Stringfellow, and James Kincheloe in 1864, Anne recorded, "the poor citizens would have to pay the penalty. At one time, they seized up all the gentlemen, all about the town, all the old men (for there was no other there). . . . And then there was an order issued that every house within five miles of the Orange and Alex—rail road was to be burned."[60] Fortunately, the Frobels were not affected.

Mosby's feats instilled pride and hope in Southern loyalists like Anne, but Kincheloe would occupy a special place in Anne's heart. Kincheloe's Prince William Rangers apparently stopped to socialize with the young ladies at a nearby house when operating in the area immediately south of Alexandria. The troopers picked up mail, papers, and packages and, in turn, left off letters to be delivered to the families of Southern soldiers. Anne was invited to be present on one occasion in 1864 when the riders appeared. At the end of the evening, Kincheloe took a button off his coat and gave it to her as a remembrance. "They were the first Confederate soldiers I had ever seen," she recorded.[61]

Southern partisans were foremost in their minds one winter night not long thereafter when a violent rapping awakened the sisters. They ran downstairs and saw a band of men through the glass panels bordering the front door. The strangers identified themselves as Mosby men and asked for something to eat. Talking through the locked door, the renegades inquired about the neighbors, their politics, the placement of pickets, and the number of men at the forts. The frightened women quickly identified the party as "yankees" from their nasal twang and refused to help them. The next day a squad of men from Fort Lyon revealed that the night callers had stolen away from camp to search and plunder houses in the vicinity.[62] The Frobels' little world was still a threatening place after three years of Federal occupation.

The disruption caused by the soldiers forced schools and churches to close in the countryside as well as the city of Alexandria. In April 1863 Lizzie's determination surfaced once again. She decided to collect some nearby children and teach them herself. It was one small way she could thank her neighbors for their many kindnesses to the lonely women on Wilton Hill. As word of the instruction spread, more youngsters came forward. Friends in town began collecting old school books and sent a whole carriageload to support the endeavor.[63] On the other hand, Mammy was uncomfortable with all those children snooping around. She insisted on keeping pots, pans, and skillets all over the stove with nothing but hot water under their covers. "You think I'm guine to let em think I got no dinner cokin, an nothin to eat, and den run home an tell it." Anne explained, "She feels all this a great degradation, and thinks it is her province to keep up the honour and dignity of the family. She has a vast deal of family pride."[64]

Charles returned from Alexandria one day to report that five hundred blacks had enlisted in the army. The recruiter tried to interest him, Charles said, but he was savvy enough not to be enticed to go off and dig breastworks. Besides, like many others in the black and white communities, he was gainfully engaged in making and selling pies and other treats to the soldiers. Charles used his profits to buy a house and lot in

Washington, where he began to spend more and more time. On May 23, 1863, he disappeared for good. "He has gone to look for freedom," concluded Mammy weeks later.[65]

As the war dragged on, a pattern became discernible in the occupation of Alexandria. The city and county were either bulging with troops or almost deserted, depending on the phase of military operations. Anne first made note of the steady stream of soldiers passing by on July 17, 1861. Pro-Union neighbors stood along the roadside, wishing the bluecoats Godspeed. For days thereafter, everything was quiet. Finally, on July 23, Anne learned of "the most glorious victory," the first she had heard of the battle at Manassas in her isolation at Wilton. Lizzie came back from town talking about exhausted Federal soldiers lying around everywhere, at least one moaning, "Defeated, defeated."[66]

The cycle was repeated on March 17, 1862, when the soldiers nearby on Wilton Hill broke camp and marched to Alexandria to board ships for the Peninsula Campaign. The Frobels were so elated to be free of their tormentors that they began planting corn, raising fowl, laying out a large garden, and restoring the fence line. It was not many days later, however, when five hundred members of the Twentieth Michigan descended on their property, returning it to an active encampment. After the Battle of Second Manassas, "the earth filled up again with old broken down dilapidated soldiers—all Cameron valley and all down the railroad." On September 21, when the sisters drove to church, "The town seemed entirely cleared of soldiers. I have not seen it so quiet since the war." Within days, the Yankees were back from Antietam. In early December, a vast number of wagons and rail cars were on their way to Richmond, Anne was told. By the end of the month, deserters from Fredericksburg were again infesting the area. In February 1863, the streets of both Alexandria and Washington were thronged with soldiers, many suffering from smallpox, typhoid, and other diseases infecting the local residents. Anne's journal does not reflect that the confrontation at Chancellorsville directly impacted Alexandria, but within weeks rumors exploded that J. E. B. Stuart's "army," two hundred thousand strong, was only miles from the city, causing a frenzy of fresh trench digging. Lee's invasion of the North in late June unnerved the force manning Alexandria's garrisons but did not seem to affect the number of soldiers. The last surge came after the final surrender, when Anne observed tents filling Cameron Valley as Grant and Sherman's armies tramped in for the grand victory parade.[67]

Despite being mistreated by soldiers, blue and gray, Southern women like the Frobels could not turn their backs on individuals in need, regardless of the uniform on their backs. When Maj. Gen. John Pope's demoralized army arrived from Second Manassas, the sympathetic women of

Wilton Hill pitched in to help them. Anne declared, "Lizzie and I have been for months gratuitously feeding and attending to their sick, whenever we have the opportunity. It is the yankees I'm talking about. We never saw a Confed the whole time of the war." A couple months later she returned to the subject. "But when they come sick and hungry—and looking so miserable and wishful it is impossible for us to refuse them something to eat. The yankee people about here will not give them a mouthful."[68]

Anne was aware that women in town were ministering to sick and wounded Southern soldiers captured by the Federals. The most celebrated was the "Angel of Mercy," Kate Hooper. A native of Centreville, she had married a clerk and settled in Alexandria in 1855. When cars arrived at the city's railway depots loaded with famished rebels, Kate and her band of Samaritans found a way to pass meat, bread, and other nourishment to them through the doors and windows. Kate also visited the city's prisons and hospitals to dispense aid and collect mail to send to homefolks. When able to obtain a pass, she comforted Confederates being confined in Washington as well.[69]

Anne Frobel's diary is notable for the absence of references to national sin. God-fearing Southerners tended to conceive of the conflict as a struggle between good (equated with their cause) and evil (the Northern infidels). Surely, the Lord was on the side of the right. But if the people of the South had abandoned God's ways, they deserved to be punished, and the enemy would triumph.[70] It is doubtful that this interpretation was preached at Christ Church in Alexandria, where the Frobels worshiped. Even if at one time she subscribed to the rationale, this point of view would have seemed far less compelling when Anne reconstructed her account after the war. Yet, on the inside of the diary's back cover, Anne scrawled a verse from the Book of Isaiah (60:10): "In my wrath, I smote thee but in my favour have I had mercy on thee."[71]

Smuggling through the lines is a staple of wartime reminiscences. Rewriting her experiences after the conflict, Anne could have taken pride in tying contraband items on her hoopskirt, but apparently this was not part of her story. The sisters never went outside the Federal lines. The picket posts separating Wilton from Alexandria became increasingly troublesome as military requirements for passes tightened, but the guards generally did not search them for scarce goods. The only complication became the despised oath of allegiance required for authorized passage.

Whites farther south lived in dread of rebellious slaves. There is no such fear in Anne's wartime account; rather, it was the demons in blue who worried her. For protection, she often turned to Charles, and for comfort, when Lizzie was away from the house, Anne sought the companionship of Mammy, a tendency that became more common with women in slaveholding areas as the war progressed.[72] Only after the cannon fell silent did the high expectations of Negroes cause Anne to worry.

The shooting in Virginia stopped at Appomattox, but the suffering continued for folks like the Frobels. The women "did not take any notice, did not put the slightest faith in the report [of Lee's surrender], had learned of it so often in the past two or three years."[73] But they soon became convinced. Bushrod was captured in Georgia. David was paroled and sent letters home complaining of destitution and want of money. The residents of Northern Virginia were subject to another round of searches after the killing of the president. Anne heard of fresh atrocities committed in the guise of finding John Wilkes Booth: "Whenever the yankees feel like committing any violence or wrong on the people of Alex or vicinity they send the soldiers round to inquire what is thought of old Lincoln's assassination, and if (as is almost invariably the case) any pleasure is expressed, that is used as an excuse for all manner of robbery and abuse."[74]

Anne's narrative is silent on her feelings about the tragedy. She does, however, label the subsequent execution of Mary Surratt "an everlasting disgrace to the nation."[75] Nor could the sisters speak their minds when soldiers gathered around the dining room table boasted of killing on the battlefield or turning women and children out of their homes. The over-wrought spinsters cried later, in private.

Anne's account of the years of occupation ends on December 25, 1865. "Christmas has come again, and we are as desolate and lonely and as badly off as at any time during the war," she wrote with a sense of hopelessness.[76] She had occupied a unique vantage point atop Wilton Hill from which to watch the struggle for nationhood unfold without witnessing the fighting or experiencing the pain of losing a loved one. The remoteness of the Frobels' home certainly had its drawbacks, but their lot was hardly tragic compared with that of so many others across the region.

There are no historical gems to be discovered in the diary of Anne Frobel. The explosion at Fort Lyon on June 9, 1863, producing more than thirty casualties, was the only local event of note, but her commentary is that of an uninformed outsider recording secondhand reports. Anne's journal is nonetheless important for telling the story of Alexandria and its environs throughout the entire war. Directly and through others, the Frobels stayed in touch with their community in order to stay abreast of happenings and glean the feelings of friends. The diary thus enables readers to follow the main currents of events and emotions as they ebbed and flowed. Anne's notations are the only extant recitation of this period in Alexandria's history from a personal perspective. The significance lies in the courage, determination, and humanitarianism shown by the sisters and those around them. Anne is representative of millions of Southern sympathizers who did not leave home to fight for what they believed but suffered adverse consequences nonetheless, both during and after the conflict.

Seven full years passed before Anne returned to her journal on January 1, 1873. She stated the reason for having "a friendly talk together" again with her old book, now openly referring to the diary as a personal confidante: "I have for some time thought of writing down certain events as they occur that are of interest to me, or that I may wish to remember."[77] Her good intentions were hardly realized, as the pages reflect primarily the misery and frustrations of a destitute pair of old maids during Reconstruction. Anne escaped her own travail by recounting the troubles confronting other family members far away or, more happily, recalling her father's life and pleasant memories of her mother.

The themes are continuations of those expressed during the Civil War. Anne wrote of heartless Northern neighbors, vandals and thieves, and unreliable blacks. The sisters tried to support themselves by taking in boarders, but with the same unpleasant results. Their old homestead was literally falling down, the house leaking in every rainstorm and freezing cold throughout the winter months. Linens and bedclothes were worn, mildewed, or gone entirely. As in wartime, shoes were in constant shortage. They attempted to sell the place to no avail. Periodically, Bushrod kept their heads above water by sending money, which often went to pay taxes. Dolly, an old horse probably acquired through Bushrod's largesse, was stolen, returned, and then beaten to death with fence rails by a local drunkard. The sisters sought to raise money by signing on a string of tenant farmers, but the women's share was always nothing.

Reflecting despair reminiscent of Wilton during the worst of the Yankee occupation, Anne cried, "In our isolated condition all these sad things, and terrible accounts makes us feel more lonely and gloomy than I can tell."[78] Nighttime seemed the most threatening. Anne rationalized, "There is little or nothing to induce any one to rob us, and there is always a revolver at hand, and the whole neighborhood knows we keep one, and Lizzie has the credit of being more expert in the use of it than she really is."[79]

Slowly, the sisters sank to new depths. In the early 1870s, they could afford to pay a servant or two to cook and tend the garden. By the end of the decade, however, they were faced with doing the same chores that many plantation mistresses and sharecroppers' wives across the South had been forced to shoulder during the war. "So low in purse we cannot hire any one to help us—every thing to do ourselves. House work—cooking, washing and ironing, milking, feeding and attending to the horse and cows, pigs and poultry, and to make the fires and water the plants in the green house."[80]

Life at Wilton had been irreparably changed, but their pride remained intact. "We do up all our work as early in the morning as possible and as late in the evenings as possible, so as not to be seen by passers by or any one coming to the house. . . . Our table is always set with care and neatness," even though they were reduced to one cracked pot and a broken cooking stove.[81] The destitution suffered by the Frobel sisters was consistent with conditions in Alexandria, which did not experience full economic recovery until World War I.

The two old women continued struggling and succeeded in staying at Wilton until Lizzie died in 1898. Her funeral took place at Christ Church. Anne moved to Alabama to live with relatives and died there on April 16, 1907. For one last time she was the beneficiary of someone else's largesse as her body was carried back home to Alexandria, where she lays at rest in Ivy Hill Cemetery along with David Funsten, Frank Stringfellow, Edgar Warfield, and so many other Southern sympathizers.

CHAPTER FOURTEEN

CHRONICLER
✭✭✭ ALEXANDER HUNTER

ALEXANDER HUNTER'S ACCOUNT OF THE CIVIL WAR MAY
be placed in the same genre as those of Sam Watkins in Tennessee,
Randolph Shotwell in North Carolina, and J. J. Womack in Texas, among
many others. Each presents the war from the enlisted soldier's perspective. Hunter's facility with the written word distinguishes his narration
from many others who served in the rank and file. His work also stands
apart by interweaving reflections of Southern leaders after the war—
Robert E. Lee, Fitzhugh Lee, John B. Gordon, and Tom Rosser being the
most notable—with excerpts from accounts of battlefield commanders
and the official records of the war. His studied approach provides a more
complete story than those first-person accounts of his enlisted peers, but
without taking away from the fresh, colorful portraits of human beings
engaged in the unfamiliar business of killing each other.

The author depicts battles through the eyes of an individual combatant. Consequently, the portrayal is limited to the information known to a
single soldier. Before or after this ground-level view, he presents the big-
ger picture, complete with numbers of troops, order of battle, and postwar recollections. Hunter's classical education also permits him to inject
comparisons with engagements and leaders in ancient times and on the
battlefields of Europe.

Hunter's commentary lay largely unpublished for forty years before
Johnny Reb and Billy Yank was released in 1905. He had compiled notes
throughout the conflict and occasionally quoted from them in his narrative. A manuscript was initially completed in 1866, entitled "Four Years
in the Ranks." Selected excerpts were printed in periodicals, notably
Hunter's hometown newspaper, the *Alexandria Gazette, Confederate Veteran,*
and as far afield as *New England Magazine.* His commentary on the battle

of Sharpsburg (or Antietam), attributed to "A High Private," received three printings in the *Southern Historical Society Papers*. During the later decades of the nineteenth century, he reflected further upon his experiences and collected observations from other sources, making the final version more comprehensive and richer in detail than the initial account of his own personal war.

Hunter portrays the conflict in human terms, viewing it as a contest between men of common nature, flesh and blood, only attired in different uniforms. He recalls the joys of picket duty early in the war, when soldiers on the perimeter conversed freely with their counterparts across the lines and later relaxed with their chums who formed the reserve. Hunter tells readers, "A camp-fire is the delight of a soldier's life," an opportunity for sharing stories, as well as a welcomed source of warmth.[1] The author repeatedly returns to the joys of tobacco as a constant companion to pass the time when alone or to share with a fellow soldier. At the war's outset, Johnny Reb is pictured as a carefree, fun-loving adventurer, ridiculing, for example, fancy fashion donned by comrades in arms or, especially, civilians. The author rails at the larceny of sutlers and laughs at a column of troops breaking ranks to chase a rabbit. Soldiers were also likely to fall out when passing cherry trees or mulberry bushes.

Hunter was a seventeen-year-old student at Episcopal High School when word arrived of South Carolina's secession.[2] Personal letters and daily papers fueled rumors and imagination until an overflow of enthusiasm sent the scholars home to join the cause of Southern nationalism. Alexander Hunter's life, like that of his native South, was thereby set on a new course.

Born in 1843, he was descended from two first families of Virginia, not surprisingly, the Alexanders and the Hunters. His uncle, Gen. Alexander Hunter, had helped defend Washington, D.C., during the British invasion in 1814. The general's namesake was the only son of Bushrod W. Hunter, a lieutenant in the U.S. Navy when the Civil War broke out. Father and son cast their lots with Virginia, Bushrod accepting a commission as a major of heavy artillery. Marching off to war, the Hunters left behind the estate of Abingdon in Alexandria County, listed as worth thirty thousand dollars in the 1860 census, along with various personal property, including twenty-seven slaves valued at forty thousand dollars. The house's foundations now seem misplaced amidst the terminals, runways, and parking lots of Reagan National Airport. To the north stands Arlington, the Custis home occupied by the family of Robert E. Lee. Young Alexander had inherited Abingdon from his uncle. Like Arlington, it was occupied by Federal troops and confiscated by the U.S. government in 1864, and, like the Lees, the Hunters had to litigate for repossession after the war, in Alexander's case with the legal assistance of future president James A. Garfield.[3]

Alexander Hunter
in the early 1860s.
From Alexander
Hunter, *The Women
of the Debatable Land*
(Washington, D.C.:
Corden Publishing
Company, 1912).

Hunter joined the Alexandria Riflemen, a militia company under command of the corpulent Morton Marye, a native of Fredericksburg who occupied a prominent place in Alexandria as lawyer and merchant. Once Virginia seceded, the unit converted into Company A of the Seventeenth Virginia Infantry.

Like any new recruit, Hunter's wide-eyed impressions of his first days in uniform are filled with amazement at the contrast from his prior life. As a slender young man weighing ninety-seven pounds, Hunter naturally worried about becoming engaged in mortal combat with an adversary the size of the large fellows enlisting with him. He recalls the long days (2:00 P.M.: "The old hour for napping"), military vocabulary (dress parade: "Oh! The mockery of that name"), and a sergeant's absolute dictatorship.[4] His introduction to hunger in uniform occurred at Manassas Junction, where Southern forces congregated after Alexandria was occupied on May 24, 1861. Appetites stimulated by the rigors of living and training outdoors could only be fully satisfied by foraging. Citizen soldiers lost individual freedom under the regimen imposed by Gen. P. G. T. Beauregard, as guards restricted movement through the encampment's perimeter, "police duty" required gentlemen in the enlisted ranks to act like mere scavengers, and the regular tap of a drum accompanied meals.

Hunter approached the war's opening engagement with the same wonderment. He provides reaction to the long drum roll announcing the threat; officers shouting, "Fall in, men!" and privates filling their knapsacks to the limit, when later, as veterans, they carried little upon entering combat. Then, there was the waiting, seemingly interminable. Volunteers were best kept busy, the author observes, moving constantly from place to place in order to keep their minds occupied. When the filth became unbearable, a "dry wash" sufficed, "rubbing the face on a jacket sleeve."[5] Hunter portrays raw troops waiting before their first battle—fearful, curious, and nervous. Many turned to prayer.

Once firing began at Blackburn's Ford on July 18, three days before the more celebrated battle known as Bull Run or First Manassas, the defenders of the Seventeenth Virginia were sobered by the frightening sound of artillery shells overhead. Hunter recalls, "The ground was covered with leaves and twigs cut off by the leaden and iron shower."[6] After the skirmish, the elated survivors engaged in "tremendous bragging," displaying holes torn in caps and jackets. Their euphoria soon diminished, however, with the frightful sight of less fortunate comrades and enemy dead lying in front of their lines. Hunter's regiment played no active role in the fighting on the twenty-first, but his eyes were opened by the wealth of goods abandoned by the enemy in its campsites—arms and ammunition, accoutrements, officers' swords and crimson sashes, and baskets of champagne, along with official orders, papers, and letters with unbroken seals. Hunter poses the now-familiar question, wondering why the victors were stopped from pursuing the vanquished all the way to Washington.

After the clash at Bull Run, food was plentiful as farmers traded vegetables, butter, and eggs for beef and salt pork, which the Southern army had in abundance at that time. Hunter's narrative confirms that human nature has not changed. Soldiers and civilians engaged in the common pastime of criticizing conduct of the war. Complacent after battle, men gathered around campfires to review the engagement from first to last, assimilating new information until the pieces fit together in a harmonious, if not factual whole.

The infantrymen from Alexandria were heavily engaged in action at Seven Pines on the Peninsula in the spring of 1862. Their initial suffering caused them to brighten later on at the prospect of fighting behind the protection of breastworks. Ever attuned to the human dimension, Hunter noted a tendency for the cowardly to rush to accompany wounded comrades to the rear. He also observed that units advancing to the front invariably encountered the slightly wounded, abandoning the battlefield and reciting the same exaggerated tale of fighting against fearful odds up ahead.

Just as Bull Run brought home to Washington the realities of war, so, Hunter points out, casualties from the clash at Seven Pines, within earshot of the Confederate capital, produced a powerful impact on Richmond's residents. Secession meant men wounded and dying, many being transported into this genteel society. Hunter contrasts the sobriety observed in Richmond with the lavishness he later noted in the capital one hundred miles to the north.

Enlisted men had no illusions about the capabilities of their officers. Hunter castigates the Confederate Congress for decreeing in 1861 that leaders be popularly elected the following spring. Blunders were consequently made by the Southern army due to the ineptness of "men of no military training and who possessed no soldierly qualities."[7] In particular, the author derides "the incompetency and criminal ignorance of our [brigade] commanding officer" at Seven Pines, Col. James Kemper.[8] Yet it would appear that officers selected under the Southern system were no worse than those commissioned by the Federal government or the men and women thrust into leadership positions in modern times. The influence of politics seems pervasive in every army.

Some things remained constant throughout the war—the omnipresence of whiskey, flies, and camp fever, notably dysentery and diarrhea. Hunter exalts the ubiquitous vermin, tracing its lineage back to ancient Egypt, before detailing the extraordinary lengths taken to expunge these creatures from body and clothing. The verbal artist also paints a stark picture of soldiers thirsting for water, especially during, but not limited to, the height of the Southern summer.

In a subsequent engagement on the Peninsula at Frayser's Farm, Hunter and some comrades were lost in the confusion of intermingling battle lines and taken prisoner by the bluecoats. During one of several retrogrades caused by Southern counterattacks, Hunter was questioned by a brigadier general. "What are you Rebels fighting for, anyway?" After consideration, the prisoner replied, "We are fighting to protect our mint-beds."[9] Fortunately for Hunter, his interrogators laughed at the response, recalling the Virginia julep.

The second dimension of his book's title is made credible by insights gained into Billy Yank during Hunter's repeated imprisonments by the Federals. When first captured, he took note of the abundance of equipment and accessories available to his adversaries and the high state of their morale. His captors were generous with their hot coffee, even if they could not influence their officers to move Hunter out of the muddy hollow in which he was being held. En route to Massachusetts, via steamship, rebel prisoners were subjected to brutality at the hands of militia guards on Governor's Island, New York, causing Hunter to remark that "veteran soldiers never illtreated their prisoners, such was the experience on both sides."[10] Later, Hunter observed the wounded, blue and gray, lying together in a common area, joking, singing songs, telling camp stories, and drinking coffee from the same cup. He concludes, "The privates of both armies never personally disliked one another; they were the best friends in the world as soon as they met on neutral ground."[11]

The seventy-five detainees from the Seventeenth Virginia were the first rank and file to be incarcerated at Fort Warren in Boston Harbor. Prior to their arrival, the facility was used for political prisoners and high-ranking captives, notably Brig. Gen. Simon Bolivar Buckner. "Certainly no prisoners of war had ever been treated so luxuriously before, nor were they ever afterwards," Hunter muses about his own experience.[12] Provisions and accommodations were far better than those provided Southern soldiers in the field. Food, clothing, books, and other luxuries arrived from families in Alexandria. "Those were halcyon days; those days of July 1862."[13] In contrast, when exchanged after forty-five days and returned to Confederate lines on the James River, the Seventeenth Virginians encountered comrades who had been imprisoned at Fort Delaware, whose countenance Hunter describes as "the saddest sight that our eyes had ever looked upon."[14]

Back in the ranks in time for Second Manassas, Hunter relates his regiment's charge near the Chinn House. He digresses to evaluate the minié musket, with which they were armed, as "worthless" because it quickly became fouled.[15] Instead, he preferred the Enfield. War had not become so commonplace that the combatants were blind to "the horribly sickening sight" of the dead resting as they fell, faces contorted, limbs ripped off, bodies torn and mangled, blood sprayed on the ground. Each had been searched, everything of value taken. Hunter believes, "A true soldier rarely condescends to strip his fallen enemies"; removing a pair of boots out of necessity being far different, in his eyes, than robbing the dead of their wealth.[16] The body of a boy scarcely fourteen years old was found, attired in a fresh, handmade uniform. "How anxious they must be at home about him," lamented a Confederate colleague.[17]

Crossing into Maryland, the Army of Northern Virginia encountered unexpected coolness from the residents of Frederick County. Hunter was once again captured when the Seventeenth Virginia was overrun on the right Confederate flank at Antietam. The Yankees were amazed at the ragged, emaciated condition of their prisoners. On reflection, Hunter attributes the lost opportunity at Sharpsburg to half of the Southern army being absent due to straggling. He writes that Lee had excused soldiers without shoes from the invasion. Some Confederates threw away their footgear to take advantage of this offer, while thousands of others were genuinely barefoot, starving, and sick.

Soon after the battle, more than five hundred Confederates, including Hunter, were paroled and released at the Potomac River. They were officially exchanged a few weeks later. Hunter rejoined his regiment at Fredericksburg, where the Seventeenth Virginia was held in reserve during the December battle. After a harsh winter with insufficient nourishment, it is hardly surprising that Hunter was hospitalized in the spring of 1863. Consequently, he missed the fighting at Chancellorsville but did record the outpouring of grief in the Confederate capital over the loss of Thomas "Stonewall" Jackson. The subsequent reversals in Southern fortunes would not have occurred if Jackson had lived, Hunter believes. Nevertheless, "America would doubtless have been one country, as destiny determined it should be—but the shame of defeat, the horrors of reconstruction would have been spared the South."[18] Hunter provides no further elaboration on this apparent contradiction.

After two years of suffering in the infantry, Hunter was ready to consider another way to serve the Confederate cause. He acknowledges that foot soldiers castigated the cavalry for leading an "easy, careless, roaming life," while, in truth, envying the troopers.[19] He mustered courage to approach General Lee for a transfer. Bushrod Hunter had served as a pallbearer at the burial of George Washington Parke Custis, and so Alexander enjoyed special entrée, but the chronicler contends that any soldier was free to speak with the commanding general. Hunter later attests, "General Lee was always accessible. The humblest private found in him a kind and gentle friend; and it is no wonder they followed him with absolute confidence and unbounded love."[20] With renowned grace, Lee acceded to the young visitor's request.

Hunter did not catch up with the Southern cavalry in time to participate in the battle at Gettysburg. In describing this watershed event, he produced the longest chapter of the book. From a postwar prospective, Hunter is prescient in characterizing the conflict as "the one battle above all others that America, North and South alike, will always take most pride in."[21] This time, Lee's advance across the Potomac was not hindered by straggling. The ranks were full, soldiers adequately clothed, stomachs well fed. Hunter's assignment of blame is of note. To begin, he describes Stuart's raid into Pennsylvania as "the greatest fiasco ever committed by a veteran soldier."[22] A. P. Hill is faulted for lack of assertiveness in not occupying the hills around Gettysburg on the first day. Hunter goes on to cite an additional failure, "the truth is that Lee himself at the supreme hour failed to rise to the occasion."[23] "On the evening of the 1st he was on the battle-field in person" and did not push his commanders to take the high ground from its Federal defenders. Again, on the second day of the encounter, in Hunter's judgment, the Confederates missed an opportunity to triumph by not pressing their advantage. He alleges that Billy Yanks who fought in the battle later told him, "The Rebs had us whipped once at Gettysburg, but did not know it . . . about sunset on the second day."[24] In addition, James Longstreet is criticized for disobeying orders and dallying. Finally, Hunter quotes Lee as saying, "Had Stonewall Jackson been at Gettysburg, I would have established the Southern Confederacy."[25]

Eventually, Hunter joined up with his new unit, the Fourth Virginia, whose Company H was known as the Black Horse Troop. His portrayal of the fortunes of this famous troop, published a century ago, corresponds with what is now the accepted characterization of the heights and depths of Southern cavalry. During the first two years of the conflict, Black Horse soldiers represented the cream of Virginia gentry, fine horsemen and expert marksmen. Their mounts were, of course, coal black. By the summer of 1863, when Hunter joined them at Fredericksburg, their uniforms were ragged and their horses of all breeds, sizes, and colors. The most frightening aspect to Hunter, however, was the infusion "of the most trifling, scary, no-account men."[26] Consequently, there was little discipline. The introduction of breech-loading firearms made the saber obsolete. The author observes that by the end of the war, Northern cavalrymen not only outnumbered their counterparts but also were better mounted and armed with superior Spencer and Henry repeating rifles. Despite these improvements in weaponry, however, Hunter is perceptive in realizing that "for deciding the fortunes of great battles the day of cavalry is numbered."[27]

Fredericksburg was a deserted village when Hunter returned, and Southern horsemen occupied themselves with stealing produce. Vedettes traded tobacco with Billy Yanks for coffee, sugar, and newspapers. By late 1863, men and horses were starving in Madison County, which was completely bare of food. Consequently, Hunter and a half dozen other troopers walked into Fauquier County, behind Yankee lines, to try to surprise Federal cavalrymen and steal their mounts. The author asserts that a single Confederate scout could escort a handful of bluecoats for days back to Southern lines. Instead of taking prisoners, however, Hunter himself was captured in January 1864 while hiding from a Yankee patrol in a church loft near Warrenton.

Extended observation of his counterparts in blue once again permitted Hunter to compare the fighting men of the two armies. "Billy Yank was comfortable in body and stuffed to the throat with the good things of life. Certainly, fifty per cent of the men were better clothed, better paid and better fed than they were at home. Besides this, his duties were generally light, especially during six months of the year."[28] In contrast, Hunter writes, Johnny Reb's clothing was ragged; half of the men were without an overcoat and not one in five was wearing a pair of socks. A solitary blanket provided warmth, day and night. His war steed was thin and attenuated.

Hunter and twenty other captives were transferred to Old Capitol Prison in Washington, D.C., where the inmates eagerly sought news from Dixie. Ironically, the fare was more wholesome and in greater quantity than that served in military camps in the South. Nevertheless, Hunter prepared to escape by sawing the bars with two knives stolen from the supper table. Hours before he planned to flee, Hunter was added to a contingent for transfer to Point Lookout, Maryland, about which he had heard appalling tales of mistreatment by the Negro guards. As the four hundred rebels were herded through Washington's streets to the wharf, Hunter stripped off his gray uniform to uncover civilian attire sent by friends in Alexandria and, at an opportune moment, broke from the column and blended into a crowd of onlookers.

Thus began a long journey back to Confederate lines. The escapee was sheltered, first by an uncle in Washington and then by Southern sympathizers in Baltimore and Frederick after taking the cars between these locales. Hunter's account reads like an escape from Devil's Island or Alcatraz. He tried unsuccessfully to cross the Potomac by raft; was recaptured and imprisoned at Wheeling, West Virginia; escaped while being transferred to the depot by using his patented ruse; trekked with a comrade through the snow and cold for several days; was briefly recaptured; climbed out the chimney of a guardhouse and plunged into the icy Potomac below; and finally tramped seventy miles to Woodstock, Virginia, and safety.

Along the way, the chronicler observed inmates being mistreated by an outfit of German immigrants until relieved by a New Hampshire regiment which restored civility. When looking for assistance behind enemy lines, the author contends, rebels often sought out Irishmen, who could relate the South's plight to that of Ireland and tended to side with the underdog. The South encompassed more Catholics than the North, Hunter asserts, and, consequently, the pope recognized the Confederacy. Here, as at other points in his writing, Hunter's exuberance led him to mischaracterization. The Vatican never formally recognized the Confederacy. Pope Pius IX wrote to President Jefferson Davis, characterizing him as "Illustrious and Honorable," a salutation usually reserved for heads of state, but there was no formal acknowledgment of the Confederacy's legal standing as a government.[29]

After a furlough to recover from his ordeal, Hunter rejoined the Black Horse in time for the Overland Campaign. Hanging sabers and revolvers on the pummels of their saddles, the troopers fought with carbines as foot soldiers. At times, Hunter's account lapses into romanticism. "The cannoneers were stripped to the waist, displaying their brawny arms and hairy chests. They swung the guns around as if steel and brass had lost their weight and were the playthings of the hour. In loading, the men would throw themselves unconsciously into attitudes and magnificent poses which, could a sculptor have caught, would have made his fame."[30] Lying on his back beside other wounded soldiers on the Spotsylvania courthouse green, after being shot in the leg at Todd's Tavern, the young narrator recalls being awed by skies full of stars, "so bright and radiant."

Once again, the chronicle plummets from heaven to hell. Hunter was evacuated to Chimborazo Hospital in Richmond. It is ironic that while imprisonment at Fort Warren was his most luxurious time of the war, "The three days I spent in that hospital [in the Confederate capital] were the most terrible of my life."[31] Fortunately, he was soon rescued by a sister and placed in a private clinic.

Convalescence in Richmond provided the invalid an opportunity to reflect upon the South's morale. In late summer of 1864, the citizenry anticipated victory, he reports. Beauregard was holding Ben Butler in check outside Petersburg; John C. Breckinridge had stopped Franz Sigel in the Shenandoah Valley; the Federals had suffered heavy losses against Lee at Cold Harbor; and there was a lull in Yankee cavalry raids directed at the railroad south of the capital. Furthermore, Hunter asserts that every private in the Army of Northern Virginia expected success. "After the Battle of Cold Harbor the Army of Northern Virginia never felt so proud and jubilant. It is true the soldiers were more enthusiastic on the march to Gettysburg a year before, but they did not possess then that implicit confidence in themselves. These troops had fought five engagements on May 6th, five on May 12th, and over a score since Grant crossed the Rapidan, and with one exception had held their ground in every one of them."[32] Conversely, he believes, despair weighed upon the Federal Army of the Potomac after suffering casualties equivalent to half of its officers and men during the summer offensive. Gloomy foreboding excerpted from Northern newspapers was reprinted in the Richmond press, cheering citizen and soldier alike.

The rebel capital received a dose of reality when a nearby battery was taken by enemy troops. Southern military personnel in the city were ordered to report to their units. Hunter's pass was not recognized as valid, as it was not signed by the provost marshal, Brig. Gen. John Winder, and the convalescent was arrested and held in Castle Thunder, a prison crowded with soldiers and civilians. One night was enough for Hunter, and the next day he and a Marylander scaled the wall surrounding the exercise yard and ran through the city streets to freedom.

Back with the Black Horse in the fall of 1864, Hunter and his comrades were again looking for mounts. On one foray, he and a chum walked to the outskirts of Washington, D.C., around Burke's Station, twelve miles west of Alexandria. Dressed in full uniform, so as not to be treated as spies if captured, and armed with double-barreled shotguns, they waited like highwaymen for vulnerable Federal riders, first between Burke's and Springfield Stations and then on the turnpike between Falls Church and Fairfax Court House. Eventually, they captured three blue-coats and absconded with them, their two horses, and a pair of mules, leading pursuers on a merry chase, which Hunter compares to a fox hunt and empathizes with the prey.

The winter of 1864–65 was unusually severe. For the first time, troop morale was shattered as soldiers verged on starvation. In Hunter's estima-tion, cavalry and artillery soldiers suffered more than infantry, because they had to share any nourishment with their horses, which were reduced to skin and bones. Enlistees from the far Southern states deserted to return to their families behind Federal lines. Those left behind could harbor no deep-seated anger over their departure, the author opines, for they had already proved their devotion to the cause through several years of service.

Hunter's leg wound reopened in a skirmish with Federal cavalry, and he returned to Richmond to recuperate. He found there a sense of over-whelming doom. Food and clothing were scarce, but the city's women were more defiant than ever. When eventually venturing into Chester-field County to return to his unit, he saw a countryside denuded of trees, the populace surviving on cornbread and sorghum molasses. Upon first hearing of Lee's surrender, Hunter did not believe it. "The end of the war was so different from that predicted by every soldier: they all thought that if Richmond was taken, every troop would take to the mountains and swamps, and carry on the struggle as did the guerilla in Spain against Napoleon, and as [Thomas] Sumter and [Francis] Marion, later on, waged against the British."[33] (His chronology was wrong.)

Paroled at Petersburg, Hunter began his journey home to Alexandria, stopping briefly on Franklin Street in Richmond to chat with General Lee. The expression of feelings about his idol is among Hunter's most personal writing.

> I could never analyze the feeling that General Lee inspired in me. I had visited at his home at Arlington before the war, his son [Robert E. Lee Jr.] being a schoolmate of mine, and I had seen him there, and he was my boyish hero, but afterwards, when a reckless, careless soldier, with not one atom of reverence in my make-up, he subdued me by his very pres-ence. It was not fear, it was a mixed feeling of homage, adoration and awe. His was not an obtrusive personality, but there enveloped him a nameless grandeur, a simple yet immaculate dignity, a kingly presence that made one unconsciously take off his hat and stand bareheaded in his presence.

> I have met some of the greatest men of the times, but I merely felt a pro-
> found respect for their genius of talent, nothing more. . . .
> I believed then, and I believe now, that no man born of woman ever
> stood so close to the Immortal as Robert E. Lee.[34]

Hunter reached home in time to stand on Pennsylvania Avenue in Washington and watch the last review of the Army of the Potomac in late May 1865. He admired the veterans of what he considered the finest fighting force the world had ever seen and, consequently, felt no shame that his side had been vanquished by this juggernaut. Hunter explains, "to those whose sympathies were with the South there is every proof that the soldiers in the field did their part, the women at home did theirs, but that the Government failed lamentably."[35] The commentator is not blind to the extraordinary challenge before the nascent Confederacy. "The South was overweighted from the start," he admits.[36] In Hunter's judgment, there were many reasons for the defeat. Access to storehouses in the West was denied with the surrender of Vicksburg, closing the Mississippi River. Blockading the ports of Charleston and Wilmington starved the South. The Army of the Potomac could not have won without the mighty Federal warships, concludes the author, the son of a career naval officer.

First and foremost, Hunter believes, the South was doomed by the selection of Jefferson Davis as its national leader. Every one of his favorite generals brought disaster. As an unabashed admirer of Abraham Lincoln, whom he calls "the genius of the century," Hunter was among the first commentators to speculate about the outcome if the two sides had exchanged presidents.[37]

Hunter is especially critical of the appointment of Jubal Early to an independent command in the Shenandoah Valley in 1864. His opinions were, in all likelihood, influenced by conversations with John B. Gordon and Tom Rosser, two Confederate generals who stumped the South for decades after the war, attempting to shape its history from their own personal points of view. The chronicler credits Gordon's account of Early restraining him from annihilating the U.S. Sixth Corps at Cedar Creek. Hunter also subscribes to Rosser's criticisms of Early's generalship, which showed him unfit for leadership and consequently disliked by his own troops.[38] Hunter does not shy away from Rosser's comment to Early that "it was General R. E. Lee's mistake in trusting [you with] so important a command."[39]

Among the most interesting contributions of Hunter's commentary are his observations on high morale within the Army of Northern Virginia during most of the conflict. Southern boys rushed to enlist in the summer of 1861, expecting a short, victorious war. At the close of 1862, after the terrible Yankee casualties at Fredericksburg, Hunter reports that Lee's troops thought they were on the verge of triumph. Six months later, morale was even better: "As one of Lee's soldiers, I know that never was the *esprit de corps* of our army so high as when on that eventful June day in '63 they crossed the Potomac on their way northward."[40] A year later, he made a similar observation. "At no time during the war was the army in such superb condition as in the spring of sixty-four . . . There was not a private soldier in the Army of Northern Virginia who did not believe that the coming year would find the South victorious . . . Only one more grand campaign, they thought, said, and wrote; only one more great, united struggle—and then a glorious peace."[41] Conversely, after the army endured the winter of 1864–65 in the trenches outside Petersburg, Hunter filed a far different report: "What I saw made me feel faint and heart-sick. The soldiers, gaunt, bony, wild-eyed and sullen, sat on the side of the road listless. No jokes, no laughter, no groups of social fellows squatted on a blanket playing seven-up or draw-poker, no jibes greeted me as I rode through."[42] This was a different Johnny Reb than the one ennobled by Hunter.

Although proudly serving four years in the enlisted ranks, Hunter resented what he observed as the South's policy of nonpromotion for valor and skill. Privates who displayed extraordinary courage and commitment, he writes, remained privates. Nevertheless, Hunter concludes his saga, "Johnny Reb did the best he knew how; he fought anything and everything and never counted the odds; he labored and slaved for years without pay and without reward."[43]

After lying fallow for four decades, Hunter's chronicle was finally released in 1905 by the Neale Publishing Company.[44] Enough time had elapsed since the fighting to soften automatic rejection of all things Southern. Confederate heroes had become popular, epitomized, of course, by the icon Robert E. Lee. In the minds of many, the South no longer bore responsibility for slavery or the war. The Lost Cause had been transformed in the national mind from military defeat to a romantic quest to preserve superior values that were being lost in industrialized America as she turned the corner into the twentieth century. Virginia writers were at the forefront in redefining the Confederate cause and portraying the charm of Southern culture. Hunter's erudite treatment of the war and Southern society was but one in a series of writings beginning with John Esten Cooke and Thomas Nelson Page and continuing with an assortment of Virginia men and women who published warm reminiscences of life before and during the conflict.[45]

Hunter's portrayal of Lee, on the other hand, cut against the crusade to canonize the beloved military leader, thereby redeeming the South but dehumanizing its idol in the process. By refusing to absolve Lee from responsibility for the defeat at Gettysburg, Hunter contradicted the historical revisionism of John B. Gordon, the old corps commander who led the United Confederate Veterans for the fifteen years preceding publication of *Johnny Reb*. Hunter did, however, contribute to the portrayal of Lee as a conciliator when recalling the general's advice to him shortly after Appomattox. "'Your first duty,' he said, 'is to go home and make your mother's heart glad, and your next is to Virginia. She needs all her sons more now than ever.'"[46]

Virginia also relied upon her daughters, as Hunter explained in later writings. *The Women of the Debatable Land* was intended, the author says in its preface, to encourage his commonwealth to erect a monument "to the women of Virginia who sacrificed their all that the cause they loved should never die."[47] The book itself is a memorial to their contribution.

Published in 1912, the volume is an expanded version of an article that appeared in *Confederate Veteran* in 1907.[48] The "debatable land" is defined as "the theater where the most stirring and sensational war drama was played" (an analogy familiar to the writer, as discussed later). It was also known as "Mosby's Confederacy" for the control exercised over Virginia's piedmont by his Rangers, despite the frequent presence of Federal troopers. In Hunter's telling, the debatable land encompassed the counties of Fairfax, Prince William, Culpeper, and Fauquier. Modern historians also include southern Loudoun County.

Hunter begins with the seemingly obligatory comparison of the South's struggle with those of the Highlanders and Lowlanders, the Scots and the English. He ties his tragedy to the siege of Troy, the irregulars who followed Marion and Sumter, and the heroism of American Indians and pioneers in frontier America. Having paid his respects to the South's adopted forebears, the author embarks upon his narrative.

The heroines of this account are women in no-man's land between the lines, alone and isolated, often living hand to mouth with their children. Hunter relates the stories of women who, despite their own personal vulnerability, risked safety and security to help soldiers in gray. They hid Black Horse troopers and Mosby's Rangers, nursed the sick and wounded, collected information on Federal forces, and warned of ambushes. Their comfort was by no means restricted to Confederates, as illustrated by the many wounded Yankees who were brought into Warrenton and cared for by maidens and matrons serving as sympathetic nurses. In this regard, Hunter contrasts these women with the damsels of New Orleans who insulted their conquerors. Hunter's paragons "could be proud and cold, but never offensive."[49]

Hunter digresses repeatedly to venerate the deeds of Southern cavaliers, operating independently or in small squads in opposition to organized units of bluecoat riders. In the author's terminology, "the king of the debatable land" was the guerilla leader, John Singleton Mosby. Hunter's portrait of the partisan, however, varies from the popular image of this storied figure.

Mosby, unlike most leaders of men, had no magnetism; he was as cold as an iceberg, and to shake hands with him was like having the first symptoms of a congestive chill. He was positive, evidence of a self-centered man; and he did not know what human sympathy was . . . Mosby was fond of reading the old English literature, and was . . . a born soldier, a light cavalryman by instinct, and a partisan who, under no orders, could accomplish wonders, but in the regular army he would, in all probability, never have been heard of.[50]

It is difficult to imagine such a leader holding together a band of independent combatants. Hunter's characterization might well have evolved from a rivalry between the Black Horse and its more celebrated counterparts riding with Mosby.

The Women of the Debatable Land provides arguably the best contemporary account of the Jessie Scouts. The appellation was given to a battalion of Union cavalrymen attired in Confederate uniforms to obtain information on the whereabouts of rebel soldiers. Their deception added to confusion caused by Southern horsemen attired by necessity in portions of Federal uniforms, along with accoutrements obtained from their counterparts. Consequently, it was incumbent upon the inhabitants of Northern Virginia to maintain a healthy suspicion of every stranger and not presume one's allegiance solely by the coat on his back.

It is also interesting to note the presentation of additional information elaborating upon the women introduced in *Johnny Reb and Billy Yank*. When making their way back to Confederate lines from Wheeling, West Virginia, for example, Hunter and his comrade pretended to be going to enlist in the Northern army, thereby obtaining the assistance of a pretty girl encountered along the way who was sympathetic to the Union. The trip into Fairfax County to steal horses was proposed, readers are now told, by a venerable Southern patriot who shared her observations of lax discipline within the Federal lines, thus providing the opportunity to capture horses and take prisoners.

Hunter's second book provides an opportunity to return to some of his favorite messages from *Johnny Reb*. "One of the great mistakes the Confederate Government made was in not enlisting the blacks and giving to them and their families their freedom," he asserts.[51] Although acknowledging that many younger slaves sided with the North, Hunter points out that house retainers were staunchly loyal to their masters.

Once again Hunter hammers out a sympathetic portraiture of the enlisted man, North and South. He seems to take special delight in acknowledging the chivalry of his opponents. The chronicler glorifies "the grandest charge ever made by mortal men, that of Meagher's brigade of Irishmen against Marye's Heights" in the battle of Fredericksburg.[52]

At another point, he gushes that "one act, especially of a Federal soldier, was so chivalric that its parallel can hardly be matched in the annals of war."[53] Bluecoats are credited with freely sharing pork and hardtack with hungry local families. When breaking camp, it was not uncommon for the Federals to leave behind large quantities of provisions, which often kept local residents from starvation. This depiction of Yankee generosity would certainly have provoked an argument with Anne Frobel. Yet *Women of the Debatable Land* was offered for sale early in the twentieth century, when writers and publishers were once again interested in appealing to readers on both sides of the Mason-Dixon line.

The xenophobic characterization of Federal enlisted men, initially presented in *Johnny Reb and Billy Yank,* is repeated. "The worst pillagers in the Army of the Potomac were men of foreign birth; and after them were the Pennsylvanians. Many of them were of mixed nationality, who inherited a love of looting."[54] At another point, the author rails, "It was rarely that a self-respecting native-born Northerner, with malice prepense, applied the torch. It was the foreigners and the riff-raff, or the hired substitutes and bounty jumpers, who joined the army for plunder who committed these outrages."[55] Conversely, Hunter embraces the Irish, who were familiar from his formative years in Alexandria. "Women in distress found in every Irishman, high and low, big and little, a defender," he writes.[56]

The author also revisits his stereotype of Southern soldiers as "the wealthiest and brightest youths in the land," accepted by Confederate officers and civilians alike as saviors of the South. In contrast, a private in a blue blouse was not welcome among his own officers. By the third year of the war, in the author's estimation, Northern ranks were filled mainly with foreigners or hirelings, as opposed to native-born enlisted men fighting for a cause, the figures esteemed in Hunter's writings on the war.

Although the work was intended to memorialize the deeds of Southern women, Hunter's opus closes with yet another tribute to the Confederate soldier. At war's end, he lamented, "his once gray uniform was patched, hit or miss, and in an active campaign, discolored with earth, tarnished with battle smoke, and torn by the briers."[57] That description could serve as a metaphor for destruction across the South, as well as for changes in Hunter's hometown, as he found upon returning after Appomattox.

Hunter's role as a chronicler for the South extended beyond remembrances of the war. He applied his literary talent to political and social commentary as an author and newspaper correspondent. This was a time when Confederate veterans were very much involved in issues being debated in Virginia, and, consequently, Hunter's observations included repeated references to them.

Hunter's political acumen was honed by representing Alexandria in Virginia's House of Delegates from 1877 to 1879. He was elected as a conservative Democrat, taking the mid-ground between adherents of the 1871 Funding Act, or Funders, who pledged to pay off the state's staggering antebellum debt at high interest, and the opposing faction known as Readjusters, who would satisfy only a portion of the obligation. The Readjusters were headed by former Maj. Gen. William Mahone. While serving in the legislature and afterward, Hunter contributed articles to the *Alexandria Gazette,* sounding a clarion call that the unwillingness of the two sides to compromise would soon lead to ascendancy of Republicans and Negroes. Hunter incorrectly forecast that Mahone's opponent would be the next U.S. senator from Virginia. When the Readjusters gained control of the legislature in 1879, the party's delegates quite naturally elected their leader to that office. Hunter then predicted, accurately this time, that Mahone could actually be a Republican in disguise, which he eventually declared after taking his seat in Washington. The Readjusters turned out veterans, many maimed and disabled, from sinecures in the state capital, whereupon Hunter again spoke out in anger. The commentator subsequently urged new leadership in the Democratic Party to enhance its appeal to the old Confederate soldiers.

When not in Richmond, Hunter was fond of retreating to Old Point Comfort, where the James River empties into the mouth of the Chesapeake Bay at Hampton Roads. During the late 1870s, a series of his articles emanated from this area. Nearby was the water, Hunter pointed out, where in 1862 the ironclad *Merrimack* (or CSS *Virginia*) rammed the Federal sloop *Cumberland,* sending her to the bottom. The resort had changed after the war from being a watering place for Northerners to a favorite of Virginians, in the correspondent's opinion, thanks to its new manager in 1878, the former chief of Lee's Third Corps artillery, Brig. Gen. Lindsay Walker. The following year, Hunter reported that the Richmond Light Infantry Blues were camped out at Old Point Comfort, causing a rush of vacationers from the capital. The Alexandria Light Infantry trained there as well, and so it is not surprising that Montgomery Corse was listed as one of the guests in 1879.

Hunter's dispatches to the *Alexandria Gazette* were signed with the nom de plume "Chasseur" (hunter or sportsman). Old Point Comfort was the departure point for outdoorsmen to enjoy the remote Virginia peninsula on the eastern shore of the Chesapeake Bay. Sportsmen would take a small boat across the mouth of the bay to the ocean side of the peninsula. First came Cape Charles and its lighthouse, then Smith Island. Eighteen miles farther was Cobb Island, with Hog Island the northernmost islet in Northampton County. Each held special attractions for hunting and fishing.

Using Cobb Island as his base of operations, Hunter composed a number of pieces for the Alexandria newspaper and, later, *Outing* magazine, published in New York.[58] They addressed such divergent matters as hunting brant (described as the "king of the waterfowl"), residents' opposition to shooting fish hawks and eagles on Hog Island, and the benefits derived from the U.S. lifesaving station on Cobb Island.

In 1908, Hunter pulled together these fragments, along with other adventures recorded in his diaries from 1880 to 1903, and published them in *The Huntsman in the South*. This volume deals solely with his experiences in Virginia and North Carolina and was intended to be the first in a series of works carrying across the Southeast. Hunter begins with recollections of hunting around Abingdon as a youngster with two slave boys as companions. He paints a picture of the Potomac reminiscent of Robert E. Lee's boyhood in Alexandria, now long forgotten.

> As for the wild fowl that haunted the river between Washington and Mount Vernon, it was simply astounding. I . . . never have seen such apparently limitless numbers of wild fowl as fed and circled in the very sight of the Capitol's dome. . . .
>
> [O]n the Virginia side the flats were bare at low water. On these shallow bottoms there grew in the greatest luxuriance an indigenous plant called wild celery, which the waterfowl preferred to any other food. About the middle of November the birds began to congregate in such huge flocks that on a clear morning, when suddenly disturbed they took to wing, they made a noise like rolling thunder.[59]

The most entertaining chapter is entitled, "A Hunt with President [Benjamin] Harrison." It concerns the chief executive's visit to the Ragged Island Club at Virginia Beach, where Hunter was a member in residence. The president is described as being clothed in a corduroy suit, "accompanied only by one colored servant," and "the only man in the club who declined to have a bracer" when awakened at three o'clock in the morning to be transported to his blind.[60] He bagged forty canvasbacks but was reported as being more excited over shooting a swan.

Ingrained in Hunter's narratives of hunting and fishing is a Southern code of honorable sportsmanship. Indeed, the author takes credit for framing the first game laws for Virginia while serving in its legislature.

The frontispiece of *The Huntsman in the South* displays a theatrical silhouette with wide-brimmed hat set at a rakish angle toward the photographer. Alexander Hunter appeared the caricature of a patrician, albeit a Virginia aristocrat down at the heels. Bereft of family estates and forced at this time to work as a government functionary with the Interior's Bureau of Land Management, Hunter was indeed playing a role.

His interest in the theater was genuine, however. Hunter's earliest reference to his fascination with the stage was in *Johnny Reb*. He writes that after escaping from Old Capitol Prison, he stopped in Baltimore and saw *The Taming of the Shrew*, the first Shakespeare play he had attended in

Alexander Hunter at the turn of the century. From Alexander Hunter, *The Huntsman in the South* (Washington, D.C.: Neale Publishing Co., 1908).

years.[61] One of his columns from Richmond after the war addressed the need for a new theater or opera house in that city. During this same period, Hunter became acquainted with the Rapley family, owners of the National Theater in Washington, D.C., which led to a commission to write a history of the playhouse's first fifty years. Published in 1885, the short volume offers a catalog of performances without engaging in artistic criticism. The National burned on three occasions and was rebuilt an additional time after a wall collapsed during a circus performance. Hunter identifies presidents attending the annual openings, revels in appearances by Jenny Lind and Lola Montez, and records the Washington debut of Theodore Hamilton. "He had been a soldier in Lee's army, and no doubt enjoyed the mimic splendor of the stage, and sweet music of the orchestra, better than standing a lonely vigil on picket duty in a blinding rain, or being chased by a score of bluecoats through fen and fallow," the author wrote with impunity twenty years after the surrender.[62] Worthy of special note are references to three separate appearances by John Wilkes Booth, playing Richard III, Romeo, and a lesser character. Seated in a private box for his first performance, on April 11, 1863, was President Lincoln.

The assassination two years later furnished the grist for Hunter's best-known writing in his day. "Booth and Bessie Hale" appeared in early June 1878 in an obscure literary magazine published in Portsmouth, Virginia. The tale is recounted with compelling naturalness in the same clear, straightforward style as his wartime narratives. Due to its controversial thesis, the piece quickly generated reaction in the nation's leading newspapers. Based on the revelations of someone identified as "one of the most brilliant society leaders in Washington," Hunter contends that Booth had assassinated the president out of jealousy over the flirtations of his true love, Bessie Hale, with the victim's eldest son, Robert Todd Lincoln. The femme fatale is identified as the daughter of John Parker Hale, a U.S. senator from New Hampshire. Elements of Hunter's theory have subsequently been entertained by Booth biographers and historians. The story's credibility suffered, however, from Robert's frequent absences from the capital during the period of the alleged dalliance while assigned to General Grant's staff, and because neither of Senator Hale's girls was known as "Bessie." The younger daughter, Elizabeth, was called "Lucy," and she was later reported to have been engaged to the actor in early 1865, a point in Hunter's favor.[63]

The timing of the publication of "Booth and Bessie Hale" was unfortunate as it coincided with coverage of the first public statement by John T. Ford, manager of the theater at the time of the assassination. The article brought only brief notoriety to Hunter before the attentions of the press moved on to new sensationalism. Hunter's existence on the fringe of Washington society, combined with his participation in the war and fondness for the theater, made this story a natural attraction for him.

Alexander Hunter's writings explored a variety of subject areas, but in none of these did he achieve lasting fame or prominence. His most important contributions are chronicles of the war years, perceptive and informative first-person narratives that record these terrible but critical times in the nation's development. Hunter gradually faded from public view, just as cognizance of his war has become fainter with each succeeding generation. He died of tuberculosis in 1914 at his home on Beech Drive in Washington's Rock Creek Park.[64] The old rebel was given full military honors, identical to those accorded Union veterans, when interred at Arlington National Cemetery in a plot overlooking his former family estate, Abingdon.[65]

There is one final irony. At his request, Hunter was buried in the uniform of a major in the Confederate cavalry, reportedly as the result of receiving a commission just before the war's close.[66] The lifelong champion of the common soldier now rests in officer's attire.

CHAPTER FIFTEEN

VETERAN

✸✸✸ EDGAR WARFIELD

NO ONE SYMBOLIZED THE CONFEDERATE VETERAN BETTER than Alexandria's Edgar Warfield. Warfield's identification with the Lost Cause spans the entire period from the city's earliest call to arms to the last hurrah for old soldiers in gray. His service during the war years is generally unremarkable, as it mirrors the campaigning of many other rebels. Indeed, a late-twentieth-century reporter went so far as to begin an article, "Though he lived to be Alexandria's oldest living Confederate soldier, Edgar Warfield can't really be called a Civil War hero."[1] In all likelihood, Warfield survived the war unscathed because for much of the conflict he was detailed as a hospital attendant, which kept him off the front lines. Warfield shines in the postwar era, when he worked tirelessly for many decades on behalf of his aging comrades in arms and the cause for which they had fought. For that reason, Warfield's story is inextricably woven into the history of the Confederate veterans camp in Alexandria.

Warfield was born in Washington, D.C., on June 7, 1842, the second son of Sarah Ann Adams and Abel Davis Warfield. Both parents were from Maryland. Edgar's father was a large man with a jovial disposition who worked as a dyer of fabric. Later that year, Abel moved the family to Alexandria, where Edgar attended the Mechanics Hall Institute on North Alfred Street. At age fourteen, he quit school to clerk in a retail drugstore. He would grow into a man of five foot six and a half inches, medium height for his day, with dark hair and hazel eyes.[2]

Five years passed and, despite its longstanding commitment to the national government, elements of Alexandria gradually became swept up in the secessionist fever moving across the South. On December 1, 1860, a notice appeared in the *Alexandria Gazette* calling for boys between the ages of sixteen and twenty to attend the organizational meeting for a new rifle company. The solicitation was signed by Edgar Warfield and a friend, each paying twenty-five cents of hard-earned money for the advertisement.[3] Five nights later, at the American Hall, sixty-eight young men formed a unit they named the "Old Dominion Rifles," with Montgomery Corse as its commander.

Warfield would not have been a credible representative of the Confederate soldier without a solid war record, but he had one. He marched out of Alexandria with the Sixth Virginia battalion in May 1861 and served continuously in uniform until paroled at Appomattox Court House on April 9, 1865. His experiences during that period were told in a work entitled *A Confederate Soldier's Memoirs,* published in 1936, and rereleased in 1996 as *Manassas to Appomattox: The Civil War Memoirs of Pvt. Edgar Warfield, Seventeenth Virginia Infantry.* The volume is based on notes jotted down some years after the war's close and expanded into a book as Warfield approached the age of ninety. The narrative is most engaging when relating anecdotes involving the author. Its impact is diluted, however, by repeated quotations from Alexander Hunter's *Johnny Reb and Billy Yank,* George Wise's histories, and the official reports of the war. The author also incorporates his understanding of important events in Alexandria's Civil War experience to ensure they are not lost to his readers, even though he did not witness them. Warfield stated that he set down this personal record for his family's use, which explains the generous references to published sources to provide context for his own reminiscences. His focus is the common soldier, and, after sixty-five years, Warfield joyfully recalls cheerful scenes of bivouac life, happy moments around the campfire, and comradeship bonded on road marches, to the exclusion of more painful experiences.[4]

The accuracy of the chronicle suffers from the lateness of its preparation. The dimming effect of intervening decades, along with a natural inclination to remember events in a certain light, calls into question some of Warfield's narrative. An example, by no means the only one, is the identification of Lt. J. E. B. Stuart as bearer of the news to Col. Robert E. Lee of the attack on Harpers Ferry in October 1859, a detail not found in any other contemporary account. Surfacing, as it did, seventy years after the incident, raises doubts about its accuracy.[5]

Nevertheless, the Warfield book has value as a firsthand perspective on the conflict, while providing many amusing vignettes. The weeks before initial combat along Bull Run were rich in human interest. Warfield recalls, for example, that the members of the new rifle company first decided to call themselves the "Alexandria Sharp Shooters" but changed their minds when they visualized the initials on their knapsacks. The most desirable posts in the city to pull guard duty were near the residences of popular young ladies. Once the Alexandrians relocated to Manassas Junction, Warfield, along with many of his comrades, was introduced to the pick and shovel for the first time in his life.[6]

Edgar Warfield in a
Confederate private's
uniform at the war's
outset. Courtesy of
Suzanne Warfield
Johnson.

Manual labor did not depress the spirits of Warfield and his chums.
One often-repeated sketch from the book concerned smuggling liquor
into camp. The author relates a sentry challenging a soldier carrying a
coffeepot. The reprobate tilted the pot, causing milk to pour out. He was
allowed entry and was soon enjoying a container full of whiskey, as the
lower end of the spout had been corked.[7]

Warfield's appreciation of the human side of war did not disappear
with his initiation into combat. He relates that during the following
spring, when the Seventeenth Regiment was deployed outside Richmond, the Alexandrians wanted to attend a minstrel show at a theater
managed by another former resident of their hometown. To enter the
capital through the cordon protecting it, they devised a ruse with
Warfield assuming the role of a prisoner under guard by his chums.[8] At

a later point, he brags about a snowball fight involving the Seventeenth Regiment that eclipsed the more famous contest at Guinea Station.[9] His most poignant episode took place a few weeks later at Frayser's Farm.

Edgar was the third member of his family to enlist, after his father and elder brother. A veteran of the Seminole War, Abel joined the Alexandria Riflemen, while George, a dyer like their father, was a member of the Mount Vernon Guards. All three took part in the action at Bull Run. The aging author recalls his pa waving as his unit crossed the stream during the skirmish on July 18, in which he was slightly wounded. With his pharmaceutical experience, Edgar was detailed as regimental apothecary. Tasked to look after the casualties at Frayser's Farm, he came across a bluecoat with a scalp injury. While bandaging the head, Warfield took note of the man's cap, which had his brother's name on the visor. Warfield asked how it came into the Yankee's possession and was told he had taken it from a dead rebel. This was how Edgar learned that George had been killed. With help from the assistant regimental surgeon, Dr. Harold Snowden, Warfield found the newly dug grave and ensured that it was marked until the remains could be returned to Alexandria after the war.[10]

Another soldier, Cpl. Pen Jordan, recounted how he was wounded three times at Frayser's Farm, captured by the Yankees, and then left by the roadside when the Federals withdrew down the Virginia peninsula. Warfield happened along with the Confederate pursuit and lay down beside Jordan to ascertain his condition and comfort him. Jordan was soon evacuated to Richmond but not before circulation of a rumor that Warfield had been hurt, based on being seen prone among a group of casualties. "Old Abe" Warfield, now working as a teamster, heard the report and frantically searched Richmond's hospitals for his only remaining son before learning that Edgar was unharmed.[11]

Warfield's narrative of the war contains two elements common to many reminiscences of Confederate soldiers. First, he was virtually barefoot much of the time. He tried to find a pair of boots on the field at Second Manassas but was thwarted by others ahead of him. By the time he reached Frederick on the way to Antietam, the soles of Warfield's footwear were held to the uppers by pieces of bandages. Second are his two vivid recollections of encountering Gen. Robert E. Lee. Retiring from Maryland, Warfield was placed in charge of a hospital train of four wagons and twelve ambulances. He was denied passage across a stream by a guard whose orders prohibited it. Warfield persisted until he heard someone nearby assert, "Those wagons can not cross there, sir." Looking up, he saw the army's commanding general and prudently selected another route. In the war's final year, Warfield recalled being told that Lee was close by and, when he passed, there must be absolutely no cheering, as the enemy was nearby. The silent body of men opened ranks. Warfield then verbally portrayed the classic Confederate image with every hat raised and waving in salute of the Southern idol.[12]

Warfield distinguished himself at Manassas Gap in July 1863, when he saved his regiment from capture or annihilation. He obtained a horse and rode to Winchester for reinforcements. A brigade arrived the following morning, just in time to repel the enemy and protect Lee's supply train. "By the chances of war," he modestly concludes, "I happened to be the agency through which the relief was brought in time."[13]

Toward the end, the tattered gray coats turned to deception. On picket duty one night, Warfield's comrades suddenly began boisterous cheering, explaining to their counterparts across the line that it signaled a great (notional) victory won by the Confederate army in the west. Yankees who deserted were deceived by being told to walk gingerly in the footsteps of their captors, as the ground was planted with hundreds of landmines ("torpedoes," in the parlance of the day). As a train passed by Warfield's campsite at Drewry's Bluff, soldiers would often erupt into cheering. When passengers poked their heads out the windows, boys with boughs separated them from their hats.[14]

In January 1865, Warfield took his only furlough of the war, a fourteen-day respite. In Richmond, he joined up with his father, who had transferred to become forage master of a Louisiana brigade. Dressed in captured Yankee clothing, the two carefully made their way northward through central Virginia, obtaining help from Southern sympathizers along the way. Warfield had written his mother that they would attempt to reach the outskirts of Alexandria and sent the note with a scout who may well have been Frank Stringfellow, as he knew her and repeatedly went behind Federal lines to enter the port city. The infiltrators finally settled into a hiding place at Burke's Station, west of Alexandria, that Edgar said was used by Stringfellow and some of Mosby's men. First they saw Edgar's oldest sister and then his mother, who stayed with them in the shelter in the woods. Within several months, the family would be reunited for good.[15]

Warfield was one of only seven Alexandrians at the surrender when the guns fell silent. For decades to come, one of his proudest possessions would be the parole signed by Col. Arthur Herbert, commanding the Seventeenth Virginia Infantry. On April 12, Warfield started for home with some companions. His shoes were worn out, and he had tailored trousers from five different colors of cloth, ranging from butternut brown to the blue used for Yankee overcoats. The comrades made it to Richmond, where the Federal provost marshal provided transportation home for the defeated rebels. The little band of four men landed in Alexandria at Wheat's Wharf, between Queen and Princess Streets, on

April 18. They were the first arrivals from Appomattox and were warmly greeted by friends who had remained behind.[16]

Within days Warfield had obtained a position as clerk in a drugstore in Washington City, a job he retained for only a short period. With a former army companion, Frank Hall, Warfield established a pharmacy on the southwest corner of Prince and Fairfax Streets in Alexandria. In addition to filling prescriptions, the druggists advertised European and domestic soaps, grooming supplies, and spices of all kinds, along with patent medicines.[17] They would remain in business together for forty years. The Warfield and Hall apothecary soon became a gathering place for ex-Confederates, regularly drawing Montgomery Corse and others around its potbelly stove. Occasionally, the shop would attract burglars, as well. A robber broke through a display window one night in 1900 and escaped with fifty cents in coins and $1.50 in stamps.[18]

Warfield soon involved himself in community activities, becoming a member of a fire company (and, later, city fire chief), the board of stewards of the Methodist Episcopal Church, and the Andrew Jackson Lodge of Masons, where he eventually became grand master.[19] Warfield was also described as "a star baseball player on the old Mount Vernon baseball team of Alexandria—one of the first baseball teams ever to play the great national game."[20] Gov. Fitzhugh Lee made the Alexandria druggist one of five appointees to the new state board of pharmacy in 1886. The initial terms of office were staggered, and Warfield drew a two-year stint. He later served a full five-year term.[21]

In the 1880s, as the war faded from public perception, friendships formed in terrible times two decades earlier became more cherished. Former soldiers, both blue and gray, began banding together as veterans. Home life had become rather dull, some of the old rebels had achieved financial security, and others were enjoying leisure time. In the city council chamber on June 30, 1884, Warfield joined with a handful of like-minded Alexandrians to establish an organization of ex-Confederates. He moved that a committee be appointed to prepare bylaws, and, as its unofficial secretary, he kept a record of what transpired. The new association called itself the R. E. Lee Camp and identified its objectives as perpetuating the memories of fallen comrades, ministering to the needs of those permanently disabled, and preserving the fraternity forged by the hardships and dangers shared during military service.[22] A call went out through the *Alexandria Gazette* for a meeting on July 7. The bylaws were adopted at this gathering and then copied into a bound book in a clear, open hand by Warfield, elected the camp's first adjutant.[23]

The selection of Warfield is intriguing. He was not the most qualified "comrade," as camp members referred to themselves. Thomas W. White had performed as General Lee's headquarters clerk, in addition to having been a local court scribe, and was active in the new brotherhood.

There were lettered members who were college educated, in contrast to Warfield, who quit school while still a youth but who as a pharmacist was obviously intelligent. The new organization needed someone to do the thankless tasks that underpin every organization. Warfield was a humble man, dedicated to the cause and not reluctant to work hard. Perhaps, as someone self-employed, he could free time for camp business, whereas others could not or would not.

In addition to keeping the minutes, Warfield corresponded with prominent former Confederates elected honorary members of the camp, sent resolutions of condolence to the families of deceased comrades, and acknowledged contributions of memorabilia on behalf of the camp. He was appointed to a committee on records to maintain the name, occupation, and residence of all members, recruit other local residents who were in Confederate States service, and contact Alexandrians living outside the city about joining the camp. He would later compile master rolls for companies of the Seventeenth Virginia at the request of the state adjutant general. Warfield was also repeatedly tasked to make travel arrangements for members attending special events, such as unveiling the George E. Pickett monument in Richmond in 1888.[24]

In its formative years, the camp was involved in a variety of activities dependent upon Warfield's competence. Membership applications needed to be accounted for, referred to committee, and, after action, retained on file. Warfield moved that a committee be formed to collect the names of Confederate dead in unmarked graves and ascertain the cost of headstones. He was subsequently designated one of its first members. The camp also solicited money to mark Confederate graves as such. Indigent veterans were a high priority. The camp bought a ton of coal for one comrade confined to home by sickness, and Warfield was directed to contact the old soldier's home in Richmond to obtain admission for another of their own.[25]

The activity that pulled the camp together, however, providing a raison d'être during its formative years, was construction of a monument commemorating the city's casualties during the war. Warfield was a central figure in this project. It all began at a camp meeting on April 6, 1885, when Warfield moved that a committee of five be designated to examine the expediency of raising money to commemorate Alexandria's Confederate dead. Upon the motion's adoption, he was quite naturally appointed to this body and soon found himself in the familiar role of record keeper.[26]

Within days, the camp approved the committee's recommendation to go forward, and Warfield became the right-hand man of the project's chairman, Montgomery Corse. The committee issued a circular soliciting contributions and over the next four years held a variety of fundraising events. The ladies of Alexandria came to the camp's aid by holding a bazaar, and, in one way or another, "the entire community enlisted in the enterprise," according to the local paper.[27] Old general Corse liked to brag that the Federals were paying for the rebel remembrance, as he earmarked his monthly pension from the Mexican War for the undertaking.[28]

The most prominent activities in support of the monument were a series of lectures delivered at the opera house on King Street, a program that stretched over several years. Warfield's camp minutes identify the speakers as including W. H. F. "Rooney" Lee, former city mayor Kosciusko Kemper, George Wise, and Dr. Bedford Brown, a new arrival from North Carolina. Frank Stringfellow enthralled an audience with tales of his three escapes from Yankee confinement and raised $60.85 in the process. Generals Eppa Hunton and W. H. F. Payne came from western Virginia to give lectures. E. V. "Lige" White from Leesburg told about his fearless Laurel Brigade. Edmund Berkley recounted the sad story of Gettysburg. Capt. S. B. Davis related his arrest as a spy and the resulting trial and conviction. Capt. Gordon McCabe journeyed from Petersburg to talk about the crater. Even the Washington Symphony Orchestra gave a concert to benefit the monument.

While the fund-raising proceeded, Corse, Warfield, and their compatriots had to agree on an appropriate memorial. John Elder, an artist from Richmond, met with the committee in July 1888 to show a model taken from his painting, "Appomattox," hanging in the library of the state capitol.[29] Richmond's *Daily Times* described the "heroic sized figure" as "dressed in the old familiar uniform of the Confederate private, [standing] with folded arms and head bowed forward as if in deep contemplation over the scenes, privation and hard fought battles through which he had passed, all for a principle which he deemed sacred and righteous, and yet all apparently for nought."[30] On the committee's recommendation, the camp voted unanimously to adopt Elder's concept. Warfield was instructed to prepare a list of the Alexandrians who had died in the war for inclusion on the base.[31]

The more controversial question was where to place the monument. One suggestion was a vacant lot across from the cotton factory on Washington Street that had served as a Union prison during the war. Another proposal was a park on an estate being developed as residences by a promoter. The camp finally settled on the intersection of Washington and Prince Streets, where the Seventeenth Regiment had formed up to march out of town. The city council endorsed the camp's decision at a meeting on November 13, 1888.[32]

The twenty-eighth anniversary of the city's evacuation was selected as the occasion to unveil the monument. As the date approached, Warfield was called upon to shoulder much of the responsibility for the project's completion. He joined the committee on a trip to New York to inspect the sculpture of "Appomattox" by Casper Buberl at the Bonard Bronze Company, which would cast the statue. With his experience in organizing the city's yearly Washington birthday celebration, it was natural to place Warfield on the committee making arrangements for the grand occasion. As adjutant, he also corresponded with other camps of Confederate veterans and the many dignitaries invited to participate.[33]

Alexandria stirred at daybreak on May 24, 1889, as fleets of carriages, boats, and other conveyances began to converge on the city. Bright sunshine and low temperatures added to the holiday atmosphere, as did buildings gaily decorated along the procession route. In mid-morning, the camp assembled at the customs house and, proceeded by the Marine Band, marched to Warfield's residence, where the veterans received the flag recently presented to the camp by ladies of the city. Returning to the monument site at noon, the old soldiers joined a crowd of thousands of onlookers. Camp commander William A. Smoot served as presiding officer and introduced a Richmond compatriot who turned over the statue on behalf of the artist. On cue, Virginia Corse, the general's eldest daughter, pulled cords unveiling the monument to applause, shouts of joy, and simultaneous music by multiple bands. Alexandrians saw what the city newspaper described as "a complete history of the lost cause graphically presented to posterity by a single figure."[34] The eight-foot warrior stood atop a rectangular pedestal with a plaque dedicating the work in memory of the ninety-nine Alexandrians listed as losing their lives in the Southern struggle.[35] Patriotic inscriptions on each side of the structure extolled the deeds of these revered casualties of war and the cause for which they died. Governor Lee then delivered the principal address, after which dignitaries and guests retired to banquets coordinated by Warfield's team.[36]

The organizing committee submitted a final report the following month, turning over fifty dollars as the balance in excess of the monument's cost of $3,500. The next January, the state's general assembly took note of the landmark by passing a bill protecting it from alteration or relocation on local authority.[37] The figure was so well received as a work of art that other communities, such as Petersburg, made plans to replicate it. Consequently, the R. E. Lee Camp obtained a copyright for its design in 1892.[38]

Ceremonies honoring Jefferson Davis and Joseph E. Johnston took place during this same period. Davis died in late 1889. The camp passed a resolution of condolence and instructed a committee of three, including Warfield, to arrange a memorial service. On December 13, the aging comrades formed in line of march and proceeded solemnly to the opera house for a tribute to the old head of state. U.S. Senators John Daniel of Virginia (a former major in gray) and James George of Mississippi and former generals Payne and "Rooney" Lee participated in the remembrance, as did John Reagan, former postmaster general of the Confederacy. Two years later, camp members, including Warfield, took a train to Washington to attend the funeral of another fallen chieftain, former General Johnston.[39]

In the summer of 1891, the Grand Camp of Virginia wrote to call attention to the need for a larger appropriation for the Robert E. Lee Camp Soldiers' Home in Richmond. Comrades were asked to call upon candidates for seats in the next legislature to obtain pledges of support. When Confederate veterans first banded together, they specifically prohibited partisan political activity, but rallying to help some of their own was different. That December, Commander Smoot and Adjutant Warfield were dispatched to Richmond on orders from the state commander to lobby the assembly for increased resources for the home.[40] The burden of caring for indigent veterans was gradually being shifted from local hands to state government.

Warfield's minutes reflect the multitude of camp activities during its heyday in the early 1890s. In addition to regularly scheduled monthly meetings, the camp gathered in special sessions to respond to invitations or plan upcoming events. The adjutant carefully listed attendees, not just at these meetings but at every funeral, ceremony, and reunion. He copied verbatim the speeches at official functions, commanders' annual reports, and personalized resolutions of sympathy regarding each passing member. It seems that the work might have been too demanding at one point, as Warfield proposed that a position of financial secretary be created to relieve him of the responsibility of accounting for dues. The innovation was apparently less than fully successful, for after a year's time, he moved that the job be abolished and its duties transferred to the treasurer. Warfield appeared to keep the records in perfect order, for when the inspector general of the Grand Camp of Virginia made an inspection of the Alexandria contingent in 1896, he assessed its administration as being in excellent condition. The adjutant and treasurer also underwent annual internal audits.[41]

As the South recovered from financial hardships brought by the war, a multitude of monuments began springing up to remember its battles and leaders. The old veterans in Alexandria were invited to many of these commemorations. They were sure to be represented at places where the Seventeenth Virginia had served. Wearing badges made especially for a particular ceremony, Warfield and his comrades participated in monument dedications at Manassas, Suffolk, Fairfax, and Fredericksburg. The largest turnout was at the presentation of Robert E. Lee's equestrian statue in Richmond, for which fifty camp members traveled to the capital, proudly bringing the camp flag, a battle flag of the Seventeenth Infantry, and the Virginia colors carried by the regiment. These appearances attained such importance for the old soldiers that the camp authorized a uniform consisting of gray frock coat and trousers. A light hat and cane were added later, bringing the total cost of the attire to $13.85.[42]

There was plenty of competition for the old veterans' money. The camp was solicited for donations to the statues of Lee and Davis in Richmond. The Ladies Memorial Society in the capital collected contributions for a Confederate museum to be housed in the president's mansion. Funds were needed locally to defray the funeral expenses of indigent members and to pay for decorating the city monument and soldiers' graves. As these demands grew, resources became constrained. In June 1892 Warfield called attention to the great number of comrades in arrears on their dues. When the situation worsened the following year, as a consequence of the depression that rocked the country, he was appointed to a committee to examine the delinquent list and cancel the accounts of those unable to pay. Monthly assessments were reduced from twenty cents to ten cents in light of the "hard times and members out of work," bringing them into closer alignment with dues in other veterans' outfits.[43] The tempo of the camp slowed but did not stop because of financial hardships. It would take a marked decline in membership to bring the veterans movement to its knees.

By the 1890s the old-timers were beginning to realize that the lore of their military service would die with them if other sympathetic individuals were not enlisted in their cause. In June 1890 Warfield and six comrades formed a committee to consider the advisability of organizing their sons as an auxiliary to the camp. Warfield reported back that the "Sons of Veterans" had held its inaugural meeting on August 28. As a consequence, Commander Smoot confidently announced an increase in the camp's ranks when delivering his annual report the following April. The gains were deceptive, however, as the sons were only afforded associate status. Membership of ex-Confederates was decidedly on the wane.[44]

In 1896 Warfield served on a committee to formally organize a local affiliate of a new society springing up across the South, known as the Sons of Confederate Veterans. The organization held its first meeting on November 2, 1896, agreeing to be known as the Montgomery D. Corse Camp, in remembrance of the general who had passed away the preceding year.[45]

The veterans camp had grown accustomed to assistance from wives and daughters of members, widows of deceased soldiers, and other sympathetic women in the community. As adjutant, Warfield regularly wrote to these ladies, thanking them for decorating the city monument and mound at Christ Church cemetery, helping to adorn graves on special occasions, performing as a choral group, and other kindnesses. In the summer of 1893, the Grand Camp recommended that its components organize ladies auxiliaries or memorial associations on the pattern of the energetic Ladies Memorial Society formed in Richmond. Warfield was a member of the committee that established an auxiliary in Alexandria. Some women wanted an organization all their own, however, and after creation of a national society in Nashville, Tennessee, formed the Mary Custis E. Lee Chapter of the United Daughters of the Confederacy in Alexandria on February 14, 1895. Another local affiliate named for the Seventeenth Virginia Regiment first met in March 1896, electing Mrs. Edgar Warfield as its second vice president. The Lee Camp could therefore look to three groups of feminine supporters.

Before entering the new century, Warfield finally had an opportunity to lead the brotherhood that had come to mean so much to him. During many of its formative years, the camp had the same primary officers: Smoot was commander from 1886 until 1895, when he was elevated to state office; Warfield served even longer as adjutant, from 1885 to 1896. In the latter year, he was elected second lieutenant commander, beginning an annual progression through first lieutenant to commander of the camp. He was formally chosen to head that fraternity on April 4, 1898.

Warfield's tenure came at the end of the vibrant period of the Confederate veterans movement. His annual report, delivered at the conclusion of his term the following spring, began by characterizing it as a "sad" year for the large number of deaths that winnowed the camp's ranks. Warfield's term began auspiciously enough in May 1898 with a call for members to escort the Alexandria Light Infantry to the rail depot as it departed for the glorious war against Spain. Sorrow replaced patriotism in September upon the death of "Winnie" Davis, daughter of the late president and star-crossed princess of the Confederacy. The camp sent its sympathies to the family and passed a resolution of condolence. Warfield offered special praise to the Mary Custis Lee Chapter and the Women's Auxiliary for their work in finishing the marking of every Confederate grave in Alexandria during his year in the top office. He also recognized the Arthur Herbert Chapter of the Children of the Confederacy, another effort to keep alive memories of the Lost Cause.[46]

After Warfield's term as commander, the camp entered an irreversible tailspin, reflecting the decline of the Confederate veterans' movement across the South.[47] Shorter minutes focused almost entirely on death, noting funerals, flowers, and grave sites. With fewer members, dues fell and attendance at gatherings waned. Warfield moved that Rev. Douglas Forrest, a former Alexandrian and lieutenant in the Seventeenth Virginia, be invited to address the camp in 1900, but speakers as a focus of meetings became less common. State headquarters and ancillary organizations—the Sons and Daughters—ascended into control of the veterans' agenda. Fewer local initiatives were undertaken; socials attained greater importance to the aging survivors than civic undertakings.

The Grand Camp had recognized its Alexandria branch with a charter dated October 17, 1896. A certificate of incorporation for "Robert E. Lee, No. 2, Camp No. 5" was recorded by the Clerk of the Corporation Court of Alexandria on June 10, 1903, which, under the authorizing legislation, permitted the camp to acquire and hold real property.[48] This designation indicated another Robert E. Lee Camp had already been established (in Richmond) and that the Alexandria unit was the fifth one formed in Virginia under auspices of the Grand Camp.[49] When later affiliating with the United Confederate Veterans, the Alexandria camp was assigned number 1801, denoting it as one of the last of 1846 subordinate units registered with that body.[50]

Flags carried during the war held special value for Warfield and his comrades. The camp suffered a scare in 1888 when it lent the battle flag of the Seventeenth Infantry to a Grand Army of the Republic post in Boston for a display of war relics. As adjutant, Warfield proudly sent along a history of the regiment raised in part in Alexandria. To everyone's horror, a few weeks later word arrived that a fire had destroyed many of the items at the exposition. It was subsequently learned, to their relief, that the Virginia banner had been spared. A few years later, Warfield exhibited the flag presented to the Alexandria Riflemen on Washington's birthday in 1861 at the city newspaper offices, after it was returned to Alexandria by a collector in the Shenandoah Valley.[51]

Of prime interest, however, were the colors of the Seventeenth Virginia that had been captured when the regiment was overrun at Antietam. For years they were on display in a showcase at the state capitol in Albany. In 1908 Arthur Herbert, by this time an influential banker in Alexandria, urged the governor of Virginia to contact his counterpart in New York and seek the flag's return. The state's adjutant general recommended instead that the camp send a formal request. A New York state legislator, who was born and raised in Alexandria and now served as chairman of the committee on military affairs, learned of the appeal and succeeded in shepherding an enabling bill through the assembly. On July 10, 1911, the camp dispatched Smoot and Warfield to Albany to recover the sacred emblem.[52]

The emissaries were warmly received. The war trophy was turned over in the governor's office, after which the Alexandrians were given a rousing reception in the assembly chamber. "This gift will make our comrades happy," Warfield exclaimed. "I can hardly wait to get back to share in their happiness in once more seeing the colors underneath which they fought."[53] Smoot and Warfield triumphantly carried home the four-foot-square battle flag, enhanced with the inscriptions "Williamsburg" and "Seven Pines," which had originally been presented to the regiment by Gov. John Letcher at Centreville in November 1861. The camp and its various ladies affiliates gathered in September to hear a presentation speech by Warfield and to welcome the banner's return. The colors remain a treasured memento to this day.[54]

On December 12, 1921, the *Alexandria Gazette* routinely announced a reception to be held at the Confederate Veterans' Building by the Mary Custis Lee–Seventeenth Virginia Chapter in honor of the R. E. Lee Camp.[55] The party was subsequently reported as marking the transfer of title for this handsome brick townhouse from the camp to the society of loyal female descendents. Still identified as adjutant, Warfield gave a short address explaining that, cognizant of its declining numbers (now consisting of only seventeen resident members), the camp wished to ensure perpetuation of its work. Warfield had long ago urged the camp to make a "will" designating who should be entrusted with custodianship of its treasured artifacts and chapter house. Years had passed before the aged veterans faced up to the question and bequeathed the historic dwelling acquired in 1903 from the descendents of Julius De Lagnel, a former Confederate colonel.[56]

Warfield now practiced pharmacology with his son and grandson at the corner of King and Pitt Streets. As the 1920s progressed, he was recognized as the oldest druggist in the state and as the oldest active pharmacist in the nation. To his membership on the board of examiners for the Virginia Pharmaceutical Society, he added the honorary title of president emeritus of the entire organization. He bragged about personally opening the drugstore each day at 8:00 A.M. and closing it every other evening. In between, Warfield attended to piles of paperwork generated by his veterans activities. In his late eighties, he also admitted to being addicted to motion pictures, a tidbit included in a sketch circulated nationwide by the United Press.[57] "I go to Washington every afternoon [to the cinema]," he told a newspaper reporter. "That's the way to keep going; keep doing things."[58]

As the 1920s drew to a close, Warfield was increasingly alone. His wife of forty-four years, Catherine Virginia Batcheller, died years earlier, and he had subsequently moved in with his eldest son, a bank vice president, in the Rosemont suburb of Alexandria. The generation that had fought America's defining war in the 1860s was steadily succumbing to old age, continuously reminding the surviving Confederate veteran of his own mortality. Warfield devoted his waning energies to transcribing notes on the war and collecting fading recollections into a book for his family. To sharpen his memory and obtain information he considered important to his narrative, Warfield wrote a series of letters to the War Department, battlefield parks, the state library, and newspapers.[59] He finally completed the manuscript in 1930, at the age of eighty-eight, although it was not published for a general readership until six years later.

By the late 1920s, the limbs of Confederate veterans' groups were withering and dying as well. For some years there had been two such organizations in the state, the Grand Camp and the Virginia Division of the United Confederate Veterans.[60] In 1929 the Grand Camp's Department of Virginia reported far more local units not submitting annual reports (forty-seven) than those that did (twenty-seven). Membership had plummeted from 1,064 in 1927 to only 386 survivors, of whom but 186 were paying dues.[61] In October, Warfield was appointed state commander at the annual meeting in Petersburg. At the same time, he continued to function as adjutant of the R. E. Lee Camp of Alexandria, even though by this time he was its sole surviving member. The last commander, Smoot, had surrendered that office long before, in 1910, after a second tenure of three years.[62]

In 1930, Warfield was chosen to command a brigade of the Virginia Division of the United Confederate Veterans, carrying with it a promotion from colonel to brigadier general. Imposters began appearing on the rolls, perhaps drawn by stipends provided to old soldiers and their widows. As chairman of the local pension board, Warfield wrote to the War Department to ascertain the credentials of claimants. The commander of the Maryland Division was summarily expelled "as a non-Confederate soldier" by the camp in Washington, D.C.[63] A thirst for power seemed to drive the few remaining members to engage in internecine warfare for control of the skeletal units, with the losers repeatedly threatening to complain to civilian legal authorities if Warfield and other senior leaders did not intervene on their behalf.[64]

Upon the incumbent's resignation in 1933, Warfield became a major general in charge of the entire Virginia Division. In the customary annual address, Warfield acknowledged the inevitability of declining membership, given their ages, but begged individual camps not to disband as long as even just two members survived. He also sought to resuscitate affiliates on the inactive list for non-payment of the yearly per capita tax.[65]

To compound the devastating reduction in numbers caused by death, Civil War veterans' organizations were hit hard by the Great Depression. The 1933 national reunion was canceled for this reason. Warfield reported, "I consider it impossible to collect any dues from the camps, sufficient to purchase stationery and stamps for its officers."[66] He was able to send out communiqué using his own money, but other old-timers were not so financially solvent, despite increases in pension payments. Knowing of Warfield's prestige in the state, he was regularly asked to help raise funds. One supplicant wanted money to disseminate a tract on Abraham Lincoln; another offered for sale three-color replicas of a memento being presented to the new president, Franklin Delano Roosevelt.[67]

Edgar Warfield in a veteran's uniform standing in front of the Confederate memorial "Appomattox" in the early 1930s. Courtesy of Suzanne Warfield Johnson.

Yet another symptom of the dying network of old rebels was the desperate effort to garner more resources from the state government. Recognizing that its days as a retirement facility were numbered, the soldiers home in Richmond launched a drive to convert its property to a permanent Confederate memorial park dedicated to the preservation of Virginia's records pertaining to the war. Warfield and other influential veterans were requested to petition their local state representatives before the assembly convened in 1934. "Get all newspaper publicity possible," implored the solicitors, prescient of the media age to come.[68]

As Civil War survivors became scarce in number, Warfield was called upon more frequently to represent his Southern brethren. Residing just across the river from the nation's capital, it was convenient for Warfield to join delegations appearing before the president. He participated in the memorable parade of United Confederate Veterans down Pennsylvania Avenue that was reviewed by Woodrow Wilson on June 7, 1917. In December 1927, he joined Calvin Coolidge and other old rebels in front of the Capitol for the return of Confederate battle flags captured by Maine regiments during the war. When Warfield met Herbert Hoover in May 1932 to arrange the chief executive's dedication of the Masonic Memorial in Alexandria, Hoover seemed more impressed that Warfield had been a Mason for sixty-two years than that he had been a soldier in the Civil War. The following March, Warfield was invited to ride with eight carloads of Confederate veterans in Roosevelt's inaugural parade.[69]

His presence was sought on a variety of other occasions as well. For example, the Reserve Officers Association made Warfield an honorary member at a state convention in 1933. He was asked to lay a wreath at Washington's grave at Mount Vernon the following year. The United Confederate Veterans designated him their representative at ceremonies at Montpelier, commemorating the anniversary of James Madison's death, and the National Fireman's Association wanted Warfield to be honorary chief marshal for a parade in Alexandria. Never a confident speaker, in his advanced years Warfield's standard role at the city's Lee-Jackson banquet each January evolved into a recitation of the general in chief's farewell address to his troops. This was a comfortable part for him to play, as Warfield had repeated these lines on numerous occasions while serving as camp adjutant in the 1880s and 1890s.[70]

The traditional times to gather in gray uniform with ladies in their finest attire were Lee's birthday (January 19) and Southern Memorial Day, recognized on April 26 in much of the South but observed on May 24 in Alexandria, the date the city's soldiers marched off to war. In his ninety-second year, Warfield once again read Lee's farewell at the general's birthday banquet in 1934. Threatening skies and a light rain moved the Confederate Memorial Day observance from the monument at Prince and Washington Streets indoors to Lee Hall, now managed by the Daughters. Despite the weather, the old warrior led the procession by foot to Christ Church Cemetery, three blocks away, for the customary tribute to thirty-four unknown dead buried beneath a mound there.[71]

Warfield's major challenge in the summer of 1934 was to plan what would be the last rebel reunion in Virginia. Bickering between the state's two organizations of Confederate veterans seemed to reach a crescendo as the Grand Camp fought what would be its final battle. It disbanded in September. Warfield disseminated a tentative program and received complaints in return. On July 27, he shared his frustrations with Homer Atkinson, the past commander in chief of the United Confederate Veterans:

> I am not in a first class physical condition. I am still at home acting under the Doctor's orders which accounts for my writing longhand, not having the opportunity to reach my typist at the store who does all that work for me. I am very much discouraged at not being able to secure a suitable Adjt. General for the division. I have a young man in view, who is a son of a Confederate soldier and who is right with me all day. He is the one I referred to as doing my typing, but unfortunately he would not be able to attend the meeting at Lynchburg where we need him.
>
> What we will do under the circumstances? I can not think of a soul. It kept me awake nearly all of last night with the worry. The Doctor came this morning. I simply told him that I had a restless night. This afternoon he has added somewhat to my troubles by putting me on a diet, the first time in my life to have that experience.[72]

At one point, Warfield became so exasperated by the contentiousness that he called off the state meeting. But the losers of America's bloodiest war would not be denied one last opportunity to give the rebel yell in Virginia. With the assistance, once again, of the Daughters of the Confederacy, the gathering took place in Lynchburg on September 11–13. Atkinson implored, "It is very important that you be there for the salvation of the Division." The weary Warfield replied, "I do feel better and hope that I will hold out," and he made the trip to southern Virginia.[73] Once more, the aged Alexandrian gathered strength and performed his duty. He concluded, "The meeting was a very pleasant and agreeable one, marred only by the fact that so many of our old comrades were absent mainly I think on account of problems caused by old age."[74] It was Warfield's last public appearance as the quintessential Confederate veteran.

As the corps of Southern veterans dwindled, its organizations leaned more and more regularly on those few survivors who were proven workers and still hearty enough to participate, regardless of age or rank dur-

ing the war. When in September 1934 the national headquarters of the
United Confederate Veterans in New Orleans informed Warfield that
he had been appointed assistant adjutant general to the commander in
chief, he drew the line. "I am sorry to write you that I can accept no
more appointments simply on account of the expenses attached thereto."
Along with his letter of declination, Warfield forwarded dues for 1935,
yet another expression of his loyalty, commitment, and optimism.[75]
Warfield did not realize that he would leave the veterans' ranks before
payment was required.

On November 18, he was admitted to the Alexandria Hospital for
infirmities related to his age. Warfield died on the evening of November
26. During his funeral two days later, the city's drugstores closed as
a mark of respect. The casket was draped with the same Confederate battle flag that the deceased brought back from Albany. The *Gazette* said
good-bye by remembering that "General Warfield's affable disposition
and pleasant smile endeared him in the hearts of all who knew him and
his friends were legion."[76]

* * *

"Thousands Line King Street" blared a headline in the *Alexandria Gazette*
in November 1934.[77] The occasion was not the funeral of Edgar Warfield.
That had taken place the day before. It was, instead, a pregame fete that
attracted six thousand onlookers to the city's main street before a match
between a team consisting of players from two city high schools and a rival
squad from Washington, D.C. Interest in a war seven decades earlier had
been eclipsed by an evolving passion for combat on the gridiron. With the
death of the community's last Confederate veteran, the Alexandrians who
fought in the mid-nineteenth century were now completely missing from
sight as well as from the public consciousness. The changing focus lost a
rich collection of individuals who took the responsibilities of citizenship
so seriously that they were willing to lay down their lives for what they
believed. It is unlikely that Americans will again see their duty in the same
way these patriots received their orders and marched off to war.

CONCLUSION

THREE DIMENSIONS OF ALEXANDRIA ACCOUNTED FOR ITS extraordinary representation in gray. The unique feature was its location across the Potomac from Washington, D.C. The county extended five miles up the river and four miles down the west bank from the Long Bridge connecting Alexandria with the capital. This proximity made Alexandria convenient as a residence for men assigned to responsible positions in the seat of government. They included senior officers who would choose to resign their commissions in service of the United States rather than take up arms against the Southern states. This sense of honor was well illustrated by Robert E. Lee and his son, Custis, Samuel Cooper, and French Forrest.

Secondly, as a focus of trade and manufacturing, antebellum Alexandria attracted talented individuals whose prospects improved in its growing economy. In contrast to the agricultural character of much of the South, a transportation hub like Alexandria offered appeal as a window on the North and the markets beyond. George Brent, David Funsten, and Wilson Presstman were drawn to the city for that reason. Montgomery Corse and Douglas Forrest prospered in the city's commerce as well. The skills they acquired prepared them to contribute to the Confederate war effort.

Thirdly, Alexandria was exceptional by Southern standards for its intellectual and cultural offerings. Lectures at the Lyceum and a first-rate daily newspaper were only the two most overt expressions. The city also claimed one of the oldest public subscription libraries in the country. Perhaps most important was the outstanding quality of its educational institutions. The premier example was Episcopal High School, which attracted students from across the South as well as from Alexandria.

Supple minds molded and disciplined "on the Hill" became contributors of note in the national contest to come. Frank Stringfellow, Randolph Fairfax, Orton Williams, Alexander Hunter, and many others used the foundation provided at Episcopal in their service to the rebel cause.

These special qualities help explain the strong representation from Alexandria in the events of the 1860s. Adding the kinds of ordinary residents found in many locales—a Patrick O'Gorman, Anne Frobel, or Edgar Warfield—provided the ingredients for a population with an exceptional amount of talent to offer a nascent country struggling to become a recognized member of the community of nations. Indeed, an argument could be made that certain of the rank and file sent off to war by Alexandria—men like O'Gorman, Fairfax, and Hunter—added more to the Southern war effort by fighting bravely and enduring hardships in the field than the actual contributions and sacrifices of other more senior and illustrious townsmen.

Alexandria was a small, closely knit society. Its citizens regularly interacted in business, religious, educational, and social activities. With their common ties, as the war progressed, it was not surprising to find David Funsten and Douglas Forrest entertaining Randolph Fairfax; Frank Stringfellow and the Warfields helping one another; French Forrest and Mrs. Samuel Cooper corresponding with Anne Frobel; George Brent seeking information from Wilson Presstman; and Alexander Hunter asking the help of Robert E. Lee.

Residents of other towns, North and South, were free to take their time in considering whether and how to contribute to the war effort. Alexandrians did not have that luxury. Alexandrians went away to war because they could not stay home and openly support the rebel cause.

Like most Southerners in the halcyon days of early 1861, Alexandrians marched off with extra liveliness in their step. In the euphoria of joining together for a glorious crusade to defend their beloved Old Dominion from invasion, these patriots were innocent of what lay ahead. Only a handful—Robert E. Lee and French Forrest being the most prominent—had ever tasted combat. It would not be long, however, before these citizen-warriors realized full well what they had volunteered to do.

For men like George Brent and Patrick O'Gorman, the war provided opportunities to develop personally in ways that would not have been possible had they remained in their civilian traces. For older participants, such as Samuel Cooper and French Forrest, who had already made an impact in their chosen careers, the conflict represented an anticlimax, as reflected in their mediocre performances. Those who lived to return home brought a shared defining experience in an unsuccessful endeavor to establish a separate nation. One of their contemporaries wondered "whether any of us will ever be able to live contented in times of peace and laziness. Our generation has been stirred up from its lowest layers and there is that in its history which will stamp every member of it until we are all in our graves. We cannot be commonplace."[1]

War changes societies as well as individuals. Nowhere in mid-nineteenth-century America was this more apparent than in Alexandria. After Appomattox, natives and newcomers alike arrived in Alexandria in ones and twos, weary and wiser, and wounded in many cases. They found the old seaport had been transformed during the battle for the union by the introduction of tens of thousands of soldiers, logisticians, contrabands, invalids, and camp followers.

Midway through the conflict, a correspondent for the *New York Herald* described what had become of Alexandria:

> Many hamlets and towns have been destroyed during the war. But, of all that in some form survive, Alexandria has most suffered. It has been in the uninterrupted possession of the Federals for twenty-two months, and has become essentially a military city. Its streets, its docks, its warehouses, its dwellings, and its suburbs, have been absorbed to the thousand uses of war . . . Alexandria is filled with like ruined people; they walk as strangers through their ancient streets, and their property is no longer theirs to possess for that has passed into the hands of the dominant nationalists.[2]

Alexandrians who escaped this fate by going south when war broke out experienced different kinds of hell. Ninety-nine of these residents in uniform did not live to see peace restored. Those who did were forever scarred by what they had experienced. The stories of the sixteen individuals related here are representative of countless men and women who risked a great deal on behalf of the Confederacy and in many cases lost everything. Whether they survived or perished, in the words of one enlisted member of the Seventeenth Virginia Regiment, these persons "yielded up their lives, though vainly, upon the altar of Southern Liberty."[3]

Appendix
✳✳✳ OTHER NOTABLE CHARACTERS

AFTER PUBLICATION OF UNTOLD NUMBERS OF HISTORIES
and biographies, the Civil War sometimes seems too massive to fully com-
prehend. Often it is easier to understand the conflict and the times in
which it erupted through the eyes and experiences of a few individual
participants. A twenty-first-century reader may find the feelings and perspectives of the 1860s not so different from those experienced today.

Hundreds of Alexandria residents fought and died for a cause in
which they fervently believed, supported the Confederate war effort in
other ways, or simply fled their hometown to escape the Federal occupation. Many were descendants of colonists who fought for independence
less than a century before and, consequently, considered themselves, first
and foremost, Virginians. Once their state decided to withdraw from the
Union, these men and women were loath to take up arms against her. For
that reason, it is difficult to find an Alexandrian who turned his back on
the Commonwealth and enlisted in Federal service.

Virtually every Southern community raised and equipped a regiment.
The history of any one of these military organizations, while seemingly
small and insignificant in comparison to the total war effort was, nevertheless, all-important to the unit members and family left behind. It
was not uncommon for the experiences of members of the same unit to
replicate one another. What makes the Alexandria story different is the
variety of ways in which its residents participated, in addition to the Seventeenth Virginia Regiment recruited in the county and nearby jurisdictions. A sampling of these characters from Alexandria's life during the
mid- and late-nineteenth century might include the following.

Morgan Davis (1841–1917). John Singleton Mosby was a hero to many
rebels, attracting Virginians like Littleton Morgan Davis to join his partisan rangers after engaging in other less glamorous military service on
foot. Davis was a carpenter who enlisted in the Alexandria Artillery in
1861. His most notable feat took place in April, when, on the orders of
Maj. Montgomery Corse, Davis seized the steamer *George Page,* a double-
ended ferry that shuttled between Alexandria and Washington. It was subsequently taken to Aquia Creek, converted into a gunboat, and christened
the *City of Richmond.* By September, Davis was complaining of a hernia and

rheumatism, which led to his discharge. The following spring, he joined the Sixth Virginia Cavalry and, after another medical discharge, Mosby's 43rd Battalion. Davis spent 1865 as a prisoner of war and returned to Alexandria in May after taking the oath of allegiance to the Union at Fort Warren, Massachusetts.[1]

George Duffey (1820–1896). The single work associated with George Duffey's name during the war was crafting a handsome pair of silver spurs in the shape of a swan's head and neck for Gen. Robert E. Lee. There is far more to remember about Duffey, however. He was born in the city and entered into the family business as a watchmaker and jeweler, at the same time learning the skills of a silversmith. Upon the outbreak of hostilities, Duffey was serving as the city's elected commissioner of revenue. Having been commander of the Alexandria Artillery before the war, he cast his lot with the Confederate military. Duffey is credited with keeping the town's earliest records intact during the years of upheaval, including an early plat of the town made by George Washington. Major Duffey spent the war as a major in the ordnance corps of the Army of Northern Virginia. When he returned home after the surrender, his fellow citizens reelected this prominent Alexandrian to his former position.[2]

William H. Fowle Jr. (1839–1903). Born and raised in Alexandria, the scion of one of the city's most prominent families, Fowle naturally joined the flourishing firm of shipping merchants founded by his grandfather. As a graduate of the Virginia Military Institute, Fowle gravitated to military service as a lieutenant in the Old Dominion Rifles when war clouds first appeared in early 1861. A year later, he was elevated to captain as commander of Company H, Seventeenth Virginia. He suffered wounds at Seven Pines and at Drewry's Bluff and ended the war on light duty. At the cessation of hostilities, Fowle returned to commercial pursuits in Alexandria. He was also elected to the city council and general assembly. During President Grover Cleveland's first term, Fowle was appointed collector of internal revenue in Northern Virginia.[3]

Arthur Herbert (1829–1919). Every resident of Alexandria is aware of the Burke and Herbert Bank, the city's financial landmark. It was founded in 1852 by John W. Burke and Arthur Herbert. The latter was a longtime resident of "Muckross" on Seminary Hill. During the war, Herbert rose from a first lieutenant in the Old Dominion Rifles through each rank until promoted to colonel of the Seventeenth Virginia. He took part in every one of the regiment's engagements, from Blackburn's Ford through Sayler's Creek, and as its commander surrendered the unit at Appomattox. Herbert returned to Alexandria to resume the banking business and help rebuild the South.[4]

James Jackson (1823–1861). "The first martyr of the Southern cause" was James Jackson. Born in Fairfax County and educated at Georgetown

College in Washington, D.C., among other places, Jackson moved to Alexandria in February 1861 as proprietor of the Marshall House. Jackson allowed a large Confederate national flag to be raised on a forty-foot staff atop the small hotel, reportedly visible even to President Abraham Lincoln in Washington. When Virginians voted to secede on May 23, Jackson joined the crowd of nationalists surging through the streets in celebration. The following morning, Federals invaded the port city. Col. Elmer Ellsworth led a detail of New York First Fire Zouaves to the southeast corner of Pitt Street, where he climbed onto the roof and tore down the colors. Jackson shot Ellsworth and was, in turn, immediately killed by a Zouave. Ellsworth's body lay in state at the White House and in prominent public buildings in other Northern cities, while, forever after, Jackson has been identified with the Confederate resistance in Alexandria.[5]

Delaware Kemper (1833–1899). A nationally known historian remarked that Delaware Kemper disappeared from view after rising to prominence at First Manassas. This is not quite accurate. Kemper achieved fame for commanding the battery that rained destruction and panic on bluecoats streaming home from the battlefield. Then, he continued to serve in uniform until the war's conclusion. Kemper was reassigned to an artillery battalion and badly wounded at Second Manassas. By special request of Gen. P. G. T. Beauregard, who had not forgotten Kemper's performance at Bull Run, he was transferred to the defense of Charleston. When Lt. Gen. William J. Hardee opposed Sherman's army in 1865, he recommended Kemper for the rank of brigadier general, but the war ended before the promotion could be effected. Kemper's life before and after the conflict was almost as colorful. After graduating from the University of Virginia, Kemper established a school for boys in Gordonsville and then in 1858 succeeded the popular Benjamin Hallowell as headmaster of the Alexandria Academy. Kemper opened a boys school in the Alexandria Lyceum in 1866 and later served as a professor of mathematics at Hampden-Sidney College, the Citadel, and Kings College, among other postings. Kemper was eventually appointed by President Cleveland as U.S. consul at Amoy, China, before finally coming home to the newspaper business in Alexandria.[6]

Sydney Smith Lee (1805–1869). Robert E. Lee's older brother spent more than four decades in the U.S. Navy, rising in rank from midshipman to commander. His most memorable assignments involved directing shore artillery alongside his sibling at the Battle of Veracruz in the Mexican War, serving as executive officer of the naval school at Annapolis, and commanding Commodore Matthew Perry's flagship when he opened Japan to the western world in 1854. Smith Lee was attached to the U.S. Coast Survey headquarters when he resigned his commission on April 22,

1861. His contributions to the Confederate navy were less impressive. Lee served for brief periods as commander of the Gosport shipyard (succeeding French Forrest), leader of naval and military forces at Drewry's Bluff, and chief of the navy's bureau of orders and details. He subsequently joined the train of officials leaving Richmond when the Confederate government collapsed. Lee died at his farm in Richland, near Aquia Creek, and is buried in Alexandria's Christ Church Cemetery.[7]

W. H. F. "Rooney" Lee (1837–1891). Gen. R. E. Lee's third child, born at Arlington House, achieved the greatest success of the seven siblings. Rooney attended Harvard until offered a direct commission in the army in 1857. He served only two years, accompanying Col. Albert Sidney Johnston in the Mormon campaign, before resigning to become a farmer on the White House, Virginia, farm inherited from his grandfather. When Virginia seceded, Lee formed a cavalry company and then steadily rose through the ranks of the Confederate army. He accompanied Maj. Gen. J. E. B. Stuart on the ride around McClellan's army, distinguished himself with bravery at South Mountain, commanded a brigade at Fredericksburg and Chancellorsville, and took part in the Chambersburg raid. Lee received a severe leg wound at Brandy Station, which led to his capture by Union troops, thereby creating a delicate situation for his father. Freed in a prisoner exchange in March 1864, Rooney became the youngest major general in the Confederate army, with the endorsement of the senior Lee. After the war, Rooney settled at Ravensworth outside Alexandria. A courteous, genial gentleman, measuring six feet two on a powerful frame, Lee was generally well liked and elected three times to the U.S. Congress.[8]

Magnus M. Lewis (1824–1884). Dr. Lewis was one of the most prominent physicians in antebellum Alexandria. Consequently, Gov. John Letcher appointed him surgeon of the local sixth militia battalion, a position that converted into identical responsibilities with the successor Seventeenth Regiment. Lewis left Alexandria with the Virginia state forces on the morning of May 24, 1861, and subsequently treated soldiers on the field of battle at Manassas, for which he received special praise from Col. Montgomery Corse. Lewis's professional competence quickly resulted in his elevation to brigade surgeon, where he served under Brig. Gen. A. P. Hill. Lewis was later reunited with his friend Corse, who had become a brigadier general. In September 1863, Lewis was appointed medical director of the Department of North Carolina. He concluded the war as Maj. Gen. George Pickett's division surgeon. Lewis was the only one of the city's doctors to return to private practice in Alexandria following the conflict. His gravestone in Christ Church Cemetery remembers "a skilful physician, a faithful friend, a noble man," and concludes, "A tribute from his patients and friends."[9]

Morton Marye (1831–1910). A lawyer and entrepreneur in Alexandria when war broke out, Morton Marye was commander of the Alexandria Riflemen, a unit in which he had served in militia status. When the Seventeenth Virginia was formed, Marye was elected to its second highest position with the rank of lieutenant colonel. Marye received accolades for leadership and courage on the battlefields at Williamsburg and Frayser's Farm. At Second Manassas, he suffered a leg wound that required amputation above the knee. He was nevertheless appointed regimental commander and promoted to colonel when Corse was elevated to brigadier general in November 1862. Marye never returned to the field, however, and retired in 1864. After the war, he served successively as merchant, clerk of the court, and state auditor in Alexandria.[10]

Charles (1840–1916) and William McKnight (1838–1927). The McKnight brothers are important to Alexandria's history for their correspondence during the Civil War. Their letters provide news and commentary on events taking place, in addition to personal accounts of their lives during this conflagration. These jottings portray dimensions of the Confederate experience uncommon in contemporary writings by Alexandrians. After losing his right arm and being captured at the Battle of Williamsburg, Charles worked as a clerk at the Bureau of Ordnance in Richmond, where he recorded his observations during the last years of the war. Glimpses of his life as a bureaucrat are provided in the diary of a coworker.[11] As the Southern capital was overrun, Charles joined functionaries fleeing south, transporting the government papers that are now the foundation for much of what is known about the Confederacy's high command. William was captured at Frayser's Farm and at Antietam, where he lost an eye. Yet he kept returning to duty. His matter-of-fact accounts, written from Federal confinement, are especially memorable. The brothers came from ordinary origins, Charles learning shorthand and William working as a seaman and carpenter in Alexandria before the war. They each enlisted in the Mount Vernon Guards in 1861, and William served with the Seventeenth Virginia throughout the war. After the conflict, both men filled white-collar positions in Alexandria.[12]

Wilmer McLean (1814–1882). "The man who could not escape the Civil War" was born in Alexandria, the son of a successful baker and founder of St. Paul's Episcopal Church. After being educated in a private school in the city, McLean entered the wholesale and retail grocery business with two family members. He had opened a branch in Centreville when war erupted. The kitchen of his home on Bull Run was damaged by Federal artillery fire and his barn was utilized for a Confederate hospital. McLean could have taken his family to the safety of Georgetown or Alexandria, but he sympathized with the Southern cause and moved to

Richmond instead. McLean exacted a price for his loyalty, however. He was soon working for the Confederate quartermaster, buying supplies in Richmond and selling them at exorbitant prices to the army at Manassas. McLean later speculated in sugar as well. Probably to continue war profiting as the army moved south, he relocated to Appomattox Court House, where McLean achieved lasting fame by another chance encounter with history. Generals Robert E. Lee and Ulysses S. Grant signed the surrender in his parlor. McLean returned to Alexandria to be buried in the graveyard of his father's church.[13]

Harold Snowden (1836–1901). Remembered as editor of the *Alexandria Gazette* for one-third of a century after the Civil War, Harold Snowden articulated the values, ideas, and customs of the Southland. He also personally reported daily news and observations from the nation's capital across the river. Less well known is Snowden's antebellum life as an Alexandria physician educated at the University of Virginia and Jefferson Medical College in Philadelphia. As surgeon of the Old Dominion Rifles, Snowden was forced to hastily evacuate the city on May 24, detouring to climb over the back fence and say good-bye to his father, who was seriously ill. Snowden succeeded Dr. Lewis as surgeon of the Seventeenth Virginia. Later in the war, he represented his hometown in the Virginia legislature and served on the Confederate Board of Medical Examiners.[14]

Mary Surratt (1823–1865). Adjudged an accomplice of John Wilkes Booth in the assassination of Abraham Lincoln, Mary Surratt was the only woman executed during the Civil War. Born Mary Jenkins in nearby Prince George's County, Maryland, she lost her father at an early age. She was, consequently, sent to Alexandria to be near relatives and attend the Sisters of Charity School, a Catholic female seminary on the southwest corner of Fairfax and Duke Streets. In 1835 Mary married John Surratt, a contractor on the Orange and Alexandria Railroad. After her husband died, she moved away from the family tavern in Maryland to open a boardinghouse in Washington, D.C.[15] Whether Surratt knew Frank Stringfellow through their Alexandria connections remains unknown. A nexus might cast doubt on his protestations that he was in no way involved in the plot against the president. If even aware of her ties to Alexandria, most current residents would wish that Surratt's roots in the city are forgotten.

Chatham Roberdeau Wheat (1826–1862). At six foot four, 275 pounds, Chatham Roberdeau Wheat was a handsome man with dark hair and moustache and flashing black eyes. His biographer claims that Wheat was the most experienced campaigner in either army when war broke out, based upon his antebellum adventures as a soldier of fortune in Mexico, Cuba, Nicaragua, and Italy. Wheat was universally liked. With his size, combat credentials, and courage under fire, he was able to lead the otherwise uncontrollable band of dock workers, ex-convicts, and hooligans who made up the unit of Louisiana Zouaves known as the "Tigers" (First Special Louisiana Battalion). These ruffians distinguished themselves at Manassas, where Wheat took a bullet through both lungs, diagnosed as fatal. Wheat exclaimed, "I don't feel like dying yet," and recovered. He was not so fortunate at Gaines Mill when a musket ball passed through his head. "Bury me on the field, boys," he murmured, and they did. Wheat had been born in Alexandria, the son of an Episcopal clergyman. He was educated for a year at Episcopal High School before receiving a degree in law at the University of Nashville, where his father had been reassigned.[16]

Thomas W. White (1829–1918). The *Alexandria Gazette* characterized Thomas W. White as "among the best of men. Careful and methodical in every duty of life, he was a man whose word was his bond." This kind of soldier was attractive to Gen. Robert E. Lee, who chose White as the chief clerk at his headquarters. It was said that Lee earlier had been sent two candidates, one of whom smelled of alcohol and the other of smoking. Lee asked for a third choice and selected the Alexandrian. It was in keeping with White's personality that, after the war, he never succumbed to enticements to reveal what he knew about the workings of Lee's inner circle. White was a bookkeeper at a coal company before the war, as well as a deputy court clerk. As an enlisted member of the Alexandria Riflemen, he marched out of town with the local militia. After returning four years later, White worked for several Alexandria businesses.[17]

George N. Wise (1840–1923). Since 1870, George Wise's *History of the Seventeenth Virginia Infantry, C.S.A.*, now in reprint, has been the authoritative text on Alexandria's regiment. Based in large part on his 1861–63 diary, this concise volume weaves personal anecdotes with excerpts from official reports but suffers irreparably from Wise's absence from the regiment during the final dark months of the war. Its author enlisted in the Old Dominion Rifles on the day the Virginia convention voted to secede and rose to regimental ordnance sergeant the following year. In late 1863 Wise transferred to the First Regiment, Engineer Troops, where he served until the end of the conflict. A coal dealer in the city before the war, Wise worked afterward for the railroad and ran a fire and life insurance business. Wise also authored a second book, entitled *Campaigns and Battles of the Army of Northern Virginia.*[18]

John R. Zimmerman (1838–1926). One of the few Alexandrians to surrender at Appomattox, John Zimmerman joined the Alexandria Riflemen in 1859 and served as a private with Company A, Seventeenth Virginia throughout the war. The sole interruption was a nine-month period spent at Point Lookout, Maryland, after being captured at Manassas Gap in 1863. Zimmerman's distinguishing contribution to the memory of the war is his voluminous diary, now accessible to researchers in the city's public library. Over nine hundred pages in length, the journal's accuracy and objectivity are compromised to some degree by having been recopied in part on the writer's postwar business stationery (and, quite likely, reworked). Zimmerman clerked for various Alexandria merchants before 1861 and operated his own coal firm and salt brokerage at the foot of Queen Street after the conflict. He was also active in veterans' activities, serving as commander of the Robert E. Lee Camp and a member of the monument committee that supervised acquisition and erection of the statue "Appomattox."[19]

Notes

References to the U.S. War Department's *War of the Rebellion: A Compilation of the Official Records of the Union and Confederate Armies (OR)* and the *Official Records of the Union and Confederate Navies (ORN)* are to Series I, unless otherwise indicated. The Compiled Military Service Records, War Department Collection of Confederate Records, Record Group 109, National Archives, Washington, D.C., is indicated as CMSR. "Record Group" is abbreviated as RG. The collection Generals, Staff Officers, and Non-Regimental Enlisted Men, C.S.A., is shortened to GSO.

INTRODUCTION

1. In 1850 a charter became effective designating the port of Alexandria as a city. It became independent of the county in 1870. The county government remained there until 1898, when a new courthouse was dedicated on Fort Myer Heights behind Arlington Mansion. In 1920 Alexandria County, less the port city, was renamed Arlington County.

2. A notable exception was in 1814, when self-preservation and economic and financial interest overcame patriotism, and the Alexandrians surrendered to the British fleet sailing up the Potomac to save the city from destruction.

3. *Alexandria Gazette,* July 31, 1860. Started in 1784, the modern-day masthead of the *Alexandria Gazette* boasts "Serving Alexandria for Over 200 Years." From 1834 until 1895, the city newspaper was known simply as the *Alexandria Gazette.* At later times during its long life, the newspaper added suffixes to its appellation, such as *Alexandria Advertiser, Virginia Advertiser,* and *Port Packet.* For brevity's sake, throughout the narrative and in the endnotes, the paper is referred to simply as the *Alexandria Gazette,* as it was known from 1834 until 1895.

4. Denys Peter Myers, "Architecture," *Alexandria: A Towne in Transition, 1800–1900* (Alexandria: Alexandria Bicentennial Commission, 1977), 156, 165.

5. Harold W. Hurst, *Alexandria on the Potomac: The Portrait of an Antebellum Community* (Lanham, Md.: Univ. Press of America, 1991), 53–54.

6. *Alexandria Gazette,* Jan. 1, 1861.

7. Ibid., Sept. 26, 1849.

8. Ibid., July 11, 1860.

9. David R. Goldfield, *Urban Growth in the Age of Sectionalism: Virginia, 1847–1861* (Baton Rouge: Louisiana State Univ. Press, 1977), 239.

10. U.S. Census Office, *Agriculture of the United States in 1860,* comp. Joseph C. G. Kennedy (Washington, D.C.: Government Printing Office, 1864), xlvi.

11. A fourth rail connection to the Long Bridge over the Potomac, known as the Alexandria and Washington Railroad, discontinued service in 1860.

12. Arthur G. Peterson, "The Alexandria Market Prior to the Civil War," *William and Mary Quarterly,* 2d ser., 11 (Apr. 1932): 113; Thomas Swiftwater Hahn

and Emory L. Kemp, *The Alexandria Canal: Its History and Preservation* (Morgantown: West Virginia Univ. Press, 1992), 27.

13. G. Terry Sharrer, "Commerce and Industry," in *Alexandria: A Towne in Transition, 1800–1900,* ed. John D. Macoll (Alexandria, Va.: Alexandria Bicentennial Commission, 1977), 24–25; Wendell Holmes Stephenson, *Isaac Franklin: Slave Trader and Planter of the Old South* (Gloucester, Mass.: Peter Smith, 1968), 22–25.

14. Goldfield, *Urban Growth,* 55–58.

15. U.S. Census Office, *Population of the United States in 1860,* comp. Joseph C. G. Kennedy (Washington, D.C.: Government Printing Office, 1864).

16. Hurst, *Alexandria on the Potomac,* 41; Goldfield, *Urban Growth,* 57.

17. Daniel W. Crofts, *Reluctant Confederates: Upper South Unionists in the Secession Crisis* (Chapel Hill: Univ. of North Carolina Press, 1989), 54.

18. *Alexandria Gazette,* Sept. 28, 1860.

19. Michael J. Dubin, *United States Presidential Elections, 1788–1860: The Official Results by County and State* (Jefferson, N.C.: McFarland & Co., 2001), 184–86.

20. *Alexandria Gazette,* Nov. 15, 1860.

21. Crofts, *Reluctant Confederates,* 188.

22. Michael F. Holt, *The Rise and Fall of the American Whig Party: Jacksonian Politics and the Onset of the Civil War* (New York: Oxford Univ. Press, 1999), 983.

23. Crofts, *Reluctant Confederates,* 176–77.

24. Ibid., 140.

25. Historian Henry T. Shanks pointed out that pro-secessionist sentiment in Virginia had gathered strength at the outset of 1861 to pressure the state legislature to call for a convention to consider the matter. Henry T. Shanks, *The Secession Movement in Virginia, 1847–1861* (Richmond, Va.: Garrett and Massie Publishers, 1934), 124.

26. Crofts, *Reluctant Confederates,* 140.

27. *Alexandria Gazette,* Dec. 5, 1860.

28. *Journals and Papers of the Virginia State Convention of 1861,* vol. 1, *Journals* (Richmond: Virginia State Library, 1966), 493–518.

29. John Pendleton Kennedy, "The Border States: Their Power and Duty in the Present Disordered Condition of the Country" (Philadelphia: J. B. Lippincott & Co., 1861), reprinted in Jon L. Wakelyn, ed., *Southern Pamphlets on Secession: Nov. 1860–Apr. 1861* (Chapel Hill: Univ. of North Carolina Press, 1996), 217–46.

30. *Alexandria Gazette,* Dec. 24, 1860.

31. A disheartened unionist from western Virginia, however, wrote to the *Alexandria Gazette* asking who could contemplate with satisfaction the Old Dominion "as the tail of a Southern Confederacy, standing as a guard, and playing patrol for 'King Cotton?'" *Alexandria Gazette,* Dec. 15, 1860.

32. *Alexandria Gazette,* Feb. 9, 1861.

33. The battalion had ten companies. The origin of the Alexandria Riflemen only dated to 1856, but the unit's lineage could be traced back to the Revolution. The Mount Vernon Guards were organized in 1842. The John Brown scare in 1859 led to formation of units in Leesburg, Haymarket, and Warrenton (Companies C, F, and K). The threat perceived by the election of Abraham Lincoln led to the creation of the Fairfax Riflemen (Company D), Old Dominion Rifles, and Warren Rifles. The two companies of Irishmen assembled in Alexandria in the spring of 1861.

34. George N. Wise, *History of the Seventeenth Virginia Infantry, C.S.A.* (Baltimore: Kelly, Piet & Co., 1870), 19.

35. Only 440 of these individuals attempted to join one of the five companies formed up in Alexandria, and not all of them were accepted or fought at Bull Run. A few of these men hailed from outside the county and therefore were not Alexandrians per se. Some volunteers were turned down or discharged due to age or medical condition. Others deserted before the opening engagement. Residents also enlisted in the Alexandria Artillery or other units, e.g. cavalry. Staff officers and enlisted men in Richmond and elsewhere are also uncounted.

36. Bell Irvin Wiley, *The Life of Johnny Reb: The Common Soldier of the Confederacy* (Baton Rouge: Louisiana State Univ. Press, 1978), 330.

37. James M. McPherson, *For Cause and Comrades: Why Men Fought in the Civil War* (New York: Oxford Univ. Press, 1997), 181.

38. Wiley, *Life of Johnny Reb*, 331.

39. Ibid., 324.

40. McPherson, *For Cause and Comrades*, 16.

41. See, for example, Peter S. Carmichael, *Lee's Young Artillerist: William R. J. Pegram* (Charlottesville: Univ. Press of Virginia, 1995), 1–5.

42. John G. Selby, *Virginians at War: The Civil War Experiences of Seven Young Confederates* (Wilmington, Del.: Scholarly Resources, 2002), xix–xx.

43. McPherson, *For Cause and Comrades*, 22–25.

44. Wiley, *Life of Johnny Reb*, 17–18. Examining an expanded sampling of resource material and more recent publications seems to confirm Wiley's findings. See, for example, James I. Robertson Jr., *Soldiers Blue and Gray* (New York: Warner Books, 1991), 3–9.

45. Wise, *History of the Seventeenth*, 9.

46. Mary Alice Wills, *The Confederate Blockade of Washington, D.C., 1861–1862* (Parsons, W.Va.: McClain Printing Co., 1975), 15, 17.

47. *Alexandria Gazette*, Apr. 19, 1861.

48. *OR*, 2:26–27.

49. *Alexandria Gazette*, May 24, 1861.

50. No place of birth is given for R. E. Lee, for example. U.S. Census Office, *Eighth Census of the United States: 1860.*

51. Edgar Warfield, *Manassas to Appomattox: The Civil War Memoirs of Pvt. Edgar Warfield, 17th Virginia Infantry* (McLean, Va.: EPM Publications, 1996), 31–32; Wise, *History of the Seventeenth*, 12.

52. *Alexandria Gazette*, May 16, 1861.

53. Ervin L. Jordan Jr., *Black Confederates and Afro-Yankees in Civil War Virginia* (Charlottesville: Univ. Press of Virginia, 1995), 102.

54. Ibid., 267.

55. William Mack Lee, *History of the Life of Rev. Wm. Mack Lee, Body Servant of General Robert E. Lee through the Civil War, Cook from 1861 to 1865* (n.p., 1918).

56. Douglas Diary, Special Collections, Alexandria Library, June 7, 1861, 3.

57. Alexandria *Local News*, Nov. 20, 1861.

58. Ibid., Dec. 12, 31, 1861.

59. Holt, *Rise and Fall*, 981.

60. Crofts, *Reluctant Confederates*, xvi, 130.

61. Alexandrians who served in the Civil War almost invariably headed south. Examples of residents enlisting in the Union effort at the outset of the conflict are scarce. An unnamed private in the Federal army, the only one of seven brothers not to wear the gray, was cited by Sylvester A. Breen in a letter to the editor of the *Alexandria Gazette* on January 27, 1934. The story of another individual is worthy of note. James Treakle lived in the port city and piloted a riverboat. After the

Federals occupied Alexandria, Treakle attempted to return to his family home in King George County, Virginia, and was apprehended as a Yankee spy by Confederate officers at Mathias Point on the Potomac. He was evidentially tried in county court and released. James Treakle, Letters and Papers, 1861, Rare Book, Manuscript, and Special Collections Library, Duke Univ., Durham, N.C.

62. *Louisville Daily Journal,* Jan. 26, 1861.

63. Alexander Hunter, *Johnny Reb and Billy Yank* (Washington, D.C.: Neale Publishing Co., 1905), 17.

CHAPTER 1. GENERAL IN CHIEF: ROBERT E. LEE

1. Margaret Sanborn, *Robert E. Lee: The Complete Man, 1861–1870* (Philadelphia: J. B. Lippincott Co., 1967), 344.

2. Michael Fellman, *The Making of Robert E. Lee* (New York: Random House, 2000), 10.

3. Only four siblings accompanied their parents to Alexandria, as the first child died in the year after his birth.

4. Henry Lee, *Memoirs of the War in the Southern Department of the United States,* ed. Robert E. Lee (New York: Univ. Publishing Co. 1870), 53.

5. Margaret Sanborn, *Robert E. Lee: A Portrait, 1807–1861* (Philadelphia: J. B. Lippincott Co., 1966), 39; Henry Lee to Anne Carter Lee, May 6, 1817, George Bolling Lee Papers, 1732–1870, Virginia Historical Society, Richmond, Va.

6. Most notable, Richard B. McCaslin, *Lee in the Shadow of Washington* (Baton Rouge: Louisiana State Univ. Press, 2001), but also, for example, David J. Eicher, *Robert E. Lee: A Life Portrait* (Dallas: Taylor Publishing Co., 1997), 11, and the classic treatment to which all others are compared, Douglas Southall Freeman, *R. E. Lee: A Biography* (New York: Charles Scribner's Sons, 1934), 1:169, 453, 4:496.

7. Joseph L. Harsh, *Confederate Tide Rising: Robert E. Lee and the Making of Southern Strategy, 1861–1862* (Kent, Ohio: Kent State Univ. Press, 1998), 72

8. McCaslin, *Lee in the Shadow,* 23.

9. Thomas L. Connelly, *The Marble Man: Robert E. Lee and His Image in American Society* (New York: Alfred A. Knopf, 1977), 171.

10. "Anecdotes of the Peninsular Campaign," *Battles and Leaders of the Civil War* (Secaucus, N.J.: Castle, 1984), 2:277.

11. Gary W. Gallagher, "Another Look at the Generalship of R. E. Lee," in *Lee the Soldier,* ed. Gary W. Gallagher (Lincoln: Univ. of Nebraska Press, 1996), 280–81; Gary W. Gallagher, *Lee and His Army in Confederate History* (Chapel Hill: Univ. of North Carolina Press, 2001), 59, 129, 153, 269.

12. McCaslin, *Lee in the Shadow,* 1.

13. Emory M. Thomas, *Robert E. Lee* (New York: W. W. Norton & Co., 1995), 34.

14. Freeman, *R. E. Lee,* 1:30.

15. Statement by William B. Leary, Feb. 15, 1824, M-619, Letters Received by the Adjutant General's Office, 1861–70, RG 94, National Archives.

16. Robert E. Lee Jr., *Recollections and Letters of General Robert E. Lee* (Garden City, N.Y.: Garden City Publishing Co., 1924), 417.

17. Thomas, *Robert E. Lee,* 38.

18. Freeman, *R. E. Lee,* 1:39–44.

19. Communiqué collected in the Robert E. Lee file, M-619, plus Ann H. Lee and R. E. Lee to John C. Calhoun, Apr. 1, 1824, Letters Received by the Adjutant General's Office, 1861–70.

20. Rose Mortimer Ellzey MacDonald, *Mrs. Robert E. Lee* (Boston: Ginn and Co., 1939), 23.

21. A. L. Long, *Memoirs of Robert E. Lee: His Military and Personal History* (Washington, D.C.: J. M. Stoddart & Co., 1886), 27–28. Interestingly, while Robert was one of Hallowell's first students, his eldest son, Custis, was one of the Quaker's last pupils.

22. Freeman, *R. E. Lee,* 1:47.

23. Ibid., 1:438, and "Cazenove Lee Remembers Robert E. Lee," *Alexandria History* 3 (1991): 21.

24. Freeman, *R. E. Lee,* 1:439; John S. Mosby, *The Memoirs of Colonel John S. Mosby,* ed. Charles Wells Russell (Boston: Little, Brown, and Co., 1917), 379.

25. Lee so informed his brother on Apr. 20, 1861. Lee, *Recollections and Letters,* 26–27.

26. *Alexandria Gazette,* Apr. 20, 1861.

27. "Memoir of Mrs. Harriotte Lee Taliaferro Concerning Events in Virginia, Apr. 11–21, 1861," *Virginia Magazine of History and Biography* 57 (Oct. 1949): 419.

28. W. W. Scott, "Some Personal Memories of General Robert E. Lee," *William and Mary Quarterly,* 2d ser., 6 (Oct. 1916): 278–79; Freeman, *R. E. Lee,* 1:637; Nelson Addington Reed, *Family Papers* (St. Louis: Patrice Press, 1990), 412–13.

29. T. Michael Miller, "My Dear Louisa ..." *Fireside Sentinel* 5 (June 1991): 71; Lee, *Recollections and Letters,* 189, 335.

30. One such silent passage was noted in the city newspaper not long after the war's conclusion. *Alexandria Gazette,* Feb. 20, 1866.

31. Freeman, *R. E. Lee,* 4:403–4.

32. *Alexandria Gazette,* May 5, 1869.

33. Lee, *Recollections and Letters,* 352.

34. *Alexandria Gazette,* July 24, 1869; Lee, *Recollections and Letters,* 361–62.

35. Freeman, *R. E. Lee,* 4:474; Mosby, *Memoirs,* 380.

36. McCaslin, *Lee in the Shadow,* 223.

37. "Cazenove Lee Remembers Robert E. Lee," 22–24; Lee, *Recollections and Letters,* 415–16.

38. Thomas, *Robert E. Lee,* 405.

39. *Alexandria Gazette,* Oct. 13, 14, 1870.

40. Ibid., Oct. 15, 1870.

41. Ibid., Oct. 18, 1870.

42. *New York Herald,* Oct. 13, 1870, 7.

43. *Alexandria Gazette,* Oct. 13, 14, 1870.

CHAPTER 2. SENIOR GENERAL: SAMUEL COOPER

1. Cooper lost his seniority on January 23, 1865, when the Congress in Richmond passed an act designating Gen. Robert E. Lee as general in chief of the armies of the Confederate States.

2. Jefferson Davis, *The Rise and Fall of the Confederate Government* (New York: Thomas Yoseloff, 1958), 598; C. Vann Woodward, ed., *Mary Chesnut's Civil War* (New Haven, Conn.: Yale Univ. Press, 1981), 572.

3. Samuel Cooper, "Recollections of Incidents and Characters during Fifty Years Military Service," in Marion Dawson, "Be It Known to All Men: The Story of General Samuel Cooper, CSA, 1798–1876" (master's thesis, Salisbury Univ., Maryland, 2000).

4. Anne Hollingsworth Wharton, *Social Life in the Early Republic* (Philadelphia: J. B. Lippincott Co., 1902), 226. Sarah Maria's sister, Ann Maria Mason, married Sydney Smith Lee, brother of Robert E. Lee, and was the mother of Fitzhugh Lee.

5. Arthur D. Howden Smith, *Old Fuss and Feathers* (New York: Greystone Press, 1927), 167–68.

6. Cooper, "Recollections of Incidents," 21, 62.

7. Ibid., 63.

8. Ibid., 24–25.

9. John K. Mahon, *History of the Second Seminole War, 1835–1842* (Gainesville: Univ. of Florida Press, 1967), 295.

10. Worth to the Secretary of War, Mar. 1, 1848, Dawson, "Be It Known to All Men," 58.

11. Cooper, "Recollections of Incidents," 36–40.

12. List signed by Cooper accompanying Worth to the Adjutant General, Apr. 25, 1842, M-567, Letters Received by the Adjutant General's Office, 1822–60, Main Series, File W-177 (1842), RG 94, National Archives.

13. In his truncated autobiography, Cooper described the Indian war in great detail, presenting it, at one point, as a play with the scene introduced and characters assigned speaking parts. The narrative focuses on events taking place in Florida but, with the exception of Cooper's trip to Washington, is silent on his role in the conflict. Cooper, "Recollections of Incidents," 32–48.

14. Scott to his wife, Feb. 22, 1845, Dawson, "Be It Known to All Men," 49.

15. Cooper, "Recollections of Incidents," 66–81.

16. "Letter from Ex-President Davis [to Gen. Fitzhugh Lee]," *Southern Historical Society Papers* 3 (May–June 1877): 274–75.

17. The future general's son, Samuel, made handwritten notes in 1889 indicating that his father used $2,000 received from sale of the book on tactics to purchase the property. Dawson, "Be It Known to All Men," 19. The prewar census reflected two slaves remaining in the possession of the Coopers.

18. Elizabeth Lindsay Lomax, *Leaves from an Old Washington Diary,* ed. Lindsay Lomax Wood (Mount Vernon, N.Y.: Books, Inc., 1943), 29.

19. *OR,* 1:187.

20. Cooper departed for the Confederate capital at Montgomery, Alabama, on March 12. The caretaker left behind at Cameron later wrote to Mrs. Cooper, acknowledging receipt of $100 from the Corse Brothers banking firm in Alexandria. R. W. Sebastian to Mrs. Maria Cooper, May 19, 1861, Dawson, "Be It Known to All Men."

21. Mason's fame was ensured by the *Trent* affair, when he and a fellow southern diplomat, John Slidell, were removed from a British mail steamer and taken away aboard a Union warship, precipitating an international crisis that generated considerable sympathy in England for the Confederacy.

22. Fitzhugh Lee, for one, completely rejected the view that Cooper followed the advice of Davis and Mason in tying his fortunes to the new Confederacy. Fitzhugh Lee, "Sketch of the Late General S. Cooper," *Southern Historical Society Papers* 3 (May–June 1877): 272–73.

23. "Letter from Ex-President Davis [to Gen. Fitzhugh Lee]," *Southern Historical Society Papers* 3 (May–June 1877): 274–76.

24. Davis to Fitz Hugh Lee, Apr. 27, 1877, Dawson, "Be It Known to All Men," 82.

25. Joseph E. Johnston, *Narrative of Military Operations, Directed, During the Late War Between the States* (New York: D. Appleton and Co., 1874), 72–73; Jefferson

Davis, *The Papers of Jefferson Davis, 1861* (Baton Rouge: Louisiana State Univ. Press, 1992), 7:335–40; Mallory, Diary, #2229, Stephen R. Mallory Papers, Southern Historical Collection, Chapel Hill, N.C.

26. Johnston's biographer agrees that the issue of seniority was the genesis of his animosity with the Confederate president. Craig L. Symonds, *Joseph E. Johnston: A Civil War Biography* (New York: W. W. Norton & Co., 1992), 125–29. A noted biographer of the chief executive alludes to stories that the Davis-Johnston feud could have originated during their cadet days at West Point but goes on to acknowledge that the two were never "open and cordial" after the tempest over ranking Confederate generals in 1861. William C. Davis, *Jefferson Davis: The Man and His Hour* (New York: Harper Collins, 1991), 356–61.

27. William C. Davis, *"A Government of Our Own": The Making of the Confederacy* (New York: Free Press, 1994), 274; Thomas C. DeLeon, *Four Years in Rebel Capitals: An Inside View of Life in the Southern Confederacy, from Birth to Death* (Mobile, Ala.: Gossip Printing Co., 1890), 25.

28. "Rummaging Through Rebeldom," *New York Citizen,* June 1, 1867, 1.

29. Interview with Samuel Cooper Dawson, great-grandson of his noted forebear, Feb. 11, 2000, Alexandria, Va.

30. *OR,* 1:454–55.

31. J. B. Jones, *A Rebel War Clerk's Diary at the Confederate States Capital* (New York: Old Hickory Bookshop, 1935), 1:43.

32. *OR,* 4:362–63.

33. Ibid., ser. II, 1:541.

34. Ibid., 5:1064.

35. Ibid., 32, pt. 3:580–81.

36. Jones, *Rebel War Clerk's Diary,* 2:269.

37. *OR,* 5:961.

38. Alfred Roman, *The Military Operations of General Beauregard* (New York: Da Capo Press, 1994), 1:87; P. G. T. Beauregard, "The First Battle of Bull Run," *Battles and Leaders of the Civil War* (Secaucus, N.J.: Castle, 1984), 1:198.

39. Woodward, *Mary Chesnut's Civil War,* 103.

40. Jones, *Rebel War Clerk's Diary,* 1: 135.

41. Susan P. Lee, *Memoirs of William Nelson Pendleton* (Philadelphia: J. B. Lippincott Co., 1893), 318.

42. *OR,* 42, pt. 3:1181.

43. "Rummaging Through Rebeldom," *New York Citizen,* July 20, 1867, 1.

44. *OR,* 17, pt. 2:595.

45. Ibid., 23, pt. 1:583–84.

46. Ibid., 33:1289–90.

47. George G. Kundahl, *Confederate Engineer: Training and Campaigning with John Morris Wampler* (Knoxville: Univ. of Tennessee Press, 2000), 81.

48. Davis, *"A Government of Our Own,"* 216.

49. Edward Younger, ed., *Inside the Confederate Government: The Diary of Robert Garlick Hill Kean* (New York: Oxford Univ. Press, 1957), 77.

50. Douglas Southall Freeman, *Lee's Lieutenants: A Study in Command* (New York: Charles Scribner's Sons, 1942), 3:7.

51. Stanley F. Horn, *The Army of Tennessee* (Norman: Univ. of Oklahoma Press, 1953), 190.

52. B. F. Cheatham to Cooper, Nov. 1, 1863, Benjamin Franklin Cheatham Papers, Tennessee State Library and Archives, Nashville.

53. *OR*, 31, pt. 1:467–68.

54. Freeman, *Lee's Lieutenants*, 2:416. Trimble was probably referring to the capture of Manassas Junction during the campaign of Second Manassas.

55. Maj. Henry A. Peyton to Capt. J. Morris Wampler, June 11, 1863. Copy in author's collection.

56. *OR*, 38, pt. 5:885.

57. Ibid., 5:1062.

58. Jones, *Rebel War Clerk's Diary*, 1:53; Freeman, *Lee's Lieutenants*, 3:435.

59. Jones, *Rebel War Clerk's Diary*, 2:168.

60. *OR*, 32, pt. 1:613.

61. Ibid., 4:445.

62. Ibid., 31, pt. 2:682.

63. Ibid., 31, pt. 1:467–70.

64. Younger, *Inside the Confederate Government*, 141.

65. Jones, *Rebel War Clerk's Diary*, 1:70, 222, 245; 2:338.

66. Younger, *Inside the Confederate Government*, 187.

67. "Rummaging Through Rebeldom," *New York Citizen*, Apr. 13, 1867, 2.

68. Ibid., July 20, 1867, 1; Jones, *Rebel War Clerk's Diary*, 1:73.

69. Jones, *Rebel War Clerk's Diary*, 1:117; George Green Shackelford, "George Wythe Randolph," *Encyclopedia of Confederate Biography*, ed. Richard N. Current (New York: Simon and Schuster, 1993), 3:1305–6.

70. Younger, *Inside the Confederate Government*, 30.

71. Ibid., 171.

72. DeLeon, *Four Years in Rebel Capitals*, 40.

73. Younger, *Inside the Confederate Government*, 30.

74. Samuel Cooper, GSO, CMSR.

75. Younger, *Inside the Confederate Government*, 87–88.

76. Woodward, *Mary Chesnut's Civil War*, 316, 394.

77. Younger, *Inside the Confederate Government*, 128.

78. "Rummaging Through Rebeldom," *New York Citizen*, July 20, 1867, 1.

79. Burton N. Harrison, "The Capture of Jefferson Davis," *Century* 27 (Nov. 1883): 135.

80. Ibid.

81. Younger, *Inside the Confederate Government*, 206–7.

82. *OR*, 47, pt. 3:842. Kean, J. E. Johnston, and Cooper were not the only senior Confederates to claim credit for preserving the records of the defunct government. P. G. T. Beauregard related that he ordered sentinels to guard the documents after coming upon soldiers engaged in throwing government records from boxcars at the Greensboro, N.C., depot. Roman, *Military Operations*, 2: 410.

83. A smaller collection of papers remained with Kean. After the war, he informed the president of the Southern Historical Society, former Lt. Gen. Jubal Early, that he had been entrusted by Breckinridge with custody of the status reports submitted by Generals Lee and Johnston and the War Department's bureau chiefs in response to its request circulated in February 1865. Kean returned to Virginia with these documents, which were deemed important as documentation of the condition of the Confederacy's defenses at the war's conclusion. "Resources of the Confederacy in February, 1865," *Southern Historical Society Papers* 2 (Sept. 1876): 56–57.

84. Cooper to President Andrew Johnson, Oct. 28, 1865, M-1003, Case Files of Applications from Former Confederates for Presidential Pardons, 1865–67, RG 94, National Archives; Cooper, GSO, CMSR.

85. Cooper to Seward, Dec. 4, 1865, Case Files of Applications from Former Confederates for Presidential Pardons, 1865–67, RG 94, National Archives.

86. Dawson, "Be It Known to All Men," 88–89.

87. Lee, *Recollections and Letters*, 420–21; Freeman, *R. E. Lee*, 4:451.

CHAPTER 3. FIELD COMMANDER: MONTGOMERY CORSE

1. *Alexandria Gazette*, Feb. 11, 1895; F. L. Brockett and George W. Rock, *A Concise History of the City of Alexandria, Va., from 1669 to 1883* (Alexandria: Gazette Book and Job Office, 1883), 10; Montgomery B. Corse, "Biography of General Montgomery D. Corse," MS, 1–2, Corse Family Papers, Special Collections, Alexandria Library. Their mother gave Montgomery and his siblings middle names beginning with the letter *D*, so that they could more easily resume the old family name of De Coursey, should they choose to do so.

2. Corse, "Biography," 2–4.

3. Warfield, *Manassas to Appomattox*, 15.

4. Corse, "Biography," 5; Brockett and Rock, *Concise History*, 29.

5. This was the same William Smith who was later known as "Extra Billy" and commanded the Forty-ninth Virginia Infantry at the outset of the Civil War. He served another term as governor during the war.

6. *Alexandria Gazette*, Nov. 20, 23, 25, Dec. 3, 1846, Feb. 1, 1847; Brockett and Rock, *Concise History*, 29–30.

7. Brockett and Rock, *Concise History*, 8.

8. McCorkle, "Corse Annals," MS, 2, Corse Family Papers.

9. Ibid.

10. Corse, "Biography," 8–9.

11. Capt. Montgomery D. Corse, Honorable Discharge, Hq. 7th Military Depot, Fort Monroe, Va., Aug. 1, 1848, Corse Family Papers.

12. *Alexandria Gazette*, Aug. 5, 1848.

13. Corse, "Biography," 10–11.

14. Ibid., 13–15.

15. *Alexandria Gazette*, Feb. 11, 1895.

16. T. Michael Miller, "Alexandrians Off to War," MS, Special Collections, Alexandria Library.

17. Corse, "Biography," 18.

18. William B. Hurd, *Alexandria, Virginia, 1861–1865* (Alexandria: City of Alexandria, 1970), 3.

19. *Alexandria Gazette*, Dec. 7, 1860.

20. Corse to Col. Francis H. Smith, Jan. 8, 28, 1861, Archives, Preston Library, Virginia Military Institute, Lexington.

21. Corse, "Biography," 20.

22. Ibid., 19.

23. Wise, *History of the Seventeenth*, 10.

24. *OR*, 2:774.

25. Wise, *History of the Seventeenth*, 14–15; Warfield, *Manassas to Appomattox*, 40; Special Requisition, June 17, 1861, Montgomery D. Corse, 17 Virginia Infantry, CMSR.

26. *OR*, 51, pt. 1:33–34, 2:464–65, 544–45.

27. T. Michael Miller, "A Chronicle of the 17th Virginia Regiment—'The Reminiscences of Col. Arthur Herbert,'" *Alexandria History* 6 (1984): 6.

28. Wise, *History of the Seventeenth*, 44–45. Wise was an enlisted member of Company H (Old Dominion Rifles) and, presumably, was on the parade ground that day.

29. McCorkle, "Corse Annals," 6; Corse, "Biography," 25.

30. *OR*, 11, pt. 1:576–78.

31. Warfield, *Manassas to Appomattox*, 71–72.

32. James Thomas Petty, Diary, May 31, 1862, Eleanor S. Brockenbrough Library, Museum of the Confederacy, Richmond, Va.

33. Warfield, *Manassas to Appomattox*, 74.

34. *OR*, 11, pt. 1:579–80; Lee A. Wallace Jr., *17th Virginia Infantry* (Lynchburg, Va.: H. E. Howard, 1990), 33–35; *Alexandria Gazette*, Feb. 11, 1895.

35. Petty Diary, June 13, 1862; Wallace, *17th Virginia Infantry*, 35–36.

36. *OR*, 11, pt.2:763.

37. Ibid., 979.

38. Wallace, *17th Virginia Infantry*, 37–38.

39. *OR*, 12, pt. 2:625–27; 51, pt. 1:135.

40. Corse, "Biography," 30.

41. *OR*, 19, pt. 1:902; 51, pt. 1:169.

42. Corse, "Biography," 32.

43. Alexander Hunter, "The Battle of Antietam," *Southern Historical Society Papers* 31 (1903): 38–39.

44. David E. Johnston, "Concerning the Battle of Sharpsburg," *Confederate Veteran* 6 (Jan. 1898): 28.

45. Hunter, *Johnny Reb and Billy Yank*, 292; *OR*, 19, pt. 1:905.

46. Corse, "Biography," 33; Walter Harrison, *Pickett's Men: A Fragment of War History* (Baton Rouge: Louisiana State Univ. Press, 2000), 58–59.

47. *OR*, 19, pt. 2:677.

48. Ibid., 678.

49. Wallace, *17th Virginia Infantry*, 41.

50. *OR*, 19, pt. 2:683, 699.

51. Corse, "Biography," 36–37. The wedding ceremony was presided over by Rev. J. T. Johnston, former pastor of St. Paul's Church in Alexandria. Corse's adjutant, Capt. Phil Hooe, also from his hometown, served as best man.

52. Warfield, *Manassas to Appomattox*, 117; Corse, "Biography," 37–39.

53. *OR*, 18:929; Warfield, *Manassas to Appomattox*, 121; Corse to his wife, Mar. 26, 1863, Corse Family Papers.

54. James I. Robertson Jr., *Stonewall Jackson: The Man, the Soldier, the Legend* (New York: Simon & Schuster Macmillan, 1997), 757.

55. *OR*, 27, pt. 1:77, pt. 3:925–26, 944.

56. As soon as Corse's brigade left the railroad bridges to rejoin the main body of Lee's army, a Yankee raiding party from Fort Monroe succeeded in burning the trestle over the South Anna River.

57. Corse was not unique among Confederate leaders in being affected by a recent marriage. Richard S. Ewell's uneven performance of duty at Gettysburg and afterward has been explained by modern historians not just as a result of poor health related to loss of a leg, but also due to his marriage to Lizinka, who was notorious for bossing him around. See, for example, Donald C. Pfanz, *Richard S. Ewell: A Soldier's Life* (Chapel Hill: Univ. of North Carolina Press, 1998), 401, 501. Other newly wedded commanders reacted differently on the field of battle, how-

ever. Although he wrote regularly and passionately to his bride, some of Dodson Ramseur's finest combat leadership took place after his wartime nuptials. Indeed, he was killed while rallying his men at Cedar Creek, shortly after learning that his wife had given birth to their first child. The most renowned bridegroom to perish in battle, of course, was John Pegram, whose body lay in state at Richmond's St. Paul's Church, where three weeks earlier he had been married.

58. Corse to his wife, July 7, 1864, Corse Family Papers. Even more extravagant, the love-struck general often left blank the back side of his paper.

59. Corse to his wife, June 18, 1863, Corse Family Papers.

60. Warfield, *Manassas to Appomattox*, 127. Pickett complained to Gen. R. E. Lee of the loss of Corse's brigade on June 21, and two days later the commanding general wrote to Gen. Samuel Cooper asking that Corse be permitted to rejoin Pickett's division. *OR*, 27, pt. 1:77, pt. 3:910. Walter Harrison, a senior officer on Pickett's staff, repeated the same woeful cry for Corse and Jenkins, implying that the presence of their veteran troops might somehow have altered the outcome on Cemetery Ridge. Harrison, *Pickett's Men*, 98.

61. Corse, "Biography," 41.

62. Corse to his wife, July 16, 1863, Corse Family Papers.

63. Harrison, *Pickett's Men*, 108.

64. Petty Diary, July 23, 1863.

65. *OR*, 30, pt. 2:604–5, pt. 4:653; Warfield, *Manassas to Appomattox*, 135–36; Wise, *History of the Seventeenth*, 166–67.

66. *OR*, 29, pt. 2:729, 736, 756, 753; 30, pt. 2:606; 52, pt. 2:532.

67. *OR*, 29, pt. 1:409, pt. 2:788–89, 874–75, 877; 30, pt. 2:606, pt. 4:758; Corse to his wife, Nov. 14, 1863, Corse Family Papers.

68. Corse to his wife, Jan. 20, 1864, Corse Family Papers.

69. *OR*, 32, pt. 2:555.

70. Ibid., 595, 33:1099.

71. *OR*, 33:1099, 1102–3.

72. Ibid., 93–96.

73. Ibid., 1201.

74. Wallace, *17th Virginia Infantry*, 57.

75. Warfield, *Manassas to Appomattox*, 139.

76. Corse to his wife, Mar. 9, 1864, Corse Family Papers; *OR*, 33:260, 1237, 1243, 1274, 1284; 51, pt. 2:862, 863.

77. Corse to his wife, Nov. 14, 1863, Corse Family Papers.

78. "Fayette Artillery," *Southern Historical Society Papers* 25 (1897): 296.

79. Gerard A. Patterson, *Justice or Atrocity: General George E. Pickett and the Kinston, N.C. Hangings* (Gettysburg, Pa.: Thomas Publications, 1998), 51.

80. Corse, "Biography," 46.

81. *OR*, 33:1278–79.

82. Ibid., 905, 906; 36, pt. 2:207; 51, pt. 2:874.

83. George C. Cabell, "Account of the Skirmish at Swift Creek," *Southern Historical Society Papers* 16 (1888): 223–24; Arthur Herbert, "The Seventeenth Virginia Infantry at Flat Creek and Drewry's Bluff," *Southern Historical Society Papers* 12 (Jul.–Sept. 1884): 289–92.

84. Roman, *Military Operations*, 2:192; Freeman, *Lee's Lieutenants*, 4:484.

85. Warfield, *Manassas to Appomattox*, 144; Wise, *History of the Seventeenth*, 178; Herbert, "The Seventeenth Virginia," 294; P. G. T. Beauregard, "The Defense of Drewry's Bluff," *Battles and Leaders of the Civil War* (Secaucus, N.J.: Castle, 1984), 4:203; *OR*, 36, pt. 2:203.

86. *OR*, 36, pt. 3:799.

87. Charles T. Loehr, "The Battle of Milford Station," *Southern Historical Society Papers* 26 (1898): 114–15; Corse to his wife, May 23, 1864, Corse Family Papers. It was about this time that Hancock reported to his superiors that "a very intelligent Irishwoman" had provided an intelligence report on Corse's brigade. *OR*, 36, pt. 3:84.

88. "A Desperate Dash," *Southern Historical Society Papers* 21 (1893): 177–82; E. M. Morrison, "Capture and Reoccupation of the Howlett House in 1864," *Southern Historical Society Papers* 22 (1894): 21–24.

89. Wise, *History of the Seventeenth*, 188.

90. Inspection Report, Aug. 13, 1864, and Register of General Hospital No. 4, Oct. 14, 1864, M. D. Corse, GSO, CMSR; Corse to his wife, June 23, 24, 27, July 15, Oct. 11 and Nov. 15, 22, 1864, Corse Family Papers.

91. Corse to his wife, Nov. 26, 28, 1864, Corse Family Papers.

92. Lee to Longstreet, Jan. 19, 1865, Robert E. Lee Headquarters Papers, Virginia Historical Society, Richmond.

93. *OR*, 42, pt. 3: 1292–93, 45, pt. 2:945; Corse to his wife, Dec. 14, 29, 1864, Corse Family Papers.

94. Corse to his wife, June 14, 1864, Corse Family Papers; *OR*, 42, pt. 2:1291–92. On the Union side, an Irish informant talked incessantly about "Corsair's division" being here and there, which the Federals translated as "Corse's division." The Fifth Corps headquarters finally concluded that the Celt was "an ignorant fellow" and speculated that "Corsair" was really "Kershaw," a better translation than "Corse," since he commanded a brigade, not a division. At another point, Corse's brigade was erroneously reported to the chief of staff of the U.S. Army to be in Charlestown, Virginia. *OR*, 42, pt. 2:340, 341, 342; 43, pt. 1:561.

95. Corse to his wife, Dec. 2, 1864, Corse Family Papers.

96. Corse, "Biography," 52.

97. Corse to his wife, Jan. 2, 1865, Corse Family Papers.

98. *OR*, 46, pt. 2:61, pt. 3:38, 1332; Corse to his wife, Mar. 7, 17, 1865, Corse Family Papers.

99. The Federal high command was being steadily updated about the location of Confederate units. Grant was apprised of Corse's whereabouts based upon the word of "a most intelligent deserter, who says he only came in because he knocked his captain (who had insulted him) down." *OR*, 46, pt. 3:237.

100. Wise, *History of the Seventeenth*, 219–20.

101. Harrison, *Pickett's Men*, 147.

102. Warfield, *Manassas to Appomattox*, 168.

103. Corse, "Biography," 58–59.

104. John R. Zimmerman, Diary, Apr. 2, 1865, Joseph L. Martin Papers, Special Collections, Alexandria Library.

105. Wise, *History of the Seventeenth*, 230–35; C. F. James, "Battle of Sailor's Creek," *Southern Historical Society Papers* 24 (1896): 85–86; Corse, "Biography," 61; *OR*, 46, pt. 3:864.

106. *OR*, vol. 46, pt. 1:1277. The Seventeenth Virginia hid its regimental colors after the defeat at Five Forks to keep them from being captured. After the surrender, the flag was divided up, a fragment going to each surviving unit member at the war's end. Wise, *History of the Seventeenth*, 228–29.

107. Corse to his wife, Apr. 12, 1865, Corse Family Papers; "Letter of General R. S. Ewell to General Grant," *Southern Historical Society Papers* 39 (Apr. 1914): 4–5.

108. Fowle to Corse, May 9, 1865; Corse to his wife, May 15, 1865, Corse Family Papers; Corse, "Biography," 62, 66.

109. Corse to Johnson and oath by Corse, June 16, 1865, Amnesty Pardons, RG 94, National Archives; Corse oath of allegiance to the United States, July 24, 1865, Corse Family Papers. Corse's aide-de-camp, Capt. Charles U. Williams, had written to Grant on behalf of Mrs. Corse and the brigade staff officers requesting the intercession of the U.S. general in chief to release their imprisoned leader. Williams to Grant, June 5, 1865, Montgomery D. Corse, 17 Virginia Infantry, CMSR.

110. *Alexandria Gazette*, Apr. 29, 1870.

111. "Unveiling of the Valentine's Recumbent Figure of Lee at Lexington, June 28th, 1883" *Southern Historical Society Papers* 11 (Aug.–Sept. 1883): 414; "The Monument to General Robert E. Lee," *Southern Historical Society Papers* 17 (1889): 266; "Fairfax Monument," *Southern Historical Society Papers* 18 (1890): 131; "Monument to the Confederate Dead at Fredericksburg, Virginia, Unveiled on June 10, 1891," *Southern Historical Society Papers* 18 (1890): 398.

112. William B. Hurd, "Montgomery Dent Corse," *Alexandria History* 4 (1982): 11–13.

113. Corse, "Biography," 70–72; "Jacintha" to "Mr. Corse," July 2, 1946, Biography: Montgomery Corse, vertical files, Special Collections, Alexandria Library.

114. Corse, "Biography," 68–69, 72.

115. Ibid., 73.

116. *Baltimore Sun*, Feb. 14, 1895, 4.

117. Corse, "Biography," 76, 81; *Alexandria Gazette*, Feb. 11, 13, 1895. Relations between old veterans of the blue and gray armies in Alexandria began to repair on National Decoration Day (May 30) in 1891, when members of the United Confederate Veterans camp and the Grand Army of the Republic post joined to decorate graves of Union dead at the city's U.S. Cemetery. The superintendent wrote a letter of thanks to the Robert E. Lee Camp, imploring "may it be the beginning of an era of good feeling." Capt. J. V. Davis to R. E. Lee Camp, June 1, 1891, R. E. Lee Camp No. 5, minutes, Mary Custis Lee–17th Virginia Regiment Chapter, United Daughters of the Confederacy, Alexandria.

118. Corse, "Biography," 81.

CHAPTER 4. PRESIDENTIAL AIDE: G. W. CUSTIS LEE

1. George Washington Parke Custis, *Recollections and Private Memoirs of Washington, by His Adopted Son, George Washington Parke Custis, with a Memoir of the Author by His Daughter* (New York: Derry & Jackson, 1860), 67.

2. There has been no adequate biography of G. W. C. Lee. Biographical material (not always reliable) is contained in a work published in 2003 by a small distributor, Bernice-Marie Yates's *The Perfect Gentleman: The Life and Letters of George Washington Custis Lee* (Longwood, Fla.: Xulon Press, 2003). A complete account of his life is found in Sandra S. Weber's 1982 master's thesis, "George Washington Custis Lee: History's Pawn," State University of New York College at Oneonta. A more judgmental précis of Lee's personality and accomplishments is found in Connelly, *The Marble Man*, 30–31.

3. See, for example, the letter from Mary Custis Lee to a friend (unnamed and undated) in Rose Mortimer Ellzey MacDonald, *Mrs. Robert E. Lee* (Boston: Ginn and Co., 1939), 41.

4. Freeman, *R. E. Lee*, 1:178.

5. For the complete story of Reverend Smith's school at Clarens, the striking colonial structure on what is now Quaker Lane in Alexandria, see T. Michael Miller, "Clarens: A Sylvan Retreat," *Fireside Sentinel* 8 (Sept.–Oct. 1994): 54–56.

Former Virginia senator James M. Mason purchased the mansion after the Civil War and was visited there by Jefferson Davis in October 1870.

6. R. E. Lee to G. W. C. Lee, Nov. 30, Dec. 18, 1845, Robert E. Lee Correspondence, DeButts-Ely Collection, Library of Congress.

7. R. E. Lee to G. W. C. Lee, Apr. 25, 1847, Lee Family Papers, 1824–1918, Virginia Historical Society, Richmond.

8. R. E. Lee to Mary Custis Lee, Mar. 24, 1848, Lee Family Papers.

9. R. E. Lee to Scott, Feb. 5, 1850, and to Brig. Gen. R. Jones, Jan. 7, 1850, Letterbook No. 1, DeButts-Ely Collection, Library of Congress.

10. Hunter and Mason to President Polk, Jan. 19, 1849, and to President Taylor, Jan. 16, 1850; petition signed by members of the U.S. House of Representatives (undated); G. W. C. Lee to Secretary of War, Mar. 10, 1850, M-688, U.S. Military Academy Cadet Application Papers, 1805–66, RG 94, National Archives.

11. G. W. C. Lee to Mary Custis (his grandmother), Mar. 19, 1853, Robert E. Lee Correspondence.

12. Court Martial Transcript, Item HH 31, Records of the Office of the Judge Advocate General (Army), RG 153, National Archives.

13. Freeman, *R. E. Lee,* 1:317.

14. Lee, *Recollections and Letters,* 15.

15. William Woods Averell, *Ten Years in the Saddle: The Memoir of William Woods Averell,* ed. Edward K. Eckert and Nicholas J. Amato (San Rafael, Calif.: Presidio Press, 1978), 46–47.

16. Freeman, *R. E. Lee,* 1:346.

17. Mary Custis Lee to Bvt. Brig. Gen. Joseph G. Totten, July 15, 1857, G. W. C. Lee to Totten, July 18, 1857, Letters Received by the Chief of Engineers, 1838–68, RG 77, National Archives.

18. G. W. C. Lee to his mother, Sept. 3, 1857, Robert E. Lee Correspondence.

19. R. E. Lee to G. W. C. Lee, Mar. 17, 1858, R. E. Lee Papers, Rare Book, Manuscript, and Special Collections Library, Duke Univ., Durham, N.C.

20. J. William Jones, *Life and Letters of Robert Edward Lee: Soldier and Man* (Washington, D.C.: Neale Publishing Co., 1906), 97. Colonel Lee produced a drumroll of correspondence aimed at convincing his eldest son to return to Arlington, in uniform or as a civilian. One letter described difficulties finding a reliable manager. R. E. Lee to G. W. C. Lee, Jan. 17, 1858, R. E. Lee Papers. Another compared the pluses and minuses of a career as an engineer officer with other options. R. E. Lee to G. W. C. Lee, Feb. 15, 1858, R. E. Lee Papers. The estate's outstanding debt of $10,000 is cited and repeated. R. E. Lee to G. W. C. Lee, Feb. 15, Mar. 17, 1858, R. E. Lee Papers. The determined executor even lamented that his duties never permitted a holiday. R. E. Lee to G. W. C. Lee, May 30, 1859, R. E. Lee Papers.

21. R. E. Lee to G. W. C. Lee, May 30, 1859, R. E. Lee Papers; R. E. Lee to G. W. C. Lee, Aug. 19, 1859, Jones, *Life and Letters,* 93, 103.

22. See, for example, R. E. Lee to G. W. C. Lee, Feb. 28, Mar. 13, Apr. 16, Nov. 24, Dec. 5, 1860, R. E. Lee Papers.

23. G. W. C. Lee to McPherson, Nov. 19, 1860, James B. McPherson Papers, Library of Congress.

24. *OR,* 51, pt. 1:313; ser. III, 1:688–89.

25. McCaslin, *Lee in the Shadow,* 3.

26. Averell, *Ten Years in the Saddle,* 241.

27. The three Virginians conferred on Apr. 21, 1861, without convincing Custis to resign. Lomax, *Leaves from an Old Washington Diary,* 149.

28. R. E. Lee to G. W. C. Lee, Nov. 24, 1860, R. E. Lee Papers.

29. Freeman, *R. E. Lee,* 1:444.

30. *Richmond Times-Dispatch,* Mar. 10, 1904, 3.

31. G. W. C. Lee to Totten, Apr. 27, 1861, item #1784, Letters Received by the Chief of Engineers, 1838–68, RG 77, National Archives.

32. Lee, *Recollections and Letters,* 29.

33. R. E. Lee to his wife, May 11, 1861, Robert E. Lee Correspondence.

34. Mrs. William Cabell Flournoy, "Arlington," *Confederate Veteran* 31 (Apr. 1923): 135.

35. R. E. Lee to his wife, May 11, 1861, Robert E. Lee Correspondence; *OR,* 2:780.

36. Special Orders No. 85, Adjutant and Inspector General's Office, G. W. C. Lee, GSO, CMSR; *OR,* 4:651; G. W. C. Lee to W. J. Green, Feb. 19, 1909, #289, Thomas Jefferson Green Papers, Southern Historical Collection, Chapel Hill, N.C.

37. *OR,* 4:576; 51, pt. 2:359, 361, 369.

38. Davis, *Papers,* 7:313.

39. William Gordon McCabe, *Major-General George Washington Custis Lee* (Richmond: Virginia Historical Society, 1914), 5.

40. Woodward, *Mary Chesnut's Civil War,* 138.

41. As an example of Lee's ceremonial responsibilities as the president's aide-de-camp, see Richmond *Daily Dispatch,* Jan. 2, 1862.

42. *OR,* 51, pt. 2:467, 9:45; 11, pt. 3:524, 632.

43. R. E. Lee to G. W. C. Lee, Jan. 4, 1862, R. E. Lee Papers; R. E. Lee to his wife, Jan. 28, 1862, Robert E. Lee Correspondence.

44. Sally Nelson Robins, "Mrs. Lee during the War—Something About 'The Mess' and Its Occupants," ed. R. A. Brock, *General Robert E. Lee, Soldier, Citizen, and Christian Patriot* (Richmond: Royal Publishing Co., 1897), 322–42. See also Freeman, *R. E. Lee,* 3:262n; Lee, *Recollections and Letters,* 169–70.

45. Robert E. Lee to Mary Lee, Aug. 9, 1863, Lee Family Papers, Virginia Historical Society.

46. See, for example, R. E. Lee to G. W. C. Lee, Dec. 29, 1861, R. E. Lee Papers.

47. Freeman, *R. E. Lee,* 3:538.

48. R. E. Lee to Mary Lee, Sept. 29, 1862, Lee Family Papers.

49. Lee, *Recollections and Letters,* 79.

50. See, for example, *OR,* 11, pt. 3:632.

51. Oliver Crenshaw, *General Lee's College: The Rise and Growth of Washington and Lee University* (New York: Random House, 1969), 176.

52. Davis to G. W. C. Lee, Apr. 8, 1863, G. W. C. Lee, CMSR.

53. *OR,* 14:894, 899, 53:289.

54. James A. Seddon to Adjutant General, C.S.A., June 25, 1863, G. W. C. Lee, CMSR.

55. It was about this time that Custis's brother, W. H. F. "Rooney" Lee, a brigadier general of the cavalry, was captured by the Yankees. Custis was said to have offered himself in place of Rooney, as he was a single man without children and therefore with no immediate family to suffer from his imprisonment. Woodward, *Mary Chesnut's Civil War,* 450.

56. *OR,* 27, pt. 3:950, 1067.

57. Ibid., 971, 977.

58. Jones, *Rebel War Clerk's Diary,* 2:40.

59. Ibid., 2:239. The same writer had expressed his approval when Custis Lee was first reported to have succeeded the unpopular Brig. Gen. John Henry Winder as commander of Richmond's local defense troops (1:361).

60. *OR,* 52, pt. 2:556; 29, pt. 1:823; 51, pt. 2:787.

61. Ibid., 29, pt. 2:158–59.

62. After the war, Custis Lee confirmed this characterization of the unsuccessful effort to appoint him to the command in West Virginia. Hudson Strode, ed., *Jefferson Davis: Private Letters, 1823–1889* (New York: Harcourt, Brace & World, 1966), 532.

63. "Letter from President Davis," *Southern Historical Society Papers* 11 (Dec. 1883): 562–63.

64. *OR*, 43, pt. 1:992.

65. Ibid., 33:1245.

66. Jones, *Life and Letters*, 304.

67. G. Watson James, "Dahlgren's Raid," *Southern Historical Society Papers* 39 (Apr. 1914): 64–67.

68. *OR*, 51, pt. 2:996.

69. Ibid., 40, pt. 2:646.

70. Ibid., 672–74; 51, pt. 2:1015–17, 1081.

71. Magnus S. Thompson, "Plan to Release Our Men at Point Lookout," *Confederate Veteran* 20 (Feb. 1912): 69.

72. Royce Gordon Shingleton, *John Taylor Wood: Sea Ghost of the Confederacy* (Athens: Univ. of Georgia Press, 1979), 116–18.

73. *OR*, 40, pt. 3:753, 757, 761; ser. II, 7:458.

74. Lycurgus Washington Caldwell, an auditor in the Treasury Department when not soldiering for Custis Lee, agreed with Gorgas, figuring that the government's civil offices would remain closed for as long as Grant threatened Richmond. Yet he could not envision his battalion being utilized in any sector of critical importance and characterized his comrades as tired of marching, felling trees, and building breastworks. J. Michael Welton, ed., *"My Heart Is So Rebellious": The Caldwell Letters, 1861–1865* (Warrenton, Va.: Fauquier National Bank, 1991), 228.

75. Welton, *"My Heart,"* 245.

76. *OR*, 40, pt. 2:679, 1180, and pt. 3:819, 1179; Burke Davis, *To Appomattox: Nine April Days, 1865* (New York: Holt, Rinehart, Winston, 1959), 38.

77. *OR*, 40, pt. 3:814–15.

78. Ibid. 42, pt. 3:1296, 1310–11.

79. Yates, *The Perfect Gentleman*, 1:312–13.

80. Jones, *Rebel War Clerk's Diary*, 2:365.

81. *OR*, 46, pt. 2:1025.

82. Bragg to Davis, Mar. 21, 1864, G. W. C. Lee, CMSR.

83. Woodward, *Mary Chesnut's Civil War*, 578.

84. "Rummaging Through Rebeldom," *New York Citizen*, June 29, 1867, 3.

85. *OR*, 46, pt. 2:1002, 1112, 1169; 51, pt. 2:1056.

86. Ibid., 51, pt. 2:1297, 1307, pt. 3:1330, 1334, 1343.

87. "The Evacuation of Richmond," *Southern Historical Society Papers* 23 (1895): 177.

88. Clement Sulivane, "The Evacuation," *Battles and Leaders of the Civil War* (Secaucus, N.J.: Castle, 1984), 4:725.

89. One nervous officer recalled overhearing Ewell remark in the midst of the artillery bombardment, "Tomatoes are very good; I wish I had some." The humor in this incongruous aside served to dissipate the tension. R. T. W. Duke, "Burning of Richmond," *Southern Historical Society Papers* 25 (1897): 137.

90. *OR*, 46, pt. 1:1293–98; Robert Stiles, *Four Years under Marse Robert* (Washington, D.C.: Neale Publishing Co., 1903), 332–34. Stiles recounts a tragic example of the fierce man-to-man fighting: "I had cautioned my men against wearing

'Yankee overcoats,' especially in battle, but had not been able to enforce the order perfectly—and almost at my side I saw a young fellow of one of my companies jam the muzzle of his musket against the back of the head of his most intimate friend, clad in a Yankee overcoat, and blow his brains out."

91. *OR*, 46, pt. 1:1295.

92. Ibid.

93. Ibid., 1302.

94. McHenry Howard, *Recollections of a Maryland Confederate Soldier and Staff-Officer under Johnston, Jackson and Lee* (Baltimore: Williams & Wilkins Co., 1914), 390–92; Stiles, *Four Years under Marse Robert*, 238–39; *New York Herald*, Apr. 16, 1865, 2.

95. G. W. C. Lee to A. L. Rives, Oct. 19, 1865, Alfred Landon Rives Papers, Rare Book, Manuscript, and Special Collections Library, Duke Univ., Durham, N.C.

96. It sometimes said, incorrectly, that Lee occupied the same teaching position as Robert E. Rodes and Thomas J. Jackson, two generals in gray who perished during the war. Rodes was professor of applied mechanics (1848–51), Jackson served as professor of natural and experimental philosophy (1852–61), and Lee's responsibilities were civil and military engineering and applied mechanics.

97. Lee to Rives, Oct. 19, 1865, Alfred Landon Rives Papers.

98. Freeman, *R. E. Lee*, 4:192–95.

99. "General Lee Just after the War," *Confederate Veteran* 30 (June 1922): 207; Lee, *Recollections and Letters*, 171. Custis's mother was reported to be elated at having Custis by her side once again. Mrs. A. M. Fitzhugh to Francis Dickins, Jan. 12, 1866, #218, Francis Asbury Dickins Papers, Southern Historical Collection, Chapel Hill, N.C.

100. Christiana Bond, *Memories of General Robert E. Lee* (Baltimore: Norman, Remington Co., 1926), 36–37.

101. Report of the Board of Visitors, 1867, 11–12, Archives, Preston Library, Virginia Military Institute, Lexington.

102. One suitor was the Maryland Agricultural College. G. W. C. Lee to W. J. Green, Feb. 2, 1867, Thomas Jefferson Green Papers.

103. James Lewis Howe, "George Washington Custis Lee," *Virginia Magazine of History and Biography* 48 (Oct. 1940): 322–23.

104. Franklin L. Riley, *General Robert E. Lee after Appomattox* (New York: Macmillan Co., 1922), 150. The similar temperament and deportment exhibited by both men undoubtedly contributed to the impression that they looked alike. William Woods Averell, for example, observed that Custis was "very like his father in personal appearance and innate dignity of manner." Averell, *Ten Years in the Saddle*, 241.

105. Scott, "Some Personal Memories of General Robert E. Lee," 285–86.

106. Lee, *Recollections and Letters*, 164–65.

107. James Dinkins, "Famous War Horses," *Confederate Veteran* 40 (Dec. 1932): 423.

108. Crenshaw, *General Lee's College*, 179–80.

109. Yates, *The Perfect Gentleman*, 2:97, 98–99.

110. G. W. C. Lee to Stephen Lee, July 19, 1894, #2440, Stephen Dill Lee Papers, Southern Historical Collection, Chapel Hill, N.C.; to W. J. Green, May 22, 1895, Thomas Jefferson Green Papers.

111. Crenshaw, *General Lee's College*, 181.

112. Custis Lee seemed trapped in a long-term relationship with Traveller. Insight into their relative importance in the old general's mind may have been

offered by an 1866 letter in which he assured his daughter, "Traveller and Custis are both well, and pursue their usual dignified gait and habits." Lee, *Recollections and Letters*, 249.

113. Howe, "George Washington Custis Lee," 326–27; *Alexandria Gazette*, Feb. 19, 1913; George L. Christian, "General Lee's Headquarters Records and Papers—The Present Location of Some of These," *Southern Historical Society Papers* 44 (June 1923): 229–30; G. W. C. Lee, "Gen. Robert E. Lee on Traveler," *Confederate Veteran* 14 (Sept. 1906): 424; "The Anne Lee Monument," *Confederate Veteran* 5 (Mar. 1897): 123–24.

114. *Alexandria Gazette*, Feb. 19, 22, 1913.

115. McCabe, *Major-General*, 2.

116. Howe, "George Washington Custis Lee," 324.

117. His sisters by no means escaped from the heavy burden of being Robert E. Lee's daughters. None of the girls married, and only Mary (the eldest) came close to leading a normal life.

118. *Richmond Times-Dispatch*, Feb. 19, 1913, 2.

119. W. O. Hart, "Arlington," *Confederate Veteran* 30 (June 1922): 208; Flournoy, "Arlington," 134; *United States v. Lee*, 106 U.S. 196 (1882); G. W. C. Lee to Stephen Lee, Aug. 3, 1894, Stephen Dill Lee Papers.

CHAPTER 5. GENERAL STAFF OFFICER: GEORGE BRENT

1. George Brown Goode, *Virginia Cousins: A Study of the Ancestry and Posterity of John Goode of Whitby* (Bridgewater, Va.: C. J. Carrier Co., 1963), 122, 239.

2. *Alexandria Gazette*, Sept. 11, 28, Oct. 27, Nov. 2, 1860.

3. Ibid., Dec. 5, 1860.

4. Ibid., Jan. 29, 1861; Washington *Evening Star*, Jan. 30, 1861.

5. *Alexandria Gazette*, Jan. 31, 1861.

6. Ibid., Feb. 5, 1861.

7. "Rummaging Through Rebeldom," *New York Citizen*, June 8, 1867, 2.

8. Benjamin J. Hillman, ed., *Virginia's Decision: The Story of the Secession Convention of 1861* (Richmond: Virginia Civil War Commission, 1964), 5–6; *Alexandria Gazette*, Mar. 14, 1861.

9. *Journals and Papers of the Virginia State Convention of 1861* (Richmond: Virginia State Library, 1966), 1:51.

10. *Proceedings of the Virginia State Convention of 1861* (Richmond: Virginia State Library, 1965), 1:511; Hillman, *Virginia's Decision*, 4; *Alexandria Gazette*, Mar. 12, 1861.

11. *Proceedings of the Virginia State Convention of 1861*, 1:516–17.

12. *OR*, 2:445, 51:34.

13. Ibid., 2:463.

14. Pvt. John R. Zimmerman recorded in his journal in late summer that Brent transferred to the Eleventh Virginia Regiment. There is no substantiation in the regimental histories of the Eleventh or Seventeenth Virginia Regiments or in Brent's official military service record. This notation must, therefore, be dismissed as merely a rumor circulating among the enlisted troops. John R. Zimmerman, Diary, Aug. 26, 1861.

15. Roman, *Military Operations*, 1:493.

16. Wise, *History of the Seventeenth*, 55.

17. *Oliapodrida,* coll. George William Brent, Virginia Historical Society, Richmond.

18. Reports, Apr. 12, 15, 16, 21, 23, 25, 27, 1862, George William Brent, GSO, CMSR; *OR,* 8:138.

19. *OR,* 10, pt. 2:531, 602.

20. For a comprehensive study of Bragg's relationships with his senior staff officers, see June I. Gow, "Chief of Staffs in the Army of Tennessee," *Tennessee Historical Quarterly* 27 (winter 1968): 341-60.

21. Brent to Gen. Samuel Cooper, June 30, 1862, Brent, CMSR.

22. *OR,* 17, pt. 2:658; 16, pt. 2:758; 16, pt. 1:935.

23. *OR,* 16, pt. 1:1095-96.

24. *OR,* 16, pt. 1:952, 958.

25. *OR,* 20, pt. 2:411.

26. The authorship of the Brent diary is proved conclusively by June I. Gow, "The Johnston and Brent Diaries: A Problem of Authorship," *Civil War History* 14 (Mar. 1968): 46-50.

27. George W. Brent, Diary, Oct. 2, 1862, Braxton Bragg Papers, William P. Palmer Collection, Western Reserve Historical Society, Cleveland.

28. Ibid., Oct. 6, 1862.

29. Ibid., Oct. 7, 1862.

30. Ibid., Oct. 8, 1862.

31. Ibid., Oct. 11-12, 1862.

32. Ibid., Oct. 14, 1862

33. Ibid., Nov. 2, 1862.

34. One observer noted that it took a full day and a half for the long line of Confederate wagons to pass a single point on their way back to Tennessee.

35. Brent Diary, Oct. 14, 1862.

36. Ibid., Nov. 22, Dec. 2, 6, 1862.

37. Interestingly, it is a principle that Robert E. Lee repeatedly violated with impunity, most notably in his renowned victory at Chancellorsville.

38. Hardee to Bragg, Oct. 7, 1862, Military Papers, Filson Club, Louisville, Ky.

39. Brent Diary, Nov. 6, 1862.

40. Ibid., Aug. 26, Nov. 21, 1863.

41. Ibid., Jan. 8, 1863.

42. Ibid., Jan. 24-Feb. 2, Mar. 15, 1863.

43. Ibid., Apr. 13, 1863.

44. Ibid., Dec. 19, 1862.

45. Ibid., Mar. 17, 1863.

46. Ibid., Apr. 13, 1863.

47. Ironically, Brent was himself the foil in a Federal intelligence-collecting operation. Shortly before the clash at Stones River, two ladies set out in a carriage from Nashville seeking loved ones behind Confederate lines. They were assigned a driver who was a Union spy. Arriving at the southern headquarters in Murfreesboro on Christmas Day, 1862, with papers Maj. Gen. William Rosecrans had sent as a ruse to gain access for his agent, the travelers had difficulty finding anyone in authority until Colonel Brent, the chief of staff, appeared, received the documents, and explained that Bragg was out at a party with his wife. Mrs. Theodore L. Burnett, "Reminiscences of the Confederacy," *Confederate Veteran* 15 (Apr. 1907): 175.

48. Brent Diary, Mar. 20, 1863.

49. Ibid., Aug. 22, 23, Sept. 4, 1863.

50. Daniel H. Hill, "Chickamauga—The Great Battle of the West," *Battles and Leaders of the Civil War* (Secaucus, N.J.: Castle, 1984), 3:641; Stanley F. Horn, *The Army of Tennessee* (Norman: Univ. of Oklahoma Press, 1953), 249–50; Thomas Lawrence Connelly, *Autumn of Glory: The Army of Tennessee, 1862–1865* (Baton Rouge: Louisiana State Univ. Press, 1971), 166–70; Judith Lee Hallock, *Braxton Bragg and Confederate Defeat* (Tuscaloosa: Univ. of Alabama Press, 1991), 52.

51. Brent Diary, Apr. 13, 1863.

52. Ibid., Aug. 17, 1863.

53. Ibid., Oct. 16, 1863.

54. Mackall to his wife, Mar. 4, 1864, #1299, William Whann Mackall Papers, Southern Historical Collection, Chapel Hill, N.C.

55. Brent Diary, Sept. 3, 1863.

56. Ibid., Jan. 11, 1863.

57. Ibid., Jan. 13, 1863.

58. Ibid., Sept. 16, 1861.

59. *OR*, 23, pt. 2:824–25; Bragg to Cooper, May 8, 1863, Brent, CMSR.

60. *OR*, 30, pt. 3:791.

61. In February 1863, Bragg would have placed Polk under arrest were it not for intercession by Brent. Col. David Urquhart, a member of Bragg's staff, recalled Brent showing him an order from Bragg to arrest the bishop general. Urquhart subsequently intervened with Bragg, convincing him not to make a move that would be most unpopular in the ranks. David Urquhart, "Bragg's Advance and Retreat," *Battles and Leaders of the Civil War* (Secaucus, N.J.: Castle, 1984), 3:608.

62. Brent Diary, Oct. 20, 1863.

63. Ibid., Oct. 4, 1863.

64. Ibid., Oct. 30, 1863.

65. Ibid., Apr. 10, 1863.

66. Ibid., Nov. 11, 1863.

67. Nathaniel Cheairs Hughes Jr., *General William J. Hardee: Old Reliable* (Baton Rouge: Louisiana State Univ. Press, 1965), 182.

68. *OR*, 31, pt. 3:869–70.

69. Brent to Bragg, Dec. 26, 1863, Bragg Papers.

70. Brent to Bragg, Dec. 10, 1863, Bragg Papers.

71. Brent to Bragg, Dec. 31, 1863, Bragg Papers.

72. *OR*, ser. II, 6:1048–49.

73. Ibid., 52, pt. 2:652.

74. Brent to Bragg, Apr. 16, 1864, Bragg Papers.

75. *OR*, 32, pt. 3:816–17, 847; 39, pt. 2:565–66; vol. 52:669.

76. Ibid., 39, pt. 2:640–44; 32, pt. 1:617–18.

77. Roman, *Military Operations*, 2:540; Brent to Bragg, June 15, 1864, Brent, CMSR; *OR*, 40, pt. 2:662.

78. *OR*, 40, pt. 3:76, 151, 595.

79. Ibid., 39, pt. 3:785, 824.

80. Richard Taylor, *Destruction and Reconstruction: Personal Experiences of the Late War* (New York: Longmans, Green and Co., 1955), 254.

81. Beauregard to Hood, Nov. 15, 1864, Roman, *Military Operations*, 2:607–8.

82. *OR*, 45, pt. 2:720. See, also, George William Brent Papers, Duke Univ.

83. *OR*, 45, pt. 2:704–5.

84. Ibid., 742; vol. 49, pt. 1: 931; Brent to Beauregard, Nov. 14, 1864, Roman, *Military Operations*, 2:607.

85. *OR*, vol. 44: 989; vol. 45, pt. 2: 731, 738–40, 745, 751, 756, 757, 768.

86. Interestingly, an earlier correspondent in Selma, Alabama, had complained about impressing agents taking Negroes from government shops, where their value as mechanics far exceeded their importance as laborers in pioneer units. This was the same conflict Custis Lee was contending with at this time in Richmond. Maj. E. H. Ewing to Brent, Dec. 2, 1864, George William Brent Papers, Rare Book, Manuscript, and Special Collections Library, Duke Univ.

87. F. Molloy to Brent, Mar. 27, 1865, George William Brent Papers, Duke Univ.

88. Roman, *Military Operations*, 2:337–39.

89. *OR*, 47, pt. 2:1322–23. Interestingly, even in these dying days of the Division of the West (and the Confederacy), Brent was thinking and writing about progress in repairing railroads and incompatible rail gauges that needed attention.

90. T. Harry Williams, *P. G. T. Beauregard: Napoleon in Gray* (Baton Rouge: Louisiana State Univ. Press, 1955), 254; *OR*, 47, pt. 3:781.

91. Brig. Gen. Alfred Iverson to Brent, Apr. 16, 1865, George William Brent Papers, Duke Univ.

92. Roman, *Military Operations*, 1:9.

93. Deed dated Aug. 4, 1866, Benjamin Barton Papers, 1804–1913, Virginia Historical Society, Richmond.

94. "Treatment of Prisoners during the War between the States," *Southern Historical Society Papers* 1 (Mar. 1876): 208. Beauregard justified his request as retaliation for Maj. Gen. William T. Sherman pushing a mass of unarmed Confederate prisoners of war ahead of his column in Georgia for the purpose of detecting and detonating torpedoes.

95. *Alexandria Gazette*, Apr. 28–29, 1870.

96. Ibid., Jan. 3, 1872.

97. Underwood was a native New Yorker who resided in Clarke County, Virginia, for over a quarter century before the war, held strong anti-slavery sentiments, and, as a Federal jurist after the conflict affirmed the right of the United States government to confiscate the property of Confederates. He denied bail to Jefferson Davis, indicted for treason in 1866. *Encyclopedia of Virginia Biography*, ed. Lyon Gardiner Tyler (New York: Lewis Historical Publishing Co., 1915), 3:291–92.

98. *St. Mary's: 200 Years for Christ, 1795–1995* (Alexandria, Va.: St. Mary's Catholic Church, 1995), 27, 38, 40–41.

99. Brent Diary, Dec. 21, 31, 1862.

CHAPTER 6. POLITICIAN: DAVID FUNSTEN

1. *The Ancestors and Descendants of Colonel David Funsten and His Wife Susan Everard Meade*, comp. Howard S. F. Randolph (New York: Knickerbocker Press, 1926), 4, 6–7, 47, 82; Reed, *Family Papers*, 259–60; Ezra J. Warner and W. Buck Yearns, *Biographical Register of the Confederate Congress* (Baton Rouge: Louisiana State Univ. Press, 1975), 92.

2. Reed, *Family Papers*, 3; *Alexandria Gazette*, June 19, Sept. 6, 1856.

3. Funsten to his wife and children, Aug. 21, 27, Sept. 23, 24, 1858, and undated fragments, David Funsten Papers, Virginia Historical Society, Richmond.

4. Davis, *Papers*, 6:665; *Alexandria Gazette*, Aug. 30, Sept. 11, Nov. 6, 1860.

5. Peter V. Daniel Jr. to Jefferson Davis, June 10, 1863, David Funsten, 11 Virginia Infantry, CMSR; Freeman, *R. E. Lee*, 1:637–38; Reed, *Family Papers*, 412–13.

6. Susan Funsten would bear thirteen children to David. One son, Oliver, less than a year old, had died in July 1858, just prior to his father's departure for Europe.

7. Susan Meade to "Buck" Meade, May 3, 1861, *Ancestors and Descendants of Colonel David Funsten,* 10, 12.

8. Washington *Evening Star,* May 4, 1861.

9. *Alexandria Gazette,* May 9, 1861.

10. Funsten to his wife, May 12, 1861, David Funsten Papers. Funsten continued with some ill-considered bravado, "I do not think an attack is designed, tho' the original idea of occupying the old district [of Columbia, which, in Virginia, constituted the boundaries of Alexandria County] lines may be contemplated."

11. Funsten, CMSR; Reed, *Family Papers,* 420; Funsten to his wife, May 26, 1861, David Funsten Papers.

12. Robert T. Bell, *11th Virginia Infantry* (Lynchburg, Va.: H. E. Howard, 1985), 2–3, 6–7, 14.

13. Ibid., 8–11. Funsten received perfunctory recognition for his performance of duty in the reports filed by Generals Longstreet and P. G. T. Beauregard concerning the campaign. *OR,* 2:445, 463.

14. Funsten to his wife, July 29, 1861, David Funsten Papers.

15. Ibid., Aug. 17, 30, 1861.

16. Randolph Fairfax to his mother, Oct. 11, 1861, Randolph Fairfax Papers, Eleanor S. Brockenbrough Library, Museum of the Confederacy, Richmond.

17. Funsten to his daughter, Mary, Dec. 15, 1861; Funsten to Garland, Dec. 13, 1861, David Funsten Papers.

18. *Ancestors and Descendants of Colonel David Funsten,* 11–12; Reed, *Family Papers,* 459–63.

19. *OR,* vol. 11, pt. 1:575–78; Bell, *11th Virginia Infantry,* 20–22.

20. Bell, *11th Virginia Infantry,* 23–24.

21. Reed, *Family Papers,* 465–66.

22. Funsten to Davis, Dec. 17, 1862, Funsten, CMSR.

23. P. V. Daniel Jr. to Davis, Jan. 3, 10, 1863, R. G. H. Kean to James A. Seddon, Jan. 8, 1863, and J. R. Tucker to Seddon, Jan. 15, 1863, David Funsten, CMSR; Funsten to his wife, Jan. 17, 1863, David Funsten Papers. In the latter correspondence, Funsten addressed a personal quandary well known within any organization. He had declared that he would not accept an appointment out of state, as he wanted to be nearby to assist his wife and children, if needed. Yet Funsten confided to Susan that, should the war continue, he would thereby forfeit the opportunity for promotion, which, despite his short time in uniform, could be envisioned.

24. "Extra Billy" was not completely through with politics, however, as the following New Year's Day he was inaugurated once again as governor of Virginia.

25. The Confederate Congress did not set a specific date for the 1863 elections, and consequently balloting occurred throughout the latter two-thirds of the year. Wilfred Buck Yearns, *The Confederate Congress* (Atlanta: Univ. of Georgia Press, 1960), 53.

26. Reed, *Family Papers,* 473–74.

27. Thomas B. Alexander and Richard E. Beringer, *The Anatomy of the Confederate Congress: A Study of the Influences of Member Characteristics on Legislative Voting Behavior, 1861–1865* (Nashville: Vanderbilt Univ. Press, 1972), 18, 19, 25, 29, 33.

28. *Journal of the Congress of the Confederate States of America, 1861–1865* (Washington, D.C.: Government Printing Office, 1905), 6:527, 557, 7:35, 39, 466, 582.

29. Ibid., 6:718, 765–67, 834, 839, 7:34, 280, 341, 470.

30. Ibid., 6:633, 650, 801–2, 7:29, 39, 102–3, 133, 341, 633.

31. Alexander and Beringer, *Anatomy of the Confederate Congress*, 336, 340; Yearns, *Confederate Congress*, 59.

32. Alexander and Beringer, *Anatomy of the Confederate Congress*, 107.

33. *Journal of the Congress*, 7:331.

34. This position seemed to put Funsten on the fence regarding one of the most controversial questions regarding conscription, whether to exempt overseers of twenty or more slaves. This was obviously an important topic in the Deep South among ardent secessionists with whom Funsten agreed on other issues, but it was not a matter of concern with his friends and supporters in northern Virginia.

35. *Journal of the Congress*, 6:365–66, 559–61, 811; Frank E. Vandiver, ed., "Proceedings of the First Confederate Congress, Fourth Session," *Southern Historical Society Papers* 50 (1953): 115.

36. *Journal of the Congress*, 7:341, 703; Frank E. Vandiver, ed., "Proceedings of the Second Confederate Congress, Second Session in Part," *Southern Historical Society Papers* 52 (1959): 27.

37. Alexander and Beringer, *Anatomy of the Confederate Congress*, 331.

38. Ibid., 173; *Journal of the Congress*, 4:705, 7:378–80.

39. *Alexandria Gazette*, Nov. 6, 1860; *Richmond Daily Enquirer*, May 6, 1864; Funsten to Brig. Gen. Alexander R. Lawton, Mar. 31, 1864, Letters Received by the Confederate Quartermaster General, 1861–65, RG 109, National Archives; H. L. Stuart, GSO, CMSR.

40. William H. Dulany, 17 Virginia Infantry, CMSR; William H. Gaines Jr., *Biographical Register of Members, Virginia State Convention of 1861* (Richmond: Virginia State Library, 1969), 32; Funsten to James A. Seddon, June 15, 1864, Letters Received by the Confederate Adjutant and Inspector General, 1861–65, RG 109, National Archives.

41. Funsten to James A. Seddon, Dec. 23, 1864, Letters Received by the Confederate Adjutant and Inspector General, 1861–65; E. W. Hamilton, 17 Virginia Infantry, CMSR.

42. John M. Eaches to James A. Seddon, Feb. 10, 1864, Letters Received by the Confederate Adjutant and Inspector General, 1861–65; John M. Eaches, 17 Virginia Infantry, CMSR.

43. Robert P. Kidwell to James A. Seddon, Feb. 10, 1864, Letters Received by the Confederate Adjutant and Inspector General, 1861–65.

44. Davis, *Papers*, 10:212; Funsten to Gen. Samuel Cooper, Jan. 11, 1865, Letters Received by the Confederate Adjutant and Inspector General, 1861–65.

45. Funsten to James A. Seddon, Jan. 11, 1865, Letters Received by the Confederate Adjutant and Inspector General, 1861–65; Chancellor A. Nelson and Jerome B. Norvell, 49 Virginia Infantry, CMSR.

46. Funsten to his children, Aug. 8, 1865, and to his daughter, Mary, Aug. 20, 1865, David Funsten Papers.

47. Funsten to his wife, Aug. 26, 1865, and to his children, Sept. 12, 1865, David Funsten Papers.

48. Susan Funsten to her sister, Emily, Jan. 3, 1866, Reed, *Family Papers*, 535.

49. Funsten to his children, Sept. 1, Oct. 17, 1865, David Funsten Papers.

50. Funsten to his children, Oct. 17, 1865, David Funsten Papers; Susan Funsten to Emily, Jan. 3, 1866, Reed, *Family Papers*, 539; *Alexandria Gazette*, Apr. 6–8, 1866.

51. *Alexandria Gazette*, Apr. 8, 1866.

CHAPTER 7. NAVAL OFFICERS:
FRENCH AND DOUGLAS FORREST

1. *New York Times,* Feb. 12, 1862, 2.

2. *Alexandria Gazette,* June 3, 1833; Sept. 2, 1847; Apr. 28, 1849.

3. "Service Record of Late Captain French Forrest," French Forrest file, Box 81, ZB Series, Early Records Collection, Operational Archives, Naval Historical Center, Washington, D.C.; Richmond *Southern Illustrated News,* May 30, 1863.

4. California, ZE Series, Early Records Collection, Operational Archives, Naval Historical Center, Washington, D.C.

5. Clark G. Reynolds, *Famous American Admirals* (New York: Van Nostrand Reinhold Co., 1978), 129.

6. K. Jack Bauer, *The Mexican War, 1846–1848* (Lincoln: Univ. of Nebraska Press, 1992), 113, 117.

7. Forrest's contemporary recounted an amusing incident during the deployment ashore. "Forrest would have his own way: all of a sudden he called out impatiently: 'Where is that base drummer, where is that base drummer?' then pausing a moment he said quietly: 'Oh! I forgot, he broke his drum head this morning and couldn't come." William Harwar Parker, *Recollections of a Naval Officer, 1841–1865* (Annapolis, Md.: Naval Institute Press, 1985), 82–83.

8. Bauer, *Mexican War,* 241–44.

9. As a squadron commander, Forrest was addressed with the courtesy title of "Commodore." The more grandiose designation of "Flag Officer" was conveyed by legislation enacted by Congress in January 1857. As his son pointed out to the Navy Department at the close of the nineteenth century, Forrest was thus the equivalent of an admiral. With less than twenty years' service as a captain, he was considered a rear admiral and entitled to display his pennant. Reynolds, *Famous American Admirals,* v; Douglas F. Forrest to the Superintendent of the Naval War Records, Sept. 28, 1898, Douglas F. Forrest file, Box 81, ZB Series, Early Records Collection, Operational Archives, Naval Historical Center, Washington, D.C.

10. Forrest to Charles W. Welsh, Acting Secretary of the Navy, Oct. 10, 1856, M-0089, Letters Received by the Secretary of the Navy from Commanding Officers of Squadrons, 1841–86, RG 45, National Archives.

11. Forrest to J. C. Dobbin, Secretary of the Navy, Dec. 5, 1856, Letters from Commanding Officers of Squadrons, 1841–86.

12. Forrest to Colonel Jose R. Villagrau, Chief of Police of Maldonado, May 6, 1857, Letters from Commanding Officers of Squadrons, 1841–86.

13. An excellent history of the Brazil squadron, from which much of this treatment is drawn, is found in Donald W. Giffin, "The American Navy at Work on the Brazil Station, 1827–1860," *American Neptune* 19 (Oct. 1959): 237–56.

14. Forrest to President Andrew Johnson, June 1, 1865, M-1003, Case Files of Applications from Former Confederates for Presidential Pardons ("Amnesty Papers"), RG 94, National Archives. Forrest referred to himself in the third person.

15. Forrest to Gideon Welles, Secretary of the Navy, Apr. 19, 1861, Letters from Officers Tendering Their Resignations but Dismissed Instead, Nov. 1860–Dec. 1861, vol. 3, RG 45, National Archives.

16. Forrest to President Johnson, June 1, 1865, Amnesty Papers.

17. One senior captain, Isaac Mayo of Maryland, committed suicide on the day Welles signed the letter dismissing him from the service. For a full discussion of the subject, along with statistics, see William S. Dudley, *Going South: U.S. Navy*

Officer Resignations and Dismissals on the Eve of the Civil War (Washington, D.C.: Naval Historical Foundation, 1981).

18. William N. Still Jr., ed., *The Confederate Navy: The Ships, Men and Organization, 1861–65* (Annapolis, Md.: Naval Institute Press, 1997), 115.

19. Edith M. Sprouse, "Clermont: The Rest of the Story," *Fireside Sentinel* 3 (Sept. 1989): 110; *Dictionary of American Biography* (New York: Charles Scribner's Sons, 1931), 3:532; Anne S. Frobel, *The Civil War Diary of Anne S. Frobel* (McLean, Va.: EPM Publications, 1992), 41.

20. Forrest's date of rank was April 12, before the state convention voted to secede. He was quickly elevated to flag officer, effective April 23. His subsequent commission as a captain in the Confederate States Navy was dated June 11, 1861. Commissions in the Navy of Virginia and the C. S. Navy, Forrest Family Papers, pt. 1, M-2206, Southern Historical Collection, Chapel Hill, N.C.

21. Richmond *Southern Illustrated News,* May 30, 1863.

22. *ORN,* 4:311–13, 400–402, 405–6.

23. Ibid., ser. II, 1:627.

24. Parker, *Recollections of a Naval Officer,* 222; Forrest to Cdr. C. F. M. Spotswood, June 5, 1861, Forrest Family Papers, pt. 1; J. Thomas Scharf, *History of the Confederate States Navy from Its Organization to the Surrender of Its Last Vessel* (New York: Fairfax Press, 1977), 383.

25. Virgil Carrington Jones, *The Civil War at Sea: The Blockaders* (New York: Holt, Rinehart, Winston, 1960), 1:155; *ORN,* 5:801.

26. John L. Porter, "The Plan and Construction of the 'Merrimac,'" *Battles and Leaders of the Civil War* (Secaucus, N.J.: Castle, 1984), 1:716–17.

27. Forrest to Mallory, Feb. 19, 1862, Register of Letters and Telegrams Received from Various Commands, Chapter II, Military Departments, 1861–65, 433, RG 109, National Archives; General Orders, Aug. 23, Oct. 15, 1861, Forrest Family Papers, pt. 1.

28. *ORN,* 6:769–71.

29. Ibid., 7:149–50.

30. Buchanan acknowledged hearing "you did inform a friend that you were expected she [the *Virginia*] would have been *offered* to you [to command]." Buchanan to Forrest, Feb. 24, 1863, #97, Franklin Buchanan Letter Book, Southern Historical Collection, Chapel Hill, N.C.

31. *ORN,* 6:776–77.

32. Ibid., 771; Parker, *Recollections of a Naval Officer,* 272.

33. *ORN,* 7:748–49; Forrest to John L. Porter, Mar. 23, 1862; Mallory to Forrest, Mar. 24, 1862, Forrest Family Papers, pt. 1.

34. *ORN,* 7:787–88.

35. Ibid., ser. II, 1:626, 632.

36. Ibid., 18:318–20.

37. Ibid., ser. II, 2:180.

38. The South's senior officer in length of service in the U.S. Navy was Capt. Lawrence Rousseau of Louisiana. *ORN,* 2:385.

39. *ORN,* ser. II, 2:256; ser. I, 8:863.

40. Tom Henderson Wells, *The Confederate Navy: A Study in Organization* (Tuscaloosa: Univ. of Alabama Press, 1971), 31. Forrest must have been livid that he was not included among the captains elevated to admiral in the Confederate Navy during the war—Franklin Buchanan and Raphael Semmes.

41. "Rummaging Through Rebeldom," *New York Citizen,* Aug. 10, 1867, 2.

42. Richmond *Southern Illustrated News,* May 30, 1863.

43. Buchanan to Forrest, Feb. 3, 1863, Franklin Buchanan Letter Book.

44. Craig L. Symonds, *Confederate Admiral: The Life and Wars of Franklin Buchanan* (Annapolis, Md.: Naval Institute Press, 1999), 194–96.

45. "Rummaging Through Rebeldom," *New York Citizen*, Aug. 10, 1867, 2.

46. Buchanan to Mitchell, Apr. 2, 1863, Franklin Buchanan Letters, 1863–64, Virginia Historical Society, Richmond.

47. Symonds, *Confederate Admiral*, 196–97.

48. *ORN*, ser. II, 2:528.

49. John M. Coski, *Capital Navy: The Men, Ships, and Operations of the James River Squadron* (Campbell, Calif.: Savas Woodbury Publishers, 1996), 90, 94–95.

50. Ibid., 94.

51. See, for example, Forrest to Commandant of the Confederate States Marine Corps, Jan. 7, 1864; Forrest to Lt. M. F. C. Cottle, Jan. 11, 1864; Forrest to J. Pembroke Jones, Steamer *Nansemond*, Jan. 18, 1864; Forrest to Pilot Edward Moore, Jan. 20, 1864; Forrest to Mallory, Feb. 3, 1864, Forrest Family Papers, pt. 1.

52. *ORN*, 8:851–52.

53. *Charleston Daily Courier*, July 1, 1864, 1.

54. Forrest's claim may well have been for pay from March 31, 1861, the date of his last compensation by the Federal navy, until April 19, when he entered into the service of the Virginia navy. He had made this case earlier, but the outcome is unknown. Forrest to Paymaster W. H. Peters, June 5, 1861, Forrest Family Papers, pt. 1.

55. *ORN*, 10:624; "Death of General J. E. B. Stuart," *Southern Historical Society Papers* 7 (Feb. 1879): 109; 51 (1958): 259; 8 (Apr. 1880): 160. Douglas French Forrest, *Odyssey in Gray: A Diary of Confederate Service, 1863–1865*, ed. William N. Still Jr. (Richmond: Virginia State Library, 1979), 213. French Forrest, M-260, Records Relating to Confederate Naval and Marine Personnel, RG 109, National Archives.

56. Edwin G. Weed, *In Memoriam: Rev. Douglas French Forrest, D.D.* (Winchester, Va.: Eddy Press, 1902), 12.

57. Ibid., 12–14. *Obituary Record of Graduates of Yale Univ., Deceased from June, 1900, to June, 1910* (New Haven, Conn.: Tuttle, Morehouse & Taylor Co., 1910), 155; *Alexandria Gazette*, July 7, 1860; John B. Miner to J. P. Benjamin, Feb. 18, 1862, Douglas French Forrest, 17 Virginia Infantry, CMSR.

58. While Douglas Forrest's Compiled Military Service Record cites his date of enlistment as April 17, 1861, the commission signed by Gov. John Letcher on May 31, 1861, indicates his date of rank as a second lieutenant in the Virginia militia to be April 24. Commonwealth of Virginia commission, Forrest Family Papers, pt. 2.

59. Warfield, *Manassas to Appomattox*, 50.

60. *Voices of the Civil War; First Manassas* (Alexandria: Time-Life Books, 1997), 97–98.

61. D. F. Forrest, CMSR.

62. Notations in the exercise book used by Douglas F. Forrest to record journal entries from November 1863 to October 1864, Forrest Family Papers, pt. 2.

63. Buchanan to French Forrest, Feb. 18, 1862, Forrest Family Papers, pt. 1.

64. *ORN*, 7:737–39. Interestingly, when Captain Buchanan took command of the CSS *Virginia*, Secretary Mallory included in his instructions the possibility of cruising past Old Point Comfort and up the Potomac, as "its effect upon the public mind would be important to the cause." *ORN*, 6:777.

65. Forrest notations, Forrest Family Papers, pt. 2.

66. *ORN*, 7:48.

67. Forrest notations, Forrest Family Papers, pt. 2.

68. Ibid.

69. D. F. Forrest to Davis, May 12, 1862, D. F. Forrest, CMSR.

70. Douglas Forrest's nomination for appointment as an assistant paymaster had already been confirmed by the Confederate Senate on March 18, 1862. *Journal of the Confederate Congress*, 2:69.

71. Orders dated May 8, 1862, Sept. 29, 1862, May 20, 1863, Douglas F. Forrest file, Box 81, ZB Series, Early Records Collection, Operational Archives, Naval Historical Center, Washington, D.C.

72. Forrest, *Odyssey in Gray*, 37.

73. James D. Bulloch, *The Secret Service of the Confederate States in Europe, or How the Confederate Cruisers Were Equipped* (New York: G. P. Putnam, 1884), 2:265–66; *ORN*, 2:505–6. A secondary source, albeit a credible one, as it is the historian of the Confederate navy, William N. Still Jr., dates the auction as being in September 1863. Forrest, *Odyssey in Gray*, 79.

74. Richmond *Daily Dispatch*, Jan. 23, 1864.

75. For a comprehensive discussion of diplomatic maneuvering concerning the *Rappahannock*, see Lynn M. Case and Warren F. Spencer, *The United States and France: Civil War Diplomacy* (Philadelphia: Univ. of Pennsylvania Press, 1970), 500–509.

76. Douglas must have enjoyed a special rapport with the senior officer, as his father had recommended Barron for flag officer rank in the Brazil squadron. French Forrest to Charles W. Welsh, Oct. 11, 1856, M-0089, Letters from Commanding Officers of Squadrons, 1841–86.

77. Greenhow was basking in the glow of the London publication of her reminiscences, *My Imprisonment and the First Year of Abolition Rule at Washington*, which accorded her celebrity status in Europe. On her return trip to the South in the autumn of 1864, she perished while running the northern blockade outside Fort Fisher and was buried with full military honors at Wilmington, N.C.

78. Forrest, *Odyssey in Gray*, 85–86, 92–93.

79. Ibid., 87–90.

80. Bulloch, *Secret Service*, 267; Case and Spencer, *United States and France*, 504.

81. Forrest, *Odyssey in Gray*, 112–13.

82. *ORN*, ser. II, 3:1039–40.

83. Forrest, *Odyssey in Gray*, 134–35.

84. Ibid., 140.

85. *ORN*, ser. II, 3:1038–39.

86. Forrest, *Odyssey in Gray*, 152–53.

87. *ORN*, 2:820–21.

88. Chester G. Hearn, *Gray Raiders of the Sea: How Eight Confederate Warships Destroyed the Union's High Seas Commerce* (Baton Rouge: Louisiana State Univ. Press, 1992), 268–69.

89. Forrest, *Odyssey in Gray*, 174.

90. *ORN*, ser. II, 2:651.

91. Forrest, *Odyssey in Gray*, 186.

92. Ibid., 203. See, also, *ORN*, 3:700–701.

93. Bulloch, *Secret Service*, 268–69.

94. Forrest, *Odyssey in Gray*, 289.

95. Sprouse, "Clermont," 111–14; Frobel, *Civil War Diary*, 66–67, 233.

96. French Forrest to President Johnson, June 1, 1865, Amnesty Papers.

97. *A Compilation of the Messages and Papers of the Presidents,* ed. James D. Richardson (Washington, D.C.: Bureau of National Literature and Art, 1905), 6:310–12.

98. French Forrest to President Johnson, Sept. 23, 1866, Amnesty Papers.

99. Washington *Evening Star,* Nov. 23, 1866, 3.

100. *Bigelow v. Forrest,* 76 U.S. (9 Wall.), 339 (1869).

101. Weed, *In Memoriam,* 17–20; *Alexandria Gazette,* May 5, 1902; *Washington Post,* May 4, 1902, 5; Sprouse, "Clermont," 116.

CHAPTER 8. SPY: ORTON WILLIAMS

1. Margaret Sanborn, "The Ordeal of Orton Williams, U.S.A., C.S.A.," *Assembly* 28 (winter 1970): 38; Patrick J. Griffin III, "Tragedy of Two Cousins—Adventurers or Spies?" *Montgomery County Story* 34 (Nov. 1991): 180.

2. Avery Craven, ed., *"To Markie": The Letters of Robert E. Lee to Martha Custis Williams* (Cambridge, Mass.: Harvard Univ. Press, 1933), 55.

3. Mary Custis Lee DeButts, *Growing Up in the 1850s: The Journal of Agnes Lee* (Chapel Hill: Univ. of North Carolina Press, 1984), 12, 55.

4. Craven, *"To Markie,"* 36–37.

5. Ibid., 37.

6. Martha Williams to Bvt. Brig. Gen. Joseph Totten, July 15, 1857; Scott to the Secretary of War, July 22, 1857, U.S. Military Academy Cadet Application Papers, 1805–66, RG 94, National Archives; Hallowell to the Secretary of War, July 20, 1857, Martha Custis Williams Papers, Tudor Place Foundation, Washington, D.C.

7. Bache to Orton Williams, Nov. 19, 1858, Martha Custis Williams Papers.

8. R. E. Lee to G. W. C. Lee, May 30, 1859, R. E. Lee Papers.

9. Craven, *"To Markie,"* 58.

10. Otto Louis Hein, *Memories of Long Ago* (New York: G. P. Putnam's Sons, 1925), 15.

11. Orton Williams to Col. Lorenzo Thomas, Mar. 30, 1861; E. D. Townsend to Williams, Apr. 15, 1861, Letters Received by the Adjutant General's Office, 1861–70, RG 94, National Archives.

12. McCaslin, *Lee in the Shadow,* 74.

13. Sanborn, *Robert E. Lee: The Complete Man,* 8–9.

14. Mary Custis Lee to Robert E. Lee, May 9, 1861, Lee Family Papers, Virginia Historical Society, Richmond.

15. Reminiscences of Britannia Peter Kennon, Jan. 17, 1897, Armistead Peter Jr., Papers, Tudor Place Foundation, Washington, D.C.

16. Orton Williams to Scott, May 14, 1861, M-619, Letters Received by the Adjutant General's Office, 1861–70.

17. Martha Williams to Benson Lossing, Aug. 13, 1866, Martha Custis Williams Papers.

18. Williams to the Adjutant General, June 6, 1861, with subsequent notations, Letters Received by the Adjutant General's Office, 1861–70.

19. "Letters of Major Thomas Rowland, C.S.A., from the Camps at Ashland and Richmond, Virginia, 1861," *William and Mary College Quarterly Historical Magazine,* ser. I, 24 (Jan. 1916): 152.

20. William Orton Williams, GSO, CMSR.

21. Sanborn, *Robert E. Lee: The Complete Man,* 17.

22. Griffin, "Tragedy of Two Cousins," 181.

23. G. A. Williams, "Light on a War Mystery," *Confederate Veteran* 29 (July 1921): 263. Confirmed by J. T. Webster, "Another Chapter on the Mystery," *Confederate Veteran* 29 (Sept. 1921): 341. Another account in the spring of 1861 described the young U.S. cavalry officer "showing off the paces of his handsome black charger" in Georgetown. Grace Dunlop Ecker, *A Portrait of Old George Town* (Richmond: Dietz Press, 1951), 133.

24. This organization was first known as Captain Williams's, then as Captain Hoxton's, and finally as Captain Tobin's Company, Tennessee Light Artillery. W. Orton Williams, Captain Tobin's Artillery, Tennessee Light Artillery, CMSR.

25. Bromfield L. Ridley, *Battles and Sketches of the Army of Tennessee* (Mexico, Mo.: Missouri Printing & Publishing Co., 1906), 195.

26. *OR*, 7:893.

27. Charles H. Nourse, "Walter Gibson Peter Executed at Franklin," *Confederate Veteran* 15 (Dec. 1907): 551; "Capt. W. G. Peter Executed at Franklin," *Confederate Veteran* 16 (Jan. 1908): 16.

28. Nourse, "Walter Gibson Peter Executed"; *OR*, 5:369; R. W. Hunter, "Men of Virginia at Ball's Bluff," *Southern Historical Society Papers* 34 (1906): 259.

29. *OR*, 10, pt. 1:469.

30. Webster, "Another Chapter," 341.

31. *OR*, 10, pt. 1:415, 469, 830–31.

32. Orton to Gen. Samuel Cooper, Dec. (n.d.) 1862, Williams, GSO, CMSR, and Sanborn, "The Ordeal of Orton Williams," 38. The name of Orton's brother was regularly misspelled as "Lawrence Albert," when, in actuality, it was "Laurence Abert," according to Wendy Kail, archivist, Tudor Place, Washington, D.C.

33. Orton Williams to Polk, Oct. 30, 1862, Williams, GSO, CMSR.

34. Orton Williams to G. W. Brent, Chief of Staff (n.d.), William P. Palmer Collection, Western Reserve Historical Society, Cleveland, Ohio.

35. Magruder to Gen. Samuel Cooper, Dec. 6, 1862; Bragg to Secretary of War James Seddon, Dec. 6, 1862; Polk to Secretary of War George Wythe Randolph, Nov. 3, 1862, Williams, GSO, CMSR.

36. Freeman, *R. E. Lee*, 3:211.

37. *OR*, 52, pt. 2:451. Another firsthand account places Orton Williams in Tullahoma on April 2, 1863. Kundahl, *Confederate Engineer*, 205, 300–301.

38. The bride's maiden name and origin are also in dispute. One account identifies her as formerly named Hamilton of Charleston (presumably South Carolina). Chattanooga *Daily Rebel*, June 16, 1863. Another report describes her as "Miss Lane of Chattanooga." Sanborn, "The Ordeal of Orton Williams," 39.

39. Walter Gibson Peter, Captain Tobin's Artillery, Tennessee Light Artillery, CMSR.

40. *OR*, 23, pt. 2:804.

41. Ridley, *Battles and Sketches*, 195.

42. Williams, "Light on a War Mystery," 263–64.

43. *Richmond Whig*, June 19, 1863.

44. *OR*, 23, pt. 2:397, ser. II, 5:763. The quotations are basically the same, except the former specifies "horses and equipments," whereas the latter says "horse equipments," and the name "Orton" is cited in the first transcription, while "Auton" is used in the second.

45. *OR*, 23, pt. 2:425.

46. Ibid., 426–27.

47. C. J. Wood, *Reminiscences of the War* (Centreville, Ind.: n.p., 1880), 181.

48. J. L. Kirby, "Execution of Two Confederates," *Confederate Veteran* 15 (Aug. 1907): 363.

49. Ibid.

50. *OR*, 23, pt. 2:397–98.

51. Kirby, "Execution of Two Confederates."

52. This quotation appears in many accounts of the hanging at Franklin, as press reports were largely based upon a letter written by the surgeon of the 85th Indiana and reprinted widely throughout the country at the time of the incident and later. See, for example, *Nashville Press*, June 11, 1863; *Charleston Mercury*, June 18, 1863; Washington *National Intelligencer*, June 19, 1863; *Richmond Whig*, June 19, 1863; Richmond *Daily Dispatch*, June 20, 1863; *Charleston Daily Courier*, June 20, 1863; "The Execution of Williams and Peters," *Harper's Weekly* 7 (July 4, 1863): 417–18; *The Grayjackets, and How They Lived, Fought and Died, for Dixie* (Richmond: Jones Brothers & Co., 1867), 89–95; Kirby, "Execution of Two Confederates," 363–64.

53. John E. Bakeless, "Incident at Fort Granger," *Civil War Times Illustrated* 8 (Apr. 1969): 14–15.

54. *OR*, 23, pt. 2:398.

55. Ibid.

56. Ibid., 424–25.

57. William T. Crawford to W. J. Isaacs, June 27, 1909, Spy Data, Confederate Collection, Tennessee State Library and Archives, Nashville; *OR*, 23, pt. 2:415.

58. *OR*, 23, pt. 2:416.

59. Ibid., 424–25.

60. Ibid., 397.

61. The decision to execute Williams and Peter weighed heavily on Baird. He was accused of being drunk three days later when commanding his regiment in contact with the enemy. After the war, Baird admitted himself to the Indiana Hospital for the Insane, where he died in 1881. Frank J. Welcher and Larry G. Ligget, *Coburn's Brigade: 85th Indiana, 33rd Indiana, 19th Michigan, and 22nd Wisconsin in the Western Civil War* (Carmel: Guild Press of Indiana, 1999), 119, 224.

62. William Gilmore Beymer, "Williams, C.S.A.," *Harper's Monthly Magazine* 119 (Sept. 1909): 508; *On Hazardous Service: Scouts and Spies of the North and South* (New York: Harper & Brothers Publishers, 1912), 57. A divergent version by an anonymous source recalled that Peter was terrorized by the sight of the hangman's rope and began to weep. "Dry those tears and die like a man!" responded Williams in this account. Inaccuracy of other details in this narrative detracts from its credibility. "Execution of Williams and Peters [*sic*] at Franklin," *Confederate Veteran* 8 (Jan. 1900): 12–13.

63. *Richmond Whig*, June 19, 1863; Washington *National Intelligencer*, June 19, 1863; Crawford to Isaacs, June 27, 1909; Kirby, "Execution of Two Confederates," 363–64.

64. Mary Mitchell, *Divided Town* (Barre, Mass.: Barre Publishers, 1968), 113.

65. *OR*, 38, pt. 3:1008.

66. *The Grayjackets*, 95.

67. DeButts, *Growing Up in the 1850s*, 113.

68. R. E. Lee to his wife, June 14, 1863, Lee Family Papers, 1824–1918, Virginia Historical Society, Richmond.

69. Craven, *"To Markie,"* 71–72.

70. Crawford to Isaacs, June 27, 1909.

71. *OR*, 23, pt. 2:416.

72. Sanborn, *Robert E. Lee: The Complete Man*, 140.

73. Lawrence W. Orton to his sister, June 8, 1863, Martha Custis Williams Papers.

74. Nourse, "Walter Gibson Peter Executed."

75. It is natural to wonder how many other reckless individuals of questionable purpose and rationality careened about during these undisciplined times. Many elements of Orton's story are found as well, for example, in the life of Charles Webster, a renegade adventurer from Maine who drifted back and forth between the armies wearing blue and gray. Webster (née Brown) changed his name, sought to entice other impressionable young men to engage in his harebrained schemes, capriciously took the life of a fellow soldier, casually entered into marriage, dispatched an impassioned plea for clemency upon his sentence to death, and then, at age twenty-three, faced hanging at Castle Thunder in Richmond with uncharacteristic dignity. A complete account is found in Robert L. Willett, "Loyal to None," *Civil War Times* 42 (Apr. 2003): 43–47.

76. Ridley, *Battles and Sketches*, 196. Vaulx's assessment is consistent with that of another veteran who served in Bragg's headquarters at the time of the hanging. Webster, "Another Chapter," 342.

CHAPTER 9. SCOUT: FRANK STRINGFELLOW

1. Benjamin Franklin Stringfellow to Jefferson Davis, July 21, 1878, Franklin Stringfellow Papers, Virginia Historical Society, Richmond.

2. Stringfellow to Davis; "In compliance with ..." [n.d.], 2, Albert H. Small Special Collections Library, Univ. of Virginia, Charlottesville.

3. H. B. McClellan, "Scout Life in the Confederacy," Philadelphia *Weekly Times*, May 19, 1877.

4. Stringfellow to Davis, "In compliance with ... ," 4; James Dudley Peavey, ed., *Confederate Scout: Virginia's Frank Stringfellow* (Onancock, Va.: Eastern Shore Publishing Co., 1956), 24–25.

5. George F. Stringfellow, "Some Incidents in the Life of Frank Stringfellow, Famous Confederate Soldier and Scout," *William and Mary Quarterly*, 2d ser., 14 (July 1934): 231–32, and *Culpeper Virginia Star*, Aug. 4, 1932.

6. Lizzie Stringfellow Watkins, *The Life of Horace Stringfellow* (Montgomery, Ala.: Paragon Press, 1931), 6; *Dictionary of American Biography* (New York: Charles Scribner's Sons, 1958), 9:138.

7. Watkins, *Life of Horace Stringfellow*, 39.

8. *Alexandria Gazette*, Jan. 1, 1849.

9. *Catalogue of the Trustees, Officers and Students of the Episcopal High School of the Dioceses of Virginia at Howard, Fairfax County, Near Alexandria, for the Session of 1859–'60* (Washington, D.C.: George S. Gideon, 1860), 8.

10. R. Shepard Brown, *Stringfellow of the Fourth* (New York: Crown Publishers, 1960), 4.

11. Beth Freshour, Director, Noxubee County (Miss.) Library, to author, Mar. 16, 2000.

12. Brown, *Stringfellow of the Fourth*, 43.

13. Ibid., 29–34.

14. Ibid., 76–109.

15. Peavey, *Confederate Scout*, 48–49; Brown, *Stringfellow of the Fourth*, 179–80.

16. Stringfellow to Davis, "In compliance with ...," 2–7. This method of exiting the Union defenses is similar to (and perhaps a retelling of) an episode recounted by another Alexandria veteran. He wrote that his mother helped Stringfellow pass through the lines by obtaining a light wagon and disguising themselves as country people, sharing vittles with each Yankee picket they encountered, all of them "foreigners." Warfield, *Manassas to Appomattox*, 164.

17. Peavey, *Confederate Scout*, 50–51.

18. Stringfellow to Davis, "In compliance with ... ," 2.

19. "War Reminiscences: At the Foot of Loudoun Heights," unidentified newspaper article by anonymous author, Franklin Stringfellow Papers.

20. Stringfellow to Davis, "In compliance with ... ," 13.

21. Ibid., 13–14. Stringfellow wrote to General Stuart "to send me five hundred men and no commissioned officers as they would not understand the ground or my mode of warfare and would only be in the way."

22. A colorful account of this incident by one of the participating Confederates was published a half-century later. The story corresponds with few discrepancies to the one related here, but, after a half century, the veteran misidentified the target as Brig. Gen. Samuel Crawford, who commanded the Pennsylvania Reserve Corps. I. S. Curtis, "The Attempted Capture of General Crawford," *Confederate Veteran* 23 (1915): 265–66.

23. *OR*, 29, pt. 1:102–3.

24. Stringfellow was reported to have given a talk on his reconnaissance in Warrenton to a 1903 gathering of Confederate veterans in Fauquier County. Kate Mason Rowland, "Reunion in Virginia," *Confederate Veteran* 11 (1903): 547–49.

25. Peavey, *Confederate Scout*, 44–48.

26. Ibid., 8–12; see, also, John Esten Cooke, "Virginia Partisans," Philadelphia *Weekly Times*, Oct. 29, 1881.

27. The most credible account of this oft-repeated incident is contained in Stringfellow's own notes entitled "Lecture for Howitzers, Richd. 2.14.1890," Franklin Stringfellow Papers. Other versions provide additional information. One dates this episode as taking place on November 20, after a disappointing attempt by Mosby's Rangers to capture Federal ambulances loaded with medical supplies. The house is identified as "Huntley," the residence of James Skinker. Two partisans are said to have dined with Stringfellow and the Skinker family, Adolphus E. "Dolly" Richards and Ludwell Knapp. Richards allegedly escaped through the garden before the Federals entered the house. Hugh C. Keen and Horace Mewborn, *43rd Battalion, Virginia Cavalry, Mosby's Command* (Lynchburg, Va.: H. E. Howard, 1993), 90–92. See also three other secondary accounts: McClellan, "Scout Life in the Confederacy"; Cooke, "Virginia Partisans"; Peavey, *Confederate Scout*, 14–19.

28. Robert E. Lee related this remarkable story to the Confederate president (Davis to Stringfellow, Mar. 28, 1880, Franklin Stringfellow Papers). In the absence of a narrative penned by the protagonist himself, the recollections of his nephew would appear the most credible (George F. Stringfellow, "Some Incidents in the Life of Frank Stringfellow," 232–33; *Culpeper Virginia Star*, Aug. 4, 1932. See also McClellan, "Scout Life in the Confederacy"; Cooke, "Virginia Partisans"; Peavey, *Confederate Scout*, 19–22). An interesting telling, from the opposing point of view, is found in a letter to the editor by a former Pennsylvania soldier ("Stringfellow the Scout: The Other Side of One of Major McClellan's Stories, A Union Soldier's Version," Philadelphia *Weekly Times*, June 2, 1877).

29. This fantastic adventure is recounted in at least three places. The most credible, of course, is a first-person account reprinted in Peavey, *Confederate Scout,* 36–42. The twentieth-century biography of Stringfellow offers more details. Brown, *Stringfellow of the Fourth,* 224–36. A shorter, somewhat confused version, based presumably on oral family history, is found in Watkins, *Life of Horace Stringfellow,* 104–6.

30. See, for example, a report from Orange Court House, Virginia, dated Jan. 25, 1864: "Lt. Stringfellow captured on the 22d, between Warrenton and Germantown," in the Raleigh *Daily Confederate,* Jan. 27, 1864.

31. Horace Mewborn, "The Operations of Mosby's Rangers," *Blue & Gray* 17 (Apr. 2000): 17, 19. The date of capture is shown elsewhere as June 15, 1863.

32. There was confusion as to the scout's rank, as he claimed to be a private but carried a communiqué addressed to "Captain Stringfellow." Stringfellow was consequently exchanged for a Connecticut captain, according to the later recollection of the scout's niece. Brown, *Stringfellow of the Fourth,* 206–10.

33. War Department to Thomas P. Abernathy, Apr. 15, 1931, Stringfellow, Signal Corps, C.S.A., CMSR. In his classic treatise on the war, Porter Alexander postulates that Stringfellow's capture, along with Stuart's absence, denied Gen. R. E. Lee the eyes to see Hooker's army crossing the Potomac on its way to the eventual collision at Gettysburg. E. P. Alexander, *Military Memoirs of a Confederate* (Bloomington: Indiana Univ. Press, 1962), 379.

34. The other instance of Stringfellow accompanying Mosby's Rangers occurred the previous November on a foray to capture Brig. Gen. David Gregg's ambulance train near Warrenton. The raiders captured two ambulances and several wagons full of valuable medical supplies. See, especially, Stringfellow, "Lecture for Howitzers."

35. Two primary sources describing the raid on Cole's camp are *OR,* 33: 15–16, and an anonymous article signed by "Soldier," entitled "War Reminiscences: At the Foot of Loudoun Heights," and contained in the Franklin Stringfellow Papers, Virginia Historical Society. In the former report, Mosby blamed Stringfellow for the botched operation: "All my plans were on the eve of consummation when suddenly the party sent with Stringfellow came dashing over the hill toward the camp yelling and shooting. They made no attempt to secure Cole." Entertaining secondary accounts are found in the classic work on Mosby, Virgil Carrington Jones, *Gray Ghosts and Rebel Raiders* (New York: Henry Holt and Co., 1956), 211–13; James A. Ramage, *Gray Ghost: The Life of Col. John Singleton Mosby* (Lexington: Univ. of Kentucky Press, 1999), 124–29; Paul Ashdown and Edward Caudill, *The Mosby Myth: A Confederate Hero in Life and Legend* (Wilmington, Del.: Scholarly Resources, 2002), 67–69; Brown, *Stringfellow of the Fourth,* 238–41; Keen and Mewborn, *43rd Battalion,* 99–102.

36. Frank Stringfellow, *War Reminiscences: The Life of a Confederate Scout Inside the Enemy's Line* (n.p., n.d.), 3.

37. *OR,* 51, pt. 2:855–56.

38. Ibid., 2:878, 33:1326.

39. Ibid., 36, pt. 3:850–51.

40. "Plan for the Capture of Brig. Genl. Kautz U.S.A.," Franklin Stringfellow Papers.

41. Stringfellow to R. E. Lee, Feb. 24, 1865, Jefferson Davis Papers, Rare Book, Manuscript, and Special Collections Library, Duke Univ., Durham, N.C.

42. Lomax to Stringfellow, Dec. 16, 1864, Franklin Stringfellow Papers.

43. Lomax to Stringfellow, Dec. 19, 1864; Maj. John G. Parrish to Stringfellow, Jan. 7, 1865, Franklin Stringfellow Papers.

44. Lomax to Stringfellow with undated reply, Dec. 6, 1864, Franklin Stringfellow Papers.

45. Lomax to Stringfellow with undated reply, Jan. 17, 1865, Franklin Stringfellow Papers.

46. Col. J. C. Ives to Maj. Gen. James Kemper, Oct. 25, 1864, Franklin Stringfellow Papers.

47. The primary source for any account of Stringfellow's whereabouts, actions, and motivations in March and April 1965 is his letter to Jefferson Davis, written in 1880 in response to a request for information to include in the former president's book about the war years. Stringfellow to Davis; "I have made an honest effort" (n.d.), Albert H. Small Special Collections Library, Univ. of Virginia, Charlottesville, Va.

48. Watkins, *Life of Horace Stringfellow,* 125.

49. See, for example, William A. Tidwell, *Come Retribution: The Confederate Secret Service and the Assassination of Lincoln* (Jackson: Univ. Press of Mississippi, 1989), 412.

50. Stringfellow to Emma Green, Sept. 27, 1865, Franklin Stringfellow Papers.

51. Stringfellow letter (addressee unspecified), Mar. 4, 1866, Franklin Stringfellow Papers; Watkins, *Life of Horace Stringfellow,* 127; William Page Johnson, comp., *Brothers and Cousins: Confederate Soldiers and Sailors of Fairfax County, Virginia* (Athens, Ga.: Iberian Publishing Co., 1995), 2:150.

52. Stringfellow to Emma Green, May 13, 1866, Franklin Stringfellow Papers.

53. Stringfellow, *War Reminiscences,* 10; *Louisville Post,* June 10, 1892.

54. Frank Stringfellow, "Colonel McClure's Article Criticised," *Confederate Veteran* 16 (Aug. 1908): 390.

55. Stringfellow to Col. John P. Nicholson, Nov. 6, 1896, Confederate Collection, Henry E. Huntington Library, San Marino, Calif.; Stringfellow, *War Reminiscences,* 7.

56. Brown, *Stringfellow of the Fourth,* 292–93.

57. Stringfellow to his wife, Aug. 2, 1898, Franklin Stringfellow Papers.

58. Lee had not been on active duty since Appomattox, and President William McKinley seemed to share the concern about his worthiness for field command. The Seventh Corps, to which Lee was assigned command, did not participate in combat operations in Cuba. Harry Warren Readnour, "General Fitzhugh Lee, 1835–1905: A Biographical Study" (Ph.D. diss., Corcoran Dept. of History, Univ. of Virginia, Charlottesville, 1971).

59. Stringfellow to his wife, Aug. 15, Oct. 10, 1898, Franklin Stringfellow Papers.

60. Ibid., Aug. 15, 1898.

61. Ibid., Dec. 8, 30, 1898.

62. *Journal of the 119th Annual Council of the Protestant Episcopal Church in the Diocese of Virginia, Richmond, May 20–22, 1914,* 83.

63. Brown, *Stringfellow of the Fourth,* 293.

CHAPTER 10. ENGINEER: WILSON PRESSTMAN

1. William Cattell Trimble, *The Presstman Family of Baltimore* (Baltimore: J. H. Furst Co., 1989), 2–3.

2. *Baltimore Sun,* Sept. 22, 1843, 2.

3. *Alexandria Gazette*, Nov. 8, 1856; *Baltimore Sun*, Nov. 8, 1856, 2. The years of birth for both Frances and Wilson Presstman are inconsistently reported. The Fowle genealogy indicates that Frances was born in 1836. Eugene Chalmers Fowle, *Descendants of George Fowle (1610/11?–1682) of Charlestown, Massachusetts* (Boston: New England Historic Genealogical Society, 1990), 99. The Presstman family history shows Wilson born in 1827. Trimble, *Presstman Family*, 3. Rather than depend upon twentieth-century sources, however, it would seem prudent to rely on contemporary data cited in the local press and inscribed on their tombstone in Christ Church Cemetery in Alexandria. These latter sources both indicate that Frances was thirty-three years of age when she died in 1857 and that Wilson perished in 1865 at age thirty-five. Consequently, Frances would seem to have been born in 1824 and her husband in 1829 or 1830.

4. *Alexandria Gazette*, Oct. 29, Nov. 2, 1857; *Baltimore Sun*, Nov. 4, 1857, 2.

5. Warfield, *Manassas to Appomattox*, 32.

6. T. C. Holland, "What Did We Fight For?" *Confederate Veteran* 31 (Nov. 1923): 423.

7. *OR*, 51, pt. 1:33–34.

8. Stephen Wilson Presstman, 17 Virginia Infantry, CMSR.

9. There are no known records for this military organization at the National Archives, other than an entry in Presstman's military service record that he was absent from the Seventeenth Virginia while performing duty with the James Detached Corps and a requisition for forage while working with the corps in January 1862.

10. John Morris Wampler, Journal, May 15, 1862, copy in author's collection.

11. Wampler Journal, Oct. 29, Nov. 15, 1862. Returning at midnight from one assignment, Wampler found the Alexandrian asleep in his bed.

12. Bragg to Gen. Samuel Cooper, Dec. 3, 1862, Confederate Collection, Henry E. Huntington Library, San Marino, Calif.

13. Wampler Journal, Feb. 8, 1863; Special Orders 31, Feb. 3, 1863, S. W. Presstman, 3 Confederate Engineer Troops, CMSR; *OR*, 20, pt. 1:779.

14. Wampler Journal, Feb. 9–May 17, 1863.

15. Col. Jeremy F. Gilmer to Beauregard, Feb. 17, 1863; Gilmer to Bragg, Mar. 2, 1863, Letters and Telegrams Sent by the Engineer Bureau of the Confederate War Dept., 1861–64, RG 109, National Archives.

16. Presstman to Wampler, June 23, 1863, copy in author's collection.

17. Kundahl, *Confederate Engineer*, 218–50.

18. Lt. Col. Alfred L. Rives, Acting Chief of Engineers, to Presstman, Nov. 19, 1863, Letters and Telegrams Sent by the Engineer Bureau of the Confederate War Dept., 1861–64; *OR*, 31, pt. 3:581; Gilmer to Bragg, Nov. 24, 1863, Braxton Bragg Papers, William P. Palmer Collection, Western Reserve Historical Society, Cleveland, Ohio; S. W. Presstman, 3 Confederate Engineer Troops, CMSR.

19. Johnston, *Narrative of Military Operations*, 312, 345, 347, 348; Joseph E. Johnston, "Opposing Sherman's Advance to Atlanta," *Battles and Leaders of the Civil War* (Secaucus, N.J.: Castle, 1984), 4:265, 270–74.

20. Johnston, "Opposing Sherman's Advance," 274; Leigh Robinson, "General Joseph E. Johnston," *Southern Historical Society Papers* 19 (1891): 361.

21. *OR*, 38, pt. 5:930, 938.

22. Ibid., pt. 3:743–44.

23. Ibid., pt. 5:1018.

24. Connelly, *Autumn of Glory*, 490.

25. *OR*, 39, pt. 3:866, 904–5; 45; pt. 2:717; 52, pt. 2:. 772–73.

26. John Bell Hood, "The Invasion of Tennessee," *Battles and Leaders of the Civil War* (Secaucus, N.J.: Castle, 1984), 4:429.

27. *OR,* 45, pt. 2:648, 690, 721, 729.

28. S. W. Presstman, Military Records Jacket, 3 Confederate Engineer Troops, CMSR; Charles F. Baker, "Something of Battle Field Maps," *Confederate Veteran* 21 (Feb. 1913): 63.

29. *Alexandria Gazette,* Feb. 11, 1865.

CHAPTER 11. FLOWER OF THE SOUTH: RANDOLPH FAIRFAX

1. Philip Slaughter, *A Sketch of the Life of Randolph Fairfax,* 3d ed. (Richmond: William Ellis Jones, 1902), vi, 53; Mrs. Burton Harrison (Constance Cary), *Recollections Grave and Gay* (New York: Charles Scribner's Sons, 1911), 96.

2. Gay Montague Moore, *Seaport in Virginia: George Washington's Alexandria* (Richmond: Garret & Massie, 1949), 237.

3. Slaughter, *Sketch of the Life,* 5.

4. The home at 607 Cameron Street still serves as a grand representation of antebellum Alexandria.

5. Slaughter, *Sketch of the Life,* 3.

6. Ibid., 4.

7. The young scholar's name lives on at Episcopal High School in the Fairfax Literary Society and the Randolph Fairfax Memorial Prize Medal for "Character, Conduct and Scholarship." John White, *Chronicles of the Episcopal High School in Virginia, 1839–1989* (Dublin, N. H.: William Bauhan, 1989), 38.

8. Slaughter, *Sketch of the Life,* 47.

9. Ibid., 45–46.

10. John Lipscomb Johnson, *The University Memorial: Biographical Sketches* (Baltimore: Turnbull Brothers, 1871), 295.

11. Crofts, *Reluctant Confederates,* 115.

12. Randolph Fairfax, Capt. Hutter's Company, Virginia Infantry, CMSR; Johnson, *University Memorial,* 296.

13. Wiley, *Life of Johnny Reb,* 335.

14. Johnson, *University Memorial,* 297.

15. Forrest, *Odyssey in Gray,* 157.

16. Fairfax to his sister Jenny, Oct. 23, 1861, Randolph Fairfax Papers, Eleanor S. Brockenbrough Library, Museum of the Confederacy.

17. Fairfax to his mother, Sept. 26, 1861, Randolph Fairfax Papers.

18. Fairfax to his mother, Oct. 11, 1861, Randolph Fairfax Papers.

19. *OR,* 51, pt. 2:372.

20. Clement D. Fishburne, "Historical Sketch of the Rockbridge Artillery, C.S. Army," *Southern Historical Society Papers* 23 (1895): 123.

21. Fairfax to his sister Jenny, Nov. 12, 1861, Randolph Fairfax Papers.

22. Fairfax to his sister Edie, Dec. 14, 1861, Randolph Fairfax Papers.

23. Fishburne, "Historical Sketch," 124–25.

24. Fairfax to his brother Bert, Feb. 8, 1862, and to his sister Jenny, Apr. 3, 1862, Randolph Fairfax Papers.

25. Fairfax to his mother, Jan. 9, 1862, Randolph Fairfax Papers.

26. Fairfax to his brother Bert, Feb. 8, 1862, Randolph Fairfax Papers.

27. Fishburne, "Historical Sketch," 126.

28. Fairfax to his mother, Jan. 9, 1862, Randolph Fairfax Papers.

29. Robert J. Driver Jr., *The 1st and 2nd Rockbridge Artillery* (Lynchburg, Va.: H. E. Howard, 1987), 13. The name of the campsite is interesting, as Brig. Gen. Felix Zollicoffer had no connection with Confederate forces operating in Virginia. He had earned the dubious distinction of being the first southern general killed in the western theater, perishing at the battle of Mill Springs in eastern Kentucky in January 1862.

30. Fairfax to his mother, Jan. 31, 1862, Randolph Fairfax Papers.

31. Fairfax to his brother Bert, Feb. 8, 1862, Randolph Fairfax Papers; Randolph Fairfax, Capt. Archibald Graham's Company, Virginia Light Artillery, CMSR.

32. Harrison, *Pickett's Men*, 67.

33. Fairfax to his sister Monimia, Mar. 14, 1862, Randolph Fairfax Papers.

34. Fishburne, "Historical Sketch," 130.

35. Fairfax to his sister Jenny, Apr. 3, 1862, Randolph Fairfax Papers.

36. *OR*, 12, pt. 1:396–97; Fairfax to his father, Mar. 25, 1862, and to his sister Jenny, Apr. 3, 1862, Randolph Fairfax Papers.

37. Fairfax to his sister Jenny, Apr. 3, 1862, Randolph Fairfax Papers.

38. Ibid.; Fairfax to his mother, Apr. 14, 1862, and to his father, May 16, 1862, Randolph Fairfax Papers.

39. Fishburne, "Historical Sketch," 136–37; Driver, *1st and 2nd Rockbridge Artillery*, 19–20.

40. Fairfax to his father, May 16, 1862, Randolph Fairfax Papers.

41. Ibid.

42. Fairfax to his brother Bert, May 27, 1862, Randolph Fairfax Papers.

43. Ibid.

44. Fairfax to his mother, May 25, 1862, Randolph Fairfax Papers.

45. Fairfax to his sister Jenny, June 7, 1862, Randolph Fairfax Papers.

46. Fairfax to his sister Jenny, June 10, 1862, Randolph Fairfax Papers; Driver, *1st and 2nd Rockbridge Artillery*, 24.

47. Fairfax to his mother, June 14, 1862, Randolph Fairfax Papers.

48. Ibid.

49. *OR*, 12, pt. 2:762–63.

50. Fairfax to his brother Bert, June 20, 1862, and to his sister Edie, June 20, 1862, Randolph Fairfax Papers.

51. Fairfax to his mother, June 14, 1862, Randolph Fairfax Papers.

52. Fairfax to his mother, July 3, 1862, Randolph Fairfax Papers.

53. Fairfax to his sister Monimia, July 22, 1862, Randolph Fairfax Papers.

54. Fairfax to his sister Jenny, June 7, 1862, to his brother Bert, June 20, 1862, and to his mother, July 3, 1862, Randolph Fairfax Papers.

55. Fairfax to his mother, Aug. 7, 1862, Randolph Fairfax Papers.

56. Driver, *1st and 2nd Rockbridge Artillery*, 28. Jackson's engagement with Brig. Gen. Nathaniel Banks on August 9 was also referred to as Cedar Run, Slaughter Mountain, and Southwest Mountain.

57. Fairfax to his mother, Sept. 7, 1862, Randolph Fairfax Papers.

58. Ibid.

59. It is worth noting that Captain Poague and some other battery commanders were placed under arrest by Jackson for allowing their men to ride across the river on the carriages.

60. Fairfax to his mother, Sept. 7, 1862, Randolph Fairfax Papers.

61. Fairfax to his mother, Sept. 14, 1862, Randolph Fairfax Papers.

62. Fairfax to his mother, Oct. 20, 1862, Randolph Fairfax Papers.

63. Fairfax to his father, Oct. 3, 1862, Randolph Fairfax Papers.

64. Fairfax to his mother, Oct. 20, 1862, Randolph Fairfax Papers.

65. Fairfax to his sister Jenny, Nov. 15, 1862, Randolph Fairfax Papers.

66. Fairfax to his mother, Dec. 12, 1862, Randolph Fairfax Papers.

67. Fairfax to his mother, Dec. 7, 1862, Randolph Fairfax Papers.

68. *OR,* 21:639; Driver, *1st and 2nd Rockbridge Artillery,* 36.

69. Slaughter, *Sketch of the Life,* 42–43.

70. *OR,* 21:631, 633; Driver, *1st and 2nd Rockbridge Artillery,* 34–36.

71. Slaughter, *Sketch of the Life,* 43.

72. William Thomas Poague, *Gunner with Stonewall: Reminiscences of William Thomas Poague; A Memoir Written for His Children in 1903,* ed. Monroe F. Cockrell (Wilmington, N.C.: Broadfoot Publishing Co., 1987), 58, 59.

73. Fairfax to his mother, Dec. 12, 1862, Randolph Fairfax Papers.

74. Driver, *1st and 2nd Rockbridge Artillery,* 36.

75. Harrison, *Pickett's Men,* 96.

76. Johnson, *University Memorial,* 300.

77. Ibid.

78. Robert E. Lee Jr. to his mother, Dec. 18, 1862, Lee Family Papers.

79. Slaughter, *Sketch of the Life,* dedication.

CHAPTER 12. IMMIGRANT: PATRICK O'GORMAN

1. U.S. Census Office, *Population of the United States in 1860,* xxix, 520.

2. T. Michael Miller, "St. Patrick's Day—The Wearing of the Green in Alexandria," MS, Special Collections, Alexandria Library.

3. Jason H. Silverman, "Irish," *Encyclopedia of the Confederacy* (New York: Simon & Schuster, 1993), 2:822.

4. U.S. Census Office, *Population of the United States in 1860,* xxix.

5. Ella Lonn, *Foreigners in the Confederacy* (Gloucester, Mass.: Peter Smith, 1965), 3–4, 32, 53–56, 230–31.

6. Ibid., 240.

7. Patrick F. Gorman, "Personal Experiences and Anecdotes, Civil War, 1861–1865," MS (n.d.), Patrick F. Gorman Papers, Special Collections, Alexandria Library. John W. Green soon joined the southern army, serving as a quartermaster staff officer. Gorman related that whenever the major was near the battery's camp, he would come by to see the Irish enlistee.

8. P. F. O'Gorman, 18 Battalion, Virginia Heavy Artillery, CMSR.

9. *Alexandria Gazette,* June 30, 1899.

10. "The Alexandria Light Artillery: Valuable Historic Data on the Famous Kemper's Battery," MS (n.d.), introducing Patrick F. Gorman, Diary, Patrick F. Gorman Papers, Special Collections, Alexandria Library.

11. Ibid.

12. Gorman Diary, May 26–July 16, 1861; *OR,* 51, pt. 2:82.

13. Gorman, "Personal Experiences and Anecdotes."

14. *OR,* 2:129.

15. Gorman Diary, June 19, 1861.

16. William C. Davis, *Battle at Bull Run: A History of the First Major Campaign of the Civil War* (Baton Rouge: Louisiana State Univ. Press, 1981), 107–8.

17. *OR,* 2:452–53, 459; Gorman Diary, July 18, 1861.

18. Gorman, "Personal Experiences and Anecdotes."

19. Ibid.

20. Ibid.

21. *OR*, 2:523–25, 535–36; Michael J. Andrus, *The Brooke, Fauquier, Loudoun, and Alexandria Artillery* (Lynchburg, Va.: H. E. Howard, 1990), 7–9; Gorman, "Personal Experiences and Anecdotes."

22. Gorman, "Personal Experiences and Anecdotes."

23. *Alexandria Gazette*, June 30, 1899.

24. Gorman Diary, Dec. 8, 1861.

25. *OR*, 11, pt. 2:726.

26. *Alexandria Gazette*, June 30, 1899.

27. After the war, Kosciusko Kemper served as mayor of Alexandria and commander of the local camp of Confederate veterans.

28. *Alexandria Gazette*, June 30, 1899.

29. *OR*, 11, pt. 2:666, 716, 727.

30. Gorman Diary, Nov. 30, 1862.

31. Andrus, *The Brooke, Fauquier*, 14.

32. Gorman Diary, Mar. 23, Apr. 7–13, 1863.

33. Steven A. Comier, *The Siege of Suffolk: The Forgotten Campaign, Apr. 11–May 4, 1863* (Lynchburg, Va.: H. E. Howard, 1989), 128; Gorman Diary, May 7–18, 1863.

34. *OR*, 18:331; Gorman Diary, Apr. 19, 22, 1863.

35. *OR*, 18:326, 336–37, 639, 1016; *ORN*, 8:746–48; Gorman Diary, Apr. 19–20, 1863.

36. Comier, *The Siege of Suffolk*, 84; Gorman Diary, May 1–22, 1863.

37. *OR*, 27, pt. 3:1029, 1067; 29, pt. 2:691, 783, 905. Gorman Diary, May 26–Aug. 7, 1863.

38. Tracy Chernault and Jeffrey C. Weaver, *18th and 20th Battalions of Heavy Artillery* (Lynchburg, Va.: H. E. Howard, 1995), 26, 34; *OR*, 36, pt. 3:809–11; O'Gorman, CMSR.

39. This defensive position was named for the chief of the Confederate Engineer Bureau, Maj. Gen. Jeremy Gilmer.

40. Gorman Diary, Jan. 1, 1865.

41. Gorman's "Personal Experiences and Anecdotes" lists Capt. David Smoot, Oscar Tubman, Jonathan Ward, Henry Poss, Andrew Sullivan, and himself as the sole surviving Alexandrians. The regimental history of the Alexandria Artillery states that eleven (unnamed) members of the battery were captured. Andrus, *The Brooke, Fauquier*, 20.

42. Gorman, "Personal Experiences and Anecdotes."

43. Ibid.; O'Gorman, CMSR.

44. Grand Roll, St. John's Academy [Alexandria, Va.], MS Box 4, Special Collections, Alexandria Library.

45. *Alexandria Gazette*, Jan. 3, 4, 7, 1921.

46. Andrus, *The Brooke, Fauquier*, 20.

CHAPTER 13. SOUTHERN SYMPATHIZER: ANNE FROBEL

1. Frobel, *Civil War Diary*. No record has been found of an award from the government for the damage sustained at Wilton Hill.

2. Ibid., 20.

3. Drew Gilpin Faust, *Mothers of Invention: Women of the Slaveholding South in the American Civil War* (Chapel Hill: Univ. of North Carolina Press, 1996), 163–64.

4. Jacob Frobel, a native of Holland, was teaching piano to Ann Washington in Richmond when her husband, Bushrod, inherited Mount Vernon in 1804. At her urging, Frobel followed the Washingtons to northern Virginia, where he married, acquired Wilton Hill, and began a family of eight children. Two sons and three daughters were living at the time the Civil War erupted. Frobel, *Civil War Diary*, introduction, 288; Washington *Sunday Star*, Feb. 7, 1915.

5. *Alexandria Gazette*, Apr. 19, 1907. The Fairfax Court House was thirteen miles away, as the crow flies, too far to be considered anything more than the seat of government for legal matters pertaining to Wilton Hill.

6. Catherine Clinton, *The Plantation Mistress: Woman's World in the Old South* (New York: Pantheon Books, 1982), 175.

7. Bushrod Frobel's obituary in the *Atlanta Constitution* (July 13, 1888) asserts that he graduated from West Point and served in the navy prior to the Civil War. However, his name is missing from the U.S. Military Academy's *Register of Graduates and Former Cadets*. The U.S. Navy specifically denies that Frobel was an officer or enlisted man before the war. Nor can any record be found in the National Archives indicating that he was ever in the U.S. Army.

8. U.S. Revenue Marine, Register of Officers, 1790–1870, 1:191; R. J. Walker to Bushrod W. Frobel, Oct. 28, 1845, Records of the U.S. Coast Guard, RG 26, National Archives.

9. Ibid.; Frobel, *Civil War Diary*, 16.

10. *OR*, 5:998.

11. B. W. Frobel, GSO, CMSR. The Alexandrian was also closely associated with Maj. Gen. Gustavus W. Smith, who refers to Frobel in his postwar accounts of the Battle of Seven Pines and his command of Georgia militia in opposing Sherman's march to the sea. Gustavus W. Smith, "Two Days of Battle at Seven Pines (Fair Oaks)," *Battles and Leaders of the Civil War* (Secaucus, N.J.: Castle, 1984), 2:245, 261; "The Georgia Militia during Sherman's March to the Sea," *Battles and Leaders of the Civil War*, 4:669.

12. D. W. Frobel, GSO, CMSR; Frobel, *Civil War Diary*, 257.

13. Faust, *Mothers of Invention*, 32.

14. Frobel, *Civil War Diary*, 15.

15. Ibid., 16.

16. Judith W. McGuire, *Diary of a Southern Refugee, during the War* (Richmond: J. W. Randolph & English, 1889), 13–14.

17. See, for example, McGuire's description of Alexandria before May 24, 1861, with Confederate flags flying, men in uniform, martial music in the air, and the diarist's admonition against admitting weakness in their cause. McGuire, *Diary of a Southern Refugee*, 13.

18. Anne E. Lee to Mrs. Samuel F. du Pont, Dec. 24 or 29, 1862, vertical files, Biography, Mrs. Cassius Lee Letters, Papers of the Society of the Lees of Virginia, Special Collections, Alexandria Library.

19. McGuire, *Diary of a Southern Refugee*, 18–19; "Refugee in Canada," Mrs. Cassius Lee Letters. At the war's end, the McGuires were stuck in Richmond without home, job, or money.

20. Not many miles away in Fauquier County, "A newspaper was a veritable treasure with isolated homes." Alexander Hunter, "The Women of Mosby's Confederacy," *Confederate Veteran* 15 (June 1907): 262.

21. Frobel, *Civil War Diary*, 71.

22. Ibid., 181.

23. George C. Rable, *Civil Wars: Women and the Crisis of Southern Nationalism* (Urbana: Univ. of Illinois Press, 1989), 211.

24. See, for example, the comment by New York cavalryman Thomas J. Goree quoted in Noel G. Harrison, "Atop an Anvil: The Civilians' War in Fairfax and Alexandria Counties, Apr. 1861–Apr. 1862," *Virginia Magazine of History and Biography* 106 (spring 1998): 146.

25. Frobel, *Civil War Diary*, 34, 151–52.

26. Harrison, *Pickett's Men*, 135.

27. Frobel, *Civil War Diary*, 22.

28. Ibid., 24.

29. Ibid., 25; Michael Fellman, "Women and Guerrilla Warfare," in *Divided Houses: Gender and the Civil War*, ed. Catherine Clinton and Nina Silber (New York: Oxford Univ. Press, 1992), 151.

30. Frobel, *Civil War Diary*, 23.

31. McGuire, *Diary of a Southern Refugee*, 20.

32. Harrison, *Recollections Grave and Gay*, 44–45.

33. Frobel, *Civil War Diary*, 61, 86–87.

34. See, for example, Rable, *Civil Wars*, 157–58. There is at least one documented case of a desperate family giving a box of silver to the cook to hide, figuring the Federals would not search her. The rationale was sound, and the heirlooms were spared. Catherine Clinton, *Tara Revisited: Women, War, and the Plantation Legend* (New York: Abbeville Press, 1995), 124.

35. Frobel, *Civil War Diary*, 87.

36. Ibid., 117, 201.

37. Ibid., 210.

38. Ibid., 45, 164.

39. Fowle later left Virginia to wait out the war in London, where he corresponded with and later visited Douglas Forrest in France. After the fighting ended, Fowle befriended Montgomery Corse when he was imprisoned at Fort Warren.

40. Frobel, *Civil War Diary*, 108, 166, 194, 195,

41. Ibid., 37.

42. Ibid., 40–41, 82, 171.

43. Harrison, *Pickett's Men*, 161.

44. Kundahl, *Confederate Engineer*, 124.

45. Harrison, *Pickett's Men*, 145.

46. Frobel, *Civil War Diary*, 73.

47. George B. McClellan, *McClellan's Own Story: The War for the Union* (New York: Charles L. Webster & Co., 1887), 89.

48. Benjamin Franklin Cooling III and Walton H. Owen II, *Mr. Lincoln's Forts: A Guide to the Civil War Defenses of Washington* (Shippensburg, Pa.: White Mane Publishing Co., 1988), 30.

49. Frobel, *Civil War Diary*, 34.

50. Ibid., 107.

51. Welton, *"My Heart,"* 108, 112, 126–27, 138.

52. Frobel, *Civil War Diary*, 57–58.

53. Ibid., 59.

54. Ibid., 92.

55. Ibid., 174, 204.

56. Ibid., 65–66, 120–22, 124–25.

57. Fort Ellsworth was sited just to the west of Alexandria city on grounds now occupied by the George Washington Masonic National Memorial.

58. Frobel, *Civil War Diary*, 176, 194.

59. Ibid., 165.

60. Ibid., 207.

61. Ibid., 209.

62. Ibid., 213–14.

63. Ibid., 172, 187, 199.

64. Ibid., 212.

65. Ibid., 72, 157–58, 184–85, 194.

66. Ibid., 43–47.

67. Ibid., 81, 84, 93–94, 101 (quotation), 103, 137, 159, 186, 226, 228–30.

68. Ibid., 101, 133. The townspeople did not all turn their backs on Federal soldiers in need. After the Battle of Bull Run, for example, Sarah Warfield, whose husband and two sons had marched off with the Alexandria regiment, nevertheless nursed a sick, young Union enlistee brought to her home after the battle at Bull Run. The depth of her caring was evident when Mrs. Warfield put her son's clean shoes and socks on the patient. Ada Warfield Kurtz, "A Heroine on the Homefront: My Mother's Experiences during the Civil War," *Alexandria Chronicle* 7 (spring 1998): 8–9.

69. "A Southern Heroine in Need," *Confederate Veteran* 13 (June 1905): 249; *Alexandria Gazette*, Oct. 4, 1893; T. Michael Miller, "Kate Hooper: Alexandria's 'Angel of Mercy,'" *Alexandria Chronicle* 9 (spring 2002): 19–20; Frobel, *Civil War Diary*, 100–101.

70. Rable, *Civil Wars*, 216; Faust, *Mothers of Invention*, 180–87. For a frank expression of this concern by a southern woman, see Kundahl, *Confederate Engineer*, 116.

71. Frobel, *Civil War Diary*, xiii.

72. Faust, *Mothers of Invention*, 59, 61.

73. Frobel, *Civil War Diary*, 216.

74. Ibid., 219.

75. Ibid., 243.

76. Ibid., 247. The discouragement expressed by Anne was being felt at this time by other women in Alexandria as well. In the fall of 1865, Lucy Lyons Turner admitted, "I do not think I have ever been so melancholy, as now." T. Michael Miller, *Visitors from the Past: A Bi-Centennial Reflection on Life at the Lee-Fendall House, 1785–1985* (Alexandria: Virginia Trust for Historic Preservation, 1986), 148.

77. Frobel, *Civil War Diary*, 249, 252.

78. Ibid., 251.

79. Ibid., 269.

80. Ibid., 271.

81. Ibid., 266, 271.

CHAPTER 14. CHRONICLER: ALEXANDER HUNTER

1. Hunter, *Johnny Reb and Billy Yank*, 101.

2. White, *Chronicles of the Episcopal High School in Virginia*, 250.

3. *Bennett* v. *Hunter*, 76 U.S. (9 Wall.), 326 (1869). Members of the First Brigade, New Jersey militia, who bivouacked on Abingdon in 1861, dubbed it "Camp Princeton."

4. Hunter, *Johnny Reb and Billy Yank*, 25.
5. Ibid., 52.
6. Ibid., 58.
7. Ibid., 154.
8. Ibid., 135.
9. Ibid., 194.
10. Ibid., 210.
11. Ibid., 244.
12. Ibid., 218.
13. Ibid., 220.
14. Ibid., 225.
15. Hunter's "Minié musket" was probably of Continental origin, purchased at the outset of hostilities by the Confederate government in large quantity to arm its nascent army. The weapon may well have been modified after manufacture to fire the minié round. An extraordinarily tight tolerance would have resulted, causing black powder to foul the barrel after several shots, thereby inhibiting loading additional bullets without cleaning, making it a liability in the heat of combat.
16. Hunter, *Johnny Reb and Billy Yank*, 259.
17. Ibid., 258.
18. Ibid., 352.
19. Ibid., 163.
20. Ibid., 516.
21. Ibid., 382.
22. Ibid., 386.
23. Ibid., 397. The portions of Hunter's original manuscript dealing with Antietam and Gettysburg are now missing, as are the statements of his personal opinions about R. E. Lee and Jubal Early, expressed in the middle and end of the work. Alexander Hunter, "Four Years in the Ranks," MS, Alexander Hunter Papers, Virginia Historical Society, Richmond.
24. Hunter, *Johnny Reb and Billy Yank*, 408.
25. Ibid., 416.
26. Ibid., 420.
27. Ibid., 423.
28. Ibid., 455.
29. Dean B. Mahin, *One War at a Time: The International Dimensions of the American Civil War* (Washington, D.C.: Brassey's, 1999), 212.
30. Hunter, *Johnny Reb and Billy Yank*, 536.
31. Ibid., 563.
32. Ibid., 594.
33. Ibid., 702–3.
34. Ibid., 707–8.
35. Ibid., 711.
36. Ibid., 21.
37. Ibid., 373.
38. Hunter by no means restricted his opinions on military competence to officers wearing gray. He praised Maj. Gen. Phil Kearney as "the most brilliant, chivalrous, dashing officer in the Yankee Army" (267) and described Brig. Gen. Alfred Pleasanton as "that dashing trooper whom Southern cavalrymen regarded as the toughest fighter they ever met" (372). Hunter considered Irvin McDowell, Fitz John Porter, and William Franklin, among others, to have been mistreated by the U.S. government.

39. Hunter, *Johnny Reb and Billy Yank*, 656.

40. Ibid., 383.

41. Ibid., 518–19.

42. Ibid., 688.

43. Ibid., 716.

44. It is interesting to note that Hunter's account omits his father's petition in the spring of 1862 to the Confederate secretary of war requesting that Alexander be commissioned a second lieutenant of field artillery. For some unknown reason, the narrative also skips over his bout with typhoid fever during the winter of 1861–62.

45. See, for example, Cooke's articles on "Stuart and His Lady Prisoner" and "Virginia Partisans" in Philadelphia *Weekly Times,* Oct. 5, 1878, and Oct. 29, 1881, and Thomas Nelson Page's series of books on the state's civilized culture—e.g., *In Ole Virginia* (1887), *Red Rock* (1898), and *The Old Dominion* (1908).

46. Hunter, *Johnny Reb and Billy Yank*, 708.

47. Alexander Hunter, *The Women of the Debatable Land* (Washington, D.C.: Corden Publishing Co., 1912), vii.

48. Alexander Hunter, "The Women of Mosby's Confederacy," *Confederate Veteran* 15 (June 1907): 257–62.

49. Hunter, *The Women of the Debatable Land,* 116.

50. Ibid., 46.

51. Ibid., 21.

52. Ibid., 24.

53. Ibid., 215.

54. Ibid., 117–18.

55. Ibid., 56.

56. Ibid., 118.

57. Ibid., 260.

58. Hunter was also a correspondent for the *New York Herald* during this period, but since the paper did not identify the authors of its articles, it is impossible to ascertain the specific work of the Alexandrian.

59. Alexander Hunter, *The Huntsman in the South* (Washington, D.C.: Neale Publishing Co., 1908), 27.

60. Ibid., 257, 260–61.

61. Hunter, *Johnny Reb and Billy Yank*, 463.

62. Alexander Hunter and J. H. Polkinhorn, *New National Theater, Washington, D.C.: A Record of Fifty Years* (Washington, D.C.: R. O. Polkinhorn & Son, 1885), 51.

63. For a complete account of Hunter's article in *The Occasional* and the reaction it generated, see Terry Alford, "Alexander Hunter and the Bessie Hale Story," *Alexandria History* 8 (1990): 5–15.

64. Abingdon had been put up for sale in 1881.

65. In the opening months of the twentieth century, the bodies of southern soldiers interred in Arlington and at the Soldiers Home in Washington, D.C., had been reburied in a plot known as the "Confederate Section."

66. Washington *Evening Star,* July 2, 1914, 22; *Washington Post,* July 2, 1914, 5; *Washington Herald,* July 2, 1914, 10.

CHAPTER 15. VETERAN: EDGAR WARFIELD

1. *Richmond Times-Dispatch,* Jan. 19, 1997, C-2.

2. *Alexandria Gazette,* Mar. 31, 1922.

3. Ibid.

4. Warfield, *Manassas to Appomattox*, 8–9.

5. Ibid., 11. See also the newspaper account of the dedication of the tablet with an inscription coauthored by Warfield, marking the spot where Lee received his orders. *Alexandria Gazette*, Aug. 3, 1932.

6. Warfield, *Manassas to Appomattox*, 16, 23, 41.

7. Ibid., 45; *Richmond Times-Dispatch*, Jan. 19, 1997, C-2.

8. Warfield, *Manassas to Appomattox*, 72–73.

9. Ibid., 118.

10. Ibid., 49, 78–79, 81. Another Alexandrian, William McKnight, incarcerated as a prisoner of war at Fort Warren, Massachusetts, noted that Mrs. Warfield went to Fort Columbus, Governor's Island, New York, to see her son who was reportedly held there as a wounded prisoner. If so, she was terribly disappointed, as George Warfield had perished at Frayser's Farm on June 30, 1862. William McKnight to his mother, July 30, 1862, McKnight-Piercy-Jacobs Family Papers, Special Collections, Alexandria Library.

11. William M. Glasgow Jr., *Northern Virginia's Own: The 17th Virginia Infantry Regiment, Confederate States Army* (Alexandria, Va.: Gobill Press, 1989), 135.

12. Warfield, *Manassas to Appomattox*, 91, 95, 110, 146.

13. Ibid., 128–32; *Confederate Military History* (Wilmington, N.C.: Broadfoot Publishing Co., 1987), 4:1237–38.

14. Warfield, *Manassas to Appomattox*, 155–56.

15. Ibid., 159–65.

16. Ibid., 174–77; newspaper clipping, "Home 57 Years Ago from Appomattox," Apr. 22, 1922, Edgar Warfield scrapbook no. 1, Warfield Family Private Collection; John R. Zimmerman, Diary, Apr. 18, 1865, Joseph L. Martin Papers, Special Collections, Alexandria Library.

17. See, for example, the advertisement in the *Alexandria Gazette*, May 13, 1880.

18. *Alexandria Gazette*, Sept. 28, 1900. Years later, when practicing with his son, Warfield's drugstore suffered a smashed door when a runaway horse plunged into the establishment. *Alexandria Gazette*, May 5, 1917.

19. Warfield, *Manassas to Appomattox*, 178–79.

20. *Alexandria Gazette*, Jan. 27, 1934.

21. A. L. I. Winne, Secretary, Virginia Pharmaceutical Association, to Warfield, Mar. 20, 1922, Edgar Warfield Papers, Carter Batcheller Private Collection. The correspondent was responding to an inquiry by Warfield concerning the dates of his service on the board. Apparently, the memory of the elderly pharmacist was failing at age eighty-two. What does this say about the accuracy of the details in his memoirs, which were not completed until eight years later?

22. By-Laws, R. E. Lee Camp No. 5, United Confederate Veterans, minutes, 5, Mary Custis Lee–Seventeenth Virginia Regiment Chapter, United Daughters of the Confederacy, Alexandria. These objectives conformed to the motives underlying the establishment of similar local organizations throughout the South: charitable, memorial, social, and historical. William W. White, *The Confederate Veteran* (Tuscaloosa, Ala.: Confederate Publishing Co., 1962), 12.

23. R. E. Lee Camp No. 5, minutes, June 30, July 7, 1884.

24. R. E. Lee Camp No. 5, minutes, Sept. 1, 1884, July 5, 1885, Aug. 2, 1886, Oct. 1, 1888, July 6, 1891, Feb. 1, 1892. The trip to Richmond became a cause célèbre when a Philadelphia brigade refused to parade behind the Confederate colors carried by the Alexandrians. The squabble was settled amicably by the Lee Camp loaning the Yankees its U.S. flag to carry as their banner. *Alexandria Gazette*, Oct. 6, 1888.

25. R. E. Lee Camp No. 5, minutes, Feb. 3, Mar. 3, 1890.

26. Ibid., Apr. 6, 1885.

27. *Alexandria Gazette,* May 24, 1889.

28. Ibid., May 23, 1959.

29. Elder is sometimes mistakenly identified as a veteran of the Confederate military. The Lee Camp members seemed to derive some comfort that the artist was a southerner, as he hailed from nearby Fredericksburg, but he was not a former soldier in gray.

30. Richmond *Daily Times,* Aug. 10, 1888, 1.

31. R. E. Lee Camp No. 5, minutes, June 4, Sept. 3, 1888.

32. *Alexandria Gazette,* Nov. 6, 14, 1888; R. E. Lee Camp No. 5, minutes, Oct. 1, Nov. 5, 1888.

33. R. E. Lee Camp No. 5, minutes, Jan. 7, Mar. 25, Apr. 20, 1889.

34. *Alexandria Gazette,* May 24, 1889.

35. In December 1900, the camp voted to add the name of James W. Jackson, former proprietor of the city's Marshall House hotel and a southern martyr, bringing the total number of deceased residents remembered on the monument to an even one hundred.

36. *Alexandria Gazette,* May 21, May 24, 1889. Former Maj. Gen. Fitzhugh Lee was one in a series of veteran governors of Virginia, stretching from 1874 to 1901. Lee's courtship of his wife, Ellen Fowle, had taken place within a stone's throw of the monument site. He visited her at the Fowle residences on Prince Street and married her at the Lyceum in 1870, then the residence of his cousin, Philip Hooe, on the southwest corner of Prince and Washington Streets.

37. *Acts and Joint Resolutions Passed by the General Assembly of the State of Virginia during the Session of 1889–90* (Richmond, Va.: J. H. O'Bannon, 1890), ch. 119, 169.

38. Copyright 43413, Oct. 26, 1892.

39. R. E. Lee Camp No. 5, minutes, Dec. 9, 13, 1889; Mar. 24, 1891.

40. By-Laws, R. E. Lee Camp No. 5, minutes, July 7, 1884; Sept. 7, Dec. 7, 1891. The unreconstructed Rebels refused to seek veterans' handouts from the U.S. government and therefore focused their attentions on legislatures in the various states.

41. R. E. Lee Camp No. 5, minutes., Jan. 20, 1896.

42. Ibid., May 29, 1890, June 22, 1892; Jan. 19, 1893.

43. Ibid., Jan. 6, 1892, Nov. 6, 1893; Apr. 2, 1894.

44. Ibid., June 2, Sept. 1, 1890; Apr. 6, 1891. *Alexandria Gazette,* Nov. 3, 1896.

45. R. E. Lee Camp No. 5, minutes, Sept. 7, 1896; Apr. 5, 1897.

46. Ibid., Apr. 4, May 14, Nov. 7, 1898; Apr. 3, 1899.

47. The comprehensive study of the Confederate veterans movement cites 1903 as its zenith, with 1,523 camps enrolled in the United Confederate Veterans, although only half were in good standing for financial reasons. They represented about 80,000 veterans, but, again, a large proportion (35,000) were considered inactive for nonpayment of dues. White, *Confederate Veteran,* 34.

48. In 1903 the camp had requested that a charter be issued under provisions of the Act of the General Assembly of Jan. 20, 1890, which cited Edward [*sic*] Warfield as one of three Alexandrians when incorporating the Grand Camp Confederate Veterans, Dept. of Virginia. *Acts and Joint Resolutions Passed by the General Assembly,* Ch. 69, 87–88. The other two Alexandrians listed were Col. W. A. Smoot and Frank Hume.

49. There would eventually be seven Robert E. Lee Camps at different locales around the state of Virginia.

50. Grand Camp Confederate Veterans, Dept. of Virginia, charter, Mary Custis Lee–Seventeenth Virginia Regiment Chapter, United Daughters of the Confederacy, Alexandria; Certificate of Incorporation, Corporation Court of Alexandria, June 10, 1903, R. E. Lee Camp No. 5, minutes; *Organized Camps of the United Confederate Veterans*, comp. George G. Kane, Eleanor S. Brockenbrough Library, Museum of the Confederacy, Richmond, 41.

51. *Alexandria Gazette*, Nov. 6, Dec. 17, 1888; Aug. 2, 1897.

52. Charles J. Anderson, Adjutant General, to Col. Arthur Herbert, Feb. 19, 1908, Edgar Warfield Papers; *Alexandria Gazette*, July 10, Sept. 26, 1911.

53. Newspaper clipping, "State Restores a Southern Flag," July 12, 1911, Edgar Warfield scrapbook no. 1.

54. *Alexandria Gazette*, July 12, Sept. 26, 1911.

55. The two chapters merged in 1921, applying for a certificate of incorporation to permit their holding property and then receiving deed to the Confederate Veterans' Building owned by the Lee Camp.

56. *Alexandria Gazette*, Dec. 2, 6, 1921.

57. "War Vet at 90 Leads Parade at Alexandria," United Press, May 24, 1932, Edgar Warfield, 17 Virginia Infantry, CMSR.

58. *Alexandria Gazette*, Mar. 31, 1922; Nov. 27, 1934. *Washington Daily News*, May 24, 1932, 1.

59. Maj. Gen. C. H. Bridges, Adjutant General, to Warfield, July 17, 1930, June 26, 1934; Capt. Jacob Horvath, Superintendent, Antietam Battlefield, to Warfield, Nov. 4, 1924; H. R. McIlwaine, Virginia State Librarian, to Warfield, Apr. 5, 1924; Frederic J. Haskin, Director, Information Bureau, Washington Star, to Warfield, May 18, 1932, Edgar Warfield Papers.

60. The Grand Camp Confederate Veterans began in 1883, when the Robert E. Lee Camp was organized in Richmond. Intended to blanket the entire South, the Grand Camp was only powerful in Virginia and chartered no other affiliates except for nominal representation in Tennessee and Mississippi. The United Confederate Veterans held its organizational meeting in June 1889 and, while intended to unite all existing associations of Confederate veterans, never unseated the Grand Camp as the primary umbrella headquarters in Virginia. White, *Confederate Veteran*, 22.

61. "Report of the Inspector General," Headquarters, Grand Camp Confederate Veterans, Dept. of Virginia, Oct. 4, 1929, Edgar Warfield Papers.

62. *Alexandria Gazette*, Oct. 10, 1929.

63. John M. Follin, Adjutant, Camp No. 171, to Edgar Warfield, June 27, 1930, Edgar Warfield Papers.

64. Cornelius B. Hite to Homer Atkinson, Mar. 6, 1931, Edgar Warfield Papers.

65. Unsigned or dated annual address (typewritten), Edgar Warfield Papers.

66. Warfield to W. M. K. Evans, Oct. 17, 1934, Edgar Warfield Papers.

67. For example, Cornelius B. Hite to Warfield, Mar. 21, 1931; Harry Rene Lee, Tennessee Board of Pension Examiners, to Warfield, Nov. 2, 1933, Edgar Warfield Papers.

68. "Dear Friends" letter from R. E. Lee Camp, No. 1, Confederate Veterans Advisory Committee, Dec. 12, 1933, Edgar Warfield Papers.

69. *Alexandria Gazette*, June 7, 1917, May 2, 1932; *Washington Post*, Dec. 25, 1927; telegram to Homer Atkinson, June 18, 1934; *Washington Sunday Star*, Mar. 5, 1933; Edgar Warfield scrapbook no. 2, Warfield Family Private Collection.

70. Dan S. Hollenga, Alexandria Chamber of Commerce, to Warfield, Aug. 6, 1934, Edgar Warfield Papers; Washington *Evening Star*, Jan. 7, 1933; Washington

Sunday Star, Jan. 28, 1933; *Alexandria Gazette,* Apr. 24, 1933, Jan. 20, 28, Feb. 23, 1934.

71. *Alexandria Gazette,* Jan. 20, May 25, 1934. The numbers of attendees had dwindled over the years since the commemoration of "Appomattox" in 1889, and in 1936 these services at the monument were held for the final time.

72. Warfield to Homer Atkinson, July 27, 1934, Edgar Warfield Papers.

73. Atkinson to Warfield, Sept. 4, 1934; Warfield to Atkinson, Sept. 5, 1934, Edgar Warfield Papers.

74. Warfield to Atkinson, Oct. (n.d.) 1934, Edgar Warfield Papers.

75. Warfield to Winnie Booth Kernan, Assistant to the Adjutant General, Sept. 17, 1934; Kernan to Warfield, Sept. 20, 1934, Edgar Warfield Papers.

76. *Alexandria Gazette,* Nov. 27, 1934.

77. Ibid., Nov. 29, 1934.

CONCLUSION

1. Henry Adams quoted in James M. McPherson, *Battle Cry of Freedom: The Civil War Era* (New York: Oxford Univ. Press, 1988), preface, viii.

2. George Alfred Townsend, *Campaigns of a Non-Combatant, and His Romaunt Abroad during the War* (New York: Blelock & Co., 1866), 53, 55.

3. Wise, *History of the Seventeenth,* dedication.

APPENDIX

1. Warfield, *Manassas to Appomattox,* 29; Keen and Mewborn, *43rd Battalion,* 312.

2. George N. Wise, *Campaigns and Battles of the Army of Northern Virginia* (New York: Neale Publishing Co., 1916), 199; *Alexandria Gazette,* July 10, 1896; Worth Bailey, "Silversmiths of Alexandria," *Antiques Magazine* (Feb. 1945), reprint in *Twentieth Annual Washington Antiques Show* catalog (1975): 39.

3. Wallace, *17th Virginia Infantry,* 114; *Alexandria Gazette,* Dec. 7, 1903.

4. T. Michael Miller, "A Chronicle of the 17th Virginia—'The Reminiscences of Col. Arthur Herbert,'" *Alexandria History* 6 (1984): 3–4.

5. Robert Manson Myers, ed., *The Children of Pride: A True Story of Georgia and the Civil War* (New Haven, Conn.: Yale Univ. Press, 1972), 1561; *Life of James W. Jackson, the Alexandria Hero, the Slayer of Ellsworth, the First Martyr of the Cause of Southern Independence* (Richmond: West & Johnson, 1862), 26–38.

6. *Alexandria Gazette,* Aug. 2, 1897, June 30, 1899; Delaware Kemper, GSO, CMSR.

7. Frank Cunningham, "A Seafaring Lee: Almost Forgotten Today, He Trained Two Navies," *Richmond Times-Dispatch, Sunday Magazine,* Apr. 6, 1952, A-2; Sidney Smith Lee, Chronology of Service, ZB Series, Early Records Collection, Operational Archives, Naval Historical Center, Washington, D.C.

8. *Dictionary of American Biography* (New York: Charles Scribner's Sons, 1958), 6:134; Maj. Gen. J. E. B. Stuart to Gen. Samuel Cooper, Mar. 23, 1864, Fitzhugh Lee, GSO, CMSR.

9. T. Michael Miller, "Dr. Magnus M. Lewis: Confederate Surgeon and Medical Director," MS in author's collection.

10. *Confederate Military History: A Library of Confederate States History in Seventeen Volumes,* extended ed. (Wilmington, N.C.: Broadfoot Publishing Co., 1987), 1037–38; Wallace, *17th Virginia Infantry,* 127.

11. Henri Garidel, *Exile in Richmond: The Confederate Journal of Henri Garidel,* ed. Michael Bedout Chesson and Leslie Jean Roberts (Charlottesville: Univ. Press of Virginia, 2001), 175, 176, 236, 254.

12. Allan W. Robbins, "The American Civil War Letters of William and Charles McKnight of Alexandria, Virginia," MS, McKnight-Piercy-Jacobs Family Papers, Special Collections, Alexandria Library.

13. Carol Drake Friedman, "Wilmer McLean: The Centreville Years," *Historical Society of Fairfax County, Virginia* 23 (1991–92): 61–62, 78.

14. *Alexandria Gazette,* May 4, 1901.

15. Guy W. Moore, *The Case of Mrs. Surratt: Her Controversial Trial and Execution for Conspiracy in the Lincoln Assassination* (Norman: Univ. of Oklahoma Press, 1954), 4–6.

16. Charles L. Dufour, *Gentle Tiger: The Gallant Life of Roberdeau Wheat* (Baton Rouge: Louisiana State Univ. Press, 1957), 5–7, 10–11, 14, 194–95; Freeman, *Lee's Lieutenants,* 1:87–88.

17. *Alexandria Gazette,* Feb. 18, 1918.

18. Ibid., Jan. 31, 1923; Wise, *History of the Seventeenth;* Wise, *Campaigns and Battles.*

19. T. Michael Miller, "Wandering Along the Waterfront, Queen to Cameron," *Fireside Sentinel* 3 (Feb. 1989): 22–23; *Alexandria Gazette,* Feb. 26, 1926; John R. Zimmerman, Diary.

Bibliography

PRIMARY SOURCES

Manuscripts

Alexandria (Va.) Library, Special Collections
    Biography, Vertical File
    Corse Family Papers
    Douglas Diary
    Patrick F. Gorman Papers
    Joseph L. Martin Papers
    McKnight-Piercy-Jacobs Family Papers
    Society of the Lees of Virginia Papers
Carter Batcheller Private Collection, Springfield, Va.
    Edgar Warfield Papers
Duke University, Rare Book, Manuscript, and Special Collections Library
    George William Brent Papers
    Jefferson Davis Papers
    R. E. Lee Papers
    Alfred Landon Rives Papers
    James Treakle Letters and Papers, 1861
Filson Club Historical Society, Louisville, Ky.
    Military Papers
Henry E. Huntington Library, San Marino, Calif.
    Confederate Collection
George G. Kundahl, Alexandria, Va.
    John Morris Wampler Papers
Mary Custis Lee, 17th Virginia Regiment Chapter, United Daughters of the Confederacy, Alexandria, Va.
    Grand Camp Confederate Veterans, Department of Virginia, Charter
    R. E. Lee Camp No. 5, United Confederate Veterans, Minutes
Library of Congress, Washington, D.C.
    DeButts-Ely Collection
    James B. McPherson Papers
Museum of the Confederacy, Eleanor S. Brockenbrough Library, Richmond, Va.
    Randolph Fairfax Papers
    James Thomas Petty Diary

National Archives, Washington, D.C.
    RG 26, Records of the United States Coast Guard
    RG 45, Naval Records Collection of the Office of Naval Records and Library
    RG 77, Letters Received by the Chief of Engineers
    RG 94, Records of the Adjutant General's Office
    RG 109, War Department Collection of Confederate Records
    RG 153, Records of the Office of the Judge Advocate General (Army)
Naval Historical Center, Washington, D.C.
    Early Records Collection, Operational Archives
Southern Historical Collection, Chapel Hill, N.C.
    Franklin Buchanan Letter Book
    Francis Asbury Dickins Papers
    Forrest Family Papers
    Thomas Jefferson Green Papers
    Stephen Dill Lee Papers
    William Whann Mackall Papers
    Stephen R. Mallory Papers
Tennessee State Library and Archives, Nashville
    Benjamin Franklin Cheatham Papers
    Confederate Collection
Tudor Place Foundation, Washington, D.C.
    Armistead Peter Jr. Papers
    Martha Custis Williams Papers
University of Virginia, Albert H. Small Special Collections Library
    Letters to Jefferson Davis
Virginia Historical Society, Richmond
    Benjamin Barton Papers
    Franklin Buchanan Letters, 1863–64
    David Funsten Papers
    Alexander Hunter Papers
    Lee Family Papers
    George Bolling Lee Papers, 1732–1870
    Robert E. Lee Headquarters Papers
    Franklin Stringfellow Papers
Virginia Military Institute, Preston Library, Archives
    Warfield Family Private Collection
    Edgar Warfield Scrapbooks
Western Reserve Historical Society, Cleveland, Ohio
    Braxton Bragg Papers, William P. Palmer Collection

Newspapers

Alexandria Gazette, 1833–1959
Alexandria *Local News,* 1861
Atlanta Constitution, 1888
Baltimore Sun, 1843

Charleston Daily Courier, 1863–64
Charleston Mercury, 1863
Chattanooga *Daily Rebel, 1863*
Chicago *Inter-Ocean,* 1878

Culpeper *Virginia Star,* 1932
Louisville Daily Journal, 1861
Louisville Post, 1892
Nashville Press, 1863
New York Citizen, 1867
New York Herald, 1865
New York Times, 1861
Philadelphia *Weekly Times,* 1877
Raleigh *Daily Confederate,* 1864
Richmond *Daily Dispatch, 1861–64*
Richmond *Daily Enquirer, 1864*

Richmond *Daily Times,* 1888
Richmond *Southern Illustrated News,* 1863
Richmond Times-Dispatch, 1904
Richmond Whig, 1863
Washington Daily News, 1932
Washington *Evening Star,* 1861, 1914
Washington Herald, 1914
Washington *National Intelligencer,* 1863
Washington Post, 1902
Washington *Sunday Star,* 1915

Books

Alexander, E. P. *Military Memoirs of a Confederate.* Bloomington: Indiana Univ. Press, 1962.

Averell, William Woods. *Ten Years in the Saddle: The Memoir of William Woods Averell,* ed. Edward K. Eckert and Nicholas J. Amato. San Rafael, Calif.: Presidio Press, 1978.

Bond, Christiana. *Memories of General Robert E. Lee.* Baltimore: Norman, Remington Co., 1926.

Brothers and Cousins: Confederate Soldiers and Sailors of Fairfax County, Virginia. Athens, Ga.: Iberian Publishing Co., 1995.

Bulloch, James D. *The Secret Service of the Confederate States in Europe, or How the Confederate Cruisers Were Equipped.* 2 vols. New York: G. P. Putnam, 1884.

Catalogue of the Trustees, Officers, and Students of the Episcopal High School of the Dioceses of Virginia at Howard, Fairfax County, Near Alexandria, for the Session of 1859–'60. Washington, D.C.: George S. Gideon, 1860.

Craven, Avery, ed. *"To Markie": The Letters of Robert E. Lee to Martha Custis Williams.* Cambridge, Mass.: Harvard Univ. Press, 1933.

Custis, George Washington Parke. *Recollections and Private Memoirs of Washington by His Adopted Son, George Washington Parke Custis, with a Memoir of the Author by His Daughter.* New York: Derry & Jackson, 1860.

Davis, Jefferson. *The Papers of Jefferson Davis.* Vol.–. Baton Rouge: Louisiana State Univ. Press, 1992–.

———. *The Rise and Fall of the Confederate Government.* 2 vols. New York: Thomas Yoseloff, 1958.

DeButts, Mary Custis Lee. *Growing Up in the 1850s: The Journal of Agnes Lee.* Chapel Hill: Univ. of North Carolina Press, 1984.

DeLeon, Thomas C. *Four Years in Rebel Capitals: An Inside View of Life in the Southern Confederacy from Birth to Death.* Mobile, Ala.: Gossip Printing Co., 1890.

Dubin, Michael J., ed. *United States Presidential Elections, 1788–1860: The Official Results by County and State.* Jefferson, N.C.: McFarland & Co., 2001.

Forrest, Douglas French. *Odyssey in Gray: A Diary of Confederate Service, 1863–1865.* Edited by William N. Still Jr. Richmond: Virginia State Library, 1979.

Frobel, Anne S. *The Civil War Diary of Anne S. Frobel.* McLean, Va.: EPM Publications, 1992.

Garidel, Henri. *Exile in Richmond: The Confederate Journal of Henri Garidel.* Edited by Michael Bedout Chesson and Leslie Jean Roberts. Charlottesville: Univ. Press of Virginia, 2001.

Harrison, Mrs. Burton. *Recollections Grave and Gay.* New York: Charles Scribner's Sons, 1911.

Harrison, Walter. *Pickett's Men: A Fragment of War History.* Baton Rouge: Louisiana State Univ. Press, 2000.

Hein, Otto Louis. *Memories of Long Ago.* New York: G. P. Putnam's Sons, 1925.

Howard, McHenry. *Recollections of a Maryland Confederate Soldier and Staff-Officer under Johnston, Jackson, and Lee.* Baltimore: Williams & Wilkins Co., 1914.

Hunter, Alexander. *The Huntsman in the South.* Washington, D.C.: Neale Publishing Co., 1908.

———. *Johnny Reb and Billy Yank.* Washington, D.C.: Neale Publishing Co., 1905.

———. *The Women of the Debatable Land.* Washington, D.C.: Corden Publishing Co., 1912.

Johnston, Joseph E. *Narrative of Military Operations, Directed, During the Late War Between the States.* New York: D. Appleton and Co., 1874.

Jones, J. B. *A Rebel War Clerk's Diary at the Confederate States Capital.* 2 vols. New York: Old Hickory Bookshop, 1935.

Lee, Henry. *Memoirs of the War in the Southern Department of the United States.* Edited by Robert E. Lee. New York: University Publishing Co., 1870.

Lee, Robert E., Jr. *Recollections and Letters of General Robert E. Lee.* Garden City, N.Y.: Garden City Publishing Co., 1924.

Lee, William Mack. *History of the Life of Rev. Wm. Mack Lee, Body Servant of General Robert E. Lee through the Civil War, Cook from 1861 to 1865.* N.p., 1918.

Lomax, Elizabeth Lindsay. *Leaves from an Old Washington Diary.* Edited by Lindsay Lomax Wood. Mount Vernon, N.Y.: Books, 1943.

McClellan, George B. *McClellan's Own Story: The War for the Union.* New York: Charles L. Webster & Co., 1887.

McGuire, Judith W. *Diary of a Southern Refugee, during the War.* Richmond, Va.: J. W. Randolph & English, 1889.

Miller, Francis Trevelyan, ed. *The Photographic History of the Civil War.* 10 vols. New York: Review of Reviews Co., 1911.

Mosby, John S. *The Memoirs of Colonel John S. Mosby.* Edited by Charles Wells Russell. Boston: Little, Brown, and Co., 1917.

The Official Atlas of the Civil War. New York: Thomas Yoseloff, 1958.

Parker, William Harwar. *Recollections of a Naval Officer, 1841–1865.* Annapolis, Md.: Naval Institute Press, 1985.

Poague, William Thomas. *Gunner with Stonewall: Reminiscences of William Thomas Poague: A Memoir Written for His Children in 1903.* Edited by Monroe F. Cockrell. Wilmington, N.C.: Broadfoot Publishing Co., 1987.

Reed, Nelson Addington. *Family Papers.* St. Louis: Patrice Press, 1990.

Roman, Alfred. *The Military Operations of General Beauregard.* 2 vols. New York: Da Capo Press, 1994.

Stiles, Robert. *Four Years Under Marse Robert*. Washington, D.C.: Neale Publishing Co., 1903.

Stringfellow, Franklin. *War Reminiscences: The Life of a Confederate Scout Inside the Enemy's Lines*. N.p, n.d.

Strode, Hudson, ed. *Jefferson Davis: Private Letters, 1823–1889*. New York: Harcourt, Brace & World, 1966.

Taylor, Richard. *Destruction and Reconstruction: Personal Experiences of the Late War*. New York: Longmans, Green and Co., 1955.

Townsend, George Alfred. *Campaigns of a Non-Combatant, and His Romaunt Abroad during the War*. New York: Blelock & Co., 1866.

Warfield, Edgar. *Manassas to Appomattox: The Civil War Memoirs of Pvt. Edgar Warfield, 17th Virginia Infantry*. McLean, Va.: EPM Publications, 1996.

Welton, J. Michael, ed. *"My Heart Is So Rebellious": The Caldwell Letters, 1861–1865*. Warrenton, Va.: Fauquier National Bank, 1991.

Willcox, Orlando B. *Forgotten Valor: The Memoirs, Journals, and Civil War Letters of Orlando B. Willcox*. Edited by Robert Garth Scott. Kent, Ohio: Kent State Univ. Press, 1999.

Wise, George N. *History of the Seventeenth Virginia Infantry, C.S.A*. Baltimore: Kelly, Piet and Co., 1870.

Wood, C. J. *Reminiscences of the War*. Centreville, Ind.: N.p., 1880.

Woodward, C. Vann, ed. *Mary Chesnut's Civil War*. New Haven, Conn.: Yale Univ. Press, 1981.

Younger, Edward, ed. *Inside the Confederate Government: The Diary of Robert Garlick Hill Kean*. New York: Oxford Univ. Press, 1957.

Articles

"Anecdotes of the Peninsular Campaign." In *Battles and Leaders of the Civil War*, 2:275–77. Secaucus, N.J.: Castle, 1984.

Baker, Charles F. "Something of Battle Field Maps." *Confederate Veteran* 21 (Feb. 1913): 10–16.

Beauregard, P. G. T. "The Defense of Drewry's Bluff." In *Battles and Leaders of the Civil War*, 4:195–212. Secaucus, N.J.: Castle, 1984.

———. "The First Battle of Bull Run." In *Battles and Leaders of the Civil War*, 1:196–227. Secaucus, N.J.: Castle, 1984.

Burnett, Mrs. Theodore L. "Reminiscences of the Confederacy." *Confederate Veteran* 15 (Apr. 1907): 173–75.

Cabell, George C. "Account of the Skirmish at Swift Creek." *Southern Historical Society Papers* 16 (1888): 223–24.

"Cazenove Lee Remembers Robert E. Lee." *Alexandria History* 3 (1991): 21–25.

Christian, George L. "General Lee's Headquarters Records and Papers—The Present Location of Some of These." *Southern Historical Society Papers* 44 (June 1923): 229–31.

Curtis, I. S. "The Attempted Capture of General Crawford." *Confederate Veteran* 23 (1915): 265–66.

Davis, Jefferson. "Andersonville and Other War Prisons." *Confederate Veteran* 15 (Mar. 1907): 107–13.

"A Desperate Dash." *Southern Historical Society Papers* 21 (1893): 177–83.

Duke, R. T. W. "Burning of Richmond." *Southern Historical Society Papers* 25 (1897): 134–38.

"The Evacuation of Richmond." *Southern Historical Society Papers* 23 (1895): 175–81.

"The Execution of Williams and Peters." *Harper's Weekly* 7 (July 4, 1863): 417–18.

"Fairfax Monument." *Southern Historical Society Papers* 18 (1890): 120–32.

Fishburne, Clement D. "Historical Sketch of the Rockbridge Artillery, C. S. Army." *Southern Historical Society Papers* 23 (1895): 98–158.

"General Lee Just after the War." *Confederate Veteran* 30 (June 1922): 207.

"The Georgia Militia during Sherman's March to the Sea." In *Battles and Leaders of the Civil War*, 4:667–69. Secaucus, N.J.: Castle, 1984

Harrison, Burton. "The Capture of Jefferson Davis." *Century* 27 (Nov. 1883): 130–45.

Herbert, Arthur. "The Seventeenth Virginia Infantry at Flat Creek and Drewry's Bluff." *Southern Historical Society Papers* 12 (July–Sept. 1884): 289–94.

Hill, Daniel H. "Chickamauga—The Great Battle of the West." In *Battles and Leaders of the Civil War*, 3:638–62. Secaucus, N.J.: Castle, 1984.

Holland, T. C. "What Did We Fight For?" *Confederate Veteran* 31 (Nov. 1923): 423.

Hood, John Bell. "The Invasion of Tennessee." In *Battles and Leaders of the Civil War*, 4:425–37. Secaucus, N.J.: Castle, 1984.

Hunter, Alexander. "The Battle of Antietam." *Southern Historical Society Papers* 31 (1903): 32–45.

———. "A Close Call: An Episode of Brant Shooting." *Outing* 45 (Jan. 1905): 401–5.

———. "Confederate Prisoners in Boston." *New England Magazine* 23 (Feb. 1901): 683–97.

———. "Jack Mason, of Penjemoy, and Other Old-Time Sportsmen." *Outing* 41 (Dec. 1902): 307–12.

———. "Plain Bob-Pointer." *Outing* 45 (Dec. 1904): 284–89.

———. "The Rebel Yell." *Confederate Veteran* 21 (1913): 218–19.

———. "Thirteenth Virginia Infantry—Humor." *Confederate Veteran* 16 (July 1908): 339–43.

———. "The Women of Mosby's Confederacy." *Confederate Veteran* 15 (June 1907): 257–62.

James, C. F. "Battle of Sailor's Creek." *Southern Historical Society Papers* 24 (1896): 83–88.

James, G. Watson. "Dahlgren's Raid." *Southern Historical Society Papers* 39 (Apr. 1914): 63–72.

Johnston, David E. "Concerning the Battle of Sharpsburg." *Confederate Veteran* 6 (Jan. 1898): 27–29.

Johnston, Joseph E. "Opposing Sherman's Advance to Atlanta." In *Battles and Leaders of the Civil War*, 4:260–77. Secaucus, N.J.: Castle, 1984.

Kennedy, John Pendleton. "The Border States: Their Power and Duty in the Present Disordered Condition of the Country." Reprinted in Jon L. Wakelyn, ed., *Southern Pamphlets on Secession, November 1860–April 1861*. Chapel Hill: Univ. of North Carolina Press, 1996.

Lee, Fitzhugh. "Sketch of the Late General S. Cooper." *Southern Historical Society Papers* 3 (May–June 1877): 269–74.

Lee, G. W. C. "Gen. Robert E. Lee on Traveler." *Confederate Veteran* 14 (Sept. 1906): 424.

"Letter from Ex-President Davis [to Gen. Fitzhugh Lee]." *Southern Historical Society Papers* 3 (May–June 1877): 274–76.

"Letter from President Davis." *Southern Historical Society Papers* 11 (Dec. 1883): 560–64.

"Letter of General R. S. Ewell to General Grant." *Southern Historical Society Papers* 39 (Apr. 1914): 4–5.

"Letters of Major Thomas Rowland, C.S.A., from the Camps at Ashland and Richmond, Virginia, 1861." *William and Mary College Quarterly Historical Magazine* 24 (Jan. 1916): 145–53.

Loehr, Charles T. "The Battle of Milford Station." *Southern Historical Society Papers* 26 (1898): 110–15.

"Memoir of Mrs. Harriotte Lee Taliaferro Concerning Events in Virginia, April 11–21, 1861." *Virginia Magazine of History and Biography* 57 (Oct. 1949): 416–20.

"Monument to the Confederate Dead at Fredericksburg, Virginia, Unveiled on June 10, 1891." *Southern Historical Society Papers* 18 (1890): 397–406.

"The Monument to General Robert E. Lee." *Southern Historical Society Papers* 17 (1889): 187–335.

Morrison, E. M. "Capture and Reoccupation of the Howlett House in 1864." *Southern Historical Society Papers* 22 (1894): 20–24.

Nourse, Charles H. "Walter Gibson Peter Executed at Franklin." *Confederate Veteran* 15 (Dec. 1907): 551.

Porter, John L. "The Plan and Construction of the 'Merrimac.'" In *Battles and Leaders of the Civil War,* 1:716–17. Secaucus, N.J.: Castle, 1984.

"Resources of the Confederacy in February, 1865." *Southern Historical Society Papers* 2 (Sept. 1876): 113–28.

Rowland, Kate Mason. "Reunion in Virginia." *Confederate Veteran* 11 (Dec. 1903): 547–49.

Scott, W. W. "Some Personal Memories of General Robert E. Lee." *William and Mary Quarterly,* 2d ser., 6 (Oct. 1926): 277–88.

Smith, Gustavus W. "Two Days of Battle at Seven Pines (Fair Oaks)." In *Battles and Leaders of the Civil War,* 2:220–63. Secaucus, N.J.: Castle, 1984.

Stringfellow, Frank. "Colonel McClure's Article Criticised." *Confederate Veteran* 16 (Aug. 1908): 390.

Sulivane, Clement. "The Evacuation." In *Battles and Leaders of the Civil War,* 4:725–26. Secaucus, N.J.: Castle, 1984.

"Treatment of Prisoners during the War between the States." *Southern Historical Society Papers* 1 (Mar. 1876): 113–327.

"Unveiling of the Valentine's Recumbent Figure of Lee at Lexington, June 28th, 1883." *Southern Historical Society Papers* 11 (Aug.–Sept. 1883): 337–88.

Urquhart, David. "Bragg's Advance and Retreat." In *Battles and Leaders of the Civil War,* 3:600–609. Secaucus, N.J.: Castle, 1984.

Vandiver, Frank E., ed. "Proceedings of the First Confederate Congress, Fourth Session." *Southern Historical Society Papers* 50 (1953): 1–463.

————. "Proceedings of the Second Confederate Congress, First Session, Second Session in Part." *Southern Historical Society Papers* 51 (1958): 1–475.

————. "Proceedings of the Second Confederate Congress, Second Session in Part." *Southern Historical Society Papers* 52 (1959): 1–500.

Webster, J. T. "Another Chapter on the Mystery." *Confederate Veteran* 29 (Sept. 1921): 341–42.

Williams, G. A. "Light on a War Mystery." *Confederate Veteran* 29 (July 1921): 263–64.

Public Documents

Acts and Joint Resolutions Passed by the General Assembly of the State of Virginia during the Session of 1889–90. Richmond, Va.: J. H. O'Bannon, 1890.

A Compilation of the Messages and Papers of the Presidents. Edited by James D. Richardson. 20 vols. Washington, D.C.: Bureau of National Literature and Art, 1905.

Journal of the Congress of the Confederate States of America, 1861–1865. 7 vols. Washington, D.C.: U.S. Government Printing Office, 1905.

Journals and Papers of the Virginia State Convention of 1861. 3 vols. Richmond: Virginia State Library, 1966.

Official Records of the Union and Confederate Navies in the War of the Rebellion. 30 vols. Washington, D.C.: U.S. Government Printing Office, 1922.

Proceedings of the Virginia State Convention of 1861. Edited by George H. Reese. 4 vols. Richmond: Virginia State Library, 1965.

U.S. Census Office. *Agriculture of the United States in 1860.* Compiled by Joseph C. G. Kennedy. Washington, D.C.: U.S. Government Printing Office, 1864.

————. *Eighth Census of the United States. 1860.*

————. *Population of the United States in 1860.* Compiled by Joseph C. G. Kennedy. Washington, D.C.: U.S. Government Printing Office, 1864.

U.S. War Dept. *The War of the Rebellion: A Compilation of the Official Records of the Union and Confederate Armies.* 128 vols. Washington, D.C.: U.S. Government Printing Office, 1880–1901.

Unpublished Material

"The Alexandria Light Artillery: Valuable Historic Data on the Famous Kemper's Battery." MS, Patrick F. Gorman Papers, Special Collections, Alexandria Library.

Cooper, Samuel. "Recollections of Incidents and Characters during Fifty Years Military Service." In Marion Dawson, "Be It Known to All Men: The Story of General Samuel Cooper, CSA, 1798–1876." Master's thesis, Salisbury University, Maryland, 2000.

Corse, Montgomery B. "Biography of General Montgomery D. Corse." Corse Family Papers, Special Collections, Alexandria Library.

Gorman, Patrick F. "Personal Experiences and Anecdotes, Civil War, 1861–1865." MS, Patrick F. Gorman Papers, Special Collections, Alexandria Library.

Grand Roll, St. John's Academy [Alexandria, Va.]. MS, Special Collections, Alexandria Library.

Hunter, Alexander. "Four Years in the Ranks." MS, Alexander Hunter Papers, Virginia Historical Society, Richmond, Va.

McCorkle, Eva. "Corse Annals." MS, Corse Family Papers, Special Collections, Alexandria Library.

Miller, T. Michael. "Alexandrians Off to War." MS, Special Collections, Alexandria Library.

———. "Dr. Magnus M. Lewis: Confederate Surgeon and Medical Director." Author's collection.

———. "St. Patrick's Day—The Wearing of the Green in Alexandria." MS, Special Collections, Alexandria Library.

Oliapodrida. Collected by George William Brent. Virginia Historical Society, Richmond.

Organized Camps of the United Confederate Veterans. Compiled by George G. Kane. MS, Eleanor S. Brockenbrough Library, Museum of the Confederacy, Richmond, Va.

Readnour, Harry Warren. "General Fitzhugh Lee, 1835–1905: A Biographical Study." Ph.D. diss., Univ. of Virginia, Charlottesville, 1971.

Weber, Sandra S. "George Washington Custis Lee: History's Pawn." Master's thesis, State Univ. of New York College at Oneonta, 1982.

SECONDARY MATERIALS

Books

Alexander, Thomas B., and Richard E. Beringer. *The Anatomy of the Confederate Congress: A Study of the Influences of Member Characteristics on Legislative Voting Behavior, 1861–1865*. Nashville, Tenn.: Vanderbilt Univ. Press, 1972.

The Ancestors and Descendants of Colonel David Funsten and His Wife, Susan Everard Meade. Compiled by Howard S. F. Randolph. New York: Knickerbocker Press, 1926.

Andrus, Michael J. *The Brooke, Fauquier, Loudoun, and Alexandria Artillery*. Lynchburg, Va.: H. E. Howard, 1990.

Ashdown, Paul, and Edward Caudill. *The Mosby Myth: A Confederate Hero in Life and Legend*. Wilmington, Del.: Scholarly Resources, 2002.

Bauer, K. Jack. *The Mexican War, 1846–1848*. Lincoln: Univ. of Nebraska Press, 1992.

Bell, Robert T. *11th Virginia Infantry*. Lynchburg, Va.: H. E. Howard, 1985.

Brockett, F. L., and George W. Rock. *A Concise History of the City of Alexandria, Va. from 1669 to 1883*. Alexandria: Gazette Book and Job Office, 1883.

Brown, R. Shepard. *Stringfellow of the Fourth*. New York: Crown Publishers, 1960.

Carmichael, Peter S. *Lee's Young Artillerist: William R. J. Pegram*. Charlottesville: Univ. Press of Virginia, 1995.

Case, Lynn M., and Warren F. Spencer. *The United States and France: Civil War Diplomacy*. Philadelphia: Univ. of Pennsylvania Press, 1970.

Chernault, Tracy, and Jeffrey C. Weaver. *18th and 20th Battalions of Heavy Artillery*. Lynchburg, Va.: H. E. Howard, 1995.

Clinton, Catherine. *The Plantation Mistress: Woman's World in the Old South*. New York: Pantheon Books, 1982.

————. *Tara Revisited: Women, War, and the Plantation Legend.* New York: Abbeville Press, 1995.

Comier, Steven A. *The Siege of Suffolk: The Forgotten Campaign, April 11–May 4, 1863.* Lynchburg, Va.: H. E. Howard, 1989.

Confederate Military History: A Library of Confederate States History in Seventeen Volumes. Extended ed. Wilmington, N.C.: Broadfoot Publishing Co., 1987.

Connelly, Thomas L. *Autumn of Glory: The Army of Tennessee, 1862–1865.* Baton Rouge: Louisiana State Univ. Press, 1971.

————. *The Marble Man: Robert E. Lee and His Image in American Society.* New York: Alfred A. Knopf, 1977.

Cooling, Benjamin Franklin, III, and Walton H. Owen II. *Mr. Lincoln's Forts: A Guide to the Civil War Defenses of Washington.* Shippensburg, Pa.: White Mane Publishing Co., 1988.

Cooney, David M. *A Chronology of the U.S. Navy: 1775–1965.* New York: Franklin Watts, 1965.

Coski, John M. *Capital Navy: The Men, Ships, and Operations of the James River Squadron.* Campbell, Calif.: Savas Woodbury Publishers, 1996.

Crenshaw, Oliver. *General Lee's College: The Rise and Growth of Washington and Lee University.* New York: Random House, 1969.

Crofts, Daniel W. *Reluctant Confederates: Upper South Unionists in the Secession Crisis.* Chapel Hill: Univ. of North Carolina Press, 1989.

Davis, Burke. *To Appomattox: Nine April Days, 1865.* New York: Holt, Rinehart, Winston, 1959.

Davis, William C. *Battle at Bull Run: A History of the First Major Campaign of the Civil War.* Baton Rouge: Louisiana State Univ. Press, 1981.

————. *"A Government of Our Own": The Making of the Confederacy.* New York: Free Press, 1994.

————. *Jefferson Davis: The Man and His Hour.* New York: Harper Collins Publishers, 1991.

Dictionary of American Biography. 11 vols. New York: C. Scribner's Sons, 1964.

Driver, Robert J., Jr. *The 1st and 2nd Rockbridge Artillery.* Lynchburg, Va.: H. E. Howard, 1987.

Dudley, William S. *Going South: U.S. Navy Officer Resignations and Dismissals on the Eve of the Civil War.* Washington, D.C.: Naval Historical Foundation, 1981.

Dufour, Charles L. *Gentle Tiger: The Gallant Life of Roberdeau Wheat.* Baton Rouge: Louisiana State Univ. Press, 1957.

Ecker, Grace Dunlop. *A Portrait of Old George Town.* Richmond, Va.: Dietz Press, 1951.

Eicher, David J. *Robert E. Lee: A Life Portrait.* Dallas: Taylor Publishing Co., 1997.

Faust, Drew Gilpin. *Mothers of Invention: Women of the Slaveholding South in the American Civil War.* Chapel Hill: Univ. of North Carolina Press, 1966.

Fellman, Michael. *The Making of Robert E. Lee.* New York: Random House, 2000.

Fowle, Eugene Chalmers. *Descendants of George Fowle (1610/11?–1682) of Charlestown, Massachusetts.* Boston: New England Historic Genealogical Society, 1990.

Freeman, Douglas Southall. *Lee's Lieutenants: A Study in Command.* 4 vols. New York: Charles Scribner's Sons, 1942–46.

————. *R. E. Lee: A Biography.* 4 vols. New York: Charles Scribner's Sons, 1934–35.

Gaines, William H., Jr. *Biographical Register of Members, Virginia State Convention of 1861.* Richmond: Virginia State Library, 1969.

Gallagher, Gary W. *Lee and His Army in Confederate History.* Chapel Hill: Univ. of North Carolina Press, 2001.

———, ed. *Lee the Soldier.* Lincoln: Univ. of Nebraska Press, 1996.

Glasgow, William M., Jr. *Northern Virginia's Own: The 17th Virginia Infantry Regiment, Confederate States Army.* Alexandria, Va.: Gobill Press, 1989.

Goldfield, David R. *Urban Growth in the Age of Sectionalism: Virginia, 1847–1861.* Baton Rouge: Louisiana State Univ. Press, 1977.

Goode, George Brown. *Virginia Cousins: A Study of the Ancestry and Posterity of John Goode of Whitby.* Bridgewater, Va.: C. J. Carrier Co., 1963.

The Grayjackets and How They Lived, Fought and Died for Dixie. Richmond, Va.: Jones Brothers & Co., 1867.

Hahn, Thomas Swiftwater, and Emory L. Kemp. *The Alexandria Canal: Its History and Preservation.* Morgantown: West Virginia Univ. Press, 1992.

Hallock, Judith Lee. Braxton Bragg and Confederate Defeat. Tuscaloosa: Univ. of Alabama Press, 1991.

Harsh, Joseph L. *Confederate Tide Rising: Robert E. Lee and the Making of Southern Strategy, 1861–1862.* Kent, Ohio: Kent State Univ. Press, 1998.

Hearn, Chester G. *Gray Raiders of the Sea: How Eight Confederate Warships Destroyed the Union's High Seas Commerce.* Baton Rouge; Louisiana State Univ. Press, 1992.

Hillman, Benjamin J., ed. *Virginia's Decision: The Story of the Secession Convention of 1861.* Richmond: Virginia Civil War Commission, 1964.

Holt, Michael F. *The Rise and Fall of the American Whig Party: Jacksonian Politics and the Onset of the Civil War.* New York: Oxford Univ. Press, 1999.

Horn, Stanley F. *The Army of Tennessee.* Norman: Univ. of Oklahoma Press, 1953.

Hughes, Nathaniel Cheairs, Jr. *General William J. Hardee: Old Reliable.* Baton Rouge: Louisiana State Univ. Press, 1965.

Hunter, Alexander, and J. H. Polkinhorn. *New National Theater, Washington, D.C.: A Record of Fifty Years.* Washington, D.C.: R. O. Polkinhorn & Son, 1885.

Hurd, William B. *Alexandria, Virginia, 1861–1865.* Alexandria, Va.: City of Alexandria, 1970.

Hurst, Harold W. *Alexandria on the Potomac: The Portrait of an Antebellum Community.* Lanham, Md.: Univ. Press of America, 1991.

Johnson, John Lipscomb. *The University Memorial: Biographical Sketches.* Baltimore: Turnbull Brothers, 1871.

Jones, J. William. *Life and Letters of Robert Edward Lee: Soldier and Man.* Washington, D.C.: Neale Publishing Co., 1906.

Jones, Virgil Carrington. *The Civil War at Sea.* Vol. 1, *The Blockaders.* New York: Holt, Rinehart, Winston, 1960.

———. *Gray Ghosts and Rebel Raiders.* New York: Henry Holt and Co., 1956.

Jordan, Ervin L., Jr. *Black Confederates and Afro-Yankees in Civil War Virginia.* Charlottesville: Univ. Press of Virginia, 1995.

Journal of the 119th Annual Council of the Protestant Episcopal Church in the Diocese of Virginia. Richmond, 1914.

Keen, Hugh C., and Horace Mewborn. *43rd Battalion, Virginia Cavalry, Mosby's Command.* Lynchburg, Va.: H. E. Howard, 1993.

Kundahl, George G. *Confederate Engineer: Training and Campaigning with John Morris Wampler.* Knoxville: Univ. of Tennessee Press, 2000.

Lee, Susan P. *Memoirs of William Nelson Pendleton.* Philadelphia: J. B. Lippincott Co., 1893.

Life of James W. Jackson, the Alexandria Hero, the Slayer of Ellsworth, the First Martyr of the Cause of Southern Independence. Richmond, Va.: West & Johnson, 1862.

Long, A. L. *Memoirs of Robert E. Lee: His Military and Personal History.* Washington, D. C.: J. M. Stoddart & Co., 1886.

Lonn, Ella. *Foreigners in the Confederacy.* Gloucester, Mass.: Peter Smith, 1965.

Luraghi, Raimondo. *A History of the Confederate Navy.* Annapolis, Md.: Naval Institute Press, 1996.

MacDonald, Rose Mortimer Ellzey. *Mrs. Robert E. Lee.* Boston: Ginn and Co., 1939.

Mackall, William W. *A Son's Recollections of His Father.* New York: E. P. Dutton & Co., 1930.

Mahin, Dean B. *One War at a Time: The International Dimensions of the American Civil War.* Washington, D.C.: Brassey's, 1999.

Mahon, John K. *History of the Second Seminole War, 1835–1842.* Gainesville: Univ. of Florida Press, 1967.

McCabe, William Gordon. *Major-General George Washington Custis Lee.* Richmond: Virginia Historical Society, 1914.

McCaslin, Richard B. *Lee in the Shadow of Washington.* Baton Rouge: Louisiana State Univ. Press, 2001.

McPherson, James M. *Battle Cry of Freedom: The Civil War Era.* New York: Oxford Univ. Press, 1988.

———. *For Cause and Comrades: Why Men Fought in the Civil War.* New York: Oxford Univ. Press, 1997.

Miller, T. Michael. *Visitors from the Past: A Bi-Centennial Reflection on Life at the Lee-Fendall House, 1785–1985.* Alexandria, Va.: Virginia Trust for Historic Preservation, 1986.

Mitchell, Mary. *Divided Town.* Barre, Mass.: Barre Publishers, 1968.

Moore, Gay Montague. *Seaport in Virginia: George Washington's Alexandria.* Richmond, Va.: Garret & Massie, 1949.

Moore, Guy W. *The Case of Mrs. Surratt: Her Controversial Trial and Execution for Conspiracy in the Lincoln Assassination.* Norman: Univ. of Oklahoma Press, 1954.

Myers, Robert Manson, ed. *The Children of Pride: A True Story of Georgia and the Civil War.* New Haven, Conn.: Yale Univ. Press, 1972.

Obituary Record of Graduates of Yale University, Deceased from June, 1900, to June, 1910. New Haven, Conn.: Tuttle, Morehouse & Taylor Co., 1910.

On Hazardous Service: Scouts and Spies of the North and South. New York: Harper & Brothers Publishers, 1912.

Patterson, Gerard A. *Justice or Atrocity: General George E. Pickett and the Kinston, N.C. Hangings.* Gettysburg, Pa.: Thomas Publications, 1998.

Peavey, Dudley, ed. *Confederate Scout: Virginia's Frank Stringfellow.* Onancock, Va.: Eastern Shore Publishing Co., 1956.

Pfanz, Donald C. *Richard S. Ewell: A Soldier's Life.* Chapel Hill: Univ. of North Carolina Press, 1998.

Powell, Mary G. *The History of Old Alexandria, Virginia, from July 13, 1749 to May 24, 1861.* Richmond, Va.: William Byrd Press, 1928.

Rable, George C. *Civil Wars: Women and the Crisis of Southern Nationalism.* Urbana: Univ. of Illinois Press, 1989.

Rammage, James A. *Gray Ghost: The Life of Col. John Singleton Mosby.* Lexington: Univ. of Kentucky Press, 1999.

Reynolds, Clark G. *Famous American Admirals.* New York: Van Nostrand Reinhold Co., 1978.

Ridley, Bromfield L. *Battles and Sketches of the Army of Tennessee.* Mexico, Mo.: Missouri Printing & Publishing, 1906.

Riley, Franklin L. *General Robert E. Lee after Appomattox.* New York: Macmillan Co., 1922.

Robertson, James I., Jr. *Soldiers Blue and Gray.* New York: Warner Books, 1991.

———. *Stonewall Jackson: The Man, the Soldier, the Legend.* New York: Simon & Schuster Macmillan, 1997.

Royce, Gordon Shingleton. *John Taylor Wood: Sea Ghost of the Confederacy.* Athens: Univ. of Georgia Press, 1979.

Sanborn, Margaret. *Robert E. Lee: The Complete Man, 1861–1870.* Philadelphia: J. B. Lippincott, 1967.

———. *Robert E. Lee: A Portrait, 1807–1861.* Philadelphia: J. B. Lippincott, 1966.

Scharf, J. Thomas. *History of the Confederate States Navy from Its Organization to the Surrender of Its Last Vessel.* New York: Fairfax Press, 1977.

Selby, John G. *Virginians at War: The Civil War Experiences of Seven Young Confederates.* Wilmington, Del.: Scholarly Resources, 2002.

Shanks, Henry T. *The Secession Movement in Virginia, 1847–1861.* Richmond, Va.: Garrett and Massie Publishers, 1934.

Shingleton, Royce Gordon. *John Taylor Wood: Sea Ghost of the Confederacy.* Athens: Univ. of Georgia Press, 1979.

Slaughter, Philip. *A Sketch of the Life of Randolph Fairfax.* 3d ed. Richmond, Va.: William Ellis Jones, Book and Job Printer, 1902.

Smith, Arthur D. Howden. *Old Fuss and Feathers.* New York: Greystone Press, 1927.

St. Mary's: Two Hundred Years for Christ, 1795–1995. Alexandria, Va.: St. Mary's Catholic Church, 1995.

Stephenson, Wendell Holmes. *Isaac Franklin: Slave Trader and Planter of the Old South.* Gloucester, Mass.: Peter Smith, 1968.

Still, William N., Jr., ed. *The Confederate Navy: The Ships, Men, and Organization, 1861–65.* Annapolis, Md.: Naval Institute Press, 1997.

———. *Iron Afloat: The Story of the Confederate Armorclads.* Nashville, Tenn.: Vanderbilt Univ. Press, 1971.

Symonds, Craig L. *Confederate Admiral: The Life and Wars of Franklin Buchanan.* Annapolis, Md.: Naval Institute Press, 1999.

———. *Joseph E. Johnston: A Civil War Biography.* New York: W. W. Norton & Co., 1992.

Thomas, Emory M. *Robert E. Lee.* New York: W. W. Norton & Co., 1995.

Tidwell, William A. *Come Retribution: The Confederate Secret Service and the Assassination of Lincoln.* Jackson: Univ. Press of Mississippi, 1989.

Trimble, William Cattell. *The Presstman Family of Baltimore.* Baltimore: J. H. Furst, 1989.

Tyler, Lyon Gardiner, ed. *Encyclopedia of Virginia Biography.* 5 vols. New York: Lewis Historical Publishing, 1915.

Voices of the Civil War: First Manassas. Alexandria, Va.: Time-Life Books, 1997.

Wallace, Lee A., Jr. *17th Virginia Infantry.* Lynchburg, Va.: H. E. Howard, 1990.

Warner, Ezra J. *Generals in Blue: Lives of the Union Commanders.* Baton Rouge: Louisiana State Univ. Press, 1964.

————. *Generals in Gray: Lives of the Confederate Commanders.* Baton Rouge: Louisiana State Univ. Press, 1959.

Warner, Ezra J., and W. Buck Yearns. *Biographical Register of the Confederate Congress.* Baton Rouge: Louisiana State Univ. Press, 1975.

Watkins, Lizzie Stringfellow. *The Life of Horace Stringfellow.* Montgomery, Ala.: Paragon Press, 1931.

Wedderburn, Alexander J. *Wedderburn's Souvenir Virginia Tercentennial, 1607–1907.* Alexandria, Va.: [1907].

Weed, Edwin G. *In Memoriam: Rev. Douglas French Forrest, D.D.* Winchester, Va.: Eddy Press, 1902.

Welcher, Frank J., and Larry G. Ligget. *Coburn's Brigade: 85th Indiana, 33rd Indiana, 19th Michigan, and 22nd Wisconsin in the Western Civil War.* Carmel: Guild Press of Indiana, 1999.

Wells, Tom Henderson. *The Confederate Navy: A Study in Organization.* Tuscaloosa: Univ. of Alabama Press, 1971.

Wert, Jeffry D. *Mosby's Rangers.* New York: Simon and Schuster, 1990.

Wharton, Anne Hollingsworth. *Social Life in the Early Republic.* Philadelphia: J. B. Lippincott, 1902.

White, John. *Chronicles of the Episcopal High School in Virginia, 1839–1989.* Dublin, N.H.: William Bauhan, 1989.

White, William W. *The Confederate Veteran.* Tuscaloosa, Ala.: Confederate Publishing, 1962.

Wiley, Bell Irvin. *The Life of Johnny Reb: The Common Soldier of the Confederacy.* Baton Rouge: Louisiana State Univ. Press, 1978.

Williams, T. Harry. *P. G. T. Beauregard: Napoleon in Gray.* Baton Rouge: Louisiana State Univ. Press, 1955.

Wills, Mary Alice. *The Confederate Blockade of Washington, D.C., 1861–1862.* Parsons, W.Va.: McClain Printing, 1975.

Wise, George N. *Campaigns and Battles of the Army of Northern Virginia.* New York: Neale Publishing, 1916.

Yates, Bernice-Marie. *The Perfect Gentleman: The Life and Letters of George Washington Custis Lee.* 2 vols. Longwood, Fla.: Xulon Press, 2003.

Yearns, Wilfred Buck. *The Confederate Congress.* Atlanta: Univ. of Georgia Press, 1960.

Articles

Alford, Terry. "Alexander Hunter and the Bessie Hale Story." *Alexandria History* 8 (1990): 5–15.

"The Anne Lee Monument." *Confederate Veteran* 5 (Mar. 1897): 123–24.

"Arlington and Mount Vernon, 1856." *Virginia History Magazine* 57 (Apr. 1949): 140–75.

Bailey, Worth. "Silversmiths of Alexandria." *Antiques Magazine* (Feb. 1945). Reprinted in *Twentieth Annual Washington Antiques Show Catalog* (1978): 37–41.

Bakeless, John E. "Incident at Fort Granger." *Civil War Times Illustrated* 8 (Apr. 1969): 10, 14–15.

Beymer, William Gilmore. "Williams, C.S.A." *Harper's Monthly Magazine* 119 (Sept. 1909): 498–510.

"Capt. W. G. Peter Executed at Franklin." *Confederate Veteran* 16 (Jan. 1908): 16.

Cunningham, Frank. "A Seafaring Lee: Almost Forgotten Today, He Trained Two Navies." *Richmond Times-Dispatch, Sunday Magazine,* Apr. 6, 1952.

"The Death of Major-General J. E. B. Stuart." *Southern Historical Society Papers* 7 (Feb. 1879): 107–10.

Dinkins, James. "Famous War Horses." *Confederate Veteran* 40 (Dec. 1932): 423–25.

"Execution of Williams and Peters *[sic]* at Franklin." *Confederate Veteran* 8 (Jan. 1900): 12–13.

"Fayette Artillery." *Southern Historical Society Papers* 25 (1897): 288–97.

Fellman, Michael. "Women and Guerrilla Warfare." In *Divided Houses: Gender and the Civil War,* ed. Catherine Clinton and Nina Silber, 146–65. New York: Oxford Univ. Press, 1992.

Flournoy, Mrs. William Cabell. "Arlington." *Confederate Veteran* 31 (Apr. 1923): 134–36.

Friedman, Carol Drake. "Wilmer McLean: The Centreville Years." *Yearbook: The Historical Society of Fairfax County, Virginia* 23 (1991–92): 61–79.

"Gen. G. W. C. Lee." *Confederate Veteran* 21 (Apr. 1913): 178–79.

Giffin, Donald W. "The American Navy at Work on the Brazil Station, 1827–1860." *American Neptune* 19 (Oct. 1959): 237–56.

Gow, June I. "Chief of Staffs in the Army of Tennessee." *Tennessee Historical Quarterly* 27 (winter 1968): 341–60.

———. "The Johnston and Brent Diaries: A Problem of Authorship." *Civil War History* 14 (Mar. 1968): 46–50.

Griffin, Patrick J., III. "Tragedy of Two Cousins—Adventurers or Spies?" *Montgomery Country Story* 34 (Nov. 1991): 177–88.

Harrison, Noel G. "Atop an Anvil: The Civilians' War in Fairfax and Alexandria Counties, April 1861–April 1862." *Virginia Magazine of History and Biography* 106 (spring 1998): 133–64.

Hart, W. O. "Arlington." *Confederate Veteran* 30 (June 1922): 208.

Higgins, Frances Caldwell. "Life on the Southern Plantation during the War between the States." *Confederate Veteran* 21 (Apr. 1913): 161–66.

Howe, James Lewis. "George Washington Custis Lee." *Virginia Magazine of History and Biography* 48 (Oct. 1940): 315–27.

Hunter, R. W. "Men of Virginia at Ball's Bluff." *Southern Historical Society Papers* 34 (1906): 254–74.

Hurd, William B. "Montgomery Dent Corse." *Alexandria History* 4 (1982): 10–14.

Kirby, J. L. "Execution of Two Confederates." *Confederate Veteran* 15 (Aug. 1907): 363–64.

Kurtz, Ada Warfield. "A Heroine on the Homefront: My Mother's Experiences during the Civil War." *Alexandria Chronicle* 7 (spring 1998): 6–16.

Mewborn, Horace. "The Operations of Mosby's Rangers." *Blue & Gray* 17 (Apr. 2000): 6–22, 38–50.

Miller, T. Michael. "A Chronicle of the 17th Virginia—'The Reminiscences of Col. Arthur Herbert.'" *Alexandria History* 6 (1984): 3–10.

———. "Clarens: A Sylvan Retreat." *Fireside Sentinel* 8 (Sept./Oct. 1994): 49–60.

———. "Kate Hooper: Alexandria's 'Angel of Mercy.'" *Alexandria Chronicle* 9 (spring 2002): 19–20.

———. "My Dear Louisa ..." *Fireside Sentinel* 5 (June 1991): 69–77.

———. "Wandering Along the Waterfront, Queen to Cameron." *Fireside Sentinel* 3 (Feb. 1989): 16–20.

Myers, Denys Peter. "Architecture." In *Alexandria: A Towne in Transition, 1800–1900*, ed. John D. Macoll, 143–71. Alexandria, Va.: Alexandria Bicentennial Commission, 1977.

Peterson, Arthur G. "The Alexandria Market Prior to the Civil War." *William and Mary Quarterly*, 2d ser. 11 (Apr. 1932): 104–14.

Robins, Sally Nelson. "Mrs. Lee during the War—Something About 'The Mess' and Its Occupants." In *General Robert E. Lee, Soldier, Citizen, and Christian Patriot*, ed. R. A. Brock, 233–49. Richmond, Va.: Royal Publishing, 1897.

Robinson, Leigh. "General Joseph E. Johnston." *Southern Historical Society Papers* 19 (1891): 337–70.

Sanborn, Margaret. "The Ordeal of Orton Williams, U.S.A., C.S.A." *Assembly* 28 (winter 1970): 6–9, 34–40.

Shackelford, George Green. "George Wythe Randolph." In *Encyclopedia of the Confederacy*, ed. Richard N. Current, 3:1305–6. New York: Simon and Schuster, 1993.

Sharrer, G. Terry. "Commerce and Industry." In *Alexandria: A Towne in Transition, 1800–1900*, ed. John D. Macoll, 16–38. Alexandria, Va.: Alexandria Bicentennial Commission, 1977.

Silverman, Jason H. "Irish." In *Encyclopedia of the Confederacy*, ed. Richard N. Current, 2:822–23. New York: Simon & Schuster, 1993.

"A Southern Heroine in Need." *Confederate Veteran* 13 (June 1905): 249.

Sprouse, Edith M. "Clermont: The Rest of the Story." *Fireside Sentinel* 3 (Sept. 1989): 97–106; (Oct. 1989): 109–17.

Stringfellow, George F. "Some Incidents in the Life of Frank Stringfellow, Famous Confederate Soldier and Scout." *William and Mary Quarterly*, 2d ser., 14 (July 1934): 230–34.

Thompson, Magnus S. "Plan to Release Our Men at Point Lookout." *Confederate Veteran* 20 (Feb. 1912): 69–70.

Willett, Robert L. "Loyal to None." *Civil War Times* 42 (Apr. 2003): 43–47.

Witherspoon, Jean. "Woman's Part in the Confederate War." *Lost Cause* 8 (Feb. 1903): 105–9.

Index

Female spouses are indexed by their married names. Place entries without further identification were located in Alexandria, Virginia, and the environs.

Alexandria Goes to War was designed and typeset on a Macintosh computer system using QuarkXPress software. The body text is set in 10/12 New Baskerville and display type is set in Willow. This book was designed and typeset by Preston Thomas and manufactured by Thomson-Shore, Inc.